A History and Philosophy of Expertise

Also available from Bloomsbury

A Critical Introduction to Testimony, by Axel Gelfert
Critical Thinking, by Robert Arp and Jamie Carlin Watson
Expertise: A Philosophical Introduction, by Jamie Carlin Watson
Intellectual Agency and Virtue Epistemology, by Patrick R. Frierson
Skepticism: From Antiquity to the Present, by Diego Machuca and Baron Reed

A History and Philosophy of Expertise

The Nature and Limits of Authority

Jamie Carlin Watson

BLOOMSBURY ACADEMIC
LONDON • NEW YORK • OXFORD • NEW DELHI • SYDNEY

BLOOMSBURY ACADEMIC
Bloomsbury Publishing Plc
50 Bedford Square, London, WC1B 3DP, UK
1385 Broadway, New York, NY 10018, USA
29 Earlsfort Terrace, Dublin 2, Ireland

BLOOMSBURY, BLOOMSBURY ACADEMIC and the Diana logo are trademarks of Bloomsbury Publishing Plc

First published in Great Britain 2022
This paperback edition published 2023

Copyright © Jamie Carlin Watson, 2022

Jamie Carlin Watson has asserted his right under the Copyright, Designs and Patents Act, 1988, to be identified as Author of this work.

For legal purposes the Acknowledgments on p. xviii constitute an extension of this copyright page.

Cover image: Daniel Grizelj/Getty images.

All rights reserved. No part of this publication may be reproduced or transmitted in any form or by any means, electronic or mechanical, including photocopying, recording, or any information storage or retrieval system, without prior permission in writing from the publishers.

Bloomsbury Publishing Plc does not have any control over, or responsibility for, any third-party websites referred to or in this book. All internet addresses given in this book were correct at the time of going to press. The author and publisher regret any inconvenience caused if addresses have changed or sites have ceased to exist, but can accept no responsibility for any such changes.

A catalogue record for this book is available from the British Library.

Library of Congress Cataloging-in-Publication Data
Names: Watson, Jamie Carlin, author.
Title: A history and philosophy of expertise: the nature and limits of authority / Jamie Carlin Watson.
Description: London; New York: Bloomsbury Academic, 2021. | Includes bibliographical references and index.
Identifiers: LCCN 2021023564 (print) | LCCN 2021023565 (ebook) | ISBN 9781350216488 (hb) | ISBN 9781350217676 (paperback) | ISBN 9781350217669 (epdf) | ISBN 9781350216495 (ebook)
Subjects: LCSH: Authority. | Expertise. | Knowledge, Theory of. | Testimony (Theory of knowledge) | Evidence. Classification: LCC BD209 W65 2021 (print) | LCC BD209 (ebook) | DDC 121/.6-dc23
LC record available at https://lccn.loc.gov/2021023564
LC ebook record available at https://lccn.loc.gov/2021023565

ISBN: HB: 978-1-3502-1648-8
PB: 978-1-3502-1767-6
ePDF: 978-1-3502-1766-9
eBook: 978-1-3502-1649-5

Typeset by Deanta Global Publishing Services, Chennai, India

To find out more about our authors and books visit www.bloomsbury.com and sign up for our newsletters.

For Laura

If, therefore, you have understanding of what is good and evil, you may safely buy knowledge (*epistemon*) of Protagoras or of any one; but if not, then, O my friend, pause, and do not hazard your dearest interests at a game of chance. For there is far greater peril in buying knowledge than in buying meat and drink.
(Plato, *Protagoras*, 313e–314a, trans, Jowett, 1892)

Contents

List of Figures	viii
Preface: What Do Experts Look Like?	ix
Acknowledgments	xviii
1 Expertise and Its Discontents	1
2 English and Ancient Roots	31
3 Expertise from the Middle Ages to the Twentieth Century	65
4 A Brief History of Expertise Studies	89
5 Epistemic Placement and Expert Testimony	105
6 Expert Authority	125
7 The Easy Recognition Problem for Expertise	157
8 The Hard Recognition Problem, Disagreement, and Trust	193
Notes	217
References and Further Reading	229
Index	262

Figures

1.1	Follow the numbers strategy	20
2.1	The continuum of domain access	54
2.2	A continuum of competence in a domain	58
5.1	The overlap between the domains of medicine and subjective experiences	116
5.2	Epistemic placement in a domain	118
5.3	Epistemic placement in a domain, alternate	118
5.4	A taxonomy of epistemic placement in a domain	120
6.1	Accounts of authority, administrative and epistemic	128
6.2	Accounts of authority, physical and ontological control	131
6.3	Accounts of authority, doxastic control	136
6.4	Accounts of authority, normative presumption	153
7.1	Nguyen's epistemic geography of expertise	181
7.2	Nguyen's epistemic geography of expertise, revised	182
8.1	*Rapport Du Comité D'Orientation* 1 (2016: 69). Translated from French by Dr. Loïc Boulanger	202
8.2	*Rapport Du Comité D'Orientation* 2 (2016: 156). Taken from Jin J. (2014)	203

Preface

What Do Experts Look Like?

[A] Wise [person] doth like an Expert Chymist, that can Extract Cordials out of Poison, but a Fool Converts Cordials into Poison by wrong Application...

(Margaret Cavendish, Letter 102, 1664)

Experts are people with a high degree of competence in a domain. Because of this, we often look for experts when we need to know or do something that's beyond our abilities, such as filing a lawsuit, remodeling our bathroom, or doing our taxes. Sometimes we do a good job of choosing experts—the attorney who got us more than we expected from our legal claim, excellent craftwork in our bathroom, and so on. Other times, we don't. The people who would seem to be able to help us turn out not to be very good. We want experts, and we get hobbyists or, worse, frauds.

How could we not get it right? We did our homework. We looked for someone with good credentials. We checked their customer ratings on the internet. We asked them pointed questions about how they would do the work. And yet...

The Trouble with Identifying Experts

Let's call anything that would tell us something about someone's competence an *indicator of expertise*. Some indicators are *direct*, such as past track records of success (a heart surgeon's statistics) or overt demonstrations of competence (someone who claims to be an expert juggler juggles for you). Other indicators are *indirect*, such as degrees, credentials, and reviews. Now we can ask: If there are indicators of expertise, why do we have trouble recognizing them?

One reason is that many indicators set too low a bar for expert-level performance in a domain. We likely know people who skated through college and got a degree without learning much of anything, or who barely skimmed by in their EMT classes or tax prep classes and got certified despite lacking important skills. Even if someone performed well on a task in the past, under different conditions, that is no guarantee that they will perform well for *you*. Further, just because I can do something doesn't mean I am an expert at it. I can change the oil in my truck, check my brake fluid, and refill my windshield wiper fluid. Because of this, I could probably get a job at a thirty-minute oil-change place. But having that job (and that ability) does not make me an expert at auto maintenance. So, even if experience or a degree or a credential, or even an ability, is an indirect indicator of expertise, there are cases where these are too weak to be of much help.

A second reason is that, even when indicators do a good job of tracking expert-level competence, we may be mistaken about the sort of expertise they indicate. It is easy to think that anyone with an MD is a medical expert. Yet, someone just out of medical school, with little experience in an actual clinic, has a medical doctorate (MD). An MD is a reasonably good measure of a type of expertise, namely, they know far more than the person on the street about medicine. But they are not yet licensed to practice medicine. Getting licensed requires another few years of residency and usually a one- or two-year fellowship. But most of us don't know that. An MD indicates expertise, but only a very weak version of it. Without realizing that, we may become disillusioned with medical expertise *in general* because the medical resident (with an MD) who is treating us turns out to be incompetent.

A third reason is that even adequate indicators may only track *general* competence when our needs are *specific*. Our attorney may have passed the bar, but if she did not specialize in tort law, she may not be competent to help us with a tort claim. Our contractor may be excellent with new construction work (setting foundations, framing, roofing, etc.) but lack skill in finishing (molding, fixtures, wall texture, etc.). As long as experts are transparent about their specific skills, this doesn't usually present a problem. But when experts attempt to work outside their specialized training, we may think we're getting an expert when we are getting only an approximation.

Fourth, regardless of how good indicators are, as domains get more complicated and there is more at stake for us—politically, religiously, ethically, and so on—a number of psychological and social factors can distort our ability to use those indicators to identify experts. For example, research suggests that the less competent people are in a domain, the more confident they feel at assessing expert-level claims (the Dunning-Kruger effect). Other distorting factors include tribal epistemology, standpoint bias, filter bubbles, and echo chambers (see Watson 2020: 14–26 for a review of each of these). These are less concerning when we're choosing a contractor or a family doctor, but as our needs grow in significance—for instance, we need a good divorce attorney, someone to handle a tricky public relations problem, or someone to advise us how to treat a rare medical diagnosis—they increasingly influence which people we turn to.

Finally, there are, of course, genuine experts who behave badly. Though they have a high degree of competence in a domain, they have misused that competence, thus undermining the authority they had to speak or work in that domain. When this happens, it doesn't matter whether any indicators adequately reflect expertise in a domain. Rather than sorting experts from nonexperts, we face the additional task of sorting well-behaved experts from poorly behaved ones.

The problem is that identifying experts—real experts who are genuinely interested in helping us and who are not bad actors—is difficult business. The more we get it wrong, the more skeptical we are likely to become of experts. We might become skeptical whether anyone in a particular field really has expertise, or we might become skeptical of the whole notion of expertise. Or, perhaps worst of all, we may become skeptical of real experts but then invest trust in people who claim expertise that they don't possess.

In some cases, expert skepticism is warranted. We have good reason to believe that financial analysts do no better than chance at choosing stocks (see Tetlock 2005). Some doctors keep using treatments long after empirical research has shown them to be ineffective (see Prasad and Cifu 2015). But in other cases, skepticism is unfounded, as when your doctor tells you that vaccines do not cause autism. The trick is knowing when to trust and how much. Those are the main topics of this book.

The Aim of This Book

In Watson (2020a), I identified five "big questions" that expertise studies aim to answer:

(1) What is an expert?
(2) How does someone become an expert?
(3) What does it mean to say that an expert has "authority," and how much should we trust authorities?
(4) How does anyone recognize an expert, and how do we choose which experts to listen to?
(5) How do we decide what to believe or do when experts disagree?

There, I focused on questions (1) and (2), explaining various approaches to answering them and four central accounts of expertise. For example, some argue that experts have more true beliefs in a domain than most other people (Goldman 2001; Coady 2012). Others stipulate that experts are people who demonstrate superior performance domain, irrespective of what they know, and argue that they acquire this high degree of competence through a very specific kind of training (Ericsson and Charness 1994; Ericsson and Pool 2016). Still others argue that an expert is someone who can meaningfully interact with others in that domain (what sociologist Harry Collins (2014) calls "interactional expertise") or contribute to a domain ("contributory expertise"), and this usually does require both knowledge and the ability to do something in that domain. On this view, people acquire expertise through immersion in the culture and practice of domain.

I argued that each of these accounts captures something important about expertise and that we can incorporate the most plausible aspects of them into a general account of expertise that I call the *cognitive systems* account. On this account, *expertise* is a high degree of competence in a domain at a time, and an *expert* is something like the following:

> **Expert:** A subject S is an expert in domain D if and only if **(a)** S has a high degree of competence in D that **(b)** is acquired through rigorous training along one of two cognitive systems, and **(c)** that is confirmed to be high enough by the current state of skills and information in D at that time.[1]

By "competence," I mean the knowledge or skill to engage meaningfully with a domain, and what that looks like will depend on what meaningful engagement looks like in that domain. The phrase "domain at a time" means that expertise is relative to the current state of expert-level competence in that domain at a time. This is why Isaac Newton would have been an expert in physics when he was alive but would not be today, and why physicists who are experts now may not be in 500 years. What counts as expert-level work depends on what level of competence current experts are working at.

An explanation of the cognitive systems involved in acquiring expertise requires more space than is available here. But the key is that competence in a domain is essential to being an expert. Yet, even this seemingly uncontroversial point raises difficult philosophical questions. If experts really are competent in their domains, then it would seem they have some authority in those domains. In other words, there are normative implications of being an expert (something required of the experts when they speak or perform in their domains, perhaps transparency, honesty, and good faith), and something required of others, whether novices or other experts, when they encounter experts (perhaps trust, deference, humility, etc.). What does that authority look like? What does it entitle experts to do? What precisely does it require of others? How do people know when the person claiming authority is really an expert and not an imposter? In this book, I focus on these questions, which comprise the remaining big questions on my list: What does it mean for an expert to have authority and what does that mean for us, how do we identify experts, and how should we respond when experts disagree?

Plan of the Book

In Chapter 1, I explore four prominent types of expert skepticism. Throughout, I highlight nuances that make a difference to a philosophical analysis of expertise, such as the conditions under which these types of skepticism are more and less plausible. It turns out that some instances of expert skepticism are not as worrisome as some scholars have suggested, but it is also the case that determining when skepticism is warranted is not always straightforward. At the end, I review what I call the "standard response" to expert skepticism and show several ways it is inadequate.

In Chapters 2 and 3, I sketch the origins of the concept of expertise, including its early association with cunning, skill, knowledge, and artisanship. This discussion lays the groundwork for much that follows, including what it means to have "access" to a domain, degrees of expert competence, and the sort of training that ancient thinkers believed was required for expertise. In Chapter 3, I explore how expertise was regarded as a type of "genius" or "innate talent" in medieval education, how it evolved in early psychological studies of "intelligence," and how it emerged in the legal system to refer to witnesses who were called to testify about scientific matters. I close by showing the connection between these past uses and our contemporary dictionary definitions of expertise, which characterize it as having extensive experience, knowledge, or skill in a domain. This history not only suggests a nuanced account of expertise but also reveals that scholars have wrestled with the question of what expertise implies, how to identify them, and whether to trust them since antiquity.

In Chapter 4, I briefly review the history of expertise studies, focusing primarily on psychological research, starting in Germany in the late 1700s, highlighting the influence of Darwin and the impact of behaviorism, its interest to computer scientists, and its transformation into the largely cognitive concept psychologists study today.

In Chapter 5, I draw on contemporary social epistemology to explore what it means to stand in different epistemic positions in a domain. I then introduce some basic concepts from the epistemology of testimony and explain how epistemic positioning accounts for what it means for someone to have an epistemic advantage over someone else. I close by describing the distinct epistemic advantage competence confers on experts and introduce a taxonomy of expertise, highlighting how epistemic placement in a domain contributes to our assessment of expert authority and the considerations that can help us decide when and how to challenge or reject that authority.

In Chapter 6, I explore what it means for experts to be "authorities" in their domains. I distinguish *administrative* from *epistemic* authority and what I call "control accounts" of authority from "normative presumption" accounts. These categories help explain how someone who is, say, an expert chemist has different degrees and types of authority depending on whether she is speaking as a researching chemist (to lay audiences or other chemists), as a professor of chemistry (to students), or as chair of a professional society of chemists (as someone charged to carry out certain tasks on behalf of the society). I argue that while control accounts of authority are the most commonly defended, they face serious objections. Instead, I show that normative presumption accounts capture what control theorists want from expert authority while avoiding the concerns about control accounts.

In Chapter 7, I introduce a problem that has faced expertise studies from its earliest discussions—the *recognition problem*. I open with a discussion of how we might delineate "domains" of expertise, which lays the foundation for the problem of identifying experts in a specific domain. I then distinguish between what I call "easy" and "hard" versions of the recognition problem and distinguish these from the novice/2-expert problem. I argue that the easy problem is not in-principle intractable, though it is not actually "easy" from a novice's perspective. However, even if the easy problem is solved—that is, even if we can reliably identify experts for most of our basic expertise needs—there remains the much harder problem of how we know when to trust experts, especially when the stakes are high or our values are threatened. In Chapter 8, I explain the hard recognition problem. I identify a set of five "compromising conditions" that underwrite the hard recognition problem. If any one of these conditions is present, the solutions used to solve the easy problem are not likely to help. Though I am not optimistic about a solution to the hard problem, I offer some suggestions about the sort of work that must be done for a solution to be plausible.

Also in Chapter 8, I explain the novice/2-expert problem and argue that it is a species of the more general epistemological problem of everyday disagreement. I contend that solving this problem depends, in important ways, on how we respond to disagreement generally. Further, I argue that it also depends on how we navigate the difference between expert testimony and expert advice. I show that expert testimony is normatively different from expert advice because every instance of expert advice overlaps with a domain in which hearers are well placed, namely, the domain of their own values. Whether a piece of advice is good for me depends, in large part, on whether I judge the purported outcome of that advice to be better than alternatives. To be sure, I could be wrong about what is valuable, but that suggests that decisions about whether to accept expert advice are not only about expertise but are also about which values are at stake and how we weigh those against what is valuable in alternative courses of action. I close the book by highlighting remaining important questions about expertise that I hope researchers continue pursuing.

There are a number of questions I would explore further but for time and length, such as the implications of expertise for politics and morality. I have made preliminary comments on both topics in *Winning Votes by Abusing Reason: Responsible Belief and Political Rhetoric* (2017) and, with Laura Guidry-Grimes, in the introduction to *Moral Expertise: New Essays from Theoretical and Clinical Perspectives* (2018). If nothing else, I hope this book lays a foundation for thinking more critically about these issues.

A Note on Terminology and Presentation

Though this is foremost a work of philosophy, I have tried not to presuppose any robust background in philosophy. Where I invoke philosophical debates, I try to explain them with little jargon. I hope the book proves useful to anyone working in or wishing to learn about expertise studies, including classicists, historians, psychologists, sociologists, political scientists, and neuroscientists. The literature on expertise across these domains is voluminous. Because there is so much written in each domain, it is easy to lose sight of what is being said about expertise in the others. My hope is that this book offers a constructive foundation for interdisciplinary discussions of expertise and, thereby, that it breeds more interdisciplinary study of expertise.

For the sake of simplicity and consistency, I use the word "domain" to refer generally to anything that typically goes by the names *subject matter, field of study, scope of practice, sport, area of specialization,* or *province*. It will become clear early in the book that domains are fuzzy, and determining who is an expert in what domain can be a conceptual mare's nest. Even those who work in expertise studies struggle to use the notion of a domain consistently.

I use the word "novice" synonymously with "nonexpert" or "layperson," referring to anyone who is not an expert in the domain in question, or who is new enough to a domain not to be a competent knower or practitioner in the domain. Some reserve "nonexpert" or "layperson" for people who have no experience in a domain whatsoever (e.g., most patients to their doctors) and "novice" for people just getting started in a domain (e.g., pupils to teachers and understudies to actors).[2] In general, I don't have a problem with this, I just find that it can be confusing. For example, aspects of many domains—even specialized domains, like cosmological physics—spill over into popular understanding, for example, the Big Bang theory (not the TV show) and Darwinian evolution. Are people with a high school understanding of these domains laypersons or novices? If novices, what then do we call the college senior who is majoring in evolutionary biology? I am hesitant to call them an expert in any sense, but the college senior is more competent than the high school student. Trying to carve such boundaries seems unnecessary, as it does little explanatory work. Further, some people are experts in one domain but not in another. Are they then nonexperts in the other or simply novices? I don't think the distinction in cases like these amounts to much, so I use "novice" to refer to anyone who is not, at minimum, what I call (in Chapter 2) a *localized expert*.

When I discuss words in other languages, I first render them in their original language and then give their transliteration (how they sound in English) in italics: for example, τέχνη, *techne*, σοφία, *sophia*. Afterward, I use only the italicized transliteration. When I first use a technical term I put it in quotation marks to distinguish mention from use (e.g., "expertise," "authority"). I then use italics to call attention to some later instances to cut down on clutter (*expertise, authority*).

Further, as someone writing in a domain that has traditionally favored men's voices over women's (philosophy) and that has, through its conservative commitment to a certain scholarly aesthetic, preferred masculine pronouns and masculine characters in its examples, I am sensitive to how these practices have alienated or indirectly devalued the voices and roles of women and other historically marginalized groups. In an attempt to be one small part of a trend toward correcting that, I have worked to use gender-neutral pronouns for my general examples, non-Western names in my specific examples, and I have changed masculine pronouns in quotations to gender-neutral pronouns using brackets, [ ], to indicate that these changes are mine. If readers find the number of brackets distracting, I can only reply that this is evidence of the extent of the problem.

Each chapter builds on the previous, but I have made an effort to point explicitly to the particular sections of past chapters when I reference them (e.g., "See Section 3.4"). So, if you are primarily interested in, say, authority (Chapter 6), you should be able to read it independently of the rest, turning back to specific sections to fill any gaps.

Acknowledgments

Thanks, as always, to my partner, wife, and colleague, Dr. Laura Guidry-Grimes, to whom I am deeply grateful for enduring tireless conversations on most of the topics in this book, for giving ample feedback, counterexamples, and suggestions, and for being gracious enough to help me organize my life so that I could write it all down. This book is dedicated to her.

Thank you, also, to Jesús Vega Encabo, Elizabeth Fricker, Jon Leefmann, Sophia Dandelet, Winnie Ma, Jesús Navarro, Alejandro Vesga, and Aderonke Ogundiwin. Thanks to C. Thi Nguyen for insightful conversations about expertise, trust, and echo chambers. Thanks to Gabriele Contessa for organizing a reading group on expertise. I have benefited much from discussions with him, as well as Gianluca Andresani, Tony Ward, Catherine Hundleby, Jennifer Szende, Rachel Herdy, Michel Croce, Katie Plaisance, Sushruth Ravish, Ben Almassi, and Maria Baghramian. Thanks to Nathan Nobis, Nick Byrd, and The Brains Blog for supporting my work. Thanks to Colleen Coalter and Becky Holland at Bloomsbury for advocating for this project and guiding it through to publication.

Finally, a book like this wouldn't have been possible without extensive input from experts in a variety of domains. I am grateful for suggestions, insights, critical feedback, and helpful conversations from (in alphabetical order):

Gianluca Andresani, PhD, history of expert legal testimony
Loïc Boulanger, MD, breast surgery oncology
Logan Dwyer, JD, law
Laura Guidry-Grimes, PhD, clinical ethics, disability ethics, psychiatric ethics
D. Micah Hester, PhD, American philosophy and bioethics
Jamie Michael Pearl, PhD(c), ancient philosophy
Samantha Muka, PhD, history and philosophy of science
Angela Scott, MD, PhD, medical humanities and developmental pediatrics
Joshua Byron Smith, PhD, medieval and renaissance studies
Tony Ward, PhD, history of expert legal testimony

Last, but by no means least, I could not have put this book together without the diligent, careful editing and feedback from Rebecca Mullen. Once again, many thanks.

1

Expertise and Its Discontents

Socrates: *And the same holds of the relation of rhetoric to all the other arts; the rhetorician need not know the truth about things; [they have] only to discover some way of persuading the ignorant that [they have] more knowledge than those who know?*

Gorgias: *Yes, Socrates, and is not this a great comfort?—not to have learned the other arts, but the art of rhetoric only, and yet to be in no way inferior to the professors of them?*

(Plato, *Gorgias*, 459b–c, trans. Benjamin Jowett, 1892)

Some people are skeptical of what we might call "traditional experts"—scientists, physicians, engineers, accountants, computer scientists, pharmacists, attorneys, public policymakers, toxicologists, economists, and so on, along with those who work in traditional academic disciplines. Skeptics either doubt that these folks are experts, or they accept that they are experts but doubt whether experts have authority worth taking seriously. It is noteworthy that these skeptics do not doubt that people in traditional expert domains are highly educated or extensively trained; rather, they doubt that "expert" means what has traditionally been claimed for it, namely, *authority*, that what experts say should have some bearing on their beliefs or behavior.

Popular media and political commentators have made much of what appears to be a global phenomenon of rejecting expertise, from the reinvigorated Flat Earth Society, to COVID-deniers, to an international community of anti-vaxxers. One of my favorite memes goes like this:

> 90s scientists: we cloned a sheep! we landed a robot on mars!
> scientists today: for the last time, the earth is *round*

What is frustrating is that, despite their often proud, hard-nosed doubt, expert skeptics seem to get through life pretty well. They work alongside us at our jobs, their kids are fairly normal, they vacation, they retire, they buy motor homes, and so on. Even with public health threats as seemingly well-supported as SARS-CoV-2, expertise-deniers seem to get on with their lives.

One person I know never wore a mask during the COVID-19 pandemic, and he did not stop working, which involved his being in contact with many people. His rationale? COVID-19 is a hoax perpetrated by mainstream media, mainstream medicine and pharmaceutical companies, and liberals for the purpose of making more money (for the researchers) and restricting civil liberties (for the politicians). His justification for this hoax? Among other things, he says the virus has not affected him or anyone he knows. Anyone who says it has is either lying or a dupe.

Interestingly, since we know that about 80 percent of COVID-19 cases are asymptomatic, and another percentage have mild symptoms that mimic the flu or a cold, my acquaintance may *never* know personally anyone affected by COVID-19. So, is his skepticism warranted? Even if his beliefs are false, they don't seem to be doing him or anyone else any harm. If any of us were walking in his shoes living where he lives, in a mid-sized city in a rural US state, could we say that his beliefs don't fit some rational assessment of the evidence?

It is worth noting that expert skeptics tend to choose which kind of expertise to doubt rather shrewdly. They may be happy to go to the doctor for broken bones or an ear infection even if they would never get the flu or varicella vaccine. They may be happy to ride on an airplane even if they think the moon landing was faked. They know that the daily work of software engineers, chemists, and mathematicians is far beyond anything they could comprehend. This suggests that, for the types of expertise they doubt, they perceive some lack of connection between some scientific claims and their relevance for the skeptic that motivates their skepticism. There is not enough correlation, to their minds, to justify believing there is a causal relationship. And they take themselves to be competent to judge such things. Could they be right?

Perhaps it is the non-skeptics who are too gullible. Perhaps many experts lack the importance most of us think they have. Sure, we should only hire carpenters and accountants and concert pianists who have a solid track record of competent work, but the measure of their competence is available to novices, on Angie's List and other customer review sites. But for other domains, where issues are not strongly correlated with results that novices can evaluate, it is not worth our time and energy to try to figure out when to trust them. Can we trust ourselves to evaluate everything we need to evaluate?

1.1 Expert Skepticism and the Enlightenment

As we will see in Chapter 3, the idea that we should think for ourselves and not rely on authorities has been a rallying cry for political liberalism since the Enlightenment. Early modern philosophers like René Descartes and Immanuel Kant encourage people to trust in reason rather than scholars or religious leaders. Natural philosophers like Francis Bacon and Robert Boyle encourage people to trust only what they can test with their own senses. The claim seems to be that the only epistemically responsible way to form beliefs is to think and judge for yourself. Following Kant's famous imperative, "*Sapere aude!*[1] Have the courage to think for yourself!" (1784), I will call this claim the *Enlightenment Mandate*.

We might say that early Enlightenment thinkers lived in simpler times and that they could not have imagined the complexity of technology or science, so the Enlightenment Mandate made more sense than it does today with the dizzying hyper-specialization in almost every domain. But we will also see in Chapter 3 that this interpretation of the Enlightenment Mandate was largely aspirational, even for them, and was practically impossible to follow. By 1835, Alexis de Tocqueville worried that by shifting authority from monarchs to individuals, the people of the United States would simply rely on others to do their thinking for them. Rather than turning to monarchs or experts, they would turn to their neighbors:

> In the United States, the majority takes charge of furnishing individuals with a host of ready-made opinions, and it thus relieves them of the obligation to form their own. There are a great number of theories on matters of philosophy, morality, or politics that everyone thus adopts without examination, on the faith of the public. (2010: 719)

People are busy and tired, and only have time to take an interest in so many domains of knowledge and skill. So, de Tocqueville worried that "public opinion" would, by default, become the authority, and a no less an oppressive one than a monarch. The solution? More individualism:

> As for the action that the intelligence of one man can have on that of another, it is necessarily very limited in a country where citizens, having become more or less similar, all see each other at very close range; and, not noticing in any one of them the signs of incontestable greatness and superiority, they are constantly brought back to their own reason as the most visible and nearest source of truth. Then it is not only confidence in a particular man that is destroyed, but the taste

to believe any man whatsoever on his word. So each person withdraws narrowly into himself and claims to judge the world from there. (2010: 700–1)

The problem, of course, is that we do recognize superiority in others. If not in moral qualities, at least in competence, experience, knowledge, and training. This is precisely why we go to the doctor (we want their advice, not just access to controlled substances), why we hire attorneys (who know how to navigate complex legal issues), and information technology specialists (because few of us can understand the latest technologies). The moment we acknowledge superiority in others, we are faced with a decision about how to interpret the Enlightenment Mandate.

On one interpretation, we are only justified in trusting our own abilities to understand a domain. On the other, we let expert testimony count as a source of evidence alongside that our minds and our senses. If the latter interpretation is more plausible—as even the expert skeptics seem to acknowledge, at least for some types of expertise—then both the expert skeptics and non-skeptics have to wrestle with the questions introduced in the preface: How do we distinguish genuine experts from hobbyists and frauds? What does it mean to say a genuine expert has authority? How strong is that authority for what we should believe or do, and what considerations can justifiably undermine or override it? How can we (whether we are novices or experts) assess the strength of that authority?

To answer these questions, I start with a history of expertise to get a sense of the various meanings of expertise over time and what those imply for belief and behavior. I show how these conceptions have informed a variety of empirical research on expertise. But these descriptive projects only orient us to the problem. They do not offer normative tools for assessing epistemically responsible trust in experts. For these, I turn to social epistemology, starting with the concepts of testimony and epistemic placement, and I show how these inform an adequate account of expert authority. In the final third of the book, I address the "recognition problem" for expertise, which is the challenge of how to adequately identify and assess expert competence. I close with a discussion of how my account of expert authority and solutions to the recognition problem help inform debates on the tension between expertise and democracy.

But before I dive in, we need a sense of the skeptical challenge. What does contemporary expert skepticism look like? Are some versions of it warranted, and, if so, under what conditions? What resources are available to non-skeptics for responding to expert skepticism? Are those resources enough?

1.2 Contemporary Expert Skepticism

The meme I mentioned earlier ("for the last time, the earth is *round*") suggests that expert skepticism is a relatively recent affair, as if the 2000s brought a wave of mistrust in science and medicine. But has the situation really changed much since the 1990s? Did more people accept experts in the 1990s?

The answer is complicated. Groups have long defended a flat earth, denied the moon landing, raised alarm over fluoride in tap water, spun tales of the Illuminati, and flocked to Roswell, NM, rejecting the official story that there was no "UFO incident" in hopes of getting the real story for themselves. There are also dozens of less extreme forms of expert skepticism: belief in naturopathy over and against "mainstream" medicine, belief that farming by astrological signs is more reliable than farming by growing cycles, belief that fad diets are more effective than the basics of scientific nutrition, and the belief that crystals have metaphysical "energy" that affects health and well-being. Part of the complication is that popular media outlets go through waves of reporting on these beliefs, so it is difficult to know precisely when expert skepticism is growing or when it is simply more visible to non-skeptics.

It is, however, easy to find examples that suggest expert skepticism is more prominent now than ever. In the early 2000s, South Africa's ministers of health, the president of Gambia, and a prominent group of medical physicists in Australia began publicly denying the link between HIV and AIDS. Until the end of his presidency in 2008, South African president Thabo Mbeki endorsed his ministers' recommendations to reject standard AIDS treatments in favor of unproven herbal remedies such as ubhejane, garlic, beetroot, and lemon juice (Specter 2007).

In 2007, actress and model Jenny McCarthy appeared on *Larry King Live* claiming that vaccines cause autism. McCarthy's charisma was soon combined with medical researcher Andrew Wakefield's 1998 journal article that suggested a link between the combined MMR vaccine and autism. Despite public controversy over Wakefield's article, the subsequent revelation that Wakefield had manipulated his data to promote his own financial interests, and his paper's retraction in 2010 (Rao and Andrade 2011), the anti-vax movement has now swept across the world (Hussein et al. 2018).

Starting in 2008, public trust in financial institutions dropped 20 percent over the course of two years after political and economic analysts either failed to notice or failed to act on signs of the impending financial collapse in the US mortgage lending market (Smith and Son 2013). In 2009, the emails of scientists at the University of East Anglia's Climatic Research Unit were hacked and made public in a fiasco now called "ClimateGate." One reading of these emails suggests that climate scientists were doing exactly what expert skeptics had accused them of, which was admitting their data was insufficient, fudging the data they had, and biasing the literature by collectively refusing to publish in certain journals.[2]

In her book about immunization, cultural commentator Eula Biss (2014) writes of this period:

> It was not a good season for trust. The United States was engaged in two ongoing wars that seemed to be benefiting no one other than military contractors. People were losing their houses and their jobs while the government was bailing out financial institutions it deemed too big to fail and using taxpayer money to shore up the banks. It did not seem unlikely that our government favored the interests of corporations over the well-being of its citizens. (9)

But, again, was this really any different from previous generations? There have always been skeptics, activists, fringe groups, and conspiracy theorists. Even if skepticism was aimed at new issues or became more visible in the early 2000s, this does not tell us whether expert skepticism has increased in any generally concerning way.

Perhaps surprisingly, trust in scientific experts has "remained stable for decades," though it is, admittedly, not as high as many of us believe is warranted. A Pew Research Center study found that public trust in science has remained at around 40 percent since 1973 (Funk and Kennedy 2019). This study also shows that slightly more Americans—about half—accept the almost unanimous scientific opinion that genetically modified foods are not worse for our health than non-GMO foods (Funk, Kennedy, and Hefferon 2018).

Further, while people who study expertise recognize that different expert domains have different success rates, research suggests that the novice public understands that, as well. For example, a 2013 study found that trust in financial institutions rose sharply with the economy in the 1980s and 1990s, with its roaring financial successes, but then fell sharply again from 2007 to 2010 in the wake of the housing market's collapse, while their trust in the sciences, broadly speaking, remained relatively stable over that time (Smith and Son 2013). A 2018 study of 3,367 experts and novices found a similar degree of confidence in science overall, but it noted distinct differences in confidence in climatologists, after claims about climate change became part of divisive political platforms (Beebe et al. 2019).

This evidence suggests that the novice public is more sensitive to shifts in evidence and distinctions among experts than we often give them credit for. When the public senses a potential conflict of interest in a group of experts, confidence drops. When it senses competence or demonstrable successes, confidence goes up. This means that there may be more to expert skepticism than mere ignorance or bias. If that's true, then understanding the nature of expert skepticism provides an opportunity for non-skeptics to reflect on just how much trust any given expert is due.

1.3 Types of Expert Skepticism

In this section, I look at four categories of expert skepticism: *anecdotal*, *scope*, *disagreement*, and *conflict of interest* skepticism. Though these are by no means exhaustive, many examples of expert skepticism in politics and popular culture fit squarely in one of these categories or a combination of two or more of them. My aim is to capture the main threads of expert skepticism as it is expressed in public debate. If it does, then it shows that many expert skeptics are not that different from those of us who believe we aren't skeptics. At some level of debate, skeptics and non-skeptics share a common language about and sensitivity to evidence. The challenge is to find that common ground and learn how we end up at such different conclusions. Doing so can help us better understand and engage with people who might, at first blush, seem fundamentally irrational for being skeptical of certain types of expertise, but who, on closer examination, have principled reasons for doubting that non-skeptics find compelling in other contexts. In the process, perhaps we will also have better tools for choosing which experts to trust and for deciding how much to trust them.

1.3.1 Anecdotal Skepticism: "Experts Can Be Wrong. I've Seen It!"

In *Strangers in Their Own Land: Anger and Mourning on the American Right* (2016), sociologist Arlie Russell Hochschild attempts to scale what she calls the "empathy wall" between people who share her liberal political views and conservatives in rural and suburban Louisiana by engaging with them through a series of interviews. One theme that emerges from these interviews is the lack of trust some conservatives have in some types of politicians. In many cases, we learn that the distrust is rooted in what the interviewees see as overblown confidence in expert authority.

Instead of trusting that experts tend to get it right, the interviewees focus on the times when experts are wrong. For example, Hochschild observes a conversation between family members about a case where contamination of soil from a chemical company may have compromised the integrity of an interstate bridge. While one brother in this family thought the experts had it right, the other said, "Just because some expert tells you X is true, doesn't mean X is true" (185). This second brother explained that there's a lot of money riding on those decisions, and you have to be "really convinced" before you believe something. He went on:

> Experts can be wrong. You remember in 1963, when the seat belt law hit? I had a Pontiac that had a lap seat belt and I'd sit and wear it. The Chevys and Fords didn't have them . . . . So some people believed it was a good thing and others didn't. And later on, the regulators concluded that the lap belt wasn't the answer. So we'd all agreed to a silly regulation. (185, italics removed)

Because experts have been wrong before—note, in this case, different experts on a different topic—this brother presumes that experts have a higher burden of proof in the case of the bridge's integrity.

Anecdotal skepticism is the wholesale skepticism of a domain (or multiple domains) of expertise on the basis of a selective number of experiences with experts who got it wrong. This kind of cherry-picking of examples is reminiscent of the fallacy of base rate neglect. There's an old joke that demonstrates this fallacy: "I heard that most accidents happen within two miles of my home. So, I moved." The statistic is almost laughably trivial: You are most likely to have an accident where you spend most of your time. But the response is absurd (and therefore funny) because you cannot escape the chance of an accident where you spend most of your time by not being where you spend most of your time. In other words, you can't challenge the base rate likelihood of an event (accidents where you spend most of your time) by looking at the outliers (accidents where you don't spend much time). In Hochschild's conversation, the skeptical brother is trying to challenge the chance that the experts are right by pointing at the times when they were wrong. But this cannot tell us what we need to know. We need to know if the so-called experts in this case are right more often than not. If experts' success rate outstrips their failure rate, then the second brother's objection fails.

1.3.2 Is Anecdotal Skepticism Warranted?

We can think of warrant for a belief in two ways: whether it *makes sense* that someone believes X or whether someone has *sufficient reasons* to believe X.[3] It can make sense for someone to believe something even if they shouldn't, that is, even if they don't have sufficient reasons for believing it. For example, there's an old bit of fatalistic folk wisdom that every time you wash your car, it rains, and another that every time you get in the shower, the phone rings. Psychologist Tom Gilovich (1991) says these beliefs can be explained by the fact that we remember very negative or very positive experiences more vividly than more common experiences—our brain records them differently than ho-hum events. It explains why people remember where they were when John F. Kennedy was shot or what they were doing on 9/11. Since rain on your car and the frustration of answering the phone while wet are negative experiences, these are preserved in our memory more vividly than all the times when it didn't rain after washing our cars and we had call-free showers.

Gilovich calls the vividness of these positive or negative experiences "hedonic asymmetries." They are "hedonic" because they are rooted in our experience of pleasure or frustration, and they are "asymmetric" because we give them more significance in our memories than experiences that do not pique our emotions. So, we can explain why someone would believe, "Every time I wash my car, it rains," even though, upon reflection, they would realize they do not have sufficient reason to believe it. They are ignoring the actual number of times they wash their car—another instance of base rate neglect.[4]

There are lots of reasons why someone might be skeptical of experts that could make sense to us. Maybe they were raised in a household with climate skeptics. Maybe they studied at a university or military school that presented only one perspective on national security and either ignored or dismissed other perspectives as not worth engaging with. Perhaps they had a bad experience with a doctor that triggered a hedonic asymmetry. Let's set aside the question of whether we could make sense of a type of skepticism and focus on whether skepticism about experts could be warranted in the sense of *having sufficient reasons*.

Some types of experts are notorious for being wrong. Consider skepticism about modern medicine. People who are broadly skeptical of modern medicine might concede its benefits when it comes to broken bones and antibiotics but doubt whether doctors are needed when it comes to childbirth, vaccinations, blood pressure, cholesterol, and most surgeries. They have heard horror stories about one or more of these and conclude that medicine is not really as advanced as doctors try to make out. Philosopher Steven Turner explains:

> Professional communities are routinely, if not invariably, wrong. The inductive hypothesis in the philosophy of science, to the effect that our present scientific

views can expect to be proven wrong because all past scientific views have been proven wrong, applies even more strongly to expert opinion, which seems to obey the pendular laws of fashion more often than the laws of scientific progress. To read an expert advice book from the early part of the last century is usually an exercise in the realm of the comic. Not infrequently, one sees the origins of old wives' tales believed by one's grandparents. Yet, these were often based on data and reasoning as good as or better than the data and reasoning employed today. (Turner 2014: 44)

We have already seen that the public is sensitive to revelations of expert incompetence. So, is anecdotal skepticism of medicine warranted?

To answer that, we would need some specific anecdotes to consider. Happily, medicine is no stranger to troublesome examples. We now have good evidence, for instance, that doctors routinely prescribe less pain medication to black patients than white for the same conditions and reported pain levels (Hoffman et al. 2016). They also routinely minimize the pain testimony of women and ignore patient refusals of treatment during childbirth (Hoffman and Tarzian 2001; Robertson 2014; Burns-Piper 2016; Wada, Charland, and Bellingham 2019). Further, as of 2016, medical error is the third leading cause of death in the United States (Makary and Daniel 2016). The problems are not limited to what doctors *do*. They also *say* questionable things. On the list of behaviors the American Academy of Pediatrics "strongly recommends" in 2016 is "Avoid alcohol and illicit drug use during pregnancy and after birth" (AAP Task Force on Sudden Infant Death Syndrome 2016), effectively discouraging anyone who has ever had children from drinking or using drugs. And oncologists offer a dizzying diversity of advice on when women should get breast cancer screenings (we'll look at these claims more closely in Chapter 8).

Do these anecdotes show that medical skeptics are correct? I think the answer is no. Skepticism of a sort is warranted, but not anecdotal skepticism. Why not? Anecdotal skepticism is *wholesale* distrust of a set of practitioners in a domain based on disparate pieces of *anecdotal* evidence. However troublesome anecdotal evidence is, the details matter:

- Different medical treatments have different rates of success, and the ones with higher rates of success deserve, in general, more trust (like appendectomies and penicillin).
- Multiple health factors (age, other illnesses, etc.) make these success rates less reliable for any particular patient, so trust should be lower when the medical picture is complicated.

- Different doctors weigh the value of these success rates and patients' risk factors differently, and this is why team-based medicine and extensive conversations with your doctor are so important.
- But most importantly: refusing medical treatment altogether leaves us with no fewer risks and uncertainties (and sometimes more).

Whether you should be skeptical of medicine comes down to whether you should be skeptical of a particular treatment under a specific set of circumstances. Based on the success rates, black and female patients should be more skeptical of medicine when it comes to their pain management.

The detail-oriented nature of this problem is why the practice of shared decision-making arose. Shared decision-making is a process of crafting medical information in light of a patient's values and preferences that requires extensive dialogue between provider and patient about the values at stake in the decision (Elwyn et al. 2012). It emerged in contrast to the classical practice of a physician or patient simply deciding what's best based on their own knowledge and interests. Thus, shared decision-making, if done well, mitigates, on one hand, against classical paternalistic medicine, which does not adequately account for patients' interest in a treatment plan, and, on the other, against unreflective consumerism, which leaves patients largely unsupported in making potentially life-changing medical decisions. The point is that the details of the treatment, the relationship between the provider and the patient, and the base rates of success matter. Medical experts are, in general, trustworthy to know and practice the *treatment aspects* of medicine. In many cases, there are good reasons to be skeptical of medical experts' ability to apply their expertise to patients' interests and nonmedical well-being. Yet, even in these cases, reasons for skepticism are based on trends (in medical error, pain management in women and people of color, etc.), not on anecdotes.

What's more, even in cases where experts are not highly successful, they may yet be more successful than any alternative. That matters for those of us trying to be epistemically responsible with our beliefs and trust. The trouble, of course, is figuring out which those cases are, what values are at stake, and whether the conditions for trust are met. We will revisit these issues in Chapters 7 and 8.

1.3.3 Scope Skepticism: "Experts Are 'Book Smart,' but They Don't Know X!"

To speak as an expert is, by necessity of human limitation, to speak within a certain domain of information or practice. Even narrow domains of science, such as biology or optics, are no longer small enough that any one person could master them, as say, Aristotle or Descartes once could. What's more, aspects (or subdomains) of domains overlap in sometimes surprising ways. It is perhaps not surprising that a mathematician who works in geometry and a mathematician who works in number theory are both experts in calculus. These domains overlap in intuitive ways. But it might be surprising to learn that a computer programmer is also a calculus whiz. The domains are not as clearly related in our minds. We might get downright suspicious when a climate scientist weighs in on whether a particular public policy will effectively reduce climate change (not least because it is very difficult for anyone to know when a public policy causes its intended effect rather than some extraneous set of factors).

Scope skepticism is the wholesale skepticism of an expert or group of experts on the grounds that those putative experts speak outside the scope of their domain of expertise often enough that they have lost credibility. If an expert doesn't respect their domain's boundaries, then, the argument goes, it is hard to believe they are reliable within their domain—they show no indication that they respect the limits of their competence. In some cases, experts speak outside their domains by *overstepping*, that is, by entering into other domains where they have no business. Nathan Ballantyne (2019) calls this "epistemic trespassing": "Epistemic trespassers are thinkers who have competence or expertise to make good judgments in one field, but move to another field where they lack competence—and pass judgment nevertheless" (2019: 195).

Consider the biologist and atheism promoter Richard Dawkins. Dawkins regularly makes sweeping claims about religion and the history and philosophy of religion. Since Dawkins is a well-respected expert in his domain, these claims embolden those who believe that secular biological views prove that religion is irrational and dangerous. On the other side of this issue, the educator and activist Jerry Falwell, Sr., when he was alive, made regular, sweeping claims about the limits of the sciences. This similarly emboldened those who believe that secular science has a corrupting influence on society. Such experts seem to be stepping from one domain into another for which it is unclear they are qualified. Thus, the skeptics say, we should not trust anything they say. Their testimony is forever tainted.

Scope skepticism is not always about experts overstepping their boundaries, however. In some cases, expertise has clear implications for other domains, and some experts outside those domains are, nonetheless, able to speak to those implications. For example, digital technologies have implications for ethical decision-making, medical research on opioids has implications for medical decision-making for patients with chronic pain, and expertise in energy technology has implications for public policy.

The hard question, in these cases, is how much authority transfers from one domain to the other. Can a computer scientist speak authoritatively about the ethics of a particular digital technology? Can a climate scientist say, with any confidence, whether a public policy will be successful in addressing climate change? In such cases, it may be unwise to listen to a single expert because the decision may be too complex for any single expert to have a sufficiently justified perspective on the matter. It may be better to trust, say, a report from a commission of diverse experts who have worked to piece together evidence from multiple domains.

Scope concerns are common in medical judgment due both to the vast uncertainties in medical treatments and to the need to address patients' values and interests. A physician may tell a husband that his wife is going to die from a certain condition, and the husband may reply with something like: "You know medicine, but you don't know my wife. She's a fighter. I'm not going to believe a prediction like that because I know how tough she is." In such cases, the husband is not wrong to believe that medicine affects different people differently; it does. Whatever trends are demonstrated by empirical research, there are outliers. Research does not capture the unique physiological makeup and complications of individual patients. Thus, the husband's knowledge of his wife *may* be relevant to her medical outcome. The doctor, on the other hand, can only recite what they understand of the literature and their anecdotal experiences. But the doctor may not be wrong that most people in the wife's condition die, and it would be irresponsible of the doctor not to say so. The difficulty, then, is determining where the doctor's expertise ends when it comes to individual patients and how to help people like the husband make decisions if we cannot tell.

Consider Susan Powell, a woman who refused to take statins for her high cholesterol. When interviewed about her decision, Susan explained:

> I'm very much like my father .... Everything he did, he did with gusto, always active. That's the kind of life I want to have. My father lived with a cholesterol level just like mine, and never took a pill. ... I believe that for some people a level of 240 is really dangerous. But for other people, like my family, that kind of number is not really abnormal, not dangerous. (Groopman and Hartzband 2011: 13)

One reason Powell gives for choosing not to take a statin was that she doesn't like taking pills. But the *central* reason seems to be that he has evidence that her family is immune from the negative effects of so-called high cholesterol. The doctor who interviewed her says that she clearly understood the risks of high cholesterol and that she didn't seem to be in denial that she had it (2011: 3).

Interestingly, Powell might have been right. Despite the devastatingly conclusive research on the risks of smoking, some people who have smoked most of their lives still live well into their nineties, completely free of cancer. Similarly, some people seem immune to problems associated with high cholesterol. However, the relevant questions in all these cases—the smoker's case, Powell's case, and the case of the dying wife—are: What do you gain if you're right, and what do you lose if you're wrong?

In the case of the dying wife, maybe the decision is whether to remove a breathing tube that would soon start causing pain and increase the risk of infection or aspiration pneumonia. Perhaps, to this husband, removing the breathing tube would violate their lifelong, mutual promise to care for each other to the best of their abilities. The doctor can't make a judgment about whether that's true. The doctor can only present other value considerations for the husband to weigh. Does that promise include keeping his wife alive *at all costs*? Even if there's no chance she will be conscious again to speak or interact with her loved ones?

But based on experience and the nature of medicine, the doctor is able to offer some advice relevant to his patient's moral interests. Perhaps the patient is not feeling any pain right now, but there may come a time when she will. Perhaps there will be no way to relieve or manage that pain given the limitations of medicine and the patient's extensive medical problems. The doctor should encourage the patient's husband to consider whether preventing his wife from experiencing unnecessary pain is also part of their lifelong promise, and thus, which is the more fundamental commitment of the two: to protect the loved one from pain or to continue a treatment that will prolong life in a way that will increase pain. The scope of the medical expert's authority is limited in such a case, but it is not negligible.

The expert's scope is less limited in Powell's case. Statins are extremely low risk and the benefits are significant. So, even on the rare chance that Susan Powell is right that her family has a special genetic immunity to the effects of high cholesterol, how much should she willing to bet she is right? What is more likely to cause her harm in the long run, trusting the expert or trusting her anecdotal experience of her family history? This doesn't mean the doctor has a right to override Susan's refusal (see Chapters 6 and 8 on the limits of expert authority).

But the doctor's judgment carries more epistemic weight for Powell than it does for the husband of the dying spouse.

1.3.4 Is Scope Skepticism Warranted?

These examples suggest that the answer to this question is yes. Patients and families are more likely to know what a medical treatment *means to them* than their doctors.[5] They are the ones who will live with the effects and burdens of those decisions. Doctors who presume to know better than families about what treatment means to them are violating their epistemic responsibilities and damaging their own credibility. Even though studies show that surrogate decision-makers would not choose what a patient would choose for themselves in around 32 percent of cases (Shalowitz, Garrett-Myer, and Wendler 2006), there is no evidence that doctors would choose more accurately.

This does not, however, mean that a patient or family's scope skepticism justifies rejecting or dismissing any of the doctor's contribution to the decision. The doctor is an expert on medicine even if her expertise is limited by the particulars of any given case. Scope concerns simply shift the question from *whether* the doctor is an expert to how we should *weigh* the doctor's expertise in light of their insider perspective. In Chapter 8, I will explore how drawing a distinction between expert *testimony* and expert *advice* can help novices better understand when and how much to trust experts.

In some cases, skepticism of a *whole domain* of expertise is justified on concerns about scope. It turns out, for example, that financial analysts are notoriously poor market forecasters. No matter how much experience or how many credentials a financial analyst has, research shows that their predictions are no more accurate than chance (Tetlock 2005). So, even if someone is rightly regarded as an expert on economics, how markets work, and how financial analysis should be done (and, therefore, should have their testimony taken seriously on those topics), one might nevertheless be justifiably skeptical of any advice they offer on which stocks to buy or sell. There is also ongoing controversy about the expertise of sommeliers. While some research suggests that most sommeliers guess the quality of a wine no more reliably than chance (Morrot, Brochet, and Dubourdieu 2001; Hodgson 2008, 2009; Goldstein et al. 2008), more recent research, employing a different range of tests (some including neural scans), suggests that sommeliers do have a degree of expertise, though it is narrower than previously thought and more strongly associated with the appearance and smell of the wine than its taste (Zucco et al. 2011; Spence and Wang 2019; Tempere, Revel, and Sicard 2019).

The point here is that the details matter. We cannot justifiably write off an expert or group of experts just because they disagree with our preconceived notions about how things are: "You know your worldview, but you don't know my worldview." At some level, we share an evidence base with experts, and being an intellectually responsible person means dealing responsibly with that evidence. If you believe that, in most circumstances, advanced education, training, and experience in a domain enhance someone's epistemic position and, in many cases, are sufficient for making someone an expert in that domain, you cannot simply dismiss someone with those credentials just because they disagree with you. On the other hand, we have to be realistic that an expert's authority diminishes as they broach topics outside their domain of expertise.

1.3.5 Disagreement Skepticism: "There's an Expert on Every Side of an Issue!"

TV shows like *Law & Order* highlight how attorneys encourage expert skepticism to stymie juries: "You bring your experts. I'll bring mine." The idea is that, if two people, both of whom the jury recognizes as "experts" disagree, a jury should be flummoxed. Since the jury members are not experts—so the reasoning goes—they have no reason to trust one expert over the other, and so one expert's claim cancels out the other's. This sort of strategy is played out in politics, talk shows, and undergraduate philosophy papers where, after sketching arguments on both sides of an issue, politicians, pundits, and students conclude, "And so, no one knows."

Disagreement skepticism is the wholesale skepticism of an expert or group of experts on the grounds that there is an unacceptable degree of disagreement in their domain over a significant issue. Of course, whether a degree of disagreement is "unacceptable" or an issue is "significant" varies widely among skeptics.

For some issues, the simple fact that a few people trained in a domain disagree with everyone else in their domain is enough to cast doubt on the whole domain, as we've seen with climate change (where about 97 percent of climate scientists agree and about 3 percent dissent or are unsure, Cook et al. 2013) and COVID-19 (where videos of random doctors saying that the effects of COVID-19 are overblown are used as evidence that the medical industry is ignoring doubts by experts). For other issues, disagreement is so widespread that even experts have trouble deciding what to believe or what advice to give, as in the case of how frequently women should get mammograms and whether (or which version of) string theory is a plausible account of subatomic physical interactions.

Before asking whether skepticism is warranted, it is worth noting that skepticism, or even suspending judgments, is not the only epistemically responsible response to significant disagreement. In domains where there is great uncertainty, either position may be equally justified, that is, both may be epistemically responsible judgments. For example, when two doctors in an ICU discuss and disagree about the best course of treatment for a patient, it usually means the matter is one of genuine uncertainty, that there is room for reasonable disagreement. Since, in many cases, a range of treatments can have equal benefit, there really might be no *single* right answer; several may be equally likely to be good for the patient. In other cases, holding and defending a contrary position in a disagreement requires discussion, which can reveal that the issue is more complex than initially thought, and that the disagreement was based on an oversimplified understanding of the issue. It could be that neither conflicting judgment in the disagreement was accurate, but only by pressing into the disagreement (rather than deferring to the person who might be thought "more expert") can a justified conclusion be reached. Some philosophers also defend a view like this, arguing that, in cases where two people who seem to be peers on a topic disagree, the most epistemically responsible thing to do is to hold steadfast (Van Inwagen 1996).

On the other hand, in some cases background assumptions can lead to premature abandoning of a disagreement. In some religious traditions, for example, when two people disagree, rather than presuming there is no single right answer or that pressing into the disagreement can be constructive, one person should assume that the problem is a lack of evidence, in particular, the other person doesn't have enough of it. Members are encouraged to view the matter as settled in the sense that there is a metaphysical fact of the matter (which is what they believe). Thus, if someone disagrees, this means only that the truth has not been sufficiently revealed to them. This response was common among early defenders of Creation Science, who were happy with any scientific conclusions that seemed consistent with a literal understanding of the Christian Bible but who rejected any scientific conclusion that contradicted the Bible as spurious and an unfortunate result of the secularization of science.

In contrast to these two responses, others philosophers argue that when two people are similarly situated with respect to the claims and evidence in a domain, as two experts in the same domain should be, then if they disagree, that is a signal that at least one person is wrong, and it could be *either of them*. The only justified response, these philosophers argue, is to suspend judgment, as you cannot tell which judgment is correct (Christensen 2007).

So, when two seeming experts disagree, one might allow that they could both be right, as in the case of the ICU docs, one might entrench in the hopes that the disagreement will work itself out through further research and debate, one might entrench on presuppositional grounds, or one might suspend judgment, admitting that there is no conclusive reason to prefer one judgment over the other.

None of these three responses amount to disagreement skepticism about expertise. Disagreement skeptics take a fifth route. They conclude that, in cases of disagreement among putative experts, expertise is compromised. The putative experts either aren't really experts on the matter or their expertise is not sufficient for addressing it. Either way, no one should trust or defer to experts on this matter; they should be regarded as unreliable. For example, one might argue that there are no experts in philosophy because philosophers disagree about everything. To their point, philosopher René Descartes noted that "nothing can be imagined which is too strange or incredible to have been said by some philosopher" ([1637]1988: 27). Does this mean that skeptics would be right in this case?

To be charitable to the disagreement skeptic, we have to look at the details of their case. Philosophers certainly disagree a lot. But not all philosophical disagreement has resulted in deadlock. In fact, it is odd to treat philosophy as a monolithic project. As with the sciences, there are specialties and subspecialties and sub-subspecialties in philosophy, some with better track records of success than others. David Coady (2012) points to this hyper-specialization in the sciences as a reason to believe there are no "science experts." Science is a kind of "loose baggy monster," and "no one is so well-informed about it that they should be treated as an expert on it" (54). This doesn't, of course, mean that there aren't experts in particular scientific subspecialties. So, while we might rightly dismiss disagreement skeptics for making the above argument against philosophy, this is not the only sort of argument available to the disagreement skeptic.

So, what precisely do disagreement skeptics claim? Journalist David Freedman (2010) looked for evidence in answer to the question, "Can vitamin D supplements help fend off cancer?" The results? He claims there is a hodgepodge of disagreement:

> **No, said a 1999 study.** [John et al.]
> **Yes, said a study in 2006—it cuts risk up to 50 percent.** [Garland et al.]

Yes, said a study in 2007—it cuts risk up to 77 percent. [Lappe et al.]
No, said a 2008 study. [Chlebowski et al.] **(39)**

Freedman concludes, "You'd almost have to laugh at these sorts of seesaw, yes-it-is/no-it-isn't findings, if they weren't addressing potentially life-and-death questions" (40).

Freedman is focusing on one issue in medical science and, based on this, rejecting putative expertise about homeopathic cancer treatments. Unfortunately, on inspection, this is not an especially strong case for disagreement skepticism. The problem is that this argument does not take into account just how many people are members of a domain or what sorts of disagreement that domain is subject to. The two *Nos* on Freedman's list are about *breast cancer*, while the others are about *cancer* in general. Does that make a difference? Could it not be the case that some types of cancer respond to vitamin D and other types not? Further, are the research methods similar in all four studies? Were the two *Yes* researchers using the same tools as the *No* researchers? If not, wouldn't this affect the strength of the conclusion?

One place disagreement skepticism about expertise figures into the broader social conversation is on the topic of climate change. Climate change deniers often point to testimony from actual climatologists who disagree with concerns about global warming trends or their correlation with carbon emissions or their correlation with human behavior. A skeptic motivated by disagreement may conclude that, given these scientists' dissent, there is no settled fact of the matter, and therefore, the intellectually responsible position is to suspend judgment. The problem, again, however, is the base rate of the disagreement. If 97 percent of actively publishing climatologists accept anthropogenic climate change, then the 3 percent who disagree should not engender much concern.[6]

We can imagine an odd sort of court case in which two mathematicians are testifying. One mathematician testifies against Peano's axioms of arithmetic, rejecting the truth of statements like 2 + 2 = 4. The other accepts and defends Peano's axioms. If a jury were to hear one expert reject arithmetic and the other defend it, would they reflectively conclude that there is no settled fact of the matter, or that there must be reasonable disagreement on this matter? The answer, one would hope, is no. The jury members have a much better intuitive sense of the base rate of acceptance than they do of climate scientists. The jury members could say to themselves: *This one mathematician doubts 2 + 2 = 4, but surely she is the only one!* If they are right that the first expert is soundly in the minority, this suggests that the second expert is more trustworthy than the first.

But if all you know in any given case is that two experts disagree—as in the case of many scientific claims—it is too hasty to conclude that "there's no way to know" or that "experts don't know what they're talking about."

1.3.6 Is Disagreement Skepticism Warranted?

In the mathematics court case, the details help us decide because we have good independent reasons for rejecting the outlier mathematician's claim. But in the sciences, we rarely have a toehold on any of the basic concepts needed to assess the claims. We are completely reliant on the experts to work out the issue among themselves. Is disagreement warranted in those cases?

There's a catch here, and it's a bit complicated. Suppose that the general public *knows* that only 3 percent of climate scientists dissent from the idea that climate change is happening or that it's anthropogenic, and they are *unable* to assess the evidence for themselves (unlike the mathematics case, they have no intuitive sense of what a scientist is likely to say). Is the 3 percent *no* cause for concern? The strategy I just suggested for assessing the plausibility of disagreement skepticism is called the "follow the numbers" strategy.[7] It advises us to trust that X is true if most experts believe that X and doubt that X is true as the balance of disagreement among experts approaches 50 percent. If there is significant disagreement—about half think X and half doubt X—then disagreement skepticism on this issue is justified. The rational response is to suspend judgment (see Figure 1.1).

This is good as far as it goes. But imagine the majority of experts believe some claim, X, solely *because two or three* experts believe that X. Notice that I'm not saying that two or three experts did the research, all the experts assessed it, *and all the experts concluded that it supports* X. I'm saying, instead, that two or three experts looked at the evidence and concluded that X, and *on the basis of those*

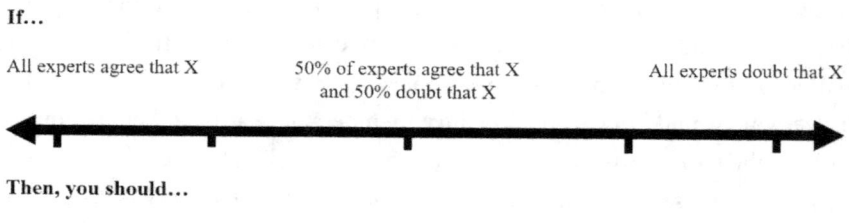

Figure 1.1 Follow the numbers strategy.

experts' testimony all the rest of the experts formed the belief that X. In this case, the majority's belief is *dependent* on the expertise of two or three people.[8] Should our trust that X is true grow just because the pool of people who believe that X grows? Not obviously. Their beliefs that X may not be sufficiently *independent* of one another to count as *additional* evidence that X is true. If Masil tells me that she saw my dog loose, and I believe her, my belief is not more justified when Masil tells Manisha and Manisha believes her.

Consensus among experts can be biased by more than just dependence, as well, and we will explore some of these in Section 8.2.2. But for now, does the possibility of dependence in the case of the 97 percent of climatologists who accept anthropogenic climate change help the disagreement skeptic's case? Not if there are good reasons for thinking the scientists formed most of their beliefs independently of one another.

Unfortunately, here is where the issue gets tricky. This is not how science (or any other domain of study, for that matter) tends to work. Experts' understanding of a domain is highly dependent on the communities in which they learn about that domain. So, most experts' beliefs will be *at least partially* dependent on the beliefs of others in their domain. Their understanding will be formed by reading past research (that they did not replicate themselves), listening to their mentors (who also didn't replicate most of the research), and working in labs where research is predicated on the findings of other labs (and where none of the labs attempted to test or reproduce the others' work).

This is not necessarily a bad thing. New medicines and technologies don't often gain momentum if they aren't doing the work the research suggests they can do. But it could be a bad thing if the majority of scientists are working from, say, the same faulty models, or are using the same faulty methodologies. A famous example from the history of science were those scientists who tried to save Ptolemy's idea that the sun and planets orbit around the earth. Anytime a celestial object moved in a way that the theory couldn't predict (such as Mars's retrograde motion), defenders would add a new orbital path for that object (called an epicycle). By the sixteenth century, defenders had added so many epicycles to explain all the aberrant motion that the theory was no longer functional.

Is the consensus on climate change a function of bad modeling? Interestingly, all predictive modeling must be regularly adjusted as new evidence comes in. Before we answer this question about climate change, consider the challenge of modeling the spread of SARS-CoV-2. Shinde et al. (2020) list fifteen variables that must be considered when trying to predict the transmission rate of the SARS-CoV-2 virus:

(a) Daily death count.
(b) Number of carriers.
(c) Incubation period.
(d) Environmental parameters, that is, temperature, humidity, wind speed.
(e) Awareness about COVID-19.
(f) Medical facilities available.
(g) Social distancing, quarantine, isolation.
(h) Transmission rate.
(i) Mobility.
(j) Geographical location.
(k) Age and Gender.
(l) Highly and least vulnerable population.
(m) Underlying disease.
(n) Report time.
(o) Strategic policies and many more.

If any one of these variables change, the predicted transmission rate can change. This makes it difficult for anyone but experts to know whether the model works. But if all nonexperts hear is that predictions are constantly changing, it sounds a lot like multiplying epicycles to save a theory.

The point is that the 3 percent of scientist climate skeptics *could* be cause for concern *if* we had good reasons to believe the 97 percent are linked by a flawed assumption or flawed belief-forming process, or are substantively dependent on the assumptions and findings of their predecessors. What's different between climate change and SARS-CoV-2 is that most epidemiologists and infectious disease researchers readily admitted that there was a great deal of uncertainty with their models—they were still learning about the virus and whether their models were up to the task of tracking it. This is not the case with climate scientists. While climate predictions change by a few degrees as they tweak their models in accordance with new data, they express less uncertainty about the models themselves (National Academy of Sciences 2001). Without additional information, we are not justified in rejecting the domain of climate science just because there is disagreement among a very small minority of climate scientists.

Disagreement skepticism is also warranted when we have good reason to believe a domain is systematically biased. As suggested on TV shows like *Law & Order*, in real-life legal cases, attorneys use conflicting expert testimony to instill doubt among juries and judges. It would be one thing if this pitting of experts against one another were in service of an honest debate among peers. Even then, it might be no small feat for a jury to assess the strength or reliability of expert testimony. But the primary goal of attorneys is to win cases (and not to prove something about nature or arithmetic). Experts are chosen according to whether they are convincing, not whether they are likely to be right.[9] As legal scholar Samuel Gross (1991) puts it: "If expert witnesses were selected by chance or by some other unbiased procedure, we might be right to give weight to" factors like "verbal fluency, ease of manner, the appearance of humility, stellar credentials, etc." Instead: "The confident expert witness is less likely to have been chosen because she is right, than to have been chosen because she is confident whether or not she is right" (1134). Confounding factors like biased interests escalate the problem: Maybe experts disagree, and maybe the experts who are less likely to be right come across just as competently as any other. In either case, novices are left in a lurch, which makes disagreement skepticism prudent. The key here is that understanding the context, the base rate of consensus, and the reasons for consensus makes a difference as to when disagreement skepticism is prudent.

1.3.7 Conflict-of-Interest Skepticism: "Experts Only Say That Because . . ."

Conflict-of-interest skepticism is the wholesale skepticism of an expert or group of experts based on suspicions that they have ulterior motives for their stated beliefs or advice. This skepticism has a long lineage. In the 300s BCE, critics of the Hippocratic physicians[10] claimed they "knowingly cared for those who would heal spontaneously while neglecting those who would die" simply "to advance their popularity and defend their art and reputations" (Bartz 2000: 9). In Plato's *Protagoras*, Socrates warns us of the ulterior motives of advertisers and food merchants: "they just recommend everything they sell" (313d).

We have good reasons to believe that financial incentives, social privilege, and other biasing interests can undermine the authority of putative experts to speak as experts. In one-off cases, this problem is known as the "poisoning the well" fallacy, as when golfer Tiger Woods promotes one brand of golf club over another. Woods is an expert golfer, and he may have chosen to promote those clubs because he genuinely prefers them. On the other hand, we have to admit that he might promote them simply because the company is paying him to. Some experts may be less susceptible to these influences than others, but few of us are in a position to tell which those are.

Recall Hochschild's interviews with conservative Louisianans. In addition to experts' tendency to be wrong, another widespread suspicion among her interviewees is that government agencies and large oil corporations have conflicts of interest that lead them to either harm the environment or unjustly curtail the rights of citizens, and, in some cases, both. For example, one interviewee pointed out that if a corporation dumped chemicals that killed a whole swamp, no one from the government would bat an eye. But if he, a private citizen, shot an eagle or drizzled a little gasoline into the water, he would be fined and likely imprisoned. Why, then, should he trust the government's "environmental experts" who advocate for more regulations that hurt people like him and benefit people who are not like him (Hochschild 2016)? Their motives undermine their ability to speak authoritatively about what regulations should be passed or enforced. Thus, for some of Hochschild's interviewees, the whole notion of *environmental expert* is tainted by conflicts of interest.

Just as perceived disagreement is a problem for experts, so is a perceived conflict of interest. During the COVID-19 pandemic of 2020, the rallying cry of people I call "COVID-deniers" was that politicians were colluding with mainstream medicine to make the pandemic seem worse than it was. It didn't matter that the majority of epidemiologists, infectious disease researchers, ICU doctors, and public health experts—most with no financial stake in the issue—testified to the dangers of SARS-CoV-2. According to the skeptics, it was the minority of dissenters, like Bakersfield, CA doctors Dan Erickson and Artin Massihi, whose YouTube "press conference" went viral, who revealed the truth about the conflicts of interest motivating the conspiracy to deceive the public.

1.3.8 Is Conflict-of-Interest Skepticism Warranted?

I think the answer has to be yes, with strong caveats. In some cases, some putative expertise—and in some cases, whole domains of putative experts—really do have conflicts of interest that incentivize bad behavior and compromise the authority of a domain (see David Coady 2012: Chapter 5). Political think tanks, for example, which tend to be organized solely for the purpose of defending a particular political position or way of approaching a political topic, have a conflict of interest that should make us question their authority to speak as experts in a domain. Note that this doesn't mean that think tank members are not genuine experts. It is that they have conflicts of interest that can prevent them from speaking on the basis of their expertise.

Political action groups like the ACLU, Southern Poverty Law Center, and PETA also engage in public activities that raise questions about their neutrality on particular issues. Economists who are known to have been trained in one style of economics rather than another can so distort empirical research that they are not trustworthy on economic matters.

In some cases, discoveries of conflict-of-interest backfire. Consider, again, Andrew Wakefield, the medical researcher who published a study suggesting that the combined MMR vaccine is correlated with occurrences of autism. He was not, contrary to popular belief, against individual vaccines for mumps, measles, and rubella, only the MMR. Nevertheless, an investigation revealed that his claim about the MMR was not based on his judgment as a scientist or his opinion as an ideologue. Instead, Wakefield had falsified his data because he was being funded by attorneys who were defending parents in lawsuits against pharmaceutical companies (Rao and Andrade 2011). Wakefield traded on his scientific expertise to produce fraudulent research, and so he really was only saying that the MMR vaccine was correlated with autism because he was being paid.

For most of us, this discovery, and the subsequent retraction of Wakefield's publications on the topic, were strong enough evidence to distrust this man and to retain our belief that no type of vaccine causes autism. But for many who were convinced by Wakefield, the evidence backfired. For the conflict-of-interest skeptics, the evidence really suggested the depths of the conspiracy to discredit him and the "real" scientific findings that vaccines can, indeed, cause autism. The conflict of interest was not with Wakefield, they argued, but with the pharmaceutical companies who were ultimately behind the investigation.

This raises the question of how we should assess conflicts of interest. Which side does a conflict impugn? How can we tell who acts from which motives? In Wakefield's case, it should be easy. Neither vaccine research nor autism research has been considered compromised by the bad behavior of one researcher. But with the proliferation of seemingly professional groups and websites advocating competing positions on topics from whether the earth is flat to whether fluoride in drinking water is poisonous, conflicts of interest are not always easy to spot. Knowing precisely when financial, ideological, or other interests are undermining what seems like expertise is difficult. Unless there is a formal investigation or information leak (by parties with no obvious conflicts of interest), it is almost impossible to be sure what's behind any particular expert's claim. This is where the issue of trust, and which social mechanisms ensure it, becomes paramount. I explore the notion of trust more thoroughly in Chapter 8.

1.4 Responding to Skepticism about Expertise

1.4.1 The Standard Response

What is the intellectually responsible reaction to expert skepticism? The simplest and most obvious response is to point out that, despite the failings of individual experts, despite the fact that every set of experts has a track record of failures, and despite serious limitations on the scope of expert authority, experts tend to be in a better position than novices to make certain claims or perform certain tasks. Pilots fly and land planes safely more often than not. Surgeons operate successfully more often than not. Not only more often than not: *much* more often than anyone who isn't a pilot or a surgeon. To be sure, not all experts need to be able to perform a task more often than not.[11] Sharpshooters hit their targets significantly more than novices, and for some domains and circumstances, that is enough, even if their overall success rate is relatively modest.

Call this descriptive principle the *Presumption of Epistemic Advantage (PEA)*:

Presumption of Epistemic Advantage (PEA): Other things being equal, experts stand in a better position than novices with respect to claims and practices in their domain of expertise.

Harry Collins and Robert Evans explain: "The assumption means simply that in spite of the fallibility of those who know what they are talking about, their advice is likely to be no worse, and may be better, than those who do not know what they are talking about" (2007: 2). Nichols also expresses a version of PEA: "[W]hile our clumsy dentist might not be the best tooth puller in town, he or she is better at it than *you*" (2017: 36, emphasis his).

The descriptive principle PEA, combined with the desire or normative demand that we novices do what we can to put ourselves in a better position, can be used to justify a normative principle to trust experts. If experts stand in a better position than novices with respect to X, and novices have a vested interest in X, then novices have a practical reason to trust experts with a claim or task. Call this the *Principle of Normative Deference (PND)*:

Principle of Normative Deference (PND): Other things being equal, novices ought to defer to the judgments of experts in a domain of knowledge or practice.

Philosopher John Hardwig (1985) gives the classic statement of PND: "[T]he lay[person] cannot rationally refuse to defer to the views of the expert or experts [they acknowledge]" (333). Hardwig continues that, even if the layperson has some reason to think the expert is wrong, "the final court of rational appeal belongs solely to one party, by virtue of that party's greater competence for and commitment to inquiry into the relevant subject matter" (333), namely, the expert's. According to Hardwig, the novice has no higher court of appeal.

In many cases, these principles capture precisely what we think expertise entails. If someone is a mathematician and you are not, they stand in a better position than you with respect to claims about mathematics. If you have an interest in some mathematical calculation—winning a bet, building a skyscraper, calculating your grades—then, other things being equal, you ought to trust the mathematician about that calculation. Let's call the combination of PEA and PND the "standard response to skepticism."

1.4.2 Limitations of the Standard Response

Unfortunately, the caveat "other things being equal" is no innocent turn of phrase.[12] Even if we accept that someone who is an expert has epistemic authority in a domain, that does not tell us everything we need to know in order to defer trust to people who claim to have expertise:

- We still don't know how to reliably identify an expert in a domain.
- We are often not sure they are speaking only in their domain. (Are we confident enough to know the difference between a molecular biologist and a geneticist? Between a pulmonologist and a cardiologist?)
- We are often not sure whether they are speaking as experts or because they have a conflict of interest (whether political, moral, religious, etc.).
- We have not addressed the question of what's at stake for us in their claim. (Is it something innocuous, like which route we should take to work? Is it something of paramount importance to us, like whether our child will go to hell if we get it wrong?)

Answering these questions is complicated in large part because expertise looks very different in different domains. Predicting the weather is very different from building a skyscraper, and both are very different from writing history. Some measures of expertise are quantitative, or at least easily accessible: How many bullseyes a sharpshooter hits relative to misses, how many free throws a basketball player makes relative to misses. Other measures of expertise are not really "measures." Consider the domain of medicine called "palliative care."

Palliative care physicians are experts in symptom management, especially pain, and end-of-life counseling and care. How does someone know whether a palliative care physician is doing a good job? Take just one aspect of palliative medicine, commonly called "comfort care." This is the care that's provided when attempts to cure an illness have failed and the remaining role of medicine is to help keep a patient comfortable until they die. We might try to come up with some observable clinical outcomes that are correlated with "good" comfort care. But what could those look like? Palliative care physician Michael Pottash is skeptical of such a project:

> If the goals of the patient and family are to prioritize symptom management over life prolongation then ask the question of every test, intervention, or medication: Does this promote quality of life? Some life-prolonging interventions can be continued without impacting quality, if the patient so chooses. This will all depend on the patient's preferences and the clinical context. That is why it is impossible to create a Comfort Care algorithm, bundle, or pathway—clinical reasoning is still required. (Pottash 2019)

The expertise of a palliative care physician, according to Pottash, is in understanding all these hypotheticals, how medicine can address them, and then helping patients and families arrive at decisions that are most comforting for them. It's not about any particular outcome—every patient and situation will be different in some relevant way. To try to compare the competence of palliative care physicians with the competence of surgeons is to misunderstand the pluralistic nature of expertise.

Even if we could answer the questions above to our satisfaction in a particular domain, there are many cases where (PEA) holds while (PND) does not. As we saw earlier, a doctor may claim to know the best medical treatment for someone's wife because the doctor knows how successful certain treatments are for certain conditions. But it is not clear that the doctor really knows the best treatment for *that woman* in light of her values and the goals she has for her health care. In this case, the doctor is an expert speaking in the domain of her expertise. But that domain has implications for other domains, domains about which the woman and (hopefully) her husband have much more intimate understanding.

To take another example from above, some experts are notoriously bad forecasters. When asked to predict events—the stock market, political shifts, the prices of precious metals, criminal recidivism, which people are likely to default on loans—some experts either miss their mark entirely or do significantly worse than some simple mathematical tools. Other experts are only marginally better at making predictions than novices. In all these cases, it may be better to trust statistical prediction rules or algorithms over expert judgments.[13] This means that the details of an expert domain matter for the scope and degree of an expert's epistemic authority.

If all this is right, then (PEA) does not strongly support (PND). The standard response to expert skepticism is not sufficient. In some cases, experts should be trusted, and in some cases skepticism about expertise is warranted.[14] In still other cases, what counts as adequate response to claims of expert authority will depend on what type of expertise is at stake and under what conditions. Claims to expertise and domains of expertise must be evaluated on a case-by-case basis. To do this, we need a richer understanding of what expertise is, what it implies for both experts and novices, and what advantages it affords in different circumstances.

1.5 Summing Up: Where Do We Go from Here?

Perhaps surprisingly, we have already made some progress. The real trouble with expertise, it turns out, is not whether experts exist or whether experts are typically more competent than novices in their domain. These claims are not, in general, controversial. We want people to go to medical school and do what doctors do, and we want the same goes for lawyers, and pilots, and so on. The real trouble is telling when someone is really an expert (rather than a fraud), assessing the extent of someone's expertise, identifying the strengths and limits of an expert's authority on a specific question, and deciding whether or how much to trust an expert in any given circumstances. It is with these questions in mind that we start our tour of the history of expertise.

2

English and Ancient Roots

Now Zeus, king of the gods, made Metis his wife first, and she was wisest among gods and mortal men. But when she was about to bring forth the goddess bright-eyed Athena, Zeus craftily deceived her with cunning words and put her in his own belly, as Earth and starry Heaven advised. . . . for very wise children were destined to be born of her, first the maiden bright-eyed [Athena], equal to her father in strength and in wise understanding.
(Hesiod, *Theogony* §§885–95, trans. Hugh G. Evelyn-White, 1914)

The phenomenon we call "expertise" is not a new concept, though it has gone by different names over the centuries. The idea that some people have privileged access to knowledge that others don't—people like politicians, doctors, orators, and ship pilots—raised a number of questions for ancient thinkers. Over the next three chapters, I sketch the lineage of our contemporary notion of expertise. I start in this chapter by exploring the roots of the English word "expert," tracing them to the Latin *expertus* (2.2). There, we find that *expertus* is mostly used of a rather weak sense of "experience"—a term better fit for a chess hobbyist than for a grandmaster—and, therefore, does not capture much of our contemporary meaning. In Section 2.3, I turn to concepts related to the current use of *expertise—authority, cunning intelligence,* and *skill*. Here, we find uses that reflect not only contemporary meaning but also discussions that inform contemporary debates. The Greek *techne* is, arguably, the word most commonly translated into English as "expert," so in Section 2.4, I explore some of its nuances. In Sections 2.5 and 2.6, I look at the relationships among *techne*, *episteme*, and the Latin *ars*, the last of which becomes "art" in English.

What emerges from this selective history is three distinct uses of the term expertise—*localized, generalized,* and *specialized* expertise. We will see that these uses are organized around the belief that competence comes in degrees; instead of being a distinct kind of epistemic state, history suggests that expertise is the upper end of quite common experiences of study and repetition. Further, we find that, rather than being the product of genius or divine dispensation, expertise is the result of extensive training and much practice. In the chapters that follow, I highlight how concepts related to expertise are used in the Middle Ages, in the Enlightenment, in the late nineteenth and early twentieth centuries, and in the history of expertise studies.

The history I sketch in these chapters is too abbreviated to do full justice to the rich domain of expertise studies. Research on expertise has grown exponentially since the mid-1980s, and my point is not to capture every nuanced development. My history is also highly selective. For example, I do not trace the emergence of neurological studies of expertise. This is partially for the sake of brevity but also partially because its history is so new that it is hard to assign it an identifiable narrative and trajectory. I also do not delve deeply into the sociological studies of expertise (the Sociology of Scientific Knowledge, or SSK), though, in Chapter 3, I highlight an important problem SSK raises for expertise studies and point to how others have wrestled with it (see, e.g., Seidel 2014). For the sake of precision, I do not explore how expertise figures in what education researchers call Activity Theory (see Engeström 2018). My goal here is only to highlight developments that help explain some of the variety in how expertise is used today and to draw some distinctions that will help enrich a philosophy of expertise. My hope is that it will clear the conceptual ground for fresh approaches to expertise and serve as a starting point for more robust histories of expertise.

2.1 The Challenge of History

Discussions of expertise often begin by narrowly defining the word in terms of one type or set of traits or skills. Some contemporary scholars, for example, study superior performance (e.g., chess grandmasters, Olympic athletes) and call this expertise. Others study the way society confers on individuals the right to speak authoritatively on a matter (e.g., expert witnesses, professors) and regard that as constitutive of expertise. Still others study expertise as the ability to perform as a professional (e.g., accountants, attorneys, mechanics). Further, some scholars start by connecting their use of the word to an older concept, like the Greek techne (τέχνη) or the Latin *expertus*. Given the complexity of the concept of expertise, this strategy of reducing the concept to a narrow, but clear, definition is often warranted. Scholars must start somewhere. In many cases, whatever narrow definition is invoked gets them enough of what they need the term for. And, of course, empirical researchers must define terms precisely enough to get clean empirical results. Such definitions are called *operational* definitions.

The danger of this sort of reductionism, however, is that it tends to favor certain aspects of expertise over others, for example, giving prominence to traits that lend themselves more easily to research (e.g., chess wins, response-time, accuracy) than others (e.g., understanding, helpfulness, qualitative judgment). This imbalance can lead to generalizing from certain types of empirical research or pragmatic uses to the concept of expertise generally. Another danger, at least for new scholars to the domain, is that it makes expertise studies seem simpler than it is: They might think expertise is merely either a matter of extensive knowledge or exceptional performance that emerges from experience, as most dictionaries have it (and far too many scholars rely on dictionaries to circumscribe technical terms). Yet, a quick tour of the history of expertise and its related concepts reveals two things. First, expertise is incredibly complex, operating in the overlap of a diversity of discussions across a diversity of languages and cultures.[1] Second, the meaning of expertise is unavoidably constrained by context; different writers use different words to highlight different functions and implications of expertise. This makes the idea that any one of them is constitutive of expertise implausible.

This does not mean that an etymological study of a complicated term like *expertise* is of little value. It just means the job is a little different than collecting instances of the word and then seeing what they have in common. An etymological study aimed at informing a philosophy of expertise requires collecting instances along with their contexts to see what work the word is intended to do in that context, and then comparing those intended uses with what conceptual analysis and empirical sciences suggest is plausible. Getting a clearer sense of how expertise and the concepts associated with it have been used can help prevent us from falling back on faulty assumptions about expertise, can help us resist generalizing hastily from overly narrow uses, and can reshape our intuitions about what experts are, how to recognize them, and how we should respond to them.

2.2 The English *Expert*

The contemporary English word "expert" is a descendent of the Latin word *expertus*, which is derived from *experior*, or "experience." Yet, while *experience*, of some sort or other, has attached itself to expertise through history, the nature of that experience is quite diverse. The statesman Cicero and the playwright Plautus, for example, used it to refer to anecdotal experiences:

> Everything which I am saying about Plancius, I say having **experienced** [*expertus*] the truth of it in my own case. (Cicero, *For Plancius*, ch. 9, § 22)

> I' faith, I find **by experience** [*experior*] how much you value your wife. (Plautus, *Amphitryon, or Jupiter in Disguise*, act 1, scene 3)

Expertus could also simply mean "to try," as in Cicero's eighth letter to Atticus and the historian Livy's *History of Rome*:

> As to your frequent remarks in your letters about pacifying my friend, I have done everything I could and **tried** [*expertus*] every expedient; but he is inveterate against you to a surprising degree, on what suspicions though I think you have been told, you shall yet learn from me when you come. I failed to restore Sallustius to his old place in his affections, and yet he was on the spot I tell you this because the latter used to find fault with me in regard to you Well, he has found by personal **experience** [*expertus*] that he is not so easy to pacify, and that on my part no zeal has been lacking either on his or your behalf. (Cicero, *Letters to Atticus*, VIII (A.I.3))

> Hannibal had **tried** [*expertni*] everything before withdrawing from the fight. (Livy, *History of Rome*, Book 30.35)

Further still, it was sometimes used to mean the experience of "testing," as in "trying something out," a sort of one-off trial. For example, the poet Ovid uses *expertus* to express Sol's outrage at Jupiter for killing his son Phaethon, saying that Jupiter should take the reins of his chariot, putting its flame-footed steeds "to the test":

> [L]et Jupiter himself do it, so that for a while at least, while he tries [*temptat*][2] to take the reins, he must put aside the lightning bolts that leave fathers bereft! Then he will know when he has **tried** [*expertus*] the strength of those horses, with hooves of fire, that the one who failed to rule them well did not deserve to be killed. (Ovid, *Metamorphoses*, Book 2: 389–93, A. S. Kline trans.)

These examples show that the Latin *expertus* does not convey, inherently, the sense of specialized skill, knowledge, or authority that seemed at stake in Chapter 1. It turns out that this sense is not found consistently in English usage until the 1780s.

The earliest known[3] English use of *expert* is as a verb (*to expert*) in the 1387 Middle English translation of Ranulf Higden's (1280–1364) Latin *Polychronicon*, which is a general history of the world:

> but the women **experte**
> the knowlege of diuerse [diverse] [people], the childer [children] of whom were callede Spartani.

Geoffrey Chaucer (*c*. 1340–1400) uses it twice as an adjective in his mid-1380s poem "Troilus and Criseyde" to describe the priest Calchas's scientific knowledge and the knowledge that comes from the experience of being in love:

Book 1—§10

Original
Now fil it so, that in the toun ther was
Dwellinge a lord of greet auctoritee,
A gret devyn that cleped was Calkas,
That in science so **expert** was, that he
Knew wel that Troye sholde destroyed be,
By answere of his god, that highte thus,
Daun Phebus or Apollo Delphicus.

Modernized
Now it fell out that in the town there was
living a lord, of great authority,
a powerful priest who was named Calchas,
in science a man so **expert** that he
knew well that Troy would fall utterly,
by the answer of his god that was called thus:
Dan Phoebus or Apollo Delphicus.

Book 2—§ 196

Original
And certainly, I noot if thou it wost,
But tho that been **expert** in love it seye,
It is oon of the things that furthereth most,
A man to have a leyser for to preye,
And siker place his wo for to biwreye;
For in good herte it moot som routhe impresse,
To here and see the giltles in distresse.

Modernized
And certainly, I know not if you know'st,
but those who are **expert** in love this say,
that it is one of the things that furthers most,
for a man to have a chance to pray
for grace, and in a proper place, if he may:
for on a good heart pity it will impress,
to hear and see the guiltless in distress.
(Trans. A. S. Kline 2001)

These English uses suggest a stronger association between "expertise" and "extensive experience" than its Latin predecessor. These early uses are also consistent with their closest linguistic cousins, the Norman *expert* and the Old French *expert* or *appert* (meaning dexterous or nimble) (Cotgrave 1611), both of which also derive from *expertus*. Other Middle English writers sometimes use the term "apert" synonymously with "expert," combining its Old French meaning of "clever" with "espert," another variation of *expertus*. The difficulty, of course, is that this range of meanings is unified—to the degree that it is—only by a vague notion of some undefined amount of experience with a domain.

Unfortunately, the difficulty is not resolved by modern English usage. William Shakespeare (1564–1616) uses the noun "expertness" as a quality of skill in combat in *All's Well That Ends Well*:

First Soldier: Well, that's set down.
[Reads]

"You shall demand of him, whether one Captain Dumain
be i' the camp, a Frenchman; what his reputation is
with the duke; what his valour, honesty, and
expertness in wars; or whether he thinks it were not 2265
possible, with well-weighing sums of gold, to
corrupt him to revolt." What say you to this? What
do you know of it? (Act 4, Scene 3, lines 1260–1268)

In *King Henry VI, Part 1*, he uses the adjective to mean someone with extensive experience as a soldier:

Lord Talbot: . . .
Now will we take some order in the town,
Placing therein some **expert** officers,
And then depart to Paris to the king. . . (Act 3, Scene 2, lines 1591–3)

In *Othello*, Shakespeare uses the adjective "expert" to indicate a highly qualified ship's captain:

Montano: Is he well shipp'ed?
Cassio: His bark is stoutly timber'd, and his pilot
Of very **expert** and approved allowance. . . (Act 2, Scene 1, lines 48–50)

None of these instances tells us precisely what kind of skill is *expert-level* skill, or how much experience makes one an expert, or what sort of experience makes one highly qualified. But we do start to see a narrowing of meaning. An experienced soldier or captain has certain advantages over someone who has never served in that role. These advantages can be used to invoke a sense of authority. The question as yet unanswered is the precise nature and implications of those advantages.

In 1612, Francis Bacon distinguishes "experts" from the "Learned": "For **expert** men can execute, & perhaps judge of particulars, one by one; but the generall counsels, and the plots, and marshalling of affaires, come best from those that are Learned" (163). In what follows, Bacon says that study perfects experience, but that study must be constrained by experience. This suggests that expertise is something like the middle-point of a continuum between two extremes: the person who simply has experience in a domain and one who simply studies it. The appropriate admixture, for Bacon, is somewhere in the overlap. An expert, in this sense, is someone whose experience has been enhanced by but not subsumed under study.

The narrower sense of experience in a domain that we now associate with specialists became firmly connected to the English word *expert* in the British legal system in the seventeenth century. Recognizing that some people were better positioned to speak on some matters than others wasn't new. Legal scholar Learned Hand (1901) says the practice of enlisting the advice of "particularly qualified" people to help decide legal cases can be traced back into fourteenth-century London. He gives examples from both civil and criminal cases, including one from 1345, in which "the court summoned surgeons from London to aid them in learning whether or not the wound was fresh" (42–3). But these requests tended to happen before any formal legal proceedings to determine whether formal legal proceedings were warranted.

By 1554, people with specialized "knowledge and skill" were regularly sought for advice in legal matters:

> If matters arise in our law which concern other sciences or faculties, we commonly apply for the aid of that science or faculty which it concerns, which is an honorable and commendable thing in our law, for thereby it appears that we do not despise all other sciences but our own, but we approve of them, and encourage them as things worthy of commendation . . . In an appeal of mayhem the Judges of our law used to be informed by surgeons whether it be mayhem or not, because their knowledge and skill can best discern it. (*Buckley v. Rice*, 1 Plowd. 125 (1554))

But even in these cases, specialists were not brought in to testify in front of juries. They were either consulted by judges and juries privately, outside of the trial, or they were asked to sit on a "special jury" of people with specialized knowledge or experience. This changed in the seventeenth century when courts requested medical testimony and reports (usually autopsies) to be presented as evidence during a trial. Autopsy reports were used as evidence in criminal cases as early as 1662 (Watson 2006: 376).

The connection between specialized knowledge or skill and the term "expertise" seems to have been made in France's legal system during the reign of Louis XIV. The king's Criminal Code, or Great Ordinance (*Grand Ordonnance*), of 1670, identifies experts as people the criminal court could turn to for review of or advice on technical matters. By 1808, the concept of an expert witness was acknowledged in Napoleon Bonaparte's Criminal Code—"No one can be a juror in the same case where he has been a judicial police officer, witness, interpreter, **expert** or party, on pain of nullity" (Section I, Article 392)—but the document does not elaborate on the concept.[4]

In the British legal system, the concept of "expert witness," that is, someone whose opinion on abstract technical matters could be presented to a jury as evidence acquired special status in 1782, in the case of *Folkes vs. Chadd*. Though the British legal system was "adversarial," that is, two parties pleaded their case before a judge or jury, people with specialized knowledge—usually doctors, ship captains, or handwriting analysts—were often treated like officers of the court in the "inquisitorial" legal systems of continental Europe—where judges were responsible for making relevant investigations and rendering judgment. The practice of "party-called" specialists was not completely new with *Folkes v. Chadd*, but the judge's decision in the case is widely regarded as legitimizing the practice (Golan 2008: 899).

In the three trials associated with the *Folkes v. Chadd* dispute (1781 and 1782), specialists were called in by each of the parties in a dispute over an embankment that was built on Wells Harbour in 1758. The harbor had started to deteriorate,[5] and "the Harbor's board of commissioners [led by a lawyer named Chadd] decided to take legal action against one of the biggest landlords [Sir Martin Browne Folkes], whose embankment, it felt, was the most harmful to its harbor" (Golan 2008: 889).

In the initial trial (1781), a specialist named Robert Mylne, who was a fellow of the Royal Society and the owner of an architecture-engineering business in London. What's noteworthy is that members of the Royal Society were pioneers in a new way of doing science (which we will see in more detail in the next chapter). The old way consisted primarily of extensive practice in a domain, for example, doctors and ship captains. The new way employed more sophisticated instruments and experiments. It came to be called "Newtonian," for all of Isaac Newton's successes (though he was not the first to practice this new scientific method). Rather than presenting their case only in terms of experience and observation, Fellows of the Royal Society appealed to general principles and predictions based on patterns in nature.

Mylne's testimony, which relied upon his extensive understanding of tides, winds, and geography, proved compelling to the special jury, and they decided the case in Folkes's favor. But his arguments were baffling to the commission and the surrounding community, who did not trust someone who had not lived near and observed the harbor for years, as they had. The novelty of Mylne's testimony was enough for the judge to grant the commission a re-trial, during which they could bring their own experts to investigate the matter.

In the second trial (1782), Folkes had another expert review the matter: John Smeaton, who was also a fellow of the Royal Society and a civil engineer, and who "was considered the highest authority on harbors in the kingdom" (Golan 2008: 892). Smeaton studied the harbor for three days and then spent time in

London studying its history. Rather than calling engineers or other scientifically trained witnesses to testify, one of the commission's barristers, named Hardinge, decided to call "a long line of mariners and navigators," who had experience with the harbor. Hardinge further objected to Smeaton's testimony on the grounds that it was "a matter of opinion, which could be no foundation for the verdict of the jury, which was to be built entirely on facts, and not on opinions" (Golan 2008: 895). The judge in that case, Chief Justice Henry Gould, accepted this reasoning and excluded Smeaton's testimony. This led Folkes to request a third trial on grounds that his witness had been inappropriately silenced.

It was the third trial (1782) that led to the landmark decision. The judge, William Murray Lord Mansfield, in addressing Hardinge's compliant, wrote:

> A confusion now arises from a misapplication of terms. It is objected that Mr. Smeaton is going to speak, not as to facts, but as to opinion. That opinion, however, is deduced from facts which are not disputed—the situation of banks, the course of tides and of winds, and the shifting of sands. His opinion, deduced from all these facts, is, that, mathematically speaking, the bank may contribute to the mischief, but not sensibly. Mr. Smeaton understands the construction of harbours, the causes of their destruction, and how remedied. In matters of science no other witnesses can be called. (Lord Mansfield's opinion of the court)

With this decision, the new experimental science of the Royal Society was legitimized. It illustrated the "growing legal recognition by the end of the eighteenth century that there was a new class of witnesses, skilled in matters of science, who could give opinions that were not based directly on the traditional trustworthiness of the senses" (Golan 2008: 902).

While this development is noteworthy, and the most commonly cited British origin for the concept of the "expert witness" (see Good 2008; Milroy 2017), I find no indication that the word "expert" is used anywhere in the proceedings. What we have, instead, is perhaps more interesting. Legal culture is unanimous that "expertise" is what was at issue in *Folkes v. Chadd* despite the fact that the word was not used. Historically, this suggests that the relationship between "expert" and specialized competence, especially competence in the empirical sciences, was solidifying.

However, this legal use of expert didn't fully constrain its meaning. The 1889 California State Legislature still used expertise as a kind of experience: "These [tables] are made at this time for the purpose of enabling me to report the balances on my books, and to facilitate the auditing and **experting** of my accounts with the Board of Trustees" (Appendix to the Journals of the Twenty-

Ninth Session). Likewise, an 1889 *Los Angeles Herald* reported: "At a meeting of the Board of Prison Directors at San Quentin, Luman Wadham, who has been **experting** the books of the Board, reported them correct" (*Los Angeles Herald*, April 1889).

By 1914, though, the connection between expertise and specialized competence seems to have fully solidified. In an article on expertise in the journal *Science*, secretary of the Boston Museum of Fine Arts Benjamin Ives Gilman writes: "By expert will here be meant a person whose achievements demand special aptitudes long exercised; and by his day a time when these developed abilities are used to the best advantage of the community" (772).

What emerges in the 1700s, then, are two distinct uses of *expertise*. On one hand, it refers to a type of authority that is personal and limited to a particular span of time and circumstances. Call this "localized expertise":

Localized Expertise: Useful beliefs or skills that emerge from the experiences of individuals as they engage with a set of information or a practice over time.

We might venture that the community of sailors and navigators around Wells Harbor had extensive localized expertise. They certainly had enough competence to do their work and to speak competently about the land and tides around the harbor. What they lacked was the competence to speak about lands and tides generally, that is, an understanding of what natural mechanisms are at work to explain the harbor's shape and composition.

For an example closer to home, imagine someone in an office who has learned to troubleshoot a cantankerous copy machine. We might call that person the "resident expert" on the copier. Similarly, someone whom we might, in a broader context, call a "hobbyist" when it comes to music history, might be our bar trivia team's "expert" on music. These are examples of localized expertise. Normatively, little follows from this kind of authority. Localized experts have some claim on their colleagues' and friends' trust in a limited number of circumstances, but the moment the copy machine repair person shows up or the music history professor from the nearby college joins the bar trivia team, the presumption of authority on the part of the localized experts is canceled out. Nevertheless, historical usage suggests this is an appropriate sense of *expert*. The question that remains is how to distinguish localized expertise from what the Fellows of the Royal Society brought to the Wells Harbor trial.

Specialization, of a sort that's much more difficult to acquire, introduced a new category of expertise, a type of competence acquired through specialized study and practice beyond even extensive experience. This category carries with it a type of authority that is interpersonal and generalizable. Though this kind of expertise is narrow in scope—restricted to specific domains—its value lies in its reliability over a variety of applications within that domain. Call this "specialized expertise":

> **Specialized Expertise: The understanding of a domain that emerges from extensive, usually structured, training in a specific body of information or practice.**

This is the expertise held by Mylne and Smeaton, the copy machine repair person and the music history professor. Much more follows, normatively, from this type of expertise. If the copy machine repair person were to disagree with her boss about a problem with the copier, we genuinely would not know who was more likely to be right. Turning to our resident expert on the copier would not resolve the matter. Specialized expertise is the sort of expertise that raises the difficult questions we encountered in the Preface, questions about the authority of scientists who weigh-in on, say, climate policy and doctors who disagree with, say, groups who think medicines like Plan-B cause abortions.

Localized expertise will come up again at several points in this book, but the important takeaway, for now, is that, while your friend the music-buff may not be the sort of (specialized) expert who can write critical music reviews for NPR, it is perfectly reasonable, historically speaking, to call her your trivia team's (localized) expert on music.

Another important takeaway is the importance of the concepts associated with expertise rather than the term itself. *Folkes v. Chadd* proved influential for understanding the authority conferred by specialized competence, even though it was not specifically called expertise.

Since the grammatical and phonetic relatives of "expert" (*expertus*, *appert*, *espert*, etc.) are (a) relatively recent and (b) refer most commonly to various types of, mostly one-off, experience (e.g., of trying or testing) or skill,[6] we must go further back in history and look at related concepts to make sense of the robust sort of authority experts, as we call them today, have.

2.3 Ancient Roots of "Expertise"

A word study of expertise is not a simple undertaking. Whether in ancient Greece or the contemporary academy, the concept of expertise is complex, allowing for a diversity of uses and implications. Since this book is aimed, broadly, at specialized expertise, we must also look for affinities among related concepts for insights into their implications and for distinctions and nuances that can help guide our contemporary project. In this section, I explore some common *traits* and *attitudes* associated with specialized expertise, namely: authority, cunning intelligence, skill, and art.[7]

2.3.1 Authority

We often say experts are "authorities" on their domain, and we use phrases like "leading authorities say. . ." or "we asked the premier authority on. . ." There is, however, an ambiguity in its meaning that is not always clear from context. Contemporary English allows us to distinguish between being *an* authority *on* something, in an epistemic sense, and being *in* authority *over* someone, in what Douglas Walton (2013) calls an "administrative" sense. But the earliest uses of authority do not typically make room for this epistemic sense.

The Greek words translated as authority—*autokrates* (αὐτοκράτης), *dunamis*, (δύναμις), *archon* (ἄρχων), *kuria* (κυρία)—refer almost exclusively to institutional hierarchies of power or control: political authorities, legal authorities, and military authorities (and, as we move into the Middle Ages, religious authorities). In Euripides's play *Andromache*, for example, we find:

> **Chorus**
> When swift breezes are hurtling sailors along, [480] a double intelligence at the helm and a throng of wise men [*sophon*, σοφῶν] put together is less effective than a lesser mind with full **authority** [*autokratous*, αὐτοκρατοῦς]. The power to bring to pass in house and in city must be a single [person's] if [people] wish [485] to find their true advantage. (479–86)

Here, we see authority linked firmly with "power."

Aristotle reserves his discussion of authority for his book *Politics* (book III, ch. 6, 1278–9), where he describes various types of authority (*archon*), including the rule of a master over a slave, the rule of a husband over a wife and children, the rule of a trainer over the gymnast, and the helmsperson over a crew. All these senses imply some degree of control.

Importantly, Aristotle thinks that anyone imbued with authority, whether by nature (as he thinks is the case with master and slave) or election (as with political leaders), rules for "the good of the governed or for the common good of both parties." He thinks this is clearest in cases of equality—where the trainer is sometimes also a gymnast, or the helmsperson is also one of the crew. In these cases, the authority receives (albeit "accidentally") the benefit of their own rule. From this, Aristotle draws an assumption about political leaders: "And so in politics: when the state is framed upon the principle of equality and likeness, the citizens think that they ought to hold office by turns" (1279, 8–10).

And in Plutarch's *Questiones Conviviales*, we find:

> after Brutus had made himself **master** [κύριος] of the city, he treated all the inhabitants very mercifully. (Book VI, Question VIII)

There is at least one exception to this theme of power and mastery, though. In *Statesman*, Plato's Socrates talks about the authority of a doctor in a way that suggests it is not grounded purely in political legitimacy, but also in the knowledge to achieve the goal of the craft (*techne*):

> Whether physicians [*iatrous*, ἰατρούς] cure us against our will or with our will, by cutting us or burning us or causing us pain in any other way, and whether they do it by written rules or without them, and whether they are rich or poor, we call them physicians just the same, so long as they exercise authority [*archein*, ἀρχὴν] by art or science [*epistatountes techne*, ἐπιστατοῦντες τέχνῃ], purging us or reducing us in some other way, or even adding to our weight, provided only that they who treat their patients treat them for the benefit of their health and preserve them better than they were. (293a–c, trans. John Burnet)

John Burnet translates *techne* as "art or science," nodding to the complex relationship in the ancient world between what we now think of as "art" and "science" (see Section 2.3.9, this chapter). What the *techne* of medicine confers, according to this passage, is an *episteme*, a type of knowledge. The idea is that people are rightly called doctors just insofar as they use the knowledge they have gained from specialized practice for the benefit of others. Specialized practice grounds their right to offer this benefit. The word Burnet translates as "authority" (*archein*) is rendered "rule" by Harold Fowler, highlighting its almost inescapable association with politics (Fowler 1921).

To be sure, doctors acquired their authority in the ancient world partly based on public trust—they were publicly authorized (as it were) to practice medicine, and for that reason, they had a type of political authority. But Plato is adding a layer of complexity to this picture. The public should authorize physicians only insofar as that authority is grounded in something else, namely, art or science. This seemingly odd use forces us to ask: Given *authority*'s historical association with political power, is Plato really referring to something different—perhaps a distinctly *epistemic* authority—or is he merely using political authority metaphorically (doctors exercise *king-like* rule over their patients because of their *episteme*)?

The Romans did not expand on this epistemic implication of authority when they cultivated the term *auctoritas*. They accepted its administrative, or "control," implications and used the term almost exclusively for political and military leaders. Historian Wilfried Nippel (2007) explains:

> In the public sphere, *auctoritas* is primarily associated with the role of the Roman senate. There are various technical meanings, as well as more general ones. *Patrum auctoritas* depicted the patrician senators' ratification of the decisions by the popular assembly concerning legislation and elections of magistrates; only thus did the assembly's votes become legally binding. (15-16)

Importantly, however, the Romans added some nuance to the concept of authority by distinguishing it from the exercise of force:

> Magistrates who were successful in quelling riots by their appearance on the spot were praised for their *auctoritas*. In 138 B.C. a consul addressed a crowd that demanded measures against an increase in corn prices by declaring that he understood the public good better than they did. The crowd fell silent "paying more regard to his authority [*auctoritas*] than to their own nutriment." . . . The same holds true for great generals. Pompeius or Caesar enjoyed the loyalty of their troops not only due to their formal competence as bearers of a military *imperium* and their military ability, but because of a personal authority that was of much greater importance, at least in critical situations. (Nippel 2007: 23)

We see an example of this in Cicero's *On the Commonwealth*:

> A statesman, therefore, who by his **authority** and by the punishments which his laws impose obliges all [people] to adopt that course which only a mere handful can be persuaded to adopt by the arguments of philosophers, should be held in even greater esteem than the teachers who make these virtues the domain of their discussions. (107)

Cicero distinguishes authority from punishments but acknowledges that it entails the right to punish. He also distinguishes it from the persuasion of arguments. This suggests that the right to command and the obligation of others to obey is a function of public office.

Similarly, E. W. Sutton translates *auctoritatem* as "authoritative judgment" in a passage of Cicero's *De Oratore*:

> I prefer to Greek instruction the **authoritative judgment** [*auctoritatem*] of those to whom the highest honors in eloquence have been awarded by our fellow countrymen. (1.6.23)

Does Cicero intend to convey something about the social position of those to whom the highest honors have been awarded? Or is he saying their insights or wisdom make them worth listening to? Without a robust sense of context and intent, it is difficult to know what grounds authority in any given use, and, therefore, what it implies for those subject to it.

By the 1400s, however, a distinction between epistemic and political authority seems to be well established. It appears in both forms in Desiderius Erasmus of Rotterdam's (1466–1536) *In Praise of Folly*, written in Latin in 1509 and published in 1511 ([1511] 1876). To make her many arguments, Folly, who is the anthropomorphized narrator of the book, calls upon the testimony of many respected writers and refers to them as *authorities*, including Homer, Horace, Sophocles, the Gospel writers, and scholars of the Catholic Church. Selections from these writers are used as testimony in favor of Folly's points, and this testimony is regarded as evidence: "For a farther confirmation whereof I have the **authority** of Homer, that captain of all poetry, who, as he gives to mankind in general, the epithet of wretched and unhappy" (48); "yet this character may more justly be assumed by me, as I can make good from the **authority** of Euripides, who lays down this as an axiom" (50); "I'll therefore draw toward an end, when I have first confirmed what I have said by the **authority** of several authors. Which by way of farther proof I shall insist upon, partly, that I may not be thought to have said more in my own behalf than what will be justified by others" (107).

But the close connection between epistemic and political authority is not lost on Erasmus. When discussing the arrogance of certain church scholars, he says their "authority" is "very considerable" and that they would have their conclusions "as irrepealably ratified as Solon's laws, and in as great force as the very decrees of the papal chair" (86).

Examples from modern English also support a distinction between epistemic and political authority. Francis Bacon (1620) writes that it is difficult for people to change their minds without the "force of authority" and that it is tempting to simply accept the testimonies of "authorities" who "lay down the law in a magisterial manner" (43, 55–6). Most of Shakespeare's uses of authority are distinctly political. When Kent enters King Lear's hall and tells the king, "[Y]ou have that in your countenance which I would fain call master." When Lear asks what that is, Kent says simply: "Authority" (1.4.29–32). Similarly, in *Antony and*

Cleopatra, Enobarbus tells Menas, "If our eyes had authority, here they might take two thieves kissing" (Act 2, Scene 6, Line 98), implying that if someone in power saw them, they might be arrested. But in *King Henry VIII*, we get a use of authority grounded more in study than in power, when Archbishop of Canterbury Cranmer says:

> Both of my life and office, I have labour'd,
> And with no little study, that my teaching
> And the strong course of my **authority**
> Might go one way, and safely; and the end
> Was ever to do well. (5.3.34)

This relatively late resolution to the ambiguity, yet still close relationship between the political and epistemic, may explain why so many contemporary thinkers draw a "control" connection between authoritative knowledge in a discipline and having authority over others (see, e.g., Arendt ([1954] 1961) and Wolff 1970). I say more about the relationship between expertise and authority in Chapters 5 and 6. The key point for this section is that the ancient conception of authority is not equivalent to what we currently mean by specialized expertise, and so its roots are not found there. Expertise may imply a type of authority, but authority does not imply expertise.

2.3.2 Cunning Intelligence

In ancient Greek myth, Metis is the goddess of wisdom, prudence, and deep thought. For a culture that would become synonymous with the reification of reason and the love of wisdom, it is not surprising that a goddess would carry the name *metis* (μῆτις), which, in broader Hellenistic use, meant *cunning intelligence* or *informed prudence*. Nor is it surprising that Metis's offspring with the powerful Zeus would be superbly competent Athena (Kerényi 1951; Graves 1960), whom classicist Emily Wilson calls the "goddess of technical expertise and strategic thinking" (2018: 34). Until the time of the Socratic philosophers, *metis* was commonly associated with a special way of performing a skill.

In the *Iliad*, Nestor tells his son Antilochus: "It is through *mêtis* rather than through strength that the wood-cutter shows [their] worth. It is through *mêtis* that the helms[person] guides the speeding vessel over the wine-dark sea despite the wind. It is through *mêtis* that the charioteer triumphs over [their] rival" (Book XXIII, 359–61, Detienne and Vernant 1991: 12). In the *Odyssey*, Homer[8] uses *metis* to describe a variety of traits we associate with expertise: Athena's use of strategy in war (in contrast to Ares's use of chaos), her especially fitting disguises (which subtly reveal her to some characters while remaining concealed from others), and her insights into human affairs (ever vigilant with bright, sharp eyes). He uses it to describe Odysseus's deceitfulness and his ability to form elaborate plans under extreme stress, sometimes using the variation *polymetis*, "a term that suggests an abundance of metis" (Wilson 2018: 36). Athena even tells Odysseus that they share this divinely favored trait:

> No man can plan and talk like you,
> And I am known among the gods for insight
> And craftiness. (13. 298–300, Wilson trans.)

Passages like these suggest that *metis* is an especially high degree of expertise, or, at the very least, an exceptional way of exerting expertise, a sign of mastery. It is noteworthy that this sign of mastery is not limited to social roles that are restricted by sex or slavery—the warrior, the homemaker. One could exhibit *metis* in any number of activities, from weaving, to shipbuilding, storytelling, navigation, sculpting, or music.

> Penelope's weaving, no less than Odysseus's fighting, is done under the aegis of Athena. Whereas Poseidon favors the untamed world of the stormy sea, Athena loves fixed settlements and the olive tree—a crop whose oil was used in archaic Greece for cooking and skin care. Poseidon makes the earth shake; Athena makes even the most rugged, barren landscape available for cultivation. (Wilson 2018: 35)

There is thoughtful order in *metis*, attention to detail and creativity, and anyone in society may possess it.

It is also noteworthy that *metis*, like many types of specialized expertise, is associated with skilled tasks that have clear success conditions. According to Marcel Detienne and Jean-Pierre Vernant (1991):

> [T]he intelligent ability referred to as *metis* comes into play on widely varying levels but in all of them the emphasis is always laid on practical effectiveness, on the pursuit of success in a particular sphere of activity: it may involve multiple skills useful in life, the mastery of the artisan in his craft, magic tricks, the use of philtres [potions] and herbs, the cunning stratagems of war, frauds, deceits, resourcefulness of every kind. (11)

It is used of Antilochus's skill in chariot racing in *Iliad* and in the Roman Poet Oppian's *Treatise on Fishing* (second century CE) to describe both the cunning of various types of fish and the fishermen who contrive traps to catch them.[9]

In many cases, the person who exhibits *metis* does so in morally questionable ways, whether deceitfully or in ways that raise suspicion of trickery. Antilochus's win over Menelaus in a chariot race, while due to his *metis*, was also a matter of cheating, an act for which Antilochus later repents. This example, combined with Odysseus's many deceits, makes it tempting to associate *metis* with morally questionable uses of expertise. But this would be too hasty. Rather, *metis* allows the already skillful artisan or athlete to see what others cannot and to act on it in a timely manner. We might think of it as the difference in play between a newly recruited NBA player and a seasoned professional. Both are experts, but the seasoned professional has a practical wisdom the younger player lacks: "Metis is swift, as prompt as the opportunity that it must seize on the wing . . . . But in no way does it act lightly (*lepté*). With all the weight of acquired experience that it carries, it involves thought that is dense, rich, and compressed (*pukiné*)" (Detienne and Vernant 1991: 15). This suggests that the athlete with *metis* is so much more advanced than everyone else that the very act of exercising their expertise can seem like a trick, as if they can see the future or contradict laws of nature. For example, Thucydides describes the political expertise Themistocles as "arriving at the most correct idea concerning the future, taking the widest point of view and foreseeing, as far as possible, the hidden advantages and disadvantages in what cannot be seen" (*History of the Peloponnesian War*, Book I, §138, trans. Detienne and Vernant). Imagine when you have observed a mathematician "seeing" connections among numbers that struck you as superhuman. Or when Olympian Simone Biles performs a floor routine that seemingly defies gravity. In both cases, it is easy to see expert performance and think, "It must be a trick!"

And yet, it is not *metis* that most ancient scholars translate into English as "expertise." Rather, researchers typically associate expertise with a *techne* (τέχνη) or specialized skill, such as blacksmithing, carpentry, and piloting a ship. To be sure, *metis* is not always used as a distinct type of specialized skill; as noted, it is often a way of exercising a *techne*, as when Penelope exhibited cunning by beguiling her arrogant suitors, weaving and unweaving Odysseus's father's burial shroud (2.89–110). And it is often used when skilled characters are in the act of deceit, trickery, or traps, which might give it a nefarious dimension that would make it seem less appropriate than *techne*. But even still, the terms *metis* and *techne* are related more intimately than adverb and verb (e.g., cunning weaving or shrewd piloting).

Before and up through the time of Plato, *techne* and *metis* were used interchangeably with *sophia* (σοφία), which is famously translated "wisdom."

During that time, *sophia* could mean knowledgeable in practical matters, shrewd, and worldly wise, much like *metis*, or it could mean skilled in a handicraft (*sophos*, σοφός), to describe poets, musicians, sculptors, and once of even hedge trimmers and ditch diggers, much like *techne*.[10] Samuel Butler (1900), for example, translates Odysseus's *metis* as "wisdom" in *Odyssey* Book II, 279. And in both *Treatise on Fishing* and *Treatise on Hunting*, Ossian refers to *techne* as a type of *metis*.[11]

To add yet more complexity, not all specialized skills were called *techne*, *sophia*, or *metis*. Mathematics and medicine—often misleadingly translated as "intellectual sciences"—are sometimes called "*epistemes*" (ἐπιστήμης) from the word commonly translated by philosophers as "knowledge," *episteme* (ἐπιστήμη). Yet, *episteme* is a richer concept than mere knowledge, as both Xenophon and Plato use *episteme* and *techne* interchangeably, depending on context and the aspects of the skill or domain at issue.[12] These distinctions show that any attempt to pin our contemporary notion of expertise to a single ancient concept is bound to miss some important nuance.

I explore *techne* in more detail later in this chapter. But for purposes of this book, let us slightly alter Ossian's conclusion, that *techne* is a type of *metis*, and say, instead, that *metis* is one way of describing *techne*; *metis* is a way of exhibiting, displaying, or exerting one's *techne*. It is tempting to do the opposite of Ossian, and say, instead, that *metis* is a type of *techne*. But as we will see later, for the ancients, *techne* reflects skill with a specific body of knowledge, and *metis* can be displayed independently of a body of knowledge. Someone can be a cunning liar, though lying is not a distinct domain. Cunning is not necessarily a feature of even superior performance: a master chess player might exhibit cunning, but could a violinist or commercial airline pilot? It seems odd to think so.[13]

Further, *techne* can be exhibited clumsily, without *metis*, as when a carpenter builds in a sloppy manner despite her ability to do otherwise. She is still a carpenter and still likely better than non-carpenters, so even her shoddy building will exhibit *techne*. But it will not exhibit a high degree of cleverness or shrewdness. Thus, I stipulate that a *techne* exhibits *metis* when *techne* is performed with *a high degree of competence in contexts that require attention to dynamic performance-related cues*. These cues are not always about working against opponents, as in chess and its uses in Homer, but it is also about working with a set of changing circumstances where fixed rules are not helpful, as in Ossian's fishing example, and as fighter pilots and firefighters have to navigate.

2.3.3 Skill

Rather than conceptualizing expertise in terms of cunning intelligence, we might search for words associated with "skill." In the Homeric epics, as we have seen, there are at least three kinds of skill: crafting (*techne*), cunning intelligence (*metis*), and wisdom (*sophia*). After Plato, when Socrates has named *sophia* one of the four central virtues (*Protagoras* 332a-ff; *Republic* 428a-ff), *sophia* becomes more closely associated with *phronesis* (φρόνησῖς): sound, right, or good judgment. This does not mean that *phronesis* is not also a kind of expertise. Khan (2005) presents a compelling argument for the claim that *phronesis* can be learned and that it plays a social role similar to other *technein* and *epistemes* (Khan 2005). Nevertheless, whether it is a distinct type of expertise, or even a type of expertise at all, is controversial, so I set it aside for my purposes.[14]

While *metis* is used extensively in Homer and Pindar (and later in Ossian) to mean skill or craft,[15] Plato uses it only to mean "counsel," "wise counsel," or "advice." In Plato, then, we find the practices we think of as types of expertise described almost exclusively as *techne* or *episteme*.

Sometimes translated "craft" or "art," philosopher James Allen (1994) explains that *techne* is characterized by at least three traits:

A *techne*:

(1) **Is a body of knowledge**
(2) **That concerns a distinct domain**
(3) **And "enables the artist to achieve a particular type of beneficial result." (83)**

Xenophon identifies as *tektonoi* many crafts that we would call *specialist* domains. In *Memorabilia*, he includes a ship's pilot, a builder, and a piper (musician) among craftspeople (Section 1.2.9). Plato includes politicians, gymnasts, doctors (*Gorgias* 464b) and sculptors, poets, painters, carpenters, and lyre-players (*Protagoras* 311b-312e).

The key implication of such specialized domains is that someone who works in those domains can actually do a good job. Xenophon, for example, attributes the view to Socrates that a true ruler is not one who has power or who was chosen at random, but someone who actually knows how to rule (*Memorabilia* 3.9.10). According to him, we should expect the same for any domain:

[T]he one who knows [*epistamenon*] rules [*archonta*] ... [E]verybody concerned with anything that needs care, look after it themselves if they think they know [*epistasthai*] how, but, if not, they obey those who know [*epistamenois*], and not only when such are present but they even send for them when absent, that they may obey them and do the right thing. (*Memorabilia* 3.9.11)

Here, we do not find a distinction between knowledge-that and knowledge-how, as contemporary philosophers are wont to draw.[16] Rather, these ancient writers seem to allow that knowledge might look different in different domains (knowledge of medicine, knowledge of building, etc.) and that the key normative implication of any of these is the same: the knowledgeable person is the one we should turn to when we need help or advice in their domain because they can actually help us.

Plato expresses this implication well in *Protagoras*:

[W]hen a decision has to be taken at the state assembly about some matter of building, they send for the builders to give their advice about the buildings, and when it concerns shipbuilding they send for the shipwrights, and similarly in every case where they are dealing with a subject which they think can be learned and taught. But if anyone else tries to give advice, who they don't regard as an [skilled craftsperson: *demiourgos*, δημιουργός], no matter how handsome or wealthy or well born he is, they still will have none of him, but jeer at him and create an uproar, until either the would-be speaker is shouted down and gives up of his own accord, or else the police drag him away or put him out on the order of the presidents. (*Protagoras* 319b–c)

A *demiourgos* (δημιουργός) is someone who possesses a *techne* (see, e.g., *Protagoras* 312b; 327c). One notable aspect of this passage is the role the community takes in regulating experts. It suggests that people are experts independently of what people think (they want someone who can *really* build buildings and who can *really* build ships), yet it also suggests that if people don't regard someone as an expert, that person will not be allowed to exercise whatever *techne* they claim to have, regardless of whether they actually have it. Does this, by default, undermine their expertise? While some argue the answer is yes (e.g., Barnes and Bloor 1982), most argue that this simply renders expertise more complex—other humans are inevitably involved in the process of becoming an expert, identifying experts, or both (see Agnew, Ford, and Hayes 1994 and Turner 2014).

It is worth noting that both Plato and Aristotle distinguish *techne* from "general education." Even if someone is fairly good at something, this does not mean they are an expert. In *Protagoras*, Plato has Socrates argue that *techne* requires more than what we might call *mere know-how*; an expert also understands their domain:

> I was saying . . . that cookery seems to me not an art [*techne*] but a habitude [*empeiria*, ἐμπειρία: experience], unlike medicine, which I argued, has investigated the nature of the person whom she treats and the cause of her proceedings, and has some account to give of each of these things; so much for medicine: whereas the other, in respect of the pleasure to which her whole ministration is given, goes to work there in an utterly inartistic [*a-technos*, ἀτέχνως]¹⁷ manner, without having investigated at all either the nature of the cause or the cause of the pleasure, and altogether irrationally—with no thought, one may say, of differentiation, relying on routine and habitude for merely preserving a memory of what is wont to result; and that is how she is enabled to provide her pleasures. (501a–b, trans. Lamb)

Socrates is saying that, because someone who cooks does so simply by memory of what tasted good in the past, their reliability is not based on expertise but on experience in cooking. Unless we're food scientists or molecular gastronomists, most of us can testify that this is, indeed, the way we cook. James Allen (1994) explains:

> While someone can pick up a knack on the basis of experience that enables him to bring about a certain kind of desirable result more frequently than a layperson who lacks that experience, if the ability depends on nothing more than a few rules of thumb, a few memorized procedures adapted to stereotypical situations, it does not yet amount to an art. (85–6)

In other words, one who practices a *techne* is able to explain *what* they are doing and *why*.

Similarly, Aristotle, in *On Sophistical Refutations*, argues that some teachers of public speaking would have their students memorize speeches and, thereby, produce an effect in the audience, but they were only transmitters of the art, not artists themselves. The teachers gave them the results of an art but not the art itself. Aristotle compares these teachers to cobblers' apprentices. Cobblers teach them how to offer customers various kinds of shoes, which really does help them, but they have not taught them the cobblers' art (183b–184a). Call these novices who understand the basics of a task and have a little experience with it, perhaps a knack for it, *people of experience*.

Thus, the person who has a *techne* can do more than perform the *actions* of an expert, they also understand why they are doing what they are doing. Richard Parry (2014) explains:

The former knows that, when Callias had such and such a disease, thus and such helped him, and the same for Socrates and many others. However, the person who has a *technê* goes beyond experience to a universal judgment . . . [T]he master crafts[person] (*technitês*) is wiser than the person of experience because he knows the cause, the reasons that things are to be done.

The ability to form a "universal judgment" shows that the person with *techne* understands their domain in general rather than isolated instances of cause and effect. Because of this, Alex John London (2000: 133) adds two other features to James Allen's account of *techne*:

(4) **The artist can give an account or explanation of these things.**

Because understanding a body of knowledge allows one to bring about a specific end relative to that knowledge (shoes from shoemaking, health from medicine, etc.), London says it follows that

(5) **This specialized knowledge is something more or less uniquely possessed by practitioners of the craft**

Plato has Socrates and Polemarchus express something very much like this in *Republic*:

> Socrates: "With respect to disease and health, who is most able to do good to sick friends and bad to enemies?"
> Polemarchus: "A doctor."
> Socrates: "And with respect to the danger of the sea, who has this power over those who are sailing?"
> Polemarchus: "A pilot." (*Republic* 332d–e, trans. Bloom)

And to Ion, Socrates says: "What we learn by mastering one profession we won't learn by mastering another" (*Ion* 537d, trans. Woodruff).

2.4 A Deeper Look at *Techne*

In addition to the five characteristics of *techne* noted earlier, three others warrant attention because they figure in so much of contemporary expertise scholarship:

(6) ***Techne* is identified by its outcomes.**
(7) ***Techne* comes in degrees.**
(8) ***Techne* requires extensive training.**

2.4.1 *Techne* Is Identified by Its Outcomes

Xenophon tells us it would be "amazing enough to me that a herdsman who lets his cattle decrease and go to the bad should not admit that he is a poor herdsman." It would be even more amazing, he tells us, if a "statesman, when he causes the citizens to decrease and go to the bad, should feel no shame nor think himself a poor statesman" (*Memorabilia* 1.2.32). While we might wonder whether politicians could ever have the skill to make people better human beings (and therefore, whether there are expert politicians), nonetheless, the point seems to be that expertise is the ability to *do* something, and how well one can do it determines just how strong an expert they are.

Cicero writes something similar of the skill of oratory: "I allowed the possession of eloquence to that man only who was able, in a style more admirable and more splendid, to amplify and adorn any subject he chose, and whose mind and memory encompassed all the sources of everything that concerned oratory" (*De Oratore* 1.20.94, trans. Sutton and Rackham). We saw a related implication with cookery in the *Protagoras* passage earlier. It is not just that someone can reliably put together a meal; there's something about the *way* they do it that matters. Since most cooks cannot explain why their meals come out so well, they cannot be considered experts.

The problem is that some domains of *techne* have outcomes that are highly accessible, while others have few demonstrable products. For example, it is often easy to tell when a musician is really good. But it is not always easy to tell whether a historian is good. Even if they write books on history, readers who are not well versed in the professional study of history may have trouble determining whether the book is good scholarship or a half-hearted and biased repackaging of others' ideas.[18] In the latter cases, presumably only other experts can assess the person's competence.

This raises a distinction we will come back to at several points in this book between *exoteric* (outward-facing) indicators of expertise and *esoteric* (inward-facing) indicators of expertise. Some domains of expertise are easily judged by those outside the domain (Figure 2.1).

Figure 2.1 The continuum of domain access.

The idea is that how easily it is to tell how good someone is at something depends on how easily we can understand what they do. These indicators fall along a continuum. In some cases, the indicators are easily accessible, even when we don't know how they do it, as with music and gymnastics. These indicators are highly exoteric. In other cases, the indicators are less easily accessible—as when a computer technician tries to tell me how to troubleshoot my laptop (they aren't just speaking gibberish, right?). These indicators are somewhat esoteric and somewhat exoteric (hey, my computer works again). In other cases, the indicators are not accessible at all; they are completely esoteric. There is nothing I could understand that would tell me whether, say, an interventional radiologist or cosmologist is good at their job.

The Hippocratic writers[19] of *On Ancient Medicine* tell us that medicine must have exoteric indicators if we are to trust doctors: "[It is] of the greatest importance that anyone speaking about this art should be intelligible to lay[people]" (quoted in Lloyd 1987: 88). Other experts may not need to demonstrate their skills to novices. Someone studying cosmological physics or topology, for example, may never need to justify their *techne* to non-physicists or non-mathematicians. Nevertheless, presumably, they should be able to demonstrate their expertise to *someone*. So, even if a domain has only esoteric indicators, peers in that domain should be able to assess competence in that domain. Unfortunately, for some domains, it is difficult for anyone to assess success—for example, teaching, counseling, and politics. In these cases, one of two things might be happening. It could be that the circumstances in which they are practiced do not allow practitioners to become experts—in which case, there may be no expert teachers or expert counselors, despite widespread belief to the contrary. On the other hand, it could be that the circumstances in which they are practiced make identifying outcomes, and, thereby, developing expertise difficult. I talk more about these latter circumstances (or "wicked environments") in Chapter 7.

Note that there is a difference between using outcomes as indicators of expertise (evidence for expertise) and saying that it is intrinsic to expertise that one produce outcomes (necessary for having expertise). Practically speaking, you must be able to demonstrate your expertise to someone; otherwise, you would have little reason to believe you are an expert in the first place. But it does seem possible to have expertise even if you don't know it, that is, to have a high degree of competence without producing any particular product and without anyone identifying you as especially good at it. We can imagine someone who practices an obscure musical instrument alone for several hours a day, and, after a time, becomes as good as any performer in the world but never plays for anyone but themselves. In such a scenario, they would have no way of knowing if they were any good.

2.4.2 *Techne* Comes in Degrees

As we have already seen, there is a difference between a generally educated person and an expert. We know that someone does not become an expert overnight. A further trait of expertise is that some experts are better than others. Some professional musicians are better than others; chess grandmasters have different Elo scores, and some Olympians have more gold medals than others. For any given *techne*, it would seem, there can be better and worse practitioners in a domain, all of whom meet the minimum conditions for expertise.

Three discussions—one from Plato and two from Aristotle—suggest that ancient thinkers held this belief, too. Aristotle frames the distinction more clearly, so I'll begin with his. First, Melissa Lane (2014) points us to a passage from Aristotle's *Politics*, where he explains three different types of "doctor": "[T]here is the ordinary practitioner, and there is the physician of the higher class, and thirdly the intelligent [person] who has studied the art" (*Politics*, Book III, ch. 11, 1282a, trans. Benjamin Jowett). The aim of the distinction is a response to an argument against democratic election by peers. If someone were to say that we should only call doctors to judge doctors, geometricians to judge geometry, and ship pilots to judge pilots. Thus, we shouldn't leave choosing leaders to the many.

In response, Aristotle notes that each type of doctor can judge the other despite the variation in their competence. Lane explains:

> [Aristotle] seems to take the status of a "general education in a craft" to apply very broadly (insofar as this conclusion is meant to defend the overall thesis endorsing participation of the general multitude in electing and inspecting officials) (1282a3–5). This can't be a specialized education. It must be more like the involvement of ordinary people, say, in medicating their children at home and so in sharing in medical practice and concerns. Aristotle's reply further erodes any sharp boundary between popular and expert knowledge, or what can be more properly considered popular judgment and expert knowledge. They are certainly distinct, but they fall on a continuum, and there will be certain habits of mind shared between them. (2014: 103)

The idea that degrees of competence (shared habits of mind) allow similarly trained people to review and evaluate one another will prove important for later discussions of epistemic placement, authority, and assessing experts. Aristotle goes on to say that "there are some arts whose products are not judged of solely, or best, by the artists themselves, namely those arts whose products are recognized even by those who do not possess the art" (*Politics*, Book III, ch. 11, 1282a). Here, Lane interprets Aristotle as distinguishing having a "general education" in the craft of medicine, be an "ordinary practitioner" of medicine, or be a "master" craftsperson in medicine (2014: 103).

Aristotle also opens *On the Parts of Animals* with a distinction between two types of competence with a body of knowledge:

> one which may be properly called scientific knowledge [*epistemein*, ἐπιστήμην] of the subject, while the other is a kind of educational acquaintance with it. For an educated [person] should be able to perform a fair off-hand judgement as to the goodness or badness of the method used by a professor in his exposition. (Book 1, 639a3-7, trans. William Ogle)

Aristotle introduces a level of competence between the pure novice and the specialist in the form of "educational acquaintance." Aristotle seems to believe that at a certain level of study, not just experience, puts one in a position to evaluate some of the methods of the specialist.

He also clarifies that this competence is not, however, a kind of meta-expertise, which is the ability to judge multiple domains. He calls this "universal education" and notes that the competence to judge specialists may be held in one or several domains:

> It will, however, be understood that we only ascribe universal education to one who in [their] own individual person is thus critical in all or nearly all branches of knowledge, and not to one who has a likeability merely in some special subject. For it is possible for a [person] to have this competence in some one branch of knowledge without having it in all. (639a8–14, trans. William Ogle)

Aristotle seems to be suggesting a distinction between generalized expertise and generalized meta-expertise, the competence to judge in multiple domains.

The notion of a generalized expertise is also suggested early in Plato's *Protagoras*. Socrates is talking with Hippocrates (not the great physician) as they are going to see the famous sophist Protagoras. Socrates asks Hippocrates what he hopes to become by studying:

> Well, look, Hippocrates, maybe this isn't the sort of education you expect to get from Protagoras. Maybe you expect to get the kind of lessons you got from your grammar instructor or music teacher or wrestling coach. You didn't get from

them technical instruction to become a professional, but a general education suitable for a gentle[person]. (*Protagoras* 312a–b, trans. Lombardo and Bell)

Hippocrates is going to learn from Protagoras, but not for the sake of becoming a sophist himself (which he finds shameful), but for a generalist education in wisdom, virtue, oratory, and reasoning. Hippocrates will then have more competence than someone who has not studied with Protagoras, but not so much that he himself could practice or teach as a sophist.

These passages suggest there is a continuum of competence from novice to specialized expert and at least two intermediate forms: the person of experience and what we might call a **generalized expert**, where generalized expertise is competence in a domain that is weaker than that of a specialized expert but stronger than that of a person of experience (Figure 2.2):

Novice　　Person of Experience　　Generalized Expert　　Specialized Expert

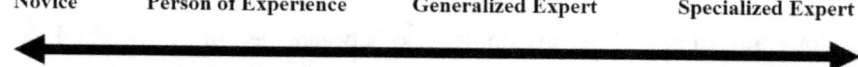

Figure 2.2 A continuum of competence in a domain.

So, while we defined specialized expertise as:

Specialized Expertise: Understanding of a domain that emerges from extensive, structured training in a specific body of information or practice.

We can now contrast this with generalized expertise:

Generalized Expertise: Useful beliefs or skills in a domain that emerge from general training (structured or unstructured) in a specific body of information or practice.

As will become evident in later discussions, these are not sharply defined categories. What counts as generalized expertise in some domains look much like specialized expertise in others. Some localized experts look more like persons of experience (e.g., a sports fanatic), while others look like generalized experts (e.g., someone who can competently use all the programs in the Microsoft Office Suite). Further, it is not always clear when one moves from one category to another—a hobbyist political forecaster can, with some dedication, become a specialized expert in political forecasting (see Watson 2021, Chapter 5). Further still, neither explains what experts can do, or for whom, or how we might recognize them, or how we should respond to them, so they are grossly underdeveloped. But they are not intended to be full-fledged accounts; they are simply starting points for orienting later discussions and, thereby, guide us as we develop a full-fledged general account of expertise.

2.4.3 *Techne* Requires Extensive Training

A key difference between *techne* on one hand and *sophia*, *metis*, and sometimes *phronesis*, on the other, is how they are obtained. While *techne* is universally thought to be a product of training and practice, the others are thought to be talents of birth (natural aptitude) or gifts of the gods. A few ancient writers believed that all talent is inborn and, while it can be honed through training, it cannot be cultivated from scratch. The Roman poet Horace writes:

> Learning promotes inborn talent,
> And the right exercises strengthen the muscles,
> But when manners falter,
> Failings mar native virtue. (*Odes*, Book IV: IV Drusus and Claudians)

But the majority suggest that a skill is not properly a *techne* if it cannot be acquired through training, for instance, if it was a gift of the gods. Note that Socrates challenges Meno over the idea that virtue is a *techne* because it does not seem something that can be learned (*Meno*). And he challenges Protagoras over the idea that politics is an art: "[W]hen it is a matter of deliberating on city management, anyone can stand up and advise them, carpenter, blacksmith, shoemaker, merchant . . .—it doesn't matter—and nobody blasts him for presuming to give counsel without any prior training under a teacher. The reason is clear: They do not think it can be taught" (*Protagoras* 319d–e, trans. Lombardo and Bell). Socrates also challenges Polemarchus, in *Republic*, over the idea that justice is an art because it seems to have no domain of information that one can learn (*Republic* 333e, trans. Bloom).

In *Laches*, Socrates allows that someone can acquire a *techne* without a teacher, but contends that such a claim demands a higher standard of proof:

> Laches: "What's that, Socrates? Haven't you ever noticed that in some matters people become more expert without teachers than with them?"
> Socrates: "Yes, I have, Laches, but you would not want to trust them when they said they were good crafts[people] unless they should have some well-executed product of their art to show—and not just one but more than one."
> (185e–186a, trans. Sprague)

Nevertheless, this passage still implies that *techne* is a learned trait.

Just how much of a *techne* must be learned to properly be a *techne* is unclear. There is a bit of tension in the texts. In the same book where he questions whether politics is a *techne*, Socrates seems to also accept the mythological account that the god Hermes distributes various *techne* to mortals as he sees fit:

> Then Hermes asked Zeus in what manner then was he to give [people] right and respect: "Am I to deal them out as the arts [*technai*] have been dealt? That dealing was done in such wise that one [person] possessing medical art is able to treat many ordinary [people], and so with the other craftsmen [*demiourgoi*; skilled worker]. Am I to place among [people] right and respect in this way also, or deal them out to all?" (*Protagoras* 322c, trans. Lamb)

Most ancient authors seem to accept some mixed view, according to which the gods are responsible for a person's having a talent, but that person is responsible for developing that talent into a *techne*.

2.5 Episteme[20]

So far, we have treated *techne* as if it were identical with *episteme*. Is there a distinction between them that lends insights to a study of expertise? Aristotle and some later writers do attempt to distinguish *techne* and *episteme*. Aristotle says that both are goals of the rational soul, but he says they refer to different types of knowledge. *Episteme* is knowledge of things that are certain and without qualification, such as geometry (*Posterior Analytics* 71b10–15), or things just short of certainty, events that have few exceptions (*Metaphysics* 1026b–1027a). If we predict extreme heat in the summer, we can do so by means of *episteme*, because such things happen "for the most part." *Techne*, on the other hand, is an art or practice aimed at producing something by way of good reasoning. *Techne* can use *episteme*, as in medicine, but this is not essential to *techne*, for Aristotle. *Techne* is skill with things that change—bringing one state out of another. But the *outcome* is also inessential to *techne*. The aim of a *techne* depends on the specific *techne*. In playing the flute, for example, the aim is the *playing* itself, because the playing and the song are part of the same process, whereas in building a ship, the *techne* aims at the *ship* rather than the process of building. The only clear connection between *episteme* and *techne*, when Aristotle defines them, is that both are distinct from pure accidents: "to accidental results there corresponds no determinate art or faculty" (*Metaphysics* 1027a).

A problem, however, is that Aristotle does not always follow his own distinction when he uses the terms. In *Nichomachean Ethics*, for example, he uses *techne* and *episteme* interchangeably to describe physicians and physical trainers (1106b). In *Metaphysics*, he says they are both capable of supporting universal judgments, in contrast with the *empeiria* (981a–b).

The Stoics (e.g., Zeno, Chrysippus, Cato) offer a variety of ways to distinguish *techne* and *episteme*, but, as with Aristotle, these are largely terms of art, coined in the context of developing philosophical positions, and neither attempt to be systematic or reflect of how the terms were commonly used. Thus, if there was either a consistent technical or colloquial difference between *techne* and *episteme*, it seems lost to history.

2.6 Art (*ars*)

As we have seen, *techne* is often translated "art," and later textual evidence supports this decision. The Latin *ars*, from which English creates "art," tracks roughly all we have said about *techne*. In *De Oratore*, Cicero uses *artium* (arts) to describe most of what is discussed in Greek as *techne* or *episteme*, including mathematics, geometry, building, medicine (1.14.61–62), music, astronomy, literature, and oratory (1.41.187). In *Gallic Wars*, Julius Caesar says the Gauls believed that Mercury invented all the *atrium* and seem to accept the standard myths about the roles of various gods in overseeing them, such as Athena's provenance over "the invention of manufacturers" (book 6, ch. 17).

Further, the traits of an *ars* are almost identical to those of *techne* and *episteme*. In *De Oratore*, Cicero quotes the Roman Crassus as explaining, an art is "defined as consisting in things thoroughly examined and clearly apprehended, and which are also outside the control of mere opinion, and within the grasp of exact knowledge" (1.23.108). Like the Greeks before him, Crassus believed that a practice was only an *ars* if it could be acquired through training. In his argument that oratory is not an *ars*, Crassus explains that, even if one understands the "principles and method of oratory," and even if an *ars* can give some "polish" to inborn talent (though what sort of art would do this is unclear), if the inborn gift is lacking "they cannot enter the ranks of the orators" (*De Oratore* 1.25.113–115). And finally, an *ars* can be lost or diminished through lack of use. While some knowledge about it may remain, Cicero notes that "even if unused, [an art] can still be retained in the form of theoretical knowledge, but virtue depends entirely upon its use" (*On the Commonwealth*, 106).

This brief survey suggests that *ars* has more in common with *techne*, and therefore, with specialized expertise, than with *expertus*. Acknowledging these differences in their lineages will, in later chapters, motivate some fine-grained distinctions among experts. It is worth noting that, slightly later in history, the Roman historian Cornelius Tacitus (56–120) would use *ars* more broadly in his *Annals of Rome*. While he sometimes means *techne*, as when he describes a doctor (*medicus arte*) (6.50), other times he seems to mean a "broad education" (*liberalium artium*) (4.13) or a person's "good qualities" (*buonem artium*) (6.46). This widening of meaning hints at other distinctions that emerge in the Middle Ages, such as that between liberal and illiberal arts, and between aesthetic arts and sciences. But it is also worth noting that, even into the 1600s, Shakespeare makes copious use of the narrower, technical sense of art, and Francis Bacon uses it to talk about natural science.

2.7 Summing Up: Is It All Just Ancient History?

From the Greeks and Romans, we see that the words *techne*, *episteme*, and *ars* reflect many of the traits we now associate with specialized expertise.
They all:

- require a combination of knowledge and ability;
- are restricted to a specific domain (what Plato calls a "body of knowledge");
- must be learned (or can be taught);
- are measured and identified by their outcomes, though those outcomes may be exoteric or esoteric;
- must be practiced;
- admit of degrees;
- can be lost;
- have "authority" (though what that means is, as yet, unclear); and
- are grounded in the ability to do something that others cannot.

We also find that concepts like *authority, cunning intelligence,* and *experience* are related to or implied by expertise but are not constitutive of it. Yet, exploring those conceptual relationships will help us better understand what experts are, what they can do for us, and how much we should trust them.

Some items on this list of traits are more controversial than others. For example, is *all* expertise aimed at measurable outcomes? As we will see in later chapters, there are good reasons for thinking the answer is no. Must all expertise be learned? What about people with seemingly special talents at an early age, or those with savant syndrome? Should we not call people experts who can perform at the same level just because they acquired their abilities differently?

Of course, there are many other unanswered questions. What sort of training makes an expert? Is it the same type of training for all types of expertise? What role does knowledge play in expertise? (Is it simply background information that allows one to train well? Is it information that is applied? Or does it grow through practice? Is it primarily knowledge-how, or is it also knowledge-that?)

I address a number of these questions in Watson (2021), so, in this book, I focus centrally on questions about authority, recognition, and trust. To see how these ancient concepts influence our understanding of authority, recognition, and trust as they are transmitted through the centuries, we turn next to the Middle Ages.

3

Expertise from the Middle Ages to the Twentieth Century

Nullius in Verba. ("Take nobody's word for it.")
(Motto of the Royal Society of London, c. 1663)

In this chapter, I review concepts associated with expertise from the Middle Ages to the middle of the twentieth century. I start with the concept of "master" as it came to be used in what are called the "cathedral schools" of Europe (Section 3.1). I then skip about 200 years to Enlightenment skepticism of the idea that experts have authority (Section 3.2). Despite this suspicion of trust, it is during this time that science started to fulfill many of its promises to improve the world, and from the end of the Enlightenment through the early twentieth century, science develops a reputation as the most reliable source of knowledge about reality. Yet, as science became more powerful, its limitations became more apparent. In the mid-twentieth century, some philosophers and sociologists became suspicious that the power of scientific expertise was due more to social structures than to scientists' connection to nature (Section 3.3). This has led to a tension between those who view science as an objective project and those who view it as a social one (Section 3.4). Upon reflection, it is difficult to doubt that science is objective in at least some sense. But it is also true that social structures like "professions," which arose to protect the interests of scientists, also serve to distort those interests and confound the concept of expertise, leading us to dismiss some real experts and to trust some nonexperts. I close by highlighting how these debates hinge on the related questions of what sort of authority experts have, how to recognize them, and when to trust them (Section 3.5).

3.1 Expertise in the Middle Ages: The Era of the Master

In the Middle Ages, discussions around what we now call specialized expertise occurred primarily in the contexts of education and guilds. Plato's Academy and

Aristotle's Lyceum set the model for the medieval schools, developed by Arabic and Western scholars to train students for roles in civil society. Outside the schools, craftspeople formed guilds to protect themselves against competition and to ensure the high quality of their products. As guild members got wealthy, they were less inclined to take on new protégées, and so the standards for entry became stricter. Not only did one have to be an excellent craftsperson, one also had to pay a fee. What is noteworthy is that the model of training both in the schools and in the guilds closely reflected the models developed in Greece and Rome: tutelage or apprenticeship under a "master" in a domain.

The school model was taken up by the Western Christian Church as early as Charlemagne in the 700s.[1] The primary aim of the schools was not to train experts, per se. The Carolingian[2] model of education (prominent from the late 700s to the early 900s) was aimed at training people for two offices, state and church, though the primary curriculum for both was Christian scripture. While "[t]he liberal arts occupied an important position," they "were ancillary to the study of scripture" (Jaeger 1994: 21).

In the 950s, a new structure of education emerged under Emperor Otto the Great (912–73) and his brother, Brun of Saxony (925–65), in Germanic and French cities, like Cologne, Worms, and Rheims. In contrast to traditional "monastery schools," which focused on spiritual development, these new "cathedral schools" focused on educating students for administrative and civil service, whether in the church or in the royal court, which meant that education of social skills took precedence over the Christian Bible. The training was "humanist" in orientation, integrating "the liberal arts into the formation of *mores*" (Jaeger 1994: 42). *Mores*, in this context, refers to secular ethics, that is, ethics not grounding the teachings of a sacred scripture or tradition. Etymologically, *more* refers broadly to cultural customs or socially dictated manners, but, because of its association with a normative demand on behavior, is also associated with principles of morality, and it is the root of the contemporary English word "moral."

Recall that both Plato and Cicero struggled with whether virtue and oratory were *technein*. These abilities were, in large part, gifts of the gods or Muses; they could not be taught. If a practice either had no comprehensive body of knowledge (as in Socrates's example of cookery) or if it could not be taught (as in the case of oratory), then it simply was not a *techne*. Medieval educators, in contrast, were convinced that virtue could be taught through the cultivation of *mores*, or habits fitting the virtuous person. Some of these habits are what we now generally regard as "the arts"—music, poetry, sculpture—and some of them are what we might call "manners"—how you dress, eat, walk, speak, and so on.

Students were taught that they should dress in moderation, that they should walk in moderation, and that their gestures should not be "effeminate or swaggering or sluggish or hasty" (Jaeger 1994: 264).

In Chapter 2, we saw that, classically, the arts included any *techne*, from shoemaking to mathematics. But in the cathedral schools, the seven "liberal" arts (grammar, rhetoric, logic, geometry, arithmetic, music, astronomy)[3] took on new significance. They were thought to have a unique power to free us (hence, "liberal") from the bonds of nature and the penalties of sin. The idea was that, without these shackles, we are free to be more human and, because humans are made in the image of God, free to be more divine:

> Why do you suppose, brothers, we are commanded to imitate the life and habits of good men, unless it be that we are reformed through imitating them to the image of a new life? For in them the form of the image of God is engraved, and when through the process of imitation we are pressed against that carved surface, we too are moulded in the likeness of that same image. (Hugh of St. Victor, *De institutione novitiorum*, ch. 8)

Poetry, music, sculpture, and architecture were praised as "overcoming nature" and the underworld, and the old gods. The medieval poem "Liège Song" says that "Facing the gods, Orpheus conquered them with his song" (Jaeger 1994: 160).

While we now distinguish art from science, it is worth noting that this belief that certain practices help cultivate virtue and, thereby, conquer nature is a likely reason. It is during this time that *ars* becomes dislodged from its association with *techne* and *episteme* and restricted to aesthetic practices. Regardless of whether cultivating these habits actually instills virtue, the liberating *artium* (liberal arts) became associated with creativity, ideals, and transcendence, while the common skills of farming, fishing, and other labors that dampen the spirit rather than lifting it were called the *illiberal arts*.[4] The key assumption, however, is that virtue can be taught. The unknown eleventh-century author of the poem *Quid suum virtutis* writes, "Scale the ladder of art wherever arduous virtue summons you!" (Jaeger 1994: 159). The liberal arts were thought powerful enough to transform character—to imbue one with virtue through their practice; poetry, especially, "soothes hard hearts and creates compassion" (1994: 148).

These cathedral schools ran from roughly 950–1200, and three features of their educational model have proved influential for later studies of expertise. First, the curriculum was taught through immersion in a community of experts. The teachers ("masters") were praised variously as "the next Cicero" or "the next

Socrates," and the schools were called "a second Athens." Brun's biographer, Sigebert of Gembloux (c. 1030–1112), says that Brun did not teach a specific content, as if from a textbook or set of rules for behavior, but rather with his personality, modeling what was expected at all times: "as steel sharpens steel, the one was edified in emulation of the other's gifts" (Sigebert, quoted in Jaeger 1994: 39). They would have endorsed Xenophon's explanation: "That is why fathers try to keep their sons, even if they are well behaved, out of bad company: for the society of honest men is a training in virtue, but the society of the bad is virtue's undoing" (*Memorabilia* 1.2.20).

Second, the curriculum was primarily practice-based and only secondarily knowledge-based. "We have to put aside the conception of school learning as primarily the transmission of knowledge: lecturing, note-taking, book-learning, the generating of understanding, the cultivation of critical thought" (Jaeger 1994: 3). Medieval scholars were under the impression that while virtue could not be taught directly, it could be cultivated through behavior, down to the finest details: how you walk, how you hold your head, how and when you speak (see also Breitenstein 2014). Further, the process was immersive: "the master is always present with [the novices] to keep watch over their discipline, to lead them to and from wherever necessity takes them."[5]

Third, the curriculum began with the assumption that great intelligence and skill were largely innate, "natural endowments," "native gifts," or "divine favors" that could be honed but not taught. Poet Godfrey of Rheims, who became chancellor of the cathedral school at Rheims in the mid-1070s, writes:

A powerful thing is genius and stronger than the sharp sword.
The eloquent tongue cuts through armed duke. (Jaeger 1994: 160)

Students were chosen carefully according to whether they had demonstrated intelligence or a tendency toward virtuous behavior. Only after the masters thought they knew a student's potential could they be confident that he would be receptive to training. While this predates the "nature vs. nurture" debate by several hundred years, this medieval commitment to innate talent is precisely what motivates that problem.

Each of these features has become a point of controversy in expertise studies. According to contemporaries, the cathedral school were a resounding success. The school at Cologne, for example, would "produce some of the most illustrious intellectuals, statesman, educators, and bishops of the next generation" (Jaeger 1994: 47). By 956, four of the first twelve major cathedral schools had developed a reputation for excellence. Yet, the generation that followed was not so complimentary. Historian C. Steven Jaeger notes that "There is a great deal of talk about flourishing schools and great teachers. But there are no intellectual achievements, and therefore the schools are judged [by historians of the eleventh century] to 'show little vitality from within'" (1994: 3).

Because the Greek notions associated with expertise were largely measured by observable outcomes, this raises the question of whether the "illustrious" progeny of these schools went on to become experts in their domains or whether they remained well-educated people of experience. Jaeger dismisses the idea that the schools were unsuccessful just because their students produced no great "texts and artifacts." Their success is found, he contends, in "personalities and in the cultivation of personal qualities." "Its works of art are men[6] whose 'manners' are 'composed.' This composition, the well-tempered man, was a major contribution of the eleventh century to 'philosophy'" (1994: 4). This does not, of course, mean these men were experts of any sort. As we saw in Plato and Aristotle, the generally educated person need not possess any specialized skills. Nevertheless, a reputation for training excellent people should not be dismissed lightly. I revisit this question of what experts must "do" and how to identify them in Chapters 7 and 8.

What is notable about this era is that, despite the apparent successes of their educational model, they conducted no study of their assumptions about learning. They seemed to hit upon some success criteria by applying ancient practices and luck. Though we might think this is because of their strict religious affiliation and political system, that is not consistent with the evidence. Tensions between the church and scholarship tended to arise only when scholarship was perceived (by someone with a vested interest in the question) to contradict a tenet of the faith.[7] Thus, Galileo Galilei was not put under house arrest for believing the Copernican doctrine, but for teaching it.[8] Even the execution of Giordano Bruno, thought by many to have been motivated by his scientific beliefs, was primarily a function of his theological writings, which the church judged to be heretical.[9] Rather, the attitude of medieval scholars seems to have been a sort of settled comfort with traditional wisdom rather than any spiritual insecurity about the aims and methods of science.

In the twelfth and thirteenth centuries, scholars started their own "guild," the "*univeristas magistribus et pupillorum*," or "guild of masters and students," to establish standards of entry into scholarly disciplines and create an agreed-upon path to becoming a "master" (Beckwith 2012: 43–5). In time, these university guilds became what we now call universities. And while some universities looked to the past, building new arguments on the old authorities, relying on the physics and biology of Aristotle and the politics of Cicero, others were looking forward. They were not content with knowledge handed down as settled, and they took such pedagogy as an insult to philosophy.

3.2 Expertise in the Enlightenment: Radically Limited Authority

Skipping ahead a couple of centuries, we find this discontent with the masters in full bloom. Giovanni Pico della Mirandola (1463–94) explicitly rejected the idea that talents were somehow distributed among humans by God, or that they had some predetermined limits. At twenty-four years old, he wrote *Oration on the Dignity of Humanity*, in which he "depicted humanity as a creature with the capacity to determine its own identity rather than be compelled to receive this in any given fixed form" (McGrath 2007: 34). He interprets God as telling humans: "You are constrained by no limits, and shall determine the limits of your nature for yourself, in accordance with your own free will, in whose hand we have placed you" (cited in McGrath 2007: 34; Pico della Mirandola 1956: 7). Thinkers from Desiderius Erasmus (1466–1536) to Thomas Jefferson (1743–1826) argued that, too often, so-called authorities have been wrong, and to simply allow the current state of "knowledge" to determine our beliefs was to (a) abdicate a clear moral responsibility to use our minds well, and (b) to miss opportunities for learning the real truth of the matter and root out mistakes and superstition.

Erasmus's *In Praise of Folly* can be interpreted as a satire of this kind of education, citing everyone from Homer to the Gospel writers as authorities and then showing how their writings can be cherry-picked to support just about any conclusion one prefers. The resulting individualism and push for autonomy in the domains of knowledge became a hallmark of the Enlightenment.[10] If one were asked to name a period of history when expertise was under attack, one could hardly do better than the Enlightenment.

René Descartes (1596–1650) was notoriously unabashed in his rejection of expert authority. In *Discourse on the Method* (1637),[11] he gives a rather conceited biographical picture of his early education, highlighting what he thought were its deficiencies. He praises the "charm" of fable, which "awakens the mind," the "beauties" of oratory, and the "ravishing delicacy and sweetness" of poetry. He also appreciates the books of ancient authors, who reveal, as if in conversation, "only the best of their thoughts." Ultimately, though, he considered all these merely "gifts of the mind rather than fruits of study." He respected mathematics as firm and certain, though he wasn't yet sure of its full potential. He was even less sanguine about the domains that used mathematics, "surprised that nothing more exalted had been built upon such firm and solid foundations" (Descartes [1637] 1988: 22–3). The study of ethics (secular ethics anyway), he argued, rested on "sand and mud," confusing virtue for "callousness, or vanity, or desperation, or parricide" (Descartes [1637] 1988: 23). Theology, he thought, is beyond human reasoning and requires divine insight. He was frustrated with philosophy because, although it has been "cultivated for many centuries by the most excellent minds," still there was no philosophical argument or conclusion "which is not disputed and hence doubtful" (Descartes [1637] 1988: 24). The other sciences rested on philosophy, and were, therefore, no better, offering "merely probable arguments and having no demonstrative basis." The sciences "do not get so close to the truth as do the simple reasonings, which a [person] of good sense, using [their] natural powers, can carry out" (Descartes [1637] 1988: 26). Descartes concludes that if he wants any firm opinion about the world, he is going to have to wipe the slate clean and start over himself. "This made me feel free to judge all others by reference to myself."

This was no small undertaking, even in his time. Perhaps due to his immense self-confidence, he undertook it as admirably as anyone, developing theories of cosmology, motion, force, analytic geometry, the physics of light, the human body, the soul, and even music (Slowik 2017). Descartes encouraged (and, if we are to believe his self-reports, modeled) what we might call "rugged individualism" about knowledge: It is primarily up to each of us, alone, to use our faculties the best we can to arrive at knowledge. His individualist influence on future discussions of knowledge cannot be overstated.

It is important to note that Descartes's doubt about expert authority need not be characterized as doubt about whether expertise exists. It certainly might, but whether it does turns on a distinction Descartes was not interested in drawing. For Descartes, what followed from being well positioned in a domain was not the ability to speak on behalf of that domain in a way that exerted normative force for others. In other words, if X is an expert in domain D, it does not follow for Descartes that you should believe X about D *simply because* X is an expert. Descartes's individualism suggests that he thinks anyone can understand a domain and come to their own *authoritative understanding* (notice where the authority is located) with the right kind of approach. Descartes's marvelous *Meditations on First Philosophy* is written in a way that exemplifies this commitment. The reader is asked to come along with the narrator to think through all the relevant points of a case, and to finally arrive at conclusions Descartes thought the reader should see as unassailable: you exist; you are not your body but an immaterial self; God exists; and because God exists, you need not doubt your senses.

Descartes and other Enlightenment thinkers started a trend, shifting discussions of knowledge away from "masters" and "officials" and "authorities" and toward individual assessment of arguments and evidence. Sociologist of science Steven Shapin points out that "The rejection of authority and testimony in favor of individual sense-experience is just what stands behind our recognition of seventeenth-century practitioners as 'moderns,' as 'like us,' and, indeed, as producers of the thing we can warrant as 'science'" (1994: 201). The question of expertise, at least among philosophers, is almost obviated during this period. Maybe there are experts, but even if so, you should pursue questions for yourself because you can be an expert with a little work. Authority rests solely in your understanding.

British philosopher John Locke echoes this sentiment: "[W]e may as rationally hope to see with other Men's Eyes, as to know by other Men's Understandings . . . The floating of other Men's Opinions in our brains makes us not a jot more knowing, though they happen to be true" (Locke 1975: 1.4.23). Consider also the opening passage of American statesman Thomas Jefferson's "A Bill for Establishing Religious Freedom":

> Well aware that the opinions and belief of men depend not on their own will, but follow involuntarily the evidence proposed to their minds; that Almighty God hath created the mind free, and manifested his supreme will that free it shall remain by making it altogether insusceptible of restraint; that all attempts to influence it by temporal punishments, or burthens, or by civil incapacitations, tend only to beget habits of hypocrisy and meanness, and are a departure from the plan of the holy author of our religion, who being lord both of body and mind, yet chose not to propagate it by coercions on either, as was in his Almighty power to do, but to extend it by its influence on reason alone; that the impious presumption of legislators and rulers, civil as well as ecclesiastical, who, being themselves but fallible and uninspired men, have assumed dominion over the faith of others, setting up their own opinions and modes of thinking as the only true and infallible, and as such endeavoring to impose them on others, hath established and maintained false religions over the greatest part of the world and through all time. (Jefferson 1776)

Here we see explicitly the claim that individuals were created to follow the "evidence proposed to their minds" and not their own will or the will of "fallible and uninspired" leaders, who are known to have propagated falsehoods throughout the world. Therefore, the burden is on each of us, as individuals, to decide for ourselves what to believe. Jefferson says that religious opinion is not the province of state authorities "any more than our opinions in physics or geometry."

Prussian philosopher Immanuel Kant warns that we have a tendency to unreflectively accept the judgments of others: "If I have a book that thinks for me, a pastor who acts as my conscience, a physician who prescribes my diet, and so on—then I have no need to exert myself. I have no need to think, if only I can pay; others will take care of that disagreeable business for me" (Kant 1784). We lack the courage to use our minds "without another's guidance." This leads to our becoming dull and submissive, and anyone who tries to perpetuate this attitude is committing "a crime against human nature whose proper destiny lies precisely in such progress." According to Kant, the motto of the Enlightenment is: "Have the courage to use your own understanding!" The claim implies that the only epistemically responsible way to form beliefs is to think and judge for yourself. Call this claim the *Enlightenment Mandate*.

If someone were to push back against the Enlightenment Mandate by saying it is too much to ask of someone to put in so much effort, saying something like, "I have no time for the long course of study which would be necessary to make me in any degree a competent judge of certain questions, or even able to understand the nature of the arguments," British philosopher W. K. Clifford (1877) replies that such a person "should have no time to believe."

Is there any room in Enlightenment thought to learn from others? The answer is yes, but only as equals learn from one another and study a domain together. In *Anthropology*, Kant explains that "the logical egoist considers it unnecessary to test his judgment by the reason of others, as if he had no need of such a touchstone" ([1785] 2006: 17). Kant is implying that we all need someone who can challenge or correct us. However, he does seem committed to the idea that no person or discipline can authoritatively dictate to another what is the case:

> One must not even say that *mathematics* is at least privileged to judge from its complete authority, for if the perceived general agreement of the surveyor's judgment did not follow from the judgment of all others who with talent and industry dedicated themselves to this discipline, then even mathematics itself would not be free from fear of somewhere falling into error. ([1785] 2006: 17)

Similarly, Locke says that, while he respects others' ideas, nevertheless, his "*greatest reverence is due to Truth*," and we would likely make more progress if we "made use rather of our own Thoughts, than other [peoples']" (Locke 1689[1975])1.4.23, p. 101, italics his).

To be sure, not every Enlightenment thinker was opposed to trusting experts on the basis of their expertise. Francis Bacon, for example, was not as enamored with human abilities as other philosophers, claiming that "the minds of [people] are so strangely disposed, as not to receive the true images of things" and that people "do not hitherto appear to be happily inclined and fitted for the sciences" ([1620]1876). Yet, he held out high hopes for a system in which people could bring their ideas and experiments together, for collaboration and innovation. He sketched how this might work in his posthumously published work of fiction *The New Atlantis* (1627). He saw this system of mutual reliance as a corrective for the isolationist and error-filled tendencies of individual experts. Giving explicit credit to Bacon, German philosopher Gottfried Wilhelm Leibniz (1646–1716) promoted the idea of a society for the promotion of the arts and sciences. Instead of the private efforts of intellectuals to build up knowledge from the foundations of pure reason, Leibniz advocated for a repository of texts and resources, and a space where "increased agreement and closer correspondence of skilled people will be aroused, creating opportunity and arrangements for many excellent and useful thoughts, inventions, and experiments" ([1671]1992: §24).[12]

Nevertheless, even for Bacon, the need for trust in experts was mostly a practical matter because people are often distracted by superstition, dogma, and other "idols" of the mind. Novices should be able, at least in principle, to assess the quality of experiments for themselves. For even though he says that "the human reason which we now have is a heap of jumble built up from many beliefs and many stray events as well as from childish notions which we absorbed in our earliest years" (1620 [2000]: 79), he has a rather optimistic view of how science can be assessed by novices:

> [I]t is our opinion that [people] could hit upon our form of interpretation simply by their own native force of intelligence, without any other art, if they had available a good history of nature and experience, and worked carefully on it.... For *interpretation* is the true and natural work of the mind once the obstacles are removed. (1620 [2000]: 101, italics his)

Interestingly, much of the overt disdain for trust in others proved implausible in practice *even for scientists*. In the mid-1600s, the work of performing experiments was constrained by a "traditional gentlemanly culture" that condemned "manual work" (Shapin 1994: 376). Robert Boyle (1627–91), for example, hired numerous assistants to actually perform his experiments and relay their findings to him. Far from relying solely on his own faculties, Boyle's lab was "an economy of trust and power relations":

> Precisely because assistants prepared, tended, and worked the instruments, Boyle was dependent upon them for his avowal that his experiments were really done, were done as he directed, and yielded the results that he would credibly relate to others. While the authorial voice was Boyle's, his narratives largely spoke for, and vouched for, what others had done, observed, and represented. (Shapin 1994: 383)

Even after the "gentlemanly culture" dissipated and scientists were more directly involved in their research, the volume, complexity, and geographic diversity of experiments left the Enlightenment rejection of expert authority looking rather quaint. Alexis de Tocqueville, in the midst of praising the intellectual and political individualism of Americans, notes an obvious limitation: "There is no philosopher in the world so great but that he believes a million things on the faith of other people and accepts a great many more truths than he demonstrates" (1835 [1963]: 9).

Historian of science Roy Porter writes, "wherever one looks, there was, during the eighteenth century, no shortage of what... we can call 'discovery,' 'invention,' or 'construction' of new knowledge" (2003: 6), and Porter cites voluminous advancements in astrophysics, mathematics, and chemistry, and the emergence of new domains, such as geology and biology. Recall from Section 2.2 that it was during this time (the middle 1600s) that courts began calling scientists as witnesses in both criminal and civil proceedings. Contrary to the advice of most Enlightenment philosophers, many of these domains were not comprised of individuals working alone. Rather, people working in one domain built upon the assumptions and findings of those in other domains, mostly without independently testing them.

Empirical research increasingly depended on the findings of others, frequently people who were in different parts of the world. Researchers had to narrowly specialize and then rely on the findings of others who narrowly specialized. This specialization meant scientists and those who rely on them needed to set up new systems of trust to ensure that what specialists were saying had been vetted and tested by other trustworthy people. Philosophers Gernot Rieder and Judith Simon explain that

> The veracity of testimony was no longer underwritten by personal virtue, but by an elaborate system of institutionalized norms and standards, rigorously policed in a great "panopticon of truth" (Shapin, 1994). A different form of trust first accompanied and then superseded the premoderns' faith in the integrity of the solitary knower and the moderns' confidence in the rigor of institutionalized expertise. (2016: 3)

Further, commercial and political interests co-opted many technologies for new uses in business and war, in a sweeping reliance on technology that users did not understand and had no interest in understanding. As these new ideas, tools, and products made their way from the minds of specialists to public use, there needed to be ways of checking plausibility and quality. Without these, any competence on the part of experts would not be perceived any more favorably than ancient authorities or charlatans—sometimes they were right; often they were wrong. We will explore this notion of a system of institutionalized norms and standards in Chapters 7 and 8, in the context of what philosopher Stephen Turner calls the "bonding" activities of experts.

The takeaway is that scientists, scholars, businesspeople, and politicians have no choice but to trust others, regardless of what Enlightenment philosophers argued was epistemically responsible. So the question is not whether to trust experts, but whether (contra the Enlightenment Mandate) trust could be justified and, if so, under what circumstances and to what degree. The challenge is to find ways of organizing expertise and information that promote and protect trust in experts. We will look at this challenge in detail in Chapters 7 and 8.

3.3 Rising Doubts about Scientific Experts

By the early twentieth century, two things were happening that could make us think that scientific experts were able to answer these questions: technologies developed through scientific methodologies were still booming, and the structure of the "profession" emerged to guard entry to specialized domains.

3.3.1 The Rise of the Scientific Expert

The invention of the jet engine, nylon, air-conditioning, plastic, radar, and frozen food, not to mention the medical discoveries of insulin, penicillin, and the polio vaccine, gave scientists a privileged place in society, seeming to establish the rightful boundary of expertise. Scientists, engineers, and doctors, it was now clear, were experts. By comparison, theologians and philosophers—especially philosophers who worked in ethics or metaphysics—were not experts in much of anything.[13] Despite centuries of debate, no theological position or philosophical argument could compete with the success of empirical research.

Further, as our knowledge of other cultures grew, we saw that fashions, miracle cures, and popular beliefs about nature, the body, and the gods were easily explained as products of cultural tradition and superstition.[14] Beliefs that seemed obviously true to one generation or culture seemed obviously false to others. Within the walls of universities, medical schools, and the private salons, the obviously false ones could be given a wink and dismissed.

To be sure, there were some folk beliefs with practical value (e.g., planting by astrological signs, administering concoctions that included calomel to purge imbalances in the humors). These were harder to dismiss, and belief in the humors persevered among medical practitioners far into the 1800s (Lagay 2002). But with the extraordinary advancements in science, these half-truths and inadequate bits of folklore were slowly replaced with more resilient theories and more successful practices. As sociologist Harry Collins notes, science offered a respite from voluminous disagreements over religion, morality, and metaphysics: "Up until the middle of the [twentieth] century . . . one could take a rest from this maelstrom of uncertainty on the calm island of the sciences and mathematics" (2014: 27–8). Philosopher Stephen Turner explains that because scientific expertise is so hard to attain and has become so influential and stable a source of information about the world "it often serves as a proxy in our thinking about knowledge in society for all experts" (882014: 6). Collins and Robert Evans (2006) call sociological research that presupposes science is the "grand metanarrative,"[15] the "First Wave" of Science Studies.

Philosopher Bertrand Russell held this lofty view of science throughout his long career. In 1912, he wrote that the sciences are the end result of successful philosophy: "[A]s soon as definite knowledge concerning any subject becomes possible, this subject ceases to be called philosophy, and becomes a separate science." He says that, while philosophy proper cannot boast of many "truths," the sciences overflow with them. "If you ask a mathematician, a mineralogist, a historian, or any other [person] of learning, what definite body of truths has been ascertained by [their] science, [their] answer will last as long as you are willing to listen" (116). In 1968, he still held that knowledge of science—its findings, not merely its methods—should be part of the fundamental training of philosophers:

> It is science that makes the difference between the modern world and the world before the 17th Century. It is science that has destroyed the belief in witchcraft, magic and sorcery. It is science that has made the old creeds and the old superstitions impossible for intelligent men to accept. (1968: 9)

The idea that scientists discover "definite knowledge" while other academics piddle in speculation has served as the touchstone for scientists and philosophers who engage in political debates against views that are inspired by or laced with religious or other metaphysical associations, such as creation science, intelligent design, and alternative medicine.

3.3.2 Empirical Limitations on Scientific Expertise

In hindsight, we might ask Russell: For *whom* has science "destroyed the belief in witchcraft, magic and sorcery"? Notorious disagreements over food science, the biology of pregnancy ("when life begins"), gender identity, disability, and the role of medicine at the end of life, many of which are fueled by religion or mysticism, permeate society and motivate public policy. There are supposedly scientific experts on both sides of these debates. That a country as technologically advanced as Japan could, in 2019, uphold a law that requires transgender individuals to be sterilized before allowing them to change their legal identities (Associated Press 2019) suggests that Russell's confidence in scientific expertise to eradicate superstition and prejudice is more a reflection of his own narrow social group than of the power of science.

Even for academics committed to a naturalistic view of the world, the eminence of scientific experts as authors of the grand "metanarrative" proved tumultuous in the twentieth century. Philosopher Thomas Kuhn famously showed that subsequent generations of scientists regularly reject the settled science of past generations (Kuhn 1962). Ptolemy's geocentric universe was overturned by Copernicus's heliocentric one. Aristotle's view that the stars were fixed in concentric crystalline spheres was overturned by Kepler's elliptical orbits. Newton's views that space could be mapped using Euclidean geometry and that it is just empty "space" were overturned by subsequent work by Lobachevsky, Riemann, and Einstein. Classical mechanics was challenged by researchers like Max Planck, Niels Bohr, and Henry Moseley. These examples are only from cosmological physics. If none of the sciences are closing in on a stable set of beliefs, why think scientists have a privileged view of reality? Why not conclude, instead, that they simply discover various ways of predicting and manipulating what we experience that are handy for our limited human interests and understanding at a given time in history?

To be sure, Kuhn did not take his findings as motivating relativism about science, and he spent the remainder of his career defending his claims against those who interpreted him that way. While he admitted that there would be "losses as well as gains" in the advancement of science, it is a problem-solving enterprise, and as long as each new paradigm solves a well-recognized problem while preserving "a relatively large part of the concrete problem-solving ability that has accrued to science through its predecessors," it retains a sufficient amount of objectivity (167, 169). Kuhn argued that scientific authorities weren't merely authorities, in the sense of being appointed advocates for one way of engaging with the world—their authority depends on whether they actually solve scientific problems.

3.3.3 Social Limitations on Scientific Expertise

Nevertheless, Kuhn's explanation of scientific progress initiated a "historical turn" in science studies, which inspired a new branch of anti-realism[16] about science that questioned the uniqueness of scientific authority among the broader pursuits of humanity. In the 1960s, sociologists of science, philosophers of science, and historians of science embarked on a research program known as "Sociology of Scientific Knowledge" (SSK), which aimed at understanding the social and historical conditions under which what counts as scientific truth emerges. Emboldened by Kuhn's work, SSK researchers highlighted the ways in which science was more than its collection of methods, observations, and theories and emphasized the ways it was also a social institution that influenced and was influenced by law, education, culture, and politics (Barnes and Bloor 1982; Collins and Evans 2007). Harry Collins (2014) explains this view:

> If *the world* changes when scientists think about it in a different way, then, not only *what counts as true* in science depends on where and when the scientists live, but what *is true* depends on where and when the scientists live: scientists who live in one place or time live in one world, while scientists who live in another place or time live in a different world. (26, italics his)

The result is a thoroughgoing relativism about knowledge and expertise, a relativism that has no teeth to compete with the various religious, folk, or mythical perspectives on the world. Collins and Evans (2006) call research that presumes that science is not an objective metanarrative but simply one among many ways of engaging with and interpreting the world, "Second Wave Science Studies."

People who work in SSK take issue with this account, arguing that it is a reductive reading of their work. Sheila Jasanoff, for example, says she does not discount the "heads and hands of skilled persons" (2003: 393) but simply emphasizes the fact that who counts as experts on what topic is largely—but not wholly or solely—shaped by the political questions asked of them at a time.

"Different bodies of expert knowledge come into being with their associated markers of excellence and credibility, through disparate contingencies of politics and knowledge production" (394). Of course, even if this more nuanced reading of the Second Wave of SSK is not a *strong* form of relativism, it is certainly not the objective picture of science the previous generations painted; it is no bulwark against the maelstrom of superstition. It leaves the notion that scientists are experts significantly weakened, if not undermined.

3.3.4 Moral Limitations on Scientific Expertise

A further concern about the authority of scientists was the uses to which they put their expertise. Like any skill, science can be put to better or worse uses, and scientists have put their skills to notoriously troubling uses. In 1945, the United States demonstrated the horrors that science can produce when it dropped two nuclear bombs on cities in Japan. From 1932 to 1972, seemingly well-meaning medical researchers financially coerced 600 black men from Tuskegee, Alabama, to participate in research on syphilis without adequately informed consent, actively prohibited them from leaving the study, and refused to offer them standard of care (penicillin) once it became available in 1945. In 1957, pharmaceutical researchers in Germany began marketing thalidomide as a cure-all for insomnia, coughs, colds, headaches, and morning sickness. Despite evidence on fetal alcohol syndrome that showed drugs could harm fetuses, researchers stubbornly maintained that chemicals could not breach the placental wall. Before thalidomide was pulled from the market in 1961, it had killed 2,000 babies and caused severe malformation of limbs (phocomelia) in 10,000 others.

We might attempt to explain all this away as a problem of *people* in science rather than *science* itself. We might note that, while certain people commit atrocities, the *practice* of science is morally and factually neutral. The method of a randomized clinical trial, for example, does not by itself discriminate against people of color or vulnerable populations, but it can certainly be used to do so. The relationships between observations, or propositions expressing those observations, and theories are an objective matter of coherence; they are not a function of scientists' judgment.[17]

While this is true, I worry it is misleading. Simply conducting an experiment is not constitutive of science. Not all scientific activities involve experiments. But even for those that do, some of what counts as science happens before those experiments, when scientists state their research questions, formulate their hypotheses, and identify their target populations.

Some of what counts as science happens after experiments, when researchers collect the data and interpret them in light of their research interests and in the context of their research institution's interest in the research, the scope of their grant (if they have a grant), and the social pressures to publish. Science is the whole bag of stuff, not just a few of its parts.

Take the act of asking a research question. Imagine you are interested in studying Down syndrome for the purpose of "curing it," that is, for reversing what you regard as a genetic "abnormality" (called trisomy 21). Your study presupposes several things about people with Down syndrome: that they have a "disability" or "disease," that their lives are somehow impoverished, perhaps that their way of experiencing the world is not as meaningful as other ways of experiencing the world, and so on. What do people with Down syndrome say about their lives? Do they view themselves as having a disability or illness? Are they interested in a "cure"?[18] What motivated you as the researcher to choose Down syndrome to study, and how is that choice expressed in the science that might emerge from the study?

Similarly biased questions from real scientific studies include:[19] Are there inherent IQ differences between X and Y populations (Murray and Herrnstein 1994)? Are men who care for their children likely to have smaller testes (Mascaro, Hackett, and Rilling 2013)? Are women more satisfied in relationships where their husband is the breadwinner (Murray-Close and Heggeness 2018)? Each of these questions is motivated by value-laden assumptions, including beliefs about intelligence, race, gender roles, biological sex, and the organization of families. While we might contend that the scientific methodologies used to study these questions are neutral to their social, moral, and metaphysical significance, we surely cannot say that the resulting findings somehow outrun their moral *implications*. If all science is beholden to the way research questions are framed and hypotheses formulated by humans with biases and subjective interests, then simply pointing to the neutral parts of science does not address the problem.

3.3.5 Conceptual Limitations on Scientific Expertise

These three phenomena—the emergence of scientific instrumentalism, the advent of SSK, and the moral horrors of science—led some philosophers much further down the path to expert skepticism. They claim that if we follow these problems to their logical ends, we should not only deny the authority of experts, irrespective of their domain, but we should also deny every author any authority over the meaning of their own words. An author writes something and puts it out into the world. But the moment someone else reads it, in a different context with different background assumptions, the author's intended meaning, whatever it might have been, is irrelevant. Philosopher Michel Foucault explains:

> Using all the contrivances that he sets up between himself and what he writes, the writing subject cancels out the signs of his particular individuality. As a result, the mark of the writer is reduced to nothing more than the singularity of his absence. (1979/2000: 337)

This "death of the author" (as literary critic Roland Barthes coined it in 1967) has startling implications for the purported expertise of scientists who claim to be discovering truths about the natural world in ways that objectively improve our lives. It implies that we should be categorically skeptical of any sort of expertise. If an author cannot impose meaning on a piece of writing, then the writing is simply a shared text (see Derrida, 1977) whose meaning (to the degree that it still counts as meaning) emerges among those who engage with it. If this were right, it would not make sense to say that a scientist (or any other expert) has authority to help us "understand our world better," as if there were something outside socially constructed meaning that could be known and that counts objectively as "our world" that could be objectively identified as "better."

Philosopher Richard Rorty sees this as a natural development of older traditions in philosophy, like Hegel's idealism. He echoes Derrida's conclusion, applying explicitly to science:

> It is useless to ask whether one vocabulary rather than another is closer to reality. For different vocabularies serve different purposes, and there is no such thing as a purpose that is closer to reality than another purpose.... Nothing is conveyed by saying... that the vocabulary in which we predict the motion of a planet is more in touch with how things really are than the vocabulary in which we assign the planet an astrological influence. (1990: 3)

Part of Rorty's point here, which he defends in his influential book *Philosophy and the Mirror of Nature* (1979), is that no one can approach a question about the world without some assumptions about the world, and those assumptions may be right or wrong, but really the only test we have for the accuracy of those assumptions is how well they cohere with one another and our experiences of the world. "It is merely to say that nothing counts as justification unless by reference to what we already accept, and that there is no way to get outside our beliefs and our language so as to find some test other than coherence" (1979: 178). We are left simply with what seems useful for specific purposes at specific times in light of our background beliefs.

3.4 Scientific Expertise despite the Skepticism

Is the sort of skepticism about scientific expertise generated by these three problems tenable? In general, the difficulty with categorical relativism or skepticism about expertise is that neither can withstand the stable, brute phenomena of suffering that attends a measles outbreak after a portion of the population stops getting vaccinated. They cannot explain why HIV can now be treated as a chronic condition rather than a terminal disease. They cannot explain how a cell phone can be tracked to a precise location within seconds. Even if, as writer Verlyn Klinkenborg says, every sentence "adheres to a set of rules—grammar, syntax, the history and customs of the language, a world of echoes and allusions and social cues—that pay no heed to your intentions" (2012: 4), this does not imply that those rules do not track something we can all identify as meaningful. Outside of academic discussions, we have good reasons to trust that airplanes will get where they're going safely,[20] skyscrapers will keep standing, elevators won't plummet to the ground, inotropes will keep hearts beating, and dialysis machines will do the work damaged kidneys cannot. Whether we can explain how all this happens in a foundational, "first philosophy" sense is beside the point for a study of expertise. We trust these things because they really work. And they work because experts understand how to build and use them. Even if we were to accept Rorty's extreme relativism, we must then accept that there's something *right*, objectively, about relativism—and that is self-defeating.[21]

Thus, behind the scenes of these skeptical concerns, and in some cases in response to them, the sciences have marched on. The successes of nineteenth-century science motivated increasingly empirical and naturalistic explanations of natural processes. Neo-Kantians, positivists, and logical empiricists advocated strongly against the previous century's rationalist and metaphysical approaches to the natural world and encouraged, instead, a purely empirical approach. They wanted to maintain the certainties of mathematics and logic but constrain their application with empirical observations. For example, in his Neo-Kantian phase, philosopher Hans Reichenbach introduced a distinction between *pure geometry* and *applied geometry* in an attempt to preserve the idea that geometric truths are necessary truths while accommodating the increasing empirical evidence that space and time as we experience them are contingent, and, therefore, very different from the concepts that rationalists and Kantians claimed to "deduce" by rigorous analyses (1958: ch. 1, §3). It was becoming widely agreed that we should only believe about nature what can be observed about nature.

During the early nineteenth century, the nature of expert skepticism shifted and narrowed. There was more outspoken doubt about ancient authorities than ever. Historian Jennifer Michael Hecht writes that "The nineteenth century was easily the best-documented moment of widespread doubt in human history: there were more doubters writing and speaking where they could be heard than ever before, and many more had come to hear them" (2003: 371). But this was not a doubt of expert authority in total, as Descartes's seemed to be. Authority was not merely relegated to each individual's ability to understand a domain. This doubt was aimed primarily at the sacred cows of religion and prejudice. "[Reformists] began the century by demanding an end to religious persecution and end it in defiance of religious support for political injustice," that is, in favor of ending slavery, women's rights, and free speech (Hecht 2003: 371). Science was gradually revealing authentic expertise and separating it from the inauthentic, traditionally ascribed authoritarian roles circumscribed by religions and governments.

But as Rieder and Simon noted above, the structure of trust also needed changing. Nonexperts needed a way to be sure they were going to the right folks for advice, and not hucksters or charlatans. Professions arose in response to rapid industrialization and the "scientizing" of disciplines who wanted a share of science's successes by association. "During the late nineteenth century, craft knowledge about everything from funerals to philanthropy became 'scientized,' as did public administration" (Noveck 2015: 28). Just as guilds emerged in the Middle Ages to guarantee quality, *professions* emerged as a gatekeeping mechanism, producing "credentials to distinguish professional from layman" (Noveck 2015: 48). Beth Simone Noveck, the White House's first deputy chief technology officer under US president Barack Obama, explains:

> Professionals are organized bodies of experts whose knowledge appears to the rest of us to be esoteric. They have elaborate systems of instruction and training. They possess and enforce a code of ethics or behavior more strict than the one the rest of us follow. They work hard to maintain their exclusivity, which affords their societies significant latitude to exclude others and to regulate and even censor members' speech like a state actor. (49)

Like their medieval counterparts, "[p]rofessions impose and police the epistemic rules for cataloguing how certain types of knowledge are produced and disseminated within their ranks and, as a result, wield tremendous political power" (49).

The benefits of this development were clear. First, professions offered efficiency in developing and identifying experts. If someone is a board-certified doctor, you can be confident that they have been well trained and well vetted by other experts to provide a certain kind of medical care. Second, professions offer legitimacy to those domains that can mirror the professional models of doctors, lawyers, and accountants. A wide array of domains, from real estate, to education, to chaplaincy, to social work, and now to clinical ethics consultants (HEC-C Certification Commission 2019), have attempted to establish legitimacy by setting up rules, policies, and procedures for demonstrating proficiency in their domains. A third benefit is financial. Also, like guilds, professions establish and protect standard salaries and fees for service.

Finally, and most significant for expertise, professions enjoy the advantage of something ethereal, namely, the sense of responsibility inherent to "serving" as a member of a profession, "a sense of duty and purpose, which breeds deference" (Noveck 2015: 48). For example, many medical schools still have students read various versions of the Hippocratic Oath, which is supposed to inspire them to practice "with uprightness and honor," to work "for the good of the sick," and to keep themselves "aloof from wrong."[22] But these oaths are taken unreflectively, and sometimes ironically. Note that, despite all the gravity that attends the phrase "do no harm,"[23] the original Oath did not include it, and most current oaths include nothing about patient rights.[24] This rite of professional passage is often little more than pomp, aimed at capturing whatever it is about their work—that special feeling of significance and responsibility—that the public is supposed to trust them with.

The structure of trust that emerges with professions has three significant impacts on expertise. First, because there is an esoteric knowledge or skill component, professionalism is often conflated with expertise. In some cases, they are coextensive. For example, one is trained to be a doctor or lawyer by doctors or lawyers in order to ensure uniformity and quality of practice, which, in turn, encourages public trust. "[B]ecause only experts can curate what is relevant, specific, and credible. . . [t]he professions have long served as a proxy for expertise" (Noveck 2015: 26–7). But in many cases, they are not coextensive. And when we conflate them, we take one of two risks, either we presume someone is an expert because they are a professional, which may not be the case, or we unnecessarily restrict ourselves to professionals when solving problems that would benefit from outside expertise (Noveck 2015: 27). Thus, it is imperative that we maintain a distinction between professionals and experts, even if some people are both.

Second, because professionalism has financial and social incentives, members of professions have strong incentives to shape and influence the world in ways that promote their interests, especially their social status. Professionals restrict access to their domains with entrance requirements, exclusionary policies, and technical jargon. This allows experts to control the markets over which they have provenance. As historian Thomas Haskell puts it: "Unchecked, the republic of letters becomes a republic of pals" (1998: 215), or, as I was raised to put it, a "good ol' boy system."

Third, professionalism can obscure the fact that expertise in different disciplines has different implications in terms of scope of authority. A cardiologist is not a pulmonologist, a pulmonologist is not a nephrologist, and a nephrologist is not an interventional radiologist, though all are licensed medical doctors. The same goes for the panoply of subspecialties in biology, physics, engineering, accounting, law, and so on. David Coady (2012) even argues that there is no such thing as "science expertise" because "no one is so well-informed about it [by which he means the whole collection of sciences] that they should be treated as an expert on it" (54). He explains:

> [B]eing a scientist is neither necessary nor sufficient for being scientifically well-informed. Although it is probably the case that most scientists are scientifically better informed than most people, there are clearly some scientists who are quite ignorant of what scientists working in other branches of science do, or who wrongly think that the methods of their branch of science characterize science as a whole. What is more, I submit that there are plenty of nonscientists who are scientifically better informed than some practicing scientists. (54)

The idea that the "profession" of scientist confers authority to speak on just any science-related matter fundamentally misunderstands the nature of expertise.

Ideally, professionalism would be a structure of trust to help circumscribe people who are trustworthy in a domain in an era where claims to knowledge and specialization are proliferating beyond what any individual or group of individuals could reasonably assess. Unfortunately, professionalism not only regularly falls short of guaranteeing expertise, in some cases it undermines experts' ability to thoroughly explore their domains, biasing them in ways that threaten their authority.

If professionalism cannot engender the trust experts need, what might? The only way, it seems, to capture the success of science without the hubris of the masters and the professions, is to devise a way to isolate the methods and findings of the science from the personalities that produced them, so they could stand on their own merits. Rather than experts' relying solely on the competence passed from their masters, perhaps groups of experts could evaluate and respond to the work of others without the biasing effects of specific teachers or schools. It was this line of thought that birthed the peer-review process.

Though the origins of the scientific journal can be traced to the Royal Societies of London and Paris in the late 1600s, it wasn't until 1731 that the Royal Society of Edinburgh set up procedures for vetting submitted articles through a set of experts (Lee et al., 2013; Spier 2002a). The Royal Society in London followed, albeit more slowly (Spier 2002a). It wasn't until 1937 that any scientific organization in the United States conducted a peer-review process, when the National Cancer Institute used it to evaluate requests for research grants (Spier 2002a; Shema 2014).

Peer review, especially blinded peer review, promises some semblance of objectivity in the scientific process, preventing the names of authors or institutions from influencing how putative expert work is assessed. Unfortunately, no system is without its flaws. Some argue that peer review keeps highly innovative work out of a domain because it conflicts with certain "settled" views that might be mistaken.[25] Further, peer review cannot detect fraud or research misconduct because reviewers do not attempt to replicate an author's research, and thus, additional protections are needed against these problems.[26] Further still, objectivity can be compromised when reviewers are working on similar projects or competing for the same grants as the anonymous author whose work they are reviewing. Thus, they may be incentivized to keep their research out of the literature until their own projects are funded or published.

None of this means that the system of vetting expertise is broken. The alternatives are clearly much worse, sending us back into the age of bloodletting and purging. It just emphasizes that becoming, identifying, and relying on experts is a fallible, human process that requires constant vigilance and reflection.

Empirical research has, without doubt, moved us forward. The age of specialization has proved a monumental boon to human quality of life. Even if we haven't yet worked all the kinks out of the system, we are at least not left in the lurches of categorical expert skepticism. It just means we have more work to do, in understanding both the structure of trust that allows scientists to make progress and the notion of expertise that underwrites such competence.

This does, however, raise questions about the empirical research on expertise itself. If we aren't yet sure how it is that some scientists become experts, how did early researchers on expertise understand the concept they were studying? Who were their models for what expertise should look like? What did they think they learned from their research? And, most importantly, how did their findings influence the current state of expertise studies?

3.5 Summing Up: *Expertise* Today

Lexicographically (according to popular use),[27] expertise is largely a matter of competence with a body of knowledge or with a skill:

Expert, *noun*

Merriam-Webster: **One with the special skill or knowledge representing mastery of a particular subject.**

Dictionary.com: **A person who has a comprehensive and authoritative knowledge of or skill in a particular area.**

English Oxford Dictionary: **A person who is very knowledgeable about or skilful in a particular area.**

Cambridge Dictionary: **A person having a high level of knowledge or skill in a particular subject.**

Technically (according to scholarly use), what counts as expertise varies according to discipline, focus, and research interest. There are four main academic domains today that study expertise: *psychology, sociology, philosophy*, and *neurology*.[28] Each brings distinct assumptions and methodologies, and these have led to a variety of conceptions of expertise. Psychologists study certain types of performance, or differences in performance among certain populations. Sociologists study how expertise is acknowledged and distributed throughout society, looking especially at how expertise is established in a community and how novices respond to experts. Philosophers wrestle with the conceptual difficulties of formulating various accounts of expertise and their implications for belief and practice. Neurologists study what experts' brains look like, how they differ from novices', and they look for changes in performance that may be due to activities like practice or environmental factors.

In the next chapter, I'll sketch the history of *expertise studies*, and we will see in the end that all of these technical uses are, despite their differences, consistent with the popular use. It would be bad for researchers if what they call "expertise" looks markedly different from what everyone else calls it. We would wonder why they chose to use the term "expertise" to begin with. But this highlights how thin the popular conception is. The popular conception doesn't help us distinguish experts from novices, or semi-experts from full experts. It doesn't tell us whom to trust when experts disagree. It doesn't tell us what to do with experts at all, or why. This book is focused on these technical uses of expertise with the aim of addressing these questions.

4

A Brief History of Expertise Studies

[I]f you had come to me for fire, and I had none in my house, you would not blame me for sending you where you might get it; . . . or did you desire to be taught music by me, and I were to point out to you a far more skilful teacher than myself, who would perhaps be grateful to you moreover for becoming his pupil, what kind of exception could you take to my behaviour?
(Xenophon, *Oeconomicus* 2.15, trans. H. G. Dakyns, 1897)

In this chapter, I trace, very roughly, the origins of empirical studies of expertise. Part of the aim is to complete the history started in Chapters 2 and 3, that is, to see how older discussions of expertise influenced early researchers, and to see which of those influences have carried into contemporary expertise studies. Another part of the aim is to highlight how assumptions about expertise influence research on expertise. If two researchers are using the term "expertise" in mutually exclusive ways, we should not be surprised if they draw incompatible conclusions. Similarly, two expertise researchers can easily talk past one another if they hold different assumptions about how expertise is acquired or its implications for society.

I begin this chapter with a review of the earliest studies of "intelligence" or "natural greatness," which became what researchers today call "superior performance" (Section 4.1). I trace this terminology through the advent of psychological behaviorism and cognitive psychology, and research on artificial intelligence (AI) (Section 4.2). In Section 4.3, I explain the major divisions of psychological research on expertise, and in Section 4.4, I introduce some basic neurological approaches to expertise. These historical developments help explain much of our contemporary use of expertise. They also explain some contemporary skepticism about experts. Most importantly, though, they highlight the need for a philosophy of expertise that takes insights from this empirical work and develops the epistemic and normative implications of expertise to help address contemporary concerns about experts.

4.1 Early Scientific Studies of Expertise

German scientist Franz Joseph Gall (1758–1828) started his exploration of superior competence by looking at what he called "natural greatness." Gall was the first to attempt to correlate natural greatness with observable bodily features, in particular the shape of a person's skull.[1] Gall hypothesized that the different parts of the brain were responsible for different cognitive activities, such as memory, mechanical ability, musical talent, combativeness, numeracy, and benevolence. The number of organs in the brain ranged from twenty-seven to forty-three, depending on which of Gall's followers you read. Gall also hypothesized that the brain was like a set of muscles that, when exercised, grew in size, pressing on the part of the skull closest to the muscle that was exercised. Even still, people with tendencies toward intellectual greatness should have larger organs than others from birth. The resulting bumps on the skull could then be correlated with the strength of intellectual abilities. Gall called his theory "cranioscopy," though one of his former assistants, Johann Gaspar Spurzheim, later changed it (much to Gall's frustration) to "phrenology." Gall collected around 300 skulls and plaster casts of skulls to compare them to biographical details about the person's intellectual abilities.

Around the same time that Gall was promoting cranioscopy, Belgian statistician and sociologist Adolphe Quetelet (1796–1874) published what is sometimes called the earliest scientific study of expertise: *A Treatise on Man and the Development of His Faculties: An Attempt at Social Physics* (1835) (Hambrick, Campitelli, and Macnamara 2018: 3). Quetelet introduced a version of mathematician Carl Friedrich Gauss's (1777–1855) "normal distribution" function—the bell curve—into social science to describe the distribution of human traits in a population. Quetelet was interested in a whole range of social phenomena, from suicide, to marriage, to crime. But he also studied human capabilities, both intellectual (the French and English dramatists, for example) and physical (the distribution of different sizes and shapes of bodies). This motivated those studying expertise to focus their attention on those who fall on the upper end of the competence distribution, one or two standard deviations above what is "normal."

Counterexample upon counterexample to Gall's hypotheses eventually discredited his views. But Gall's work set the stage for the work of English scientist Francis Galton (1822–1911), who, rather than correlating intellectual ability with observable physical traits, took cues, instead, from Charles Darwin, who was looking to the biological origins of those traits. Galton argued that, while talents could be trained and improved, heritable traits set an upper limit on how much training could help: "maximal performance becomes a rigidly determinate quantity" (Galton, cited in Ericsson 2003: 96).

All three researchers—Gall, Quetelet, and Galton—assumed that talent and skill were largely inborn, allowing for only slight variation. They seemed intent upon upsetting over a thousand years of practice-based notions of expertise grounded in the ways they had observed people become masters and artisans. Galton even coined the phrase "nature vs. nurture" in his 1869 book *Heritable Genius* to highlight what he thought was a significant discovery, that nature is primarily responsible for intelligence and ability. The Greek and Roman distinction between innate human abilities and skills that can be cultivated more or less from scratch, through effort and practice, did not figure in their work.

Nudging the pendulum in the opposite direction, philosopher Friedrich Nietzsche defended the "nurture" side of the debate. Nietzsche claimed that the nature camp was a holdout from medieval religion, according to which genius was bestowed supernaturally. But he thought such an idea was motivated by "vanity," the sense that one was favored by God. "[I]f we think of genius as something magical, we are not obliged to compare ourselves and find ourselves lacking." Instead, he contends (albeit with only anecdotal argument) that genius is developed through focused practice:

> Do not talk of gifts, of inborn talents! We could mention great men of all kinds who were but little gifted. But they obtained greatness, became "geniuses" (as they are called), through qualities of the lack of which nobody who is conscious of them likes to speak. They all had that thorough earnestness for work which learns first how to form the different parts perfectly before it ventures to make a great whole; they gave themselves time for this, because they took more pleasure in doing small, accessory things well than in the effect of a dazzling whole. (1878: §163, p. 167)

And while Nietzsche was keeping this Enlightenment-inspired, individual responsibility view alive among philosophers, similar nurture accounts of *learning* were emerging in psychology. Rather than starting with geniuses and looking for genetic and environmental causes, psychologists began with novices and focused on how they acquired information and skills in general. These studies were not aimed at discovering the path to genius, but they paved the way for more robustly empirical studies of how expertise is acquired.

William James (1842–1910), credited as the father of American psychology, was one of the earliest pioneers of the nurture theory of learning, and his work greatly influenced later work on expertise.[2] Unlike later behaviorists, who would contend that the brain is unnecessary for explaining behavior and abilities, James took the brain seriously. James hypothesized that our behaviors are solely the result of our experiences. And the way experience shapes our behavior is by shaping our brains. As we interact with the world, sensorial experiences make impressions on our brains. As experiences are repeated, those impressions are made firm and become assumptions and tendencies. At a certain level of firmness, we don't notice our reactions anymore; they have become habitual:

> [A]ctions originally prompted by conscious intelligence may grow so automatic by dint of habit as to be apparently unconsciously performed. Standing, walking, buttoning and unbuttoning, piano-playing, talking, even saying one's prayers, may be done when the mind is absorbed in other things. The performances of animal instinct seem semi-automatic, and the reflex acts of self-preservation certainly are so. Yet they resemble intelligent acts in bringing about the same ends at which the animals' consciousness, on other occasions, deliberately aims. ([1890] 1950: 5)

The idea is that, through changing our habits, the nature of one's attention (what James called *stream of thought*) is changed. It shifts from one "groove" carved by how we normally do things into another. Then, once settled into that new groove, one's conscious efforts shift from a position of *trying*, intentionally to perform each part of a task, to a general *monitoring* of the environment in which one is performing the task, taking note of where things are going wrong or need adjustments.[3] This settling into a groove frees the mind to focus on training specific aspects of a task. The freedom to focus on different aspects of a practice while practicing, contemporary scholars now agree, is what allows one the opportunity to individually develop every aspect of a practice, that is, to fully master it.

Importantly, these grooves are not so firmly fixed that we should think experts are ideologues. Such a disposition would rather cast doubt on someone's expertise. The fact that we can shift out of them and create new ones is what accounts for the possibility of mastery in the first place. For James, the attention developed by habit is "weak enough to yield to influence, but strong enough not to yield all at once" ([1890] 1950: 105). It is from James that we now have the concepts of neural "plasticity," "stream of thought" and "stream of consciousness," and the role of habit in developing our ability to perform a task (like standing and walking) automatically (a phenomenon now called "automaticity").[4]

Adapting James's insights for education, Jane Addams and John Dewey developed a learning-as-doing model of instruction. Because we learn by doing, we gain competence by practicing more. Competence emerges when the practice becomes a habit. Dewey explicitly connects the concept of "habit" with the classical sense of "art" discussed in Chapter 2: "[H]abits are arts. They involve skill of sensory and motor organs, cunning or craft, and objective materials. They require order, discipline, and manifest technique" (Dewey 1922: 15). If this is right, then it would seem that the central difference between the expert and the novice is the amount of practice one puts in to develop a habit in the domain.

But this is not the whole story for Dewey. Practice gets us only so far. The difference between someone who has extensive experience or skill and an expert is their attitude toward novel experiences. Experience and skill can set people up in positions of respect, can give them the air of authority. But, in *How We Think* (1910), Dewey explains simply being able to do something well is not the mark of expertise. A true expert can handle novel problems. So, someone may have a reputation as competent, but "mental inertia, laziness, unjustifiable conservatism" are revealed when they are presented with something new. They are not the authorities they could be.

> Certain men or classes of men come to be the accepted guardians and transmitters—instructors—of established doctrines. To question the beliefs is to question their authority; to accept the beliefs is evidence of loyalty to the powers that be, a proof of good citizenship. Passivity, docility, acquiescence, come to be primal intellectual virtues. Fact and events presenting novelty and variety are slighted, or are sheared down till they fit into the Procrustean bed of habitual belief. ([1910] 2009: 149)

Those who thoroughly understand a domain can avoid this passivity.

Expertise, then, according to Dewey, is not simply the automatic knowledge of how to do something gained through practice, but the ability to jump out of the streams of consciousness to overcome the limitations of old views and tackle new problems. Using James's imagery, Dewey writes, "Empirical inference follows the grooves and ruts that custom wears, and has no track to follow when the groove disappears" (148). As opposed to the layperson, who can answer questions in a domain only if they fall within the scope of what they've read or been taught, the expert approaches a problem "assuming that what seems to be observation to be a single total fact is in truth complex," a set of many conditions, any one of which might be relevant for addressing the question at hand and, therefore, must be considered individually (150).

4.2 Behaviorism and the Cognitive Turn in Expertise Studies

In 1913, spurred by the finding of Russian physiologist Ivan Pavlov, psychologist John Watson[5] published what is now known as the manifesto of psychological behaviorism (Watson 1913). Rejecting James's theory that consciousness is necessary to the scientific study of behavior, Watson's work led to the view sometimes called "black box" behaviorism, which is the idea that all behavior can be explained solely in terms of external stimuli. As Watson puts it, "Introspection forms no essential part of its methods, nor is the scientific value of its data dependent upon the readiness with which they lend themselves to interpretation in terms of consciousness" (158). If Watson and the behaviorists were right, then we can dispense, not just with the antiquated notion of inherited talent, as James's view suggests, but also the idea that the "mind," whatever it is supposed to be, is involved at all in the process of forming expertise.

This development shows that "nature vs. nurture" is only one dimension of this debate. An equally divisive disagreement, once one demonstrates some talent, has to do with *how* nurture strengthens one's talent. Can anyone from any background start at any point in their lives and become an expert? Or does early childhood environment shape what is possible later in life? Swiss botanist Alphonse Pyrame de Candolle (1806–93), for example, presented evidence suggesting that where one is raised in the world and under what conditions are the primary explanatory features of intelligence and ability (Hambrick, Campitelli, and Macnamara 2018: 3). Answers to this question are still debated by scientists who study expertise, whether from sociological, psychological, or neurological perspectives.

Despite the widespread influence of behaviorism, the empirical work of psychologist Edward Tolman (1886–1959) reopened the door to cognitive theories of information processing. Tolman was a devout behaviorist until a series of experiments where he ran mice through mazes but eliminated any possibility that they could learn the maze by moving their bodies in standard ways. In fact, he put some mice in tiny wheelbarrows so they couldn't physically run the maze at all—they could only be wheeled through it by a researcher. Nevertheless, all the mice learned the mazes. This showed rather conclusively that the mice were not learning the mazes through overt movement; they were learning it by sight alone. This suggested that what the mice were seeing was leaving an impression on their minds that they could recall for help in running the maze in the future. Tolman's research led to the idea that conscious experience allowed one to form "cognitive maps" (what James called "mental representations") that could be recalled later to improve performance on new tasks. No one could dismiss the role of consciousness in behavioral explanations. This discovery led to what is called the "cognitive turn" in psychology—the turn away from behaviorism and toward what would become cognitive psychology.

Tolman's findings, combined with the advent of computer technology, led to a number of mechanical views of mental phenomena, including, predominantly, the "information processing model" (Feltovich et al., 2018). Regardless of how mental phenomena occur, they must be explainable in terms of cause-and-effect relationships with the natural world. No one in the empirical sciences was returning to Cartesian dualism or Leibnizian epiphenomenalism. Even in cases where we cannot correlate specific mental states with specific stimuli, we can at least take the mental states as given and explore how they respond to various stimuli and conditions.[6] The role of mental representations in the development of expertise is now a central topic of interest in psychological expertise studies. But the mechanisms for talking about mental representations and how they were formed were not yet developed. However, computing technology suggested an answer that had not been considered before.

4.3 Artificial Intelligence and Expertise as Rule-Following

By the late 1940s, computational technology had evolved from analog to electromechanical digital processing, and it was becoming clear just how important these new Analytical Engines[7] (computers) would be for almost every area of human life. Computers also suggested a new answer to a question that philosophers had wrestled with for centuries, namely: What is a mind? If computers were able to do much of analytical reasoning in logic and math that the Greeks hailed as one of humankind's greatest attributes, and to do them much faster, it was reasonable to ask what it would mean for a computer to have a mind. In 1950, aiming to answer this question, the philosophically minded mathematician Alan Turing proposed a test, now called the Turing test: If a machine could perform in such a way that humans could not tell whether a machine did it or a human did it, then the answer would be yes, computers can have minds.[8]

Attempts to run this test have proved inconclusive. On one hand, computers do many things much better than humans—they are more accurate and exponentially faster at, for example, solving math problems and recalling stored information. Some early programs could play checkers better than the best human checkers players (Samuel 1959) and even create some novel proofs to advanced math problems (Newell and Simon 1972). So, the task we choose for the test must be one where distinctly human abilities are evident. But even here, things are not so clear. There are now computer programs that write symphonies and novels. Are these examples of computers with minds?

Consider the task of answering questions in a natural language (like Chinese or Japanese). Natural languages are a hodgepodge of rules that don't always make logical sense—meanings are influenced by use and culture, and not all natural languages express the same concepts or capture their myriad nuances in meaning. So, if there's any task that seems uniquely suited to a human, using natural language well seems like it. Even in 2021, as I am finishing this book, programs like Google Translate seem like an excellent example of how artificial language intelligence fails the Turing test.[9] However, back in 1980, philosopher John Searle proposed a thought experiment that, he believed, showed that even a successful version of Google Translate wouldn't tell Turing what he wanted to know.[10]

Imagine a person sitting in a room with an open slot in the wall. In front of them is a table on which sits a book full of symbols, which happen to be Chinese text. Next to that book is a very complex manual written in English that explains how to transform the symbols in the Chinese book into other Chinese symbols. Imagine, also, that the person in the room does not know any words or phrases in Chinese. They speak and read only English. They don't even know that the symbols are Chinese symbols. Through the slot in the wall, another book of Chinese symbols is passed, called "The questions." This book comes with a note that says: "Use the manual to answer these questions." The person then uses the manual to compare the symbols in both texts and write a third book of Chinese symbols, "The answers." The person passes this book through the slot, and the people on the outside—who do know Chinese—can read and understand the answers perfectly. The answers adequately answer the questions about the original text.

Does such a process require a mind? It seems not. Any rule-following mechanism, conscious or not, could do the job. Searle concludes that the person in the room is missing a critical component of conscious minds that the Turing test is supposed to reveal: They do not *understand* the language they are using to answer questions—they don't know what the words or phrases *mean*. So, even if a computer program were able to use natural language perfectly, this would not prove that it has a mind.

This is not, however, the end of the story.[11] Computer programmers are clever. The Chinese Room experiment, as it is now called, presupposes that computers can *only* follow rules. It does not take into account the massive complexity of *computer learning* that has emerged in recent years (facial recognition, voice recognition, emotion recognition, deep learning, etc.). Because of this, whether computers can have (already do have?) minds remains an open question.

But even so, let us grant the possibility that some computers will one day have minds (or something near enough). If so, a reasonable question to ask next is: Could computers be *experts*? Could they develop the sophisticated understanding and seemingly effortless performance that human minds and bodies are capable of? While philosophers like Hubert and Stuart Dreyfus focused the majority of their careers attempting to show that the answer is, in principle, no (see their 1986, for example, researchers in the domains of AI and machine learning remain hopeful.)

In the 1980s and 1990s, psychologists interested in expertise changed the direction of their research, reverting to the strategy used before William James. Instead of trying to explain *learning* from scratch and then extrapolating their findings to *expertise*, they observed examples of superior performance and then tried to trace back how it developed. Unlike their pre-Jamesian colleagues, they focused on what genetic or environmental factors were present in these performers; they asked, more like their Greek and Roman predecessors: What did experts *do* to become experts. How long did they practice? What was their practice like? Were they coached?

Today, it is uncontroversial that mental states are relevant to explaining expertise, but it is less clear which mental states are relevant for explaining which aspects of expertise. It is also fairly uncontroversial that environmental factors (e.g., the age at which someone starts practicing a task) and biological factors (e.g., body type) are necessary for explaining some types of performative achievement. But it is difficult to say how strongly any particular set of these factors influence the development of expertise. There remains the question of whether or to what degree mental states and environmental factors could be triggers for expert abilities latent in our genetic and neurological structures. The vast amount of research that has emerged since the 1980s has culminated into roughly four ways of approaching expertise that I label: *lab-based optimists, lab-based pessimists, natural expertise optimists,* and *natural expertise pessimists*.

4.4 The Psychology of Superior Performance: Optimists and Pessimists

Among cognitive psychologists, there are two broad ways of studying expert performance: observe expert performance under strictly controlled experimental conditions or observe expert performance as it occurs in the real world. Call the former "lab-based expertise" projects and the latter "natural expertise" projects. In both the lab-based projects and the natural projects, there are "optimists" and "pessimists," though these are no reflection on the personalities of these researchers. Optimists publish research that presumes there is expertise in the world and then aims to either explain what expertise is or show how expertise can be developed. Pessimists publish research that is skeptical of expertise and aims to either undermine the notion that there are genuine experts or explain the significant limitations of expert judgment and decision-making.

The difference between lab-based and natural experiments is not trivial (see Montero 2016: 2–4). Consider a lab-based experiment where researchers test how long it takes a person to hit a button after a light is turned on. Most people, from couch potatoes to professional athletes, take around 200 milliseconds to respond. Expert performance ability makes no difference on this isolated task (Epstein 2014a: 4ff). The same has been found to be true for every performance task that is not directly related to an expert's domain. For example, Ericsson and Smith (1991: 5) note that "research on individual differences in general memory ability has found low correlations of memory performance across different types of material and methods of testing" and "individual difference in performance of simple tasks showed disappointingly low correlations, both among tasks and between performance and indices of ability, such as grade in school." Some have found similar poor results when trying to improve medical decision-making by teaching general critical thinking skills (Rogers, Swee, and Ullian, 1991).

But in a specific domain, things are quite different. Major League baseball players can hit 95-mph fastballs, a feat which defies the biology of information processing. "The window for actually making contact with the ball, when it is in reach of the bat, is 5 milliseconds." Keeping their eye on the ball is "literally impossible" (Epstein 2014a: 9). In an early study of chess players, grandmasters memorized an arbitrarily selected organization of pieces on a board in under 3 seconds with an average of 90 percent accuracy over multiple trials, in contrast with regular players, who could memorize the board only with about 50 percent accuracy over the trials (de Groot, [1946] 1965).

However, when lab-based experiments create tasks that sufficiently mimic expert performance ("representative tasks," Ericsson 2018), the results correlate much better with real-life variations in performance between novices and experts. Figuring out which tasks are representative, then, gives us insights to the nature and limits of performative expertise. They also help inform strategies for developing expertise in natural environments (see Klein 1998). This suggests that lab-based and natural expertise projects constructively inform one another. But to get a sense of where the field now stands, we need a little background.

4.4.1 Expertise Pessimists: Lab-based and Natural

The most famous pessimistic, lab-based project is now known as the *heuristics and biases* program, which started in the late 1960s with the work of psychologists Amos Tversky and Daniel Kahneman. Tversky and Kahneman demonstrated, in experiment after experiment, that the prevailing assumption (tracing back to Adam Smith and John Stuart Mill) that humans are cost-benefit reasoners is wildly inaccurate (see Watson 2017, Chapter 5). When people are faced with identical decision tasks, especially when they make quick, intuitive judgments, they make drastically different decisions based on completely irrelevant details, such as whether the decision was framed in positive or negative language, preconceived notions about the frequency of some feature of the case, or the order in which information is presented (see Tversky and Kahneman 1974; 1981; 1986). In laboratory tests, these fast, "System 1" cognitive processes, as Kahneman calls them (see his 2011), prove unreliable (chock full of biases and faulty heuristics), and everyone—including experts—is subject to them.

Early natural expertise projects were similarly pessimistic. Researchers wanted to know if the problems Tversky and Kahneman found in the lab held for decisions in the real world. It turns out, they do (Arkes et al. 1981; McNeil et al. 1982; Koehler et al. 2002). Arkes et al. (1981), for example, found that physicians regularly overestimate how likely they were to be successful when a successful outcome was not predictable (hindsight bias). But this is not the whole story. We know there are experts in the world—people who are highly competent in their domains and people who get predictions right. How do we account for them? Enter the optimists.

4.4.2 Lab-based Expertise Optimists

The central problem with pessimists, according to the optimists, is that they start with a faulty assumption, namely, that humans *should* be excellent cost-benefit reasoners. If we should be, and the evidence shows that we aren't, then it seems we have a problem. But what if we shouldn't be? Psychologists have studied the superior decision-making skills of grandmaster chess players since the 1940s (Adriaan de Groot [1946] 1965; Chase and Simon 1973; Simon and Chase 1973), so it would seem that some people really are experts. If some people really are experts, there must be an explanation for why, and this explanation must account for how experts avoid expertise pessimism.

Early research on chess revealed two things about expert decision-making (at least in chess): Expertise is (a) primarily a matter of rich pattern memorization, which allows for quick recall, and (b) bounded rationality. With respect to the first, chess players have a better grasp of chess patterns than novices. They have spent tens of thousands of hours looking at chess boards at various stages of game play, and they remember which patterns work and which one's don't. This memorization allows for quick, intuitive recall during game play. De Groot ([1946] 1965) concluded that time playing (experience) was the key to the intuitive speed and accuracy of grandmasters. But at the time, there was little empirical study to confirm that his suspicion was more plausible than those who believed that some people just have a talent for memorization—a natural gift. Thirty years later, economist and psychologist Herbert Simon and psychologist William Chase (1973) found a strong correlation between time spent playing chess and chess expertise. They estimate that grandmasters spend anywhere from 10,000 to 50,000 hours looking at chess boards to achieve their success, and that there is no record of anyone reaching grandmaster status "with less than about a decade's intense preoccupation with the game" (402).[12] All this time looking at chess boards imprints patterns into memory as "chunks" of information that are efficiently available for easy recall when they are encountered again. This led to what is now known as the "ten-year-rule" for the development of expertise.

But isn't this the sort of intuitive, System 1 decision-making that's the problem? Simon (1957a; 1957b) thinks not. He argues that human minds are not organized to be ideal reasoners of the sort the classical cost-benefit-all-things-considered theory of rationality would suggest. Rather, taking our time to get things just right ends up taking *too much* time. So, instead of looking for the optimal solution to any problem, we look for a "good enough" solution; we are "satisficers." Satisficing is "the strategy of considering the options available to you for choice until you find one that meets or exceeds a predefined threshold—your aspiration level—for a minimally acceptable outcome" (Wheeler 2018). Consider that, from an evolutionary perspective, biases and heuristics serve us pretty well. Rather than considering all possible options and thoroughly deliberating (what Kahneman has named "System 2" cognitive processing), we choose from among a set of useful strategies that have proved good enough. This "bounded rationality" (rationality within the bounds of environmental and aspirational constraints) suggests that we can be quite reasonable in getting around in the world even if we don't meet the ideal cost-benefit (that is, utilitarian) standard. Of course, the better your pattern recognition, the better your bounded rationality works. Thus, with these two mechanisms—robust memorization and satisficing—we have an explanation for chess expertise.

Could these mechanisms work outside of the strict, rule-bound context of chess? Building on Simon's theory of bounded rationality, psychologist Gerd Gigerenzer (2007) says yes. We employ bounded rationality in many domains, and we can be pretty good at it. Gigerenzer cites twelve different studies that were initially interpreted as demonstrating erroneous reasoning but were later reevaluated as reflecting reasonable judgments in light of environmental constraints (2007: 66). Going beyond the work of Simon, Gigerenzer argues that, rather than utilitarian reasoners, humans are natural Bayesians—a theory of probability that is specifically aimed at addressing uncertainty, named after mathematician Thomas Bayes (1702–61). This suggests that the problem of heuristics and biases is only partially cognitive. In the right environments, our cognitive machinery gets us what we need. Unfortunately, given that our contemporary world doesn't look much like the one we evolved through, the challenge for mitigating the negative effects of biases and heuristics is twofold: training our cognitive machinery but also, when we can, restructuring the way we make decisions.

4.4.3 Natural Expertise Optimists

The optimism I've discussed so far has been all lab-based. Can we talk meaningfully about expertise in the real world, where there is always uncertainty and there are few reliable ways to control for extraneous variables? According to some researchers, the answer is undeniably yes. In the 1980s, psychologists

Judith Orasanu and Gary Klein started working with military leaders to study decision-making in high-stakes and wildly uncertain conditions. Their work led to a research program called "Natural Decision Making" (NDM) in contrast to the "formal decision making" research that had been taking place in laboratories. According to Klein (2016):

> [NDM aims] to study how people actually make decisions—people such as firefighters, military commanders, nurses, design engineers, pilots, and petrochemical unit managers. NDM examines the kinds of decisions they make in the course of their work, and how they use their experience to cope with challenging conditions such as time pressure, uncertainty, vague goals, high stakes, organizational constraints, and team coordination requirements.

As we saw earlier, not all "natural expertise" projects are optimistic, but NDM researchers tend to be optimists. This program not only discovered mechanisms by which expert decision-makers perform competently but also developed strategies for training natural expert decision-making.

Klein (1998) advanced the domain significantly with his study of expert judgment in firefighters and military strategists. He and his research group found that experts under pressure don't seem to deliberate at all. Instead, they use contextual cues to settle on a course of action more quickly and accurately than novices.

> The basic explanation is that skilled decision makers make sense of the situation at hand by recognizing it as one of the prototypical situations they have experienced and stored in their long-term memory. This recognition match is usually done without deliberation. Once the decision makers have arrived at a recognition match, an appropriate course of action, or decision, becomes clear. (Philips, Klein, and Sieck 2007: 305)

So, there is pattern recognition, but not of the rigid sort found in chess playing. Instead, they seem to make a rough comparison to known situations, identify the point where they are least similar, and then formulate a plan that will work within those constraints. "[T]hey seek a course of action that is workable, but not necessarily the best or optimal decision . . . In naturalistic settings, the time pressures often dictate that the situation be resolved as quickly as possible. Therefore, it is not important for a course of action to be the best one; it only needs to be effective" (Philips, Klein, and Sieck 2007: 305). Sometimes, simply being able to make a decision that works is what sets experts apart from novices. In the 1980s, Janet Starkes found similar evidence of domain-specific, mind-bogglingly fast, pattern recognition in a number of different sports (1984). Journalist David Epstein describes the significance of her findings by noting, "It was as if every elite athlete miraculously had a photographic memory when it came to her sport" (2014a: 8). This "general intuition" or "Recognition-Primed Decision-making" (Klein 1993) suggests that pattern recognition extends beyond well-structured patterns, like those found in chess, to domain-specific situations.

4.5 Neurological Approaches to Expertise

With the invention of brain imaging technology, such as MRI (magnetic resonance imaging) and CT (computed tomography) in the 1970s and the fMRI (functional MRI) in the 1990s, a new approach to expertise was possible. Studies that were previously restricted to the overt outcomes of expert performance—chess wins, violin playing, number memorization—could be combined with brain imaging to learn, at the neurological level, what makes experts different from novices.

Neurological research on expertise tends to divide along one of two methodologies. Researchers might take what Bilalić calls an *expert performance approach*, which studies similarly competent experts across similar types of tasks. Alternatively, they may take an *expertise approach*, which compares expert performance to novice performance on the same tasks (2017: 27).

Taking an example of the latter, consider a popular assumption: Experts think less about what they are doing than novices. Hubert and Stuart Dreyfus (1986) defended a version of this assumption, arguing that experts lose themselves in their performance because their competence is embodied rather than strictly a function of their brain. Psychologist Mihaly Csikszentmihalyi says this nonminded performance, which he has famously labeled "flow," is "one of the most universal and distinctive features of optimal experience" (1990: 53). And philosopher Barbara Montero (2016) highlights no less than a dozen examples of people who report the "nonminded" or "unconscious" nature of expert performance, which she calls the "just do it" principle. Though there are serious problems with identifying the phenomenology of flow with expertise (see Watson 2020: Chapter 4), it is an assumption that can be tested neurologically.

Professor of Cognitive Psychology Merim Bilalić admits, "One of the widespread assumptions about expertise is that we should see less brain activation in experts than in novices. . . . After all, experts' performance is not only highly efficient; it also seems almost effortless, unlike the ponderous performance of novices" (2017: 21). However, it turns out that, rather than having less brain activity, they have more, just in different places in the brain (Bilalić 2017: 21–2). This suggests that, at least in those cases where experts experience effortless flow, it is not because their brains are working less; it just means that phenomenology does not neatly map onto brain activity.

This is just one example of how neurology is informing expertise studies. Other examples include research on expertise with pattern recognition, facial recognition, and pitch perception.

4.6 Summing Up: Strengths and Weaknesses of Empirical Expertise Studies

Empirical studies of expertise have brought us a rich understanding of expertise, especially of how people become experts, the limits of expert performance, and the limits of empirical research. What is largely left out of these studies are questions about what expertise implies for beliefs and justification, whether experts transmit knowledge, whether an expert counts as an authority, and what that authority might imply for others. Many of these studies also reduce the recognition problem—the question of how we identify experts—to overt performance, which would be good if measurable performance were all there is to expertise. But not all expertise is aimed at a fixed set of observable results. And this research does not help us decide which expert is more trustworthy when they disagree. To address these issues, we must supplement empirical research with philosophical analyses. Turning, then, to philosophical analysis, the next chapter addresses the question of what it means to have epistemic standing in a domain.

5

Epistemic Placement and Expert Testimony

Almost all the opinions we have are taken on authority and trust; and 'tis not amiss; we could not choose worse than by ourselves, in so weak an age.
(Montaigne, "Of Physiognomy," 210, trans. Charles Cotton, 1910)

In this chapter, I explore what it is about experts that suggests they are at least prima facie trustworthy in their domains. I first introduce the concept of epistemic advantage and epistemic placement (Section 5.1), and I argue that epistemic authority in a domain is contingent upon epistemic placement in a domain. However, following Elizabeth Fricker, I distinguish between being well placed in a domain for incidental reasons (being in the right place at the right time) and being enduringly well placed (having acquired placement through training and practice). I then introduce some basic concepts in the epistemology of testimony (Section 5.2) and show how justified epistemic dependence on testimony is explained in terms of epistemic placement. In Section 5.3, I explain the epistemic significance of expert testimony for epistemic justification in light of the conceptual framework introduced in Sections 5.1 and 5.2. Along the way, we will see how various ways of being well placed in a domain show that even expert authority can be challenged by novices under some circumstances.

5.1 Epistemic Advantage and Epistemic Placement

If I know something you don't, I have an advantage over you. For instance, if I know how to wire a three-way switch, and you don't, then I have a certain kind of leg up: I can do it, and you cannot. Let's call this a *technical advantage* (borrowing from the Greek word *techne*). Similarly, if I am looking for your dog on one side of a house, and you are on the other side, I have a certain kind of advantage over you with respect to that side of the house: I can see it, and you cannot (and you have one over me, for that matter, with respect to what is on the other side of the house). Let's call this a *gnostic advantage* (borrowing, again from Greek, a word for knowledge: *gnosis*).

In both cases, this advantage is very limited. Just because I can wire a three-way switch does not mean I can wire a whole house. Further, my advantage is limited to just this activity. If you never need to install a three-way switch, then my technical advantage likely won't be all that interesting to you. The same goes for my gnostic advantage: I have access to only one side of the house, not the park down the street or even, necessarily, the neighbor's back yard. If you aren't looking for your dog or you have already found her, then my advantage won't mean much.

A technical advantage reflects what philosophers, following Gilbert Ryle (1945), call "knowledge-how" and a gnostic advantage reflects what they call "knowledge-that." Both are types of knowledge, so I call either type of advantage an *epistemic advantage* (from the Greek *episteme*).

When someone has an epistemic advantage over someone, they are better *placed* with respect to the evidence for the claim in question.[1] Elizabeth Fricker (2006) says someone properly accepts S's testimony that P only if S is "well enough placed with respect to P" (231). Placement explains the advantage.

In her explanation of being "well placed" with respect to a proposition, Fricker draws a distinction between someone's being in a different "spatiotemporal location" than another[2] and someone's having "superior skill" over another (234–5). Two examples demonstrate the difference. In some cases, someone is better placed with respect to a proposition than another by simply being, literally, in the right place at the right time. If I am in my windowless office and you are standing outside, you are in a better position than I to know whether it is raining. In other cases, someone is better placed than another if they have a greater ability to recall, discern, judge, or reason about a proposition. My wife has a stellar ability to do math in her head, while my mathematical ability stalled sometime after I stopped watching Sesame Street. So, if both of us work on a math problem, even if I come up with an answer of which I'm reasonably sure, I still regard her as better placed than I am with respect to the conclusion of the problem.

Fricker says epistemic placement is relative to a *proposition*, but this does not commit us to the objective existence of propositions (remember, placement is an epistemic issue and not inherently spatiotemporal or metaphysical), or to the idea that the propositions one is "placed" with respect to are true. Being well placed with respect to P is necessary for having access to reasons prima facie sufficient for being justified that P or not-P. And since epistemic advantage, as I have defined it, includes technical advantages in addition to gnostic advantages, epistemic placement should also accommodate placement relative to skills to do something. Thus, I define epistemic placement as follows:

> **Epistemic placement: An epistemic agent, S, is epistemically placed with respect to some proposition or practice P to the degree that S has access to evidence that P or that S has the ability to do P.**

Someone is *well* placed with respect to the *proposition* that P just in case they have evidence that P or not-P, and someone is *well* placed with respect to the *activity* P just in case that, when given the opportunity to do P, they are able to do P at a certain minimum level of competence.

And since placement explains advantage, we have

> **Epistemic advantage: An epistemic agent, S, has an epistemic advantage over another epistemic agent, R, with respect to a proposition or practice P just in case S is better placed with respect to P than R.**

But if placement explains epistemic advantage, we seem to have a problem. Imagine a person S has an advantage over person A with respect to P because S is well placed with respect to P while A is not. If S says to A that P is true, isn't person A now similarly well placed with respect to P, thus canceling S's epistemic advantage over A?

The answer is: Not necessarily. Placement, like evidence, comes in degrees. In some cases, simply telling someone something you are well placed to know is not enough to confer to them your degree of justification for that claim even if it sufficiently justifies that claim for them. Consider this example from Plato's *Republic*:

> I think we should adopt the method of investigation that we'd use if, lacking keen eyesight, we were told to read small letters from a distance and then noticed that the same letters existed elsewhere in a larger size and on a larger surface. We'd consider it a godsend, I think, to be allowed to read the larger ones first and then to examine the smaller ones, to see whether they really are the same. (368d, trans. Grube)

Imagine we are the ones who lack "keen eyesight" in this case. If someone tells us that the same letters are written elsewhere in a font large enough to read, that person is presuming to have an epistemic advantage over us: They claim to know that the words in both places are the same, while we can only read the ones in larger font. If we believe the person is trustworthy, then we have good reason to believe we know what the words in both places say. Nevertheless, simply having this good reason does not put us in the same epistemic place as the person who told us they are the same words. The person who told us is still better placed with respect to them than we are. Our understanding remains dependent on their fallible interpretation. Even Socrates acknowledges that it is prudent to check the words against one another "to see whether they really are the same."

To be sure, not all mediated evidence is necessarily weaker than unmediated evidence. Imagine I see a group of symbols I don't understand, like (X → Y), and you carefully explain that the letters stand for different propositions, that the arrow represents the operator "If. . ., then. . .," and therefore, the symbols say, "If some proposition X, then some proposition Y." Based on your testimony, I now understand what the symbols mean. You no longer have an advantage over me with respect to what the symbols mean. So, in some cases, epistemic advantage *is* canceled through sharing information. But as we will see in later chapters, that's consistent with many views about how experts train to become experts. At some point, the soon-to-be expert gains an understanding of their domain that reduces the type or amount of advantage that other experts have over them.

Why does all this matter for my purposes? Two reasons. Epistemic placement explains how someone can have an epistemic advantage over another, and thereby, the normative status of testimony (i.e., *why* testimony *should* be believed in the cases when it should). It also explains how *expert testimony* differs from other types of testimony.

How do we get from descriptive claims about epistemic placement to normative claims of expert authority? Recall from Chapter 1 that once we reject the Enlightenment Mandate, then we are forced to ask whether expert testimony can be assessed as evidence in the process of forming responsible beliefs. Unfortunately, we saw that PEA:

> **Presumption of Epistemic Advantage (PEA):** Other things being equal, experts stand in a better position than novices with respect to claims and practices in their domain of expertise.

does not support PND:

> **Principle of Normative Deference (PND):** Other things being equal, novices ought to defer the judgments of experts in a domain of knowledge or practice.

Nevertheless, epistemic placement has normative force. The aforementioned examples provide reason to believe that trusting others under the right circumstances puts us in a better epistemic position. If this is right, given the practical necessity of relying on others, especially for those who want to become experts, then relying on others is epistemically indispensable for responsible belief. John Hardwig says it well: "Those who do not trust cannot be fully rational—they often cannot have the best evidence for their beliefs. Those who do not trust often cannot know. Those who do not trust usually cannot be experts; they cannot be competent members of most professions" (1994: 89). Unfortunately, Hardwig goes too far in interpreting the normative implication as "deference." As we have already started to see, the criteria for justified deference are often not met. Further, as we will see in Chapters 7 and 8, the ability to assess the variables at stake in the phrase "other things being equal" is sometimes required for justifying trust in experts.

But if PEA doesn't support PND, what normative principle might it support? If we have good reason to believe someone is an expert, and expertise implies a thick epistemic advantage, then, much like knowing that your friend was at a concert you missed, the epistemic position of an expert constitutes a prima facie reason to trust their testimony in the domain of their expertise. Call this the *principle of* prima facie *trust* (PPT):

> **Principle of *Prima Facie* Trust (PPT): If a subject S has good reason to believe that R is an expert in domain D, S has *prima facie* reason to trust R with claims or advice in D.**

As with PND, expert testimony is defeasible; the reason to trust is prima facie. Unlike PND, in PPT there is not a normative reason to defer an expert's testimony over a novice's. Whether there are good reasons to defer will depend on a number of details. If I have good reason to believe that experts in a domain are subject to a systematic bias or conflict of interest, I have good reason not to defer to their judgments over novices.

The key to the normative PPT, then, is the degree and type of epistemic placement of the expert. This means that expert authority is simply an extension of more general testimonial authority. To see how the concepts of epistemic placement and epistemic advantage inform belief based on testimony, let's look briefly at the epistemology of testimony.

5.2 The Basics of Testimony

"Testimony" is communication that P—whether oral, written, or gestured, individual or institutional, or anonymous or attributable—that is intended as a reason to believe that P. Communication that P in a theatre production or film is not testimony because it is not intended as a reason for the audience to accept that P. Communication that P that is paired with reasons to accept that P is not testimony; that is an argument. If I perceive that you have an epistemic advantage over me, and I rely on you to form, maintain, or justify a belief, then I am relying on your *testimony* for my belief. In cases where I accept what you say on the basis of your testimony, I become "epistemically dependent" on you.[3]

In some cases, I may remain epistemically dependent on you, as when one scientist accepts and uses another scientist's findings as "given" in building a case for their own findings. They do not rerun the other scientist's experiments; instead, they take the scientist's conclusions as authoritative. In other cases, I may be epistemically dependent on you only until I've worked the matter out for myself. Maybe your testimony helped me do that, but nevertheless, my current beliefs on the matter are not dependent for their justification on your testimony. For example, if you tell me, "Hey, your mom's here," and I get up to go greet her, then once I see her, I no longer need your testimony that she is here to justify my belief that she is here. I change my reasons for that belief; I am no longer epistemically dependent on you for that information. But I wouldn't have gotten up to go see if you hadn't told me. There is a nontrivial sense in which I was dependent upon you before I came to believe for different reasons.[4]

Whether I trust your testimony depends on a number of factors. I may assess whether your tone is genuine or sarcastic. I may consider what sort of person you are—whether you are prone to lies, exaggeration, or drama. I may watch your body language or listen to how you explain something to discern whether you are defensive, and therefore, unsure about what you are saying, or whether you are confident and easy-going. I may consider your credentials or education level, your friends or profession. Any one of these factors can increase or decrease my willingness to regard you as having an epistemic advantage over me, and, therefore, the degree to which I will trust what you tell me.

Another factor that can affect my willingness to trust and the degree to which I trust is how I weigh the importance of the content of your testimony. For low-stakes claims, I may have little concern over whether you really have an epistemic advantage. *Low-stakes claims* are claims for which the epistemic or practical costs of being wrong are low. Consider some claims that could be low stakes:

- "Hey, your mom's here."
- "It's 10 AM."

- "There's a woman you work with on the news right now."
- "Some people are at higher risk for stroke than others."
- "The first life on Earth actually migrated from another planet by a meteor."

To be sure, context matters a lot as to whether these are low stakes. If you haven't seen your mom in a while, and you're really excited about it, the first one may not be low stakes for you.[5] Similarly, if something important is happening at 10, this is not a low-stakes claim. But the point is that, low-stakes claims call for a different epistemic response than high-stakes claims:

- "Hey, your mom is really sick."
- "You're late for your interview."
- "Your picture is on the news tonight."
- "That medicine you're taking will likely give you a stroke."
- "A large meteor will hit Earth in a few months."

Again, context matters. Perhaps you do not have a close relationship with your mom and so you are indifferent as to whether she is sick. Nevertheless, when a claim is high stakes, it is in my epistemic interests to be more wary. I would benefit from some additional support, beyond your simply stating these claims, that they are true. Depending on how you came to believe what you're telling me, you might offer a variety of additional evidence: "I was just talking with your mom on her porch"; "I'm sitting here looking at the TV, and your face is on the screen!" Or, in the instance you are an expert: "Look, I finished my medical residency at a hospital that does a ton of clinical drug trials. I know what I'm talking about." (I say more about the epistemic significance of low- and high-stakes claims in Chapter 7.)

Notice what is happening in the last example. Rather than giving evidence about the truth of the claim, you are giving evidence about your competence with the relevant information. This suggests there's something about *you* that counts as a reason for me to accept the claim as true. There are other reasons you are the source of evidence for a claim (e.g., the claim is about your internal states or perspective: "My head hurts"; "It happened to me"). But in this case, you are pointing to your competence as the support for your claim. Relying on your competence is especially important as domains get more complex. Even if we are both highly competent biologists, I can rely on your competence to help me confirm or disconfirm some findings in my lab. Some evidence is so difficult to interpret that it would not be epistemically responsible for anyone to rely only on their own competence to form beliefs based on it.[6] So, even if I am not strongly dependent on you (as when you see whether my mom is here and I cannot), I can be weakly dependent on you even if we are both well placed in a domain. We will return to this in the next section.

We rely on the testimony of others for all sorts of reasons. In most cases of low-stakes beliefs, we presume they are well placed with respect to the claim. In the case of some high-stakes beliefs, we presume someone is well placed because of their social role, as when we are confident someone is a doctor or accountant. Of course, the question is whether this practice is epistemically responsible.

Some philosophers argue that the considerations I enumerated earlier (confidence, character, credentials, etc.) are secondary to the basic trustworthiness of testimony. These philosophers argue that all testimony should be presumed reliable, like our senses of sight and hearing, unless there are reasons to think it isn't. With respect to sight, for example, we know that visual images can be deceiving, as when a stick looks bent in water or when the lighting in a room isn't normal, but, in general, we trust our vision unless we have reason to think we shouldn't. Similarly, with testimony, humans learn some of the most basic truths about the world and themselves when we are very young through testimony—our name, our birthday, who our parents are, how to count and name colors, etc. Testimony is as basic a source of evidence as our eyesight, and thus, should be afforded no less epistemic weight. This view is called *non-reductionism* about testimony—any particular piece of testimony is prima facie justified without any additional evidential support.[7] In other words, the justification for testimony does not *reduce* to, or depend upon, any more basic evidence.

Other philosophers, in contrast, argue that, while it is *pragmatically* useful to rely on others when we are very young, that in no way guarantees the *epistemic* value of testimony. What if those testifying were well intentioned but wildly mistaken? The accuracy of any piece of testimony depends on a complex set of evidential conditions that are far from being basic in the way that sight or hearing are.[8] Thus, while we might, in the course of a day, presume that testifiers are well placed for pragmatic reasons or because the beliefs in question are low stakes, whether we are *justified* in doing so depends on our evidence that this person is *actually* well placed with respect to the proposition. This view is called *reductionism* about testimony—a particular piece of testimony is justified just in case there are independent reasons sufficient for believing the testifier is well placed with respect to the proposition.[9] The justification for any piece of testimony reduces to, or depends on (at least in part), more basic evidence.

In addition to reductionism and non-reductionism, there are several other explanations for how testimony is justified. Some argue for "local reductionism," which is the view that we cannot identify reasons that justify testimony globally. Instead, testimonial justification must be evaluated on a case-by-case basis. Whether a bit of testimony is justified on this view depends on "some conceptual, linguistic, and other background knowledge" (Gelfert 2014: 110). There are also hybrid, or "mixed," views of testimonial authority, according to which other aspects of the giving and receiving of testimony affect whether testimony is justified (see Lackey 2006 and Faulkner 2000).

For my purposes in this book, we need not resolve the tensions among these views. Almost everyone in the debate agrees on two key points: (a) There are occasions on which we must appeal to additional evidence to confirm or justify a piece of testimony, and (b) that the testimony given by an expert in their domain often constitutes such an occasion.

5.3 The Epistemic Significance of Expert Testimony

How, then, does expert testimony differ from novice testimony? Can't we just say that we should trust anyone who has an epistemic advantage over us and drop the word "expert" altogether? I think the answer is no. There are a number of aspects of expertise that are not captured by the concept of epistemic advantage, aspects that help explain *why* experts are prima facie better placed than others, and also why experts should be trusted in some circumstances where we should not trust others.[10]

Recall the case where you're standing outside, and I am in my windowless office. You are better placed than I am to know whether it is raining. Elizabeth Fricker thinks that *your competence to know whether it is raining* combined with *your epistemic placement* is sufficient for calling your advantage with respect to the proposition "It is raining" *expertise*:

> *S is an expert about P relative to H at t* just if at t, S is epistemically well enough placed with respect to P so that were she to have, or make a judgment to form a conscious belief regarding whether P, her belief would almost certainly be knowledge; and she is better epistemically placed than H to determine whether P. (2006: 233, italics hers)

David Coady agrees: "I am significantly better informed than most people about what I had for breakfast this morning; hence I am an expert on the subject" (2012: 31).

Fricker admits that this is a rather thin notion of expertise because it is "highly accidental" and "based in a mere happenstance about our location . . . not on any more stable and intrinsic talent, skill, or base of knowledge that [S] possesses" (234). Call expertise with respect to a proposition that is based on accidental factors *thin expertise*. The fact that expertise is thin does not imply anything with respect to its epistemic value; it simply narrows its scope. For example, it would be unwise for me to contradict you about whether it is raining given my epistemic placement even if you only happen to be outside when I am inside. Similarly, it would be epistemically imprudent to contradict Coady about what he had for breakfast.

Based on these examples, it might seem that thin expertise is trivial, or at least not that interesting from a broader philosophical perspective. Coady even says he is reluctant to describe himself as an expert on what he had for breakfast, "not because it isn't true, but because it sounds as if I am boasting about something which is nothing to boast of" (2012: 31).

But consider a different example. Imagine a doctor says to a patient, "Based on your physiology and the dose of medicine I gave you, your pain should be gone," but the patient says, "I understand that, but I'm still in pain." Barring any reasons to think either party is disingenuous, it would be odd to trust the doctor over the patient. Even though the doctor is an expert in the use of medicine, the patient has an epistemic advantage with respect to the proposition at issue: whether she is in pain. The patient's advantage is thin; that is, it is limited to this one experience with the drug and this pain. Nevertheless, if anyone is well placed to know whether the patient is in pain, it is the patient.

What should we say, then, about the doctor's expertise? Is it nullified, canceled, or somehow undermined by this patient's epistemic advantage? I think not. It is simply limited by its nature (medical expertise is derived by generalizing over thousands of patients) and scope (medical expertise does not extend into the subjective physiological states of others). The doctor has an epistemic advantage that is grounded in extensive training and background knowledge and experience in her subdomain of medicine. Rather than having an epistemic advantage with respect to single propositions, the doctor has an advantage with a whole range of propositions and their relationships.

Fricker explains this type of expertise as a "complex perceptual-cum-knowledge-based skill" that "provides a superior ability to determine the truth of a range of propositions in certain circumstances" (2006: 235). Because this kind of expertise is grounded in deliberate immersion in a domain or practice, the doctor's expertise is *thick*; that is, it is expertise in a *domain* (or, in Fricker's terms, "subject matter") rather than a narrow subset of claims or activities:

> **S has an expertise relative to H on some subject matter W at a time t just if S has a superior ability at t to determine the truth of propositions in W which is based in superior perceptual and/or cognitive skills and knowledge, and is hence (in a relaxed sense) intrinsic, or has a crucial intrinsic component. (2006: 235, italics hers)**

Call expertise in a domain *thick expertise*. As with thin expertise, the word "thick" is not an indication of its epistemic value, but of its scope. Return to our patient in pain. If, before the doctor administered the drug, both the doctor and the patient were asked, "What medicine would likely relieve the pain?" we would be right to trust the doctor over the patient. The question relates to the doctor's domain of expertise, which is, necessarily, grounded in extensive training and experience. The patient, unless they are also a medical professional, is unlikely to have the thick expertise necessary for answering the question with any degree of accuracy.

So, the patient's expertise is thin with respect to this drug's effects on this pain, and the doctor's is thick. But the patient still has an epistemic advantage over the doctor. How do we explain this? And, again, what work is the word "expertise" doing for us?

While the patient and doctor are differently placed with respect to a proposition, the scope of their competence is different. It seems like we are trading off expertise against expertise (because Fricker uses "expertise" both for propositions and domains), but really, we are trading off thick expertise against a thin epistemic advantage. This suggests that there is a problem with treating expertise as if it applies both to *propositions* and to *domains*.

According to some philosophers, the idea that someone could be an expert about a proposition doesn't make sense. Scott Brewer (1998), for example, argues that expertise requires understanding, and understanding involves beliefs about relations among propositions in a domain, how those propositions are applied to solve problems, and how existing propositions and the relations among them can be used to introduce new propositions into the domain. Brewer quotes philosopher Miles Burnyeat (1987) to make this point:

> The important difference between knowledge and understanding is that knowledge can be piecemeal, can grasp isolate truths one by one, whereas understanding always involves seeing connections and relations between the

items known. "The only part of modern physics I understand is the formula '$E=mc^2$'" is nonsense. (Quoted in Brewer [2006: 113])

This suggests (compellingly, in my opinion) that what we have called *thin expertise* may be better classified as an instance of *knowledge* rather of *expertise*. To be sure, knowledge carries epistemic authority. It can confer an epistemic advantage, which is why we should trust patients who report on their own pain over doctors who dismiss such testimony.[11] But to call beliefs about what one had for breakfast "expertise" seems to stretch the notion in an unhelpful way.

Returning to the doctor-patient case, we get a much richer picture by first setting out the scope of their expertise and then seeing what this implies with respect to the proposition, "I am in pain." The doctor is an expert in the domain of medicine. It is conceivable that the patient is also an expert in her personal experiences. The patient's epistemic placement with respect to her subjective experiences could constitute thick expertise if she has extensive experience with them, and she has carefully reflected on them such that she is competent at identifying and responding to them. These domains happen to overlap where the doctor is attempting to apply medicine to change the patient's experience (Figure 5.1):

But, with respect to the patient's experience of pain with this medication, her knowledge is thin because it is accidental and not based on extensive training, experience, or knowledge. It is not a judgment based on her past experiences with her body or her understanding of how pain medicines tend to work with her.[12] It is more productively framed as a single instance of knowledge.

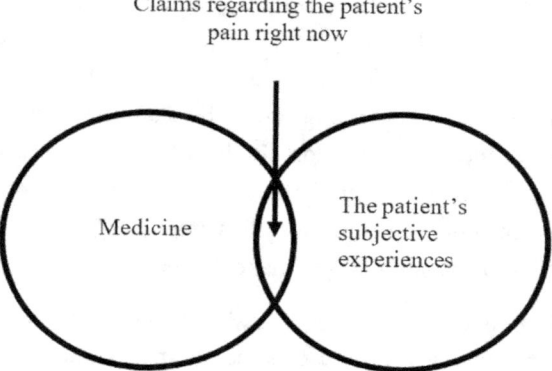

Figure 5.1 The overlap between the domains of medicine and subjective experiences.

To see the point more clearly, we can change the example to something less subjective than pain. If the patient can see the display of a heart rate monitor in her room while the doctor cannot, the patient has an epistemic advantage over the doctor as to what measurement it reads. They are well placed relative to the doctor, regardless of what the doctor, in light of their expertise, predicts it *should* read.

Thus, for now, I set aside the notion of thin expertise and focus on thick expertise, whether *localized* or *specialized*. We can continue to make use of the notion of thick and thin epistemic placement and acknowledge that someone who is thinly placed with respect to a proposition may have an epistemic advantage with respect to that proposition relative to others, and, therefore, should be trusted about it. But since we need not refer to this type of epistemic advantage as a species of expertise, and since it strikes me as confusing to do so, I set it aside, and I will return to it briefly in Chapter 8.

Importantly, even thick expertise need not be especially *strong*. Recall from Chapter 2 our discussion of *localized expertise*. Localized expertise (knowledge of the ins and outs of an office copy machine; being good at sports questions at bar trivia) is not accidental or due to happenstance. It is usually the result of extensive experience, and so it is, by our definition, thick expertise. However, it is not specialized. The testimony of a copy machine repair person or sports historian would carry more epistemic weight than the local expert. (I admit that the boundaries are fuzzy here. I've known a few sports fanatics who could probably go toe-to-toe with a sports historian, especially since historians tend to specialize narrowly, whereas the hobbyist usually has a breadth of knowledge. The key here is that with enough training, a hobbyist can become a specialized expert, but even as a hobbyist might have bits of knowledge that constitute a thin epistemic advantage over the expert.)

To make the differences in degrees of expertise clearer, consider the controversial topic of childhood vaccinations, and compare five people:

Person A, whose only knowledge of childhood vaccinations came from a single *People* magazine article.

Person B, a school nurse, who has given hundreds of vaccinations.

Person C, a second-year resident physician (a person who has an MD, but is still in training and, therefore, not a licensed physician).

Person D, a licensed physician who works in a community clinic.

Person E, a licensed physician who is also a specialist in immunology and is regularly engaged in funded research on vaccines.

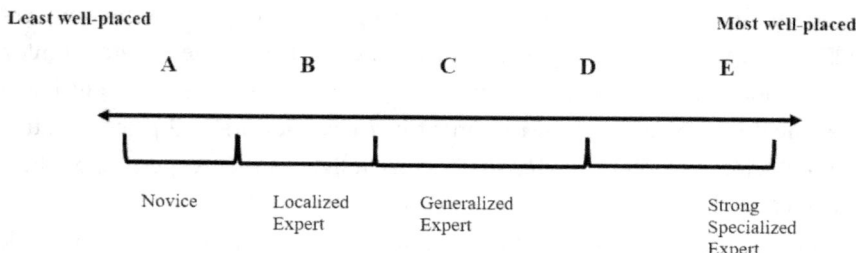

Figure 5.2 Epistemic placement in a domain.

We can arrange these people according to their epistemic placement with respect to claims about the safety of childhood vaccines (Figure 5.2). Note that I am talking about the *domain* of childhood vaccinations and not some specific *proposition* about the safety of vaccines.

I am calling B a localized expert, but I am happy to leave it an open question whether Person B is a *localized expert* or a *person of experience* (see Sections 2.3.3 and 2.3.5) based on their level of experience and understanding. If they were a person of experience and not an expert, I would draw the chart this way, with the understanding that the "borders" between any of these are fuzzy and highly dependent on the domain under consideration (Figure 5.3):

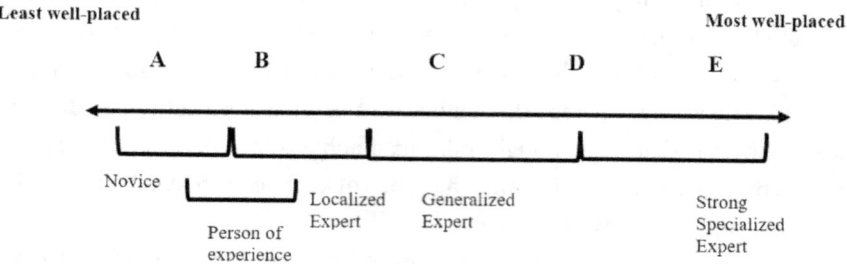

Figure 5.3 Epistemic placement in a domain, alternate.

Note that, in either figure, who has an *epistemic advantage* over whom is relative to the person seeking understanding in a domain, while someone's *degree of expertise* is relative to the domain itself. Some philosophers argue that experts are better placed in a domain *relative to others* and that this placement determines who has an epistemic advantage over whom. In other words, they argue that the strength of one's expertise depends on how many others share or lack that same expertise. If everyone is an expert in domain X, they contend, then "expertise" doesn't amount to very much, epistemically speaking. Unfortunately, this *population-relative* account of expert authority leads to trouble.

We can imagine a world where everyone except a handful of highly trained specialists in a domain is wiped out. The remaining specialists seem to retain the competence sufficient for expertise even though they are not more competent in their domain "than most people"? They still have their specialist knowledge and skills; they can still speak authoritatively about their domain to each other. Further, they can still turn to one another for a review of their own work and collaboration (in fact, they should turn to them precisely because they have that knowledge and skill). These are things they could not do with novices. If expertise is to be grounded in an objective competence in a domain, and these people lose none of their competence in cases where everyone else has disappeared, then it seems arbitrary to withhold the term "expert" from them. I propose that this *domain-linked* account is a more plausible way to ground expert authority. Nevertheless, for this section, either account will suffice.

With respect to the domain of childhood vaccinations, Person A is the least well placed. Therefore, other things being equal, everyone else has a prima facie epistemic advantage over A with respect to whether claim P in the domain of childhood vaccinations is true. There is a *normative presumption*, for example, that A should defer to C on questions about childhood vaccines.

It is not out of the question, though, that A has an epistemic advantage over C with respect to a particular claim, P, about childhood vaccinations. Perhaps A runs into E at the local pub, and they have a long conversation about childhood vaccinations. From this conversation, Person A picks up a few new pieces of information (say, propositions P, Q, and R) about childhood vaccinations that Person C is in no position to have. In that case, if Person A runs into C (say, at a different pub, because that's how A rolls) and A testifies that P, then if C had good reasons for believing that A received P from E and that A understood P well enough to transmit it successfully, C would be obliged to admit that A has an epistemic advantage (albeit thin) over C with respect to P.

To see why this is only a thin epistemic advantage, consider the following possibility: If in their conversation, C notes growing concerns over A's ability to understand P and what it means for the domain, C might lose any reason for thinking that A understood what E was talking about. The line of authority from E through A would be broken for C. But there is nothing in principle that prevents A from having this thin epistemic advantage over C in cases similar to this example.

Let's consider one more level of complexity. Let's say the scenario played out as earlier: C has reason to trust A that P. Now imagine that C leaves her conversation with A and runs into Person D on the street outside the pub. C asks D about P, and D confirms A's testimony. Because D is strongly placed with respect to P, and let's say C has good reason to believe this, then C has a reason to revise her degree of belief that P (she now has stronger evidence that P). What matters in all of these scenarios is that someone is thickly placed in the domain, whether E or D, or both.

5.4 A New Taxonomy of Expertise

Pulling together the threads of the book so far, from the ancient Greeks to contemporary social epistemology, we now have what I hope is a helpful taxonomy for talking about expertise (Figure 5.4). Consider a continuum of competence in a domain. The horizontal line reflects the continuum of placement in a domain. The further left you go, the weaker your competence in the domain; the further right you go, the stronger your competence in the domain. Above the line are types of incidental experience that confer varying degrees of thin epistemic authority. Below the line are the types of specialized training or knowledge that confers thick epistemic authority.

On the far left of the continuum are people who have very little understanding in that domain. They may understand nothing at all (much the way I felt when

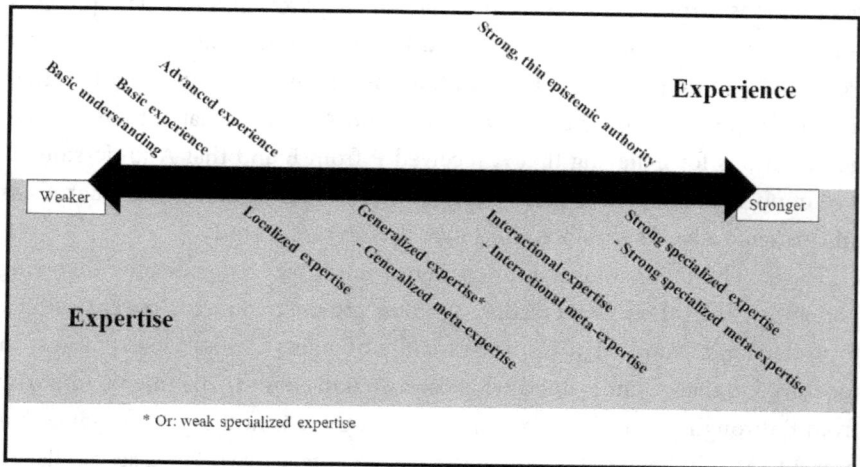

Figure 5.4 A taxonomy of epistemic placement in a domain.

I first heard of the medical specialty "interventional radiology"), or they may have a working understanding of what the domain is. A little further to the right are people who have a *basic understanding* about what the domain is and what it does. Some have even worked in the domain, gaining *basic experience*. Think of your first high school job at a dry-cleaning service (mine) or fast food restaurant. You had a sense of what was going on, but little more. For other domains, this might look like reading an article about it or listening to a few podcasts.

Moving most of the way to the right on the continuum, we find *strong, thin epistemic authority* is a type of strongly authoritative, first-person experience. If you are in pain, for example, you have the most intimate possible relationship to whether that is true, and no one is better positioned to know whether you are in pain than you. And you don't have to be an art historian to know that the statue of St. Peter at the Almudena Cathedral in Madrid is holding two keys in his hand if you are looking at the statue in person. However, this competence is extremely narrow (hence, "thin") and is usually restricted to one or a few claims in a domain. It is an incidental rather than enduring competence.

Below the line are degrees of expertise. Recall your first job. Over time, you got the hang of that job. You could explain the work, the tools, the concepts, and how to use them. You could do some basic troubleshooting of problems in that domain or use your understanding to answer questions you hadn't encountered before. This enduring experience developed in you *localized expertise* in that domain. Localized expertise is more robust than basic experience. Everyone in your office can probably use the copy machine, but if you understand how to change the toner, remove paper jams, and generally troubleshoot its problems, then you are a localized expert on the copy machine. Basic experience is only just below localized expertise because with enough experience, one usually develops localized expertise.

Generalized expertise, or weak specialized expertise, is acquired through spending time studying or practicing in a domain, and the scholars we call "generalists" are typically weak specialized experts in several domains of expertise. Graduate students in many domains and MDs who have not yet completed their residencies may be generalized experts.

There is a rich literature on *interactional expertise,* a type of expertise identified by sociologist Harry Collins and his colleagues (Collins and Evans 2007; Collins 2014). I won't delve deeply into the concept here. But the basic idea is that the social dynamics of becoming an expert are much more social than many accounts of expertise acknowledge. Experts don't just know things, and they aren't just able to do things. By being immersed in the culture of a domain—spending time with other experts, talking casually with them in the lab or around the lunch table or out for drinks—aspiring experts learn how experts think about, talk about, and approach the issues in their domain, nuances over and above what you find in a textbook or classroom. Like learning a natural language, this "linguistic socialization," as Collins and Evans call it, makes aspiring experts fluent in both the formal and informal aspects of a domain; they come to understand both its technical and nontechnical activities and practices.

Interactional expertise stops just short of what I am calling *strong specialized expertise*. For that, Collins and Evans argue that the interactional expert must progress a bit further, to the point where they can also contribute novel ideas or procedures or discoveries to their domain. So, what I am calling strong specialized expertise, Collins and Evans call "contributory expertise." Nevertheless, the majority of scientific activities—from peer review, to teaching broadly in a domain, to writing textbooks—happen through interactional expertise. A strong specialist pulmonologist, for example, is typically also an interactional expert in hematology. The pulmonologist can understand and interact with the hematologist she consults on a patient's case, and she can likely teach some basics of hematology to medical students. Interactional experts are not usually well enough placed in a domain to contribute novel ideas to or solve novel problems that domain, but they can engage with it and other experts in that domain in a meaningful and constructive way.

Interestingly, medicine is a field in which a specialist in one area of medicine is usually also an interactional expert in a number of others. The pulmonologist, for example, has a rather robust understanding of cardiology, hematology, nephrology, and so on. Given that medical specialists often have interactional expertise in a range of medical subspecialties, this suggests they have *interactional meta-expertise* across that range. Interactional meta-expertise is probably common among strong specialized experts, as most domains overlap in substantive ways with others—the topologist who is also competent in logic and calculus; the toxicologist who is also competent in biochemistry and epidemiology; and so on.

Strong specialized experts, in contrast, are well placed enough in a domain to contribute to that domain, and, given the time and energy it takes to specialize, few others are usually as well placed as they are. Finally, the *strong specialized meta-expert* are those rare people—like Amartya Sen and Queen Margrethe II of Denmark—who have specialized expertise in multiple domains.

5.5 Summing Up: Conceptual Heavy Lifting

Thus, expertise does important epistemic work. First, it establishes a distinct kind of epistemic placement in a domain, namely, thick epistemic placement. Second, the degree of an expert's competence is determined whether that placement is weak or strong. The stronger an expertise in a domain, the better placed they are with respect to any proposition in that domain at any given time. This, then, helps inform us about when we have good reason to trust experts, among others. In other words, epistemic placement helps explain expert *authority*.

Of course, this taxonomy is not the whole story. Domains overlap. Some domains are nested inside others. Experts in one domain share competencies with those in others, and experts close to another domain can use their ability to assess expertise to help novices decide whom to trust in those other domains, even if those domains are fairly esoteric. More on those complexities in Chapters 7 and 8.

In the meantime, what is "authority," and what does it mean for the receivers of expert testimony or advice that the expertise is "authoritative"? Do experts have some sort of right to compel the belief and actions of others? Do others have an obligation to defer to experts, suspending all other beliefs and reasoning? Under what circumstances can a novice reasonably question, challenge, or reject an expert's authority? And how should two experts in a domain respond to one another's testimony? To address these questions, in the next chapter, I explore four proposals for what "authority" means and highlight their implications for expert testimony.

6

Expert Authority

Physicians who cut, burn, stab, and rack the sick, demand a fee for it which they do not deserve to get.
(Heraclitus, fr. 58, trans. John Burnet, *Early Greek Philosophy*, 1908, p. 151)

In this chapter, I explore the concept of authority with the aim of illuminating the normative implications of expertise. If experts are better epistemically placed than novices in a domain, then novices have good reason to think experts can help them in that domain, whether they need information, advice, or skill. If epistemic placement counts as a reason for novices to trust someone, as we saw in the previous chapter, then experts have authority for novices in that domain. When an expert is well placed enough and for the right reasons, their authority applies to everyone, not just those who seek them out or acknowledge them as experts. They don't just have authority; they are *authorities* in that domain. But what does "authority" mean in the context of expertise?

The majority of the literature on authority has focused on political authority, and there are good historical and etymological reasons for this, as we saw in Chapter 2. But we have also seen that the authority of experts seems somehow distinct from political authority; that is, it is better understood to imply epistemic authority. Unfortunately, trying to state precisely the difference between political and epistemic authority has led to a number of confusions.

In this chapter, I distinguish *epistemic* conceptions of authority from *political* and *administrative* conceptions, and I argue that expert authority is distinctly epistemic (Section 6.1). I then review four ways of thinking about epistemic authority. We might think of it as a *control* notion—an expert has the normative right to exert *physical control* (Section 6.1.1), *ontological control* (Section 6.1.2), or *doxastic control* (Section 6.1.3) over others. The doxastic control account developed by Linda Zagzebski (2012) has been especially influential, so in

Section 6.2, I explain her arguments for it in detail. But Zagzebski's view—like other control accounts—faces a number of serious objections, which I explain in Section 6.3. In Section 6.4, drawing on the work of Jennifer Lackey and others, I develop an alternative account of epistemic authority that rejects the idea that epistemic authority entails control over other. I call this the *normative presumption account* of authority, and I argue that captures what we need from an account of expert authority while avoiding the most significant concerns for control accounts of authority.

6.1 Authority: Administrative versus Epistemic

It is important to acknowledge that testimony, which is associated with oral or written expressions of propositions, is a narrow dimension of what constitutes expertise. Expert authority extends beyond testimony to various kinds of performance, from writing scholarly works (which exhibit a proficiency beyond their content, for example, in translations of classical works) to acting, surgery, athletics, and advice. We trust Olympic swimmer Dara Torres to perform expertly as a swimmer irrespective of whether we should trust her testimony about the physiology, kinetics, or history of swimming, even Olympic swimming. Just because you can do something well, doesn't mean you can explain it well.[1] But, in many cases, a master woodworker or master distiller exhibits authority in their respective crafts by their testimony or advice about their craft. So, for simplicity, I abbreviate an expert's testimony, advice, or performance as TAP.

The idea that experts should be trusted as authorities has a complicated history. This is partly because the notion of *authority* has long been bound up with the idea of political control, while the *skilled judgment* associated with specialized expertise has more often been associated with trade work and professions. But with a little conceptual work, it becomes clear that there are important differences between being *in authority* over someone—that is, having a claim on their behavior—and being *an authority* in a domain—that is, having a claim on someone's belief or trust (Peters 1958).

Consider the requirements for the ruler of Socrates's "city in speech" in Plato's *Republic*. As we see in several of Plato's writings (*Crito, Statesman*, etc.), government is presumed to play the role of a loving and fair parent, whose aim is to protect and train citizens in virtue.[2] Yet, in *Republic*, after extensive discussion, Socrates concludes that the only people capable of adequately filling that role are philosophers (*Republic*, Book V, 473dff), in particular philosophers who don't want the job (Book VI). It is certainly not, as Socrates demonstrates to Thrasymachus, simply a matter of having physical power over others. While one can have authority as a ruler simply by having power, this is not what *legitimates* the use of force. For Socrates, the three key requirements for legitimate political authority are:

(1) **Knowledge of the people's interests;**
(2) **The *ability* to facilitate citizens' fulfilling those interests; and**
(3) **The *willingness* to facilitate their fulfilling them.**

Only philosophers, according to Plato's Socrates, are in a position to meet these criteria. In other words, the *right* to the use of political control—legitimate authority—is grounded in mastery of certain domains: practical, political, and moral.[3]

Importantly, for my purposes, Plato's criteria are not idiosyncratic. Apart, perhaps, from Machiavelli's political strategies, they form the background assumptions for almost every subsequent political philosophy's concept of legitimate political authority. Consider, for example, the divine right of kings (also called monarchical absolutism). Though defenses of the absolute legitimacy of a single sovereign's rule vary (see Burgess 1992), it is easy to make sense of monarchical authority in light of Plato's discussion. The God of classical theism is supposed to be necessarily omniscient, omnipotent, and omnibenevolent. Necessarily, then, this being fulfills Plato's three criteria. Thus, if God appoints someone king or pope, this is because God is choosing to work his perfect knowledge and virtue through this person for the good of society. Objectively, in this case, the connection between political power and legitimacy is guaranteed. Of course, from our limited perspective on things, the connection is not so clear. Many decisions by these (surely well-meaning) leaders have had disastrous and morally abhorrent effects, so that the divine seal of approval is, at minimum, suspect. Thus, we feel motivated to distribute political power to mitigate its worst effects. Monarchies transform into constitutional monarchies, democracies, or republics.

Similarly, all democratic processes, from classic, pure democracy to the more recent deliberative practices, are predicated on the assumption that individuals are in a better epistemic and moral position to know what's good for them than insulated political leaders. Even if people are not always right about what's good for them, the idea is that they have a better shot at getting it right than someone who has never met them. This distribution of authority throughout the population sits uneasy with the idea of specialized experts in politics (see, Moore 2017 for an excellent discussion of this problem). Here, it is enough to point out that, the *exercise* of political authority is distinct from whatever might *legitimize* it. For the sake of simplicity, I will assume in the remainder of this chapter that the authority in question is legitimate. The question, then, is what legitimate expert authority implies for those who are not authorities.

For clarity, I will treat "political authority" as an instance of a broader conception of authority that is strongly associated with control. Following philosopher Douglas Walton (1992: 48), I will call the right to make one's judgments binding *administrative authority*. Walton gives the example of a doctor, whose medical license and privileges in a hospital imbue them with administrative authority; in other words, it is *because of the license and privileges* that their judgments are both institutionally and legally binding.[4] Political authority is like this in that politicians and others with political power have the unilateral right to make many of their judgments binding, whether in the form of executive orders, international agreements, or military mobilization. Doctors and politicians are *in authority* because they have the right to exert control over others' behavior.

Now, contrast the doctor's right to control (prescriptions, diagnoses, write orders) with the doctor's ability to make judgments in the domain of medicine that reflect the current state of medicine. In other words, contrast the doctor's right to control aspects of the medical encounter with their competence to form appropriate judgments about those aspects. This competence is a function, not of the state or the hospital, but of the doctor's understanding and skill in their domain. Following Linda Zagzebski (2012), I will call this *epistemic authority*, which is the ability to make judgments in a domain that, other things being equal, constitute sufficient evidence for justifying those judgments for others (see Figure 6.1).

It is important to note that neither administrative nor epistemic authority implies the other. It is possible to have administrative authority without epistemic authority and vice versa. Of course, it has seemed plausible to many

Figure 6.1 Accounts of authority: Administrative and epistemic.

that epistemic authority is an essential part of what justifies or legitimates administrative authority. For example, we typically want doctors (and no others) to have the administrative authority to write medical orders in large part because they have epistemic authority. But, I will show in the following sections that even if epistemic authority is a necessary condition for legitimate administrative authority, it is not sufficient for it, and having epistemic authority, while in some sense social (see also Watson 2021), does not require having administrative authority.

6.1.1 The Physical Control Account of Authority

Some philosophers have thought that the answer is yes. Friedrich Nietzsche ([1886] 2009), for example, seems to accept Plato's criteria and his idea that people who have a certain type of epistemic authority have the right to make their judgments binding (i.e., they also have administrative authority). However, unlike Plato's Socrates, who thinks that most philosophers will believe they shouldn't accept this political role because they have better things to do with their time, Nietzsche thinks philosophers have an obligation to rule because of these qualities. He says philosophers have the "greatest responsibility" to rule because they have "the conscience for the general development of mankind" ([1886] 2009: §61). And this type of conscience engenders "authority," by which he means "a bond which binds rulers and subjects in common, betraying and surrendering to the former the conscience of the latter, their inmost heart, which would fain escape obedience" ([1886] 2009: §61). This suggests that the legitimacy of the expert philosopher implies the same demands of deference on novices that political expertise does. The problem, of course, is that Nietzsche doesn't offer a solution for the problem that beset Plato's philosopher kings and, later, claims regarding divinely appointed monarchs: There don't seem to be people who actually meet these criteria.

To be sure, it is easy to draw a connection between administrative and epistemic authority. Whether political or epistemic, authority seems to imply having control of some kind. In political contexts, authority is command over people and their behavior. In contexts of specialized skill or knowledge, authority is mastery or command over the skills and information necessary for understanding, paraphrasing, explaining, and drawing inferences about many aspects of a domain. The latter is not quite the control that an *author* has (which has the same Latin root, *auctor*, and a similar meaning in that it implies "causing something to happen" or "brings something into being"),[5] but it is a mastery compatible with authorship. For example, someone like Allan Bloom is a source of information about Plato's *Republic*—not just a translator and transmitter of it—because he understands better than most readers how the context of the writing shaped the use of the words.

But the connection between *author* and *authority* is weak (hardly even an inference), drawn between two languages in very different sociohistorical contexts. Experts cannot control their domains. The state of a domain is the product of many experts working overtime within the constraints of technology, discovery, and success conditions.

Further, even this weak conceptual relationship between administrative authority and authorial creation does not map cleanly onto the concepts we tend to identify with expertise. Someone can hold administrative authority despite incompetence to lead or govern. Someone can create (be an author of) something clumsily or hastily. So even though the English word *expert* implies a certain type of authority, many types of authority do not imply expertise.

Nevertheless, like Nietzsche, many have accepted the idea that something about an expert's epistemic placement implies some administrative right to control others. Philosopher Robert Paul Wolff (1970; 1990), for example, defines authority explicitly in terms of control: "Authority is the right to command, and correlatively, the right to be obeyed" (1990: 20). According to Wolff, authority is not the exercise of power, because the mere exercise of power is not an exercise of authority. For example, a thief who takes your money at gunpoint exercises power over you but not authority. Rather, on Wolff's view, authority is a justification for the exercise of power. The government that taxes you on pain of penalty or incarceration is claiming authority over you that would justify the penalty or incarceration were you not to obey that government.

Similarly, Benjamin Ives Gilman (1852–1933), Secretary of the Boston Museum of Fine Arts, echoes Nietzsche's reasoning, applying it to scientific experts. In an article in the journal *Science* (1914), Gilman argues that a scientist's expertise instantiates an authority that requires "a positive system of control" in which experts have a determinative influence in institutions that have an interest in the domain of their expertise: charitable foundations, libraries, hospitals, museums, and so on.

However, notice a difference between Gilman's notion of control and Wolff's. Gilman isn't claiming that scientists should help run museums on threat of imprisonment or fines. Gilman is claiming something about the integrity of institutions that have a substantive overlap with the sciences. While Gilman's

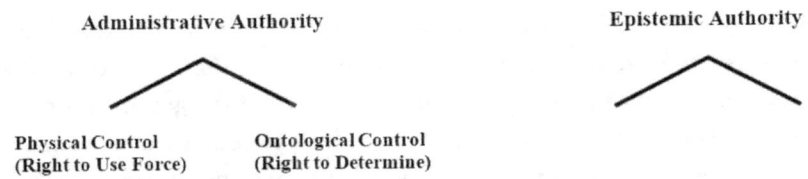

Figure 6.2 Accounts of authority: Physical and ontological control.

view still implies a "right to be obeyed" by the authority, the control need not be physical control, enforceable, for example, by the police or military.

This suggests that we should distinguish two control accounts of authority: authority as the *right to use force* and authority as the *right to determine*, or what I will call the "ontological control" model of authority (Figure 6.2).

6.1.2 The Ontological Control Account of Authority

The right to use force is clear enough. It is what Plato and Nietzsche and other political philosophers have in mind when they talk about the legitimacy of state power. What I am calling "ontological control" is subtler. And there is no abler proponent of it than philosopher Hannah Arendt ([1954] 1961).

Arendt locates the normative force of authority in mutually accepted hierarchical relationships in social institutions. Arendt rejects the idea that authority entails the right to the use of "force and violence" (Greek: *bia*, βία); however, she does contend that it "demands obedience." Further, authority is not compatible with *persuasion* (Greek: *peithein*, πείθειν); that is, the authority cannot remain in authority while attempting to persuade people of her authority. This is because persuasion presumes that people who are engaged in persuading one another are equals, reasoning together to arrive at a conclusion. As long as someone is engaged in attempts to persuade, they are forgoing any presumed authority.

For Arendt, the power of authority rests wholly with the structure of relationships among the authority figure and those over whom they have authority:

> Against the egalitarian order of persuasion stands the authoritarian order, which is always hierarchical ... (The authoritarian relation between the one who commands and the one who obeys ... is the hierarchy itself whose rightness and legitimacy both recognize and where both have their predetermined stable place.) ([1954] 1961: 93)

The idea is that a hierarchical structure of relationships among people determines who is in authority over whom.

What does an authoritative "command" amount to if not backed by force or persuasion? Presumably it is the right to proclaim definitively, for example, the Catholic Church's right to say who is a Christian, the right of a hospital to determine who has privileges, the right of scientists to declare who is a scientist.[6] Authority is a right to demarcate one's domain: it confers the power to determine what is or is not the case, what exists or doesn't exist in an institution. Therefore, I call this kind of control "ontological." The key point for Arendt is that both parties accept the authority's right to demand and regard that right as settled.[7]

To see how Arendt's account works, we can expand on Walton's example of a doctor. In hospitals, some physicians are assigned to specific patients. A physician who is assigned to a patient is called the "attending of record" or just "the attending." When another physician, presumably from another specialty, is asked by the attending to comment about a patient's condition, they are "consulting physicians." According to the hierarchy of hospital leadership, the attending of record is the authoritative voice, legally and institutionally, regarding treatments for the patient to which they are assigned. Regardless of how competent the consulting physician is, and even if they are more competent than the attending, the consultant can only make recommendations; the ultimate medical decision regarding treatment lies with the attending.

Because some of my professional work is in a hospital, I once observed a consulting physician who, after evaluating a patient, said that a patient didn't need a treatment, call it Treatment X. But when the consulting physician was told that the attending physician said the patient *did* need Treatment X, the consultant immediately retracted his claim: "Oh! Then the patient *does* need Treatment X. The attending's judgment is final." Note that, despite the fact that the doctors had similar training and had both examined the patient, the hospital hierarchy—the fact that one doctor was assigned to the patient and the other wasn't—was regarded as determining the truth value of the claim, "The patient needs Treatment X." This might lead one to believe that the doctor's *pronouncement* that the patient needed Treatment X *made it true* that patient needed Treatment X—a power that doctors (like most others) tend not to have.

Interestingly, this is the same authority Arendt ascribes to political leaders. In virtue of their role as a leader and the fact that others acknowledge that role, the leader's pronouncements demand deference. The control is ontological, determined by institutions and commitments, rather than physical, and she does not seem to draw any distinction between the authority of a politician and the authority of an expert. Unfortunately, Arendt's view has trouble explaining the legitimate use of force. In typical cases of ontological control, the authority determines whether you are part of an organization or not (employed or fired, Christian or excommunicated, whether you have agreed to an arbitration agreement or not, and so on). But what happens if you reject the results of the arbitration agreement or, in political cases, fail to pay your taxes or do something illegal? For Arendt, when one withdraws one's acknowledgment of the authority's privileged position, there is no longer any authority to appeal to. Authority ceases to exist when one or more parties withdraw their commitment from the hierarchy. Indeed, one of Arendt's motivations for developing her view is her belief that "authority has vanished from the modern world," or at least "we are no longer in a position to know what authority really *is*" ([1954]1961: 92, italics hers); therefore, the concept lacks teeth. This is concerning because governments still *claim* the justified use of force in cases of noncompliance. In those cases where they do use force on those who no longer acknowledge the legitimacy of their claim, we may rightly ask: By what authority do you impose force?

We need not work out a solution here for how government, on Arendt's view, could retain the right to use force in the face of dissenters. We have explored reasons to distinguish the ontological control model from the physical control model, and that's sufficient for my purposes here. I leave to others the question of whether Arendt's view can accommodate both the right to use force and the right to determine. The question for us is whether either of these (the physical control or ontological control conceptions of authority) successfully captures the type of authority engendered by specialized expertise. I think the answer is no.

Because there are no (and, arguably, can be no) philosopher kings, neither of these types of authority successfully elucidates the normative role of the *expert's* epistemic position. Apart from a few dissenters, most expertise scholars agree that someone's epistemic placement is not merely a function of a community's agreement or assent, and it does not always determine whether they have the right to use force. Yet, it seems reasonable to think there is an objective norm associated with an expert's TAP, that is, a prima facie obligation for novices (and maybe some other experts) to give special weight to expert judgment. If expertise is an objective state in the world, it also seems reasonable that this obligation stands regardless of whether one acknowledges the expert's standing as an expert. Thus, we must look elsewhere for a conception that captures the sort of authority implied by expertise.

6.1.3 The Doxastic Control Account of Authority

Linda Zagzebski (2012) attempts precisely this. She maintains the control element of authority but argues that the implications of that control are not the right to deploy physical or ontological force, but the right to compel assent on the part of novices. An expert is more likely than you to be right about a claim in their domain, and therefore, any reasons you have for thinking the expert is wrong are likely to lead you to the wrong conclusion. Thus, epistemically, you have an obligation to "screen off" any reasons you have for thinking the claim is true or false and trust the expert.

Zagzebski draws heavily on Joseph Raz's ([1975] 1999; [1985] 1990, 1988) work on political authority, arguing that "all of his theses can be satisfied by authority in the epistemic domain" (2012: 106). To see how, we need a brief sketch of Raz's view. Raz's account of authority is administrative in that it imbues a person with the right to be obeyed, and this right is underwritten by the justified use of force. Though Raz attempts to distance his view from physical control accounts by saying that "justified use of coercive power is one thing and authority is another" (1988: 25), he makes clear that there is no meaningful sense of authority that does not include the power to compel compliance. What makes "authority" different from the *mere* justified use of force is recognition of that justification on the part of the governed. Whereas one might be justified in physically restraining someone for their own or others' good (as in forcibly quarantining someone with Ebola), this would not, according to Raz, be an act that exhibited or derived from "authority" (though presumably only designated "authorities" would have this justified right, so there is some equivocation in Raz's account). Authority requires the assent of the governed; that is, they must acknowledge the authority's claim on their behavior or beliefs.

So far, this is consistent with Raz's primary examples, which include tax laws, military conscription, military command, and the relationship of a parent to a child. Thus, the sort of normative force of his opening examples is difficult to separate from the expectation of the use of force in cases of noncompliance. Unfortunately, Raz also introduces cases of private arbitration and the advice of a financial advisor for choosing stocks as instances of the authoritative right to be obeyed. In the case of arbitration, for example, Raz says that "the arbitrator's decision is for the disputants a reason for action. They ought to do as he says because he says so" (121). Yet, we should be clear that the conclusion of a professional arbitration is only normatively binding to the degree that an arbitration has been court-ordered, and, in those cases, failure to reach a resolution has clear legal consequences. Otherwise, a failed arbitration is simply a failed attempt to reach an agreement. Further, an arbiter's expertise is in *negotiation*, not in proffering claims or advice regarding the domain at issue. In fact, an arbiter often has no expertise with the content in dispute in an arbitration.

Similarly, to the degree that a stock advisor is an expert, perhaps one has reason to trust them, but they certainly possess no right to be obeyed. Given the possibility of empirical evidence against the reliability of professional investment advisors (see Tetlock 2005, for example), it would seem that the sort of authority entailed by this kind of expertise should be conceived differently than political authority.

Nevertheless, Raz believes that the same sense of authority is at play in all these examples because it is the *only* way to make sense of what normativity requires: "The only proper way to acknowledge the arbitrator's authority is to take it to be a reason for action which replaces the reasons on the basis of which he was meant to decide" ([1986] 1990: 122). Raz thinks authority is normatively binding in this strong sense because it exhibits two features: *dependence* and *preemptiveness*.

By "dependence," Raz means that an authority's judgment includes all considerations relevant to a judgment and has the ability to weigh them appropriately. This means that, to the extent that you accurately identify good reasons to believe something, the authority has already taken those into consideration, and to the extent that you're wrong about the value of a reason, the authority has weighed them accordingly or dismissed them altogether. This is a purely epistemic claim, of course, and does not consider whether the authority's aims align with those who are obligated to obey. For example, a commanding officer in the military (even one who holds that role legitimately and whose soldiers acknowledge that legitimacy) may give orders to pursue goals that diverge from the goals of the obeying soldier. Similarly, an arbiter may have no goals other than agreement, but this in itself does not constitute a reason for parties to an arbitration to accept any particular arrangement the arbiter may suggest.

For simplicity, let us consider only cases of *expert* authority (leaving aside the roles of military commander and legislator). According to our working account of expertise, experts have access to relevant information or evidence novices lack. Even in cases where experts do not have more relevant information or evidence than novices, experts can weigh that information and evidence more effectively. In this sense, the expert's judgment is dependent on all relevant information, whereas the novice is dependent, to a nontrivial degree, on the expert's judgment about that information.

In the expert-novice relationship, according to Raz, the expert's TAP is not merely one reason among many to accept what they say; rather, their TAP is the *ultimate* reason because it has taken into account all the other reasons and is pronouncing definitively on the matter. In cases of legitimate authority, no other reasons are sufficient for overriding the authority's judgment, even if the authority happens to be wrong in this case (121, 126).

By "preemptiveness," Raz means that the authority's judgment "is meant to replace the reasons on which it depends" (121). The authority's judgment "settles" what should be believed or done. Raz seems to think that when someone becomes an authority, this is their social function—to guide novices. Therefore, their TAP constitutes a "preemptive reason" for those who understand that they are an authority.

The resulting judgment is thus normatively binding on recipients independently of its content. Zagzebski calls the claim that the judgment's authority is independent of its content the "content-independence thesis." The authoritative judgment could have been to believe A or to believe B, and no matter what the evidence, or what the novice thinks the evidence is, the authority has the final say in whether it is A or B. Whatever the judgment, if it is authoritative, the judgment constitutes a binding reason for others to accept it.

Together, according to Raz, dependence and preemptiveness normatively bind those under an authority to the authority's judgments. There is extensive discussion in the literature about whether Raz's account is sufficient for political authority and its relationship to the justified use of force. We need not explore those here because this is where Zagzebski's view picks up and takes the concept of authority in a new direction.

Whereas Raz's conception of authority presumes a strong connection with the justified use force, Zagzebski restricts her normative claims to what one should believe or do irrespective of how others are justified in responding to us (she says "the right to command is not necessary" [102]). In other words, she aims to develop a distinctly *epistemic* conception of authority grounded in the normativity of an expert's reasons. "What is essential to authority is that it is a normative power that generates reasons for others to do or to believe something preemptively" (2012: 102).[8] Call this the "doxastic control" account of epistemic authority (Figure 6.3).[9]

Notice that, on the doxastic control account, the norms associated with authority have shifted from the perspective of the authority figure (what they have a right to do as a result of their authority, such as physically coerce others

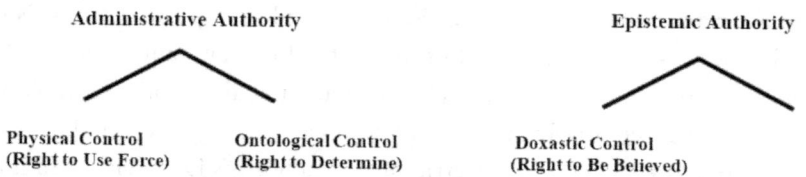

Figure 6.3 Accounts of authority: Doxastic control.

if they refuse to obey) to the perspective of the person under the scope of the authority (how a novice should receive experts, irrespective of what anyone else is authorized to do if novices refuse). This effectively suspends the question of physical or ontological control and focuses on the epistemic implications for the receiver of authoritative TAP. Under ontological control, for example, refusing to defer has certain institutional implications. You haven't necessarily done anything objectively wrong, but you may be ousted from an association or company; you may no longer be permitted certain privileges. On the doxastic control account, refusing to defer has epistemic consequences. It may violate your intellectual integrity, may constitute acting epistemically irresponsibly, or may imply that the belief you retain in contrast to the expert is not justified for you. In other words, if you refuse to defer, you are violating an epistemic norm.

Zagzebski accepts the dependence and preemptiveness features of Raz's account of authority as well as the content-independence thesis. Thus, like Raz, she holds that, when an epistemic agent acknowledges someone as an authority, they accept the authority's TAP in their domain *in lieu of any other reasons* they might have about that claim.[10] An expert's authority "preempts" or "replaces my other reasons relevant to believing *p* and is not simply added to them" (2012: 107).

In saying that an authority's TAP replaces or preempts one's reasons, Zagzebski does not mean that one *ignores* the other reasons she may have, nor does she mean that one *actively decides* to let an authority's TAP override her other reasons (in other words, deference is not primarily a question about how much control we have over our beliefs) (113). She means simply that an authority's TAP constitutes a sufficient and overriding reason to accept that TAP. Because of the strong normative requirement to defer, this is still a control-based account of expertise.

6.2 The Case for Doxastic Control

What motivates an account of epistemic authority that requires such strong deference? Zagzebski offers two lines of argument. The first is grounded in her understanding of different types of reasons. An important aspect of Zagzebski's view is her notion of "conscientious reflection," that is, "[u]sing our faculties to the best of our ability in order to get the truth" (2012: 48). Unlike evaluating evidence, which is an objective cognitive assessment of "facts that are logically or probabilistically connected to the truth of p" (64), evaluating whether someone is in a better epistemic place than I am is "irreducibly first personal" (64), a subjective cognitive assessment of someone's reliability in a domain. The former assessment involves what she calls "theoretical reasons," the latter, what she calls "deliberative reasons." To trust someone is an authority is to say: this person "can help me to believe as I would believe myself, given my desires, emotions, and other beliefs, and given that I aim to have a belief that will ultimately survive my own conscientious self-reflection" (111).

With this distinction among reasons in hand, her first line of argument says that believing a person because I believe she is better placed than I am is a different kind of reason than believing that p on the basis of evidence.[11] Trusting a person is an evaluation of someone's relative epistemic competence with respect to evidence in a domain and, therefore, has implications for how strongly I should trust myself to evaluate the evidence for any claim in that domain. Allowing someone's superior abilities to preempt my own judgment makes sense if I judge them more competent to make such judgments. Call this the "argument from conscientious self-reflection."

Her second line of reasoning is the "track-record argument." Consider Raz's financial advisor again. If the advisor is 20 percent better than I am at making stock decisions, then if I defer to him 100 percent of the time, I will be 20 percent better over time. Epistemic values suggest trusting the expert over myself every time. Zagzebski cites a study by Mlodinow (2008) that makes the same point. When animals discern that one choice is better a majority of the time, they choose that option every time. Thus, they choose the better choice most of the time; they are outcome-maximizers. Humans, on the other hand, are probability-matchers. If a choice is better about 75 percent of the time, humans will choose that option about 75 percent of the time, making it very likely that they will almost always choose the better option less than 75 percent of the time (2012: 115). Thus, in deferring to an expert, one is more likely to form a responsible belief than if they were to evaluate the reasons for that belief themselves.

With these two lines of argument in place, she formulates two versions of what she calls the "Justification Thesis for the Authority of Belief" (110–11):

Justification Thesis 1 for the Authority of Belief (JAB 1)
The authority of another person's belief for me is justified by my conscientious judgment that I am more likely to form a true belief and avoid a false belief if I believe what the authority believes than if I try to figure out what to believe myself.

Justification Thesis 2 for the Authority of Belief (JAB 2)
The authority of another person's belief for me is justified by my conscientious judgment that I am more likely to form a belief that survives my conscientious self-reflection if I believe what the authority believes than if I try to figure out what to believe myself.

JAB 1 is grounded in the track-record argument, and JAB 2 is grounded in the argument from conscientious self-reflection. The conclusion of these arguments is that novices have an epistemic obligation to defer to expert authorities' TAP.

We might think this view presupposes that coming to recognize someone as an authority is a onetime thing that cannot be revisited: I judge that someone is an expert in domain X and then start preempting all my judgments about X in deference to the authority. But it would be hasty. Zagzebski's view allows that one can stop regarding someone as an authority if, say, their claims conflict with "anything that you find trustworthy when you are conscientious," such as a doctor advising you to take 4,000 pills an hour for the rest of your life (116). Further, "If I conscientiously judge that a belief [that an authority] has in the relevant domain clearly does not survive present self-reflection and is not likely to do so in the foreseeable future, I must decide whether to change my judgment that [they are] an authority" (117). This adds a bit of nuance to the content-independence thesis. The idea seems to be that some content is more firmly set in our conscientious reflection than our beliefs about experts' reliability. Of course, determining precisely when to allow this content to influence our trust in experts is tricky, as we will see in Section 6.3.

6.3 Objections to the Doxastic Control Account

While Zagzebski's account is likely the most well-developed account of epistemic authority in the literature, there are, unfortunately, at least six problems with the doxastic control view. The first is that it has trouble with the commonsense notion that expert authority can help one accumulate degrees of confirmation for a belief. Recall from Chapter 3 that Kant rejects the idea that we can do all necessary epistemic work for ourselves: "the logical egoist considers it unnecessary to test his judgment by the reason of others, as if he had no need of such a touchstone" (*Anthropology* [1785] 2006: 17). What does "testing" our judgment by the "reason of others" look like? For Zagzebski, when the others are experts, it means suspending all our other reasons and relying solely on the expert's TAP.

But Katherine Dormandy (2017) shows that this is inconsistent with how epistemologists treat evidence generally. She asks us to imagine cases where a novice "has done some independent research into the domain and so knows a little about it, but is by no means an expert; and the domain is not totally unfathomable for non-experts" (779). Dormandy calls these "informed-amateur cases."

Let:

p = a proposition in domain D
r = a reason to believe that p
a = the belief that an expert in D believes that p

When an expert speaks in a domain, the novice could be in one of two epistemic circumstances.

$e1$ The novice has a and no other reason relevant to whether p.
$e2$ The novice has a as well as r. (adapted from Dormandy 2018: 779)

Zagzebski's account of epistemic authority, while not excluding the possibility of $e2$ (because novices get to keep their reasons), nevertheless, regards the novice in $e2$ as no better off epistemically than the novice in $e1$. This is because, given a, r adds no normative force to whether p; the novice should screen off the force of r in favor of a.

In contrast, Dormandy argues that the novice in $e2$ is in a better epistemic position with respect to p than the novice in $e1$:

> First, because p is true—so we should expect the state of affairs that it denotes to leave traces of itself in other places than just the minds of epistemic authorities. . . . Second, informed amateurs have done some research and so can be expected to turn up reasons that they can understand . . . . Third, . . . the domain is not unfathomable to [informed amateurs]. (780)

Dormandy's point is that, as long we don't assume that novices can understand nothing about a domain and have done a little homework, surely expert testimony that p confirms (rather than replaces) the evidence the novice already has that p.

Strictly speaking, it is important that the novice's evidence is independent of the expert's. If the expert learned that p from her mentor and the novice read that p in that mentor's book, it is not necessarily true that combining a and r would increase the novice's justification that p. However, if after learning that p, the expert comes to find p compelling for additional reasons related to her work in her domain, then it is plausible that the combination of a and r increases the novice's justification that p.

The notion of "informed amateur" is an important contribution to the expertise literature. Many scholars treat experts and novices as if they occupied the opposite ends of a long continuum, such that novices couldn't possibly understand what experts are doing. Dormandy's argument, and the discussion around Figures 5.2 and 5.3 from Chapter 5, show that this doesn't reflect our actual epistemic situation. In Chapters 7 and 8, we will see how acknowledging the range of epistemic placement of both novices and experts can help us overcome what is known as the "recognition problem" for expertise.

Dormandy attempts to fix this problem with Zagzebski's account by replacing what she calls Zagzebski's "total preemption" account with what she calls the "proper-basing view":

> **Proper-Basing Belief on Authority:** Believing that p on authority amounts to basing this belief on the authoritative reason and any other reasons you may have, where (i) pro-reasons exert a force for p and (ii*) *contra-reasons do not exert any force against p*. (784, italics hers)

Pro-reasons are reasons believe that p is true, and contra-reasons are reasons to believe not-p. Dormandy formulates (ii*) in order to preserve what she takes to be right about Zagzebski's argument, namely, the track-record argument. "out of a range of (hypothetical) cases in which an [novice] discovers what an authority believes, total preempting produces a *higher proportion of true beliefs* than basing his belief on other reasons too" (782–3). Dormandy calls this virtue of the preempting reasons strategy "proportional truth-conduciveness."

Interestingly, in acknowledging the possibility of the informed amateur, Dormandy raises concerns for the proportional truth-conduciveness of expertise under some circumstances. There are at least five reasons to be skeptical of the doxastic control view even after Dormandy's repair efforts:

(1) Different kinds of expertise have different epistemic strengths.
(2) Expert TAP can conflict with a novice's thin epistemic advantage.
(3) Expert domains overlap with expertise in domains of value.
(4) Expertise overlaps with other domains of expertise.
(5) Truth-conduciveness is not always relevant to expert competence.

6.3.1 Different Kinds of Expertise Have Different Epistemic Strengths

The first problem with the doxastic control account is that it presupposes expert TAP exhibits the same epistemic weight across domains of expertise. By relying on analogies from politics and formal agreements, Raz and Zagzebski conflate the administrative right of some authorities to command and dictate with epistemic justification for that role. I am justified only in either deferring to the arbiter's judgment or not. A soldier is justified only in either deferring to her commanding officer or not. In most cases, however, when presented with a statement by someone I regard as an expert, I have a much wider range of justifiable options with respect to how strongly I defer.

If I regard my doctor as an authority, and she tells me I have a nasty kind of cancer, should I allow her judgment to screen off all the things I happen to know about medicine, medical reasoning, medical research, and clinical judgment, even though I am not an expert in medicine? Imagine that I believe that no test is 100 percent reliable, that many doctors are statistically illiterate (cf. Wegwarth and Gigerenzer 2011), that medical error is prevalent (cf. Anderson and Abrahamson 2017), and that clinical judgment is subject to the same heuristics and biases that affect everyone else (cf. Saposnik et al., 2016). I presume I should not reason thusly: "Well, my doctor, being an authority in medicine, also knows all this, but has, nevertheless, formed the judgment that I have cancer. And while I have expertise in critical reasoning strategies, I am no expert in medicine. Therefore, I should screen off any reasons I have for doubting my doctor." Even under these conditions, given the vast uncertainty in medicine and the seriousness of the stakes for my well-being, I would certainly not be violating an epistemic norm by getting a second opinion, or a third. The point here is that my perception of my and my doctors' relative epistemic placement matters to whether I defer strongly or weakly to my doctor.

6.3.2 Expert TAP Can Conflict with a Novice's Thin Epistemic Advantage

A second additional problem with the doxastic control account is that it doesn't take into account the ways that expertise overlaps with domains where novices have relevant competence, even if that competence only establishes a thin epistemic advantage (as discussed in Chapter 5). Someone may be an authority in a domain, and yet be much better at *explaining* claims in that domain than *predicting* events in the world based on those explanations or advising others what to do. So, I could justifiably regard an expert as an authority in domain X and justifiably defer to their judgments about the ideas in X but also justifiably not defer to their judgments about whether those ideas are relevant for my belief or behavior.

As an example, consider that in the UK in the 1980s, farm workers raised concerns about the safety of herbicide 2,4,5-T no less than eight times to the

Advisory Committee on Pesticides (ACP) (Irwin 1995). Each time, they were assured that it was safe when used as directed. Unfortunately, the workers had a perspective on the domain that the ACP did not. "[O]nly they could say that it was impossible not to violate the precautions in use and that the herbicide was not safe in the way the scientists said it was" (Collins 2014: 40). The farmers could accept expert testimony that 2,4,5-T is safe when used correctly but still reject the use of 2,4,5-T because they had good reason to believe it could not be used "correctly." Their localized experience on the use of the herbicide put them in a better epistemic position to assess the expert's advice than the regulators who evaluated the product from a laboratory perspective. Their epistemic advantage might reasonably be called "thin," but it is nevertheless an authoritative advantage that undermines condition (ii*) in Dormandy's proper-basing view.

There are other cases where thin epistemic advantage is easier to recognize, namely, in cases experts testify to things that strike novices as patently false. This presents a challenge for Zagzebski's view because she explains that, when choosing among multiple authorities, I am to decide which authorities' judgments would more likely survive my conscientious self-reflection. Presumably, some of them would *more* likely survive than others, but how could I assess this if I couldn't already evaluate the reasons they employ in forming their judgments, or at least the reasons they give me as a novice for choosing one over the other? I have to engage in what she calls a deliberative process not just about their authority, but about how they arrive at their judgments and the judgments at which they arrive. We saw this in the case of the doctor who prescribes 4,000 pills an hour. The challenge comes with a question: How outrageous must a belief be before I reject the authority?

Jennifer Lackey (2018a) argues that Zagzebski's account "fails to provide the resources for rationally rejecting an authority's testimony when what is offered is obviously false or otherwise outrageous" (234, italics removed). Expert authorities are not only fallible; they sometimes say patently false things. Lackey gives the example of a pastor who may be highly regarded as a moral expert in a novice's community but who nevertheless makes a claim that women are morally inferior to men. If the novice is screening off other reasons, they should accept the pastor's testimony without question. Yet, even if the novice weren't a moral expert; they would likely have substantial reasons to challenge the claim.

The pastor's claim is outlandish for most of us, and so we might think that Zagzebski has it covered. But what if you were raised in an environment where that kind of claim is fairly common and regarded as normal? Even if the belief felt slightly icky to you, by what resources of your own could you conclude that you should reject the authority of the minister? This is especially problematic if you think that nothing else the minister says strikes you as icky. As Raz points out, "there is no point in having authorities unless their determinations are binding even if mistaken (though some mistakes may disqualify them)" ([1986] 1990: 126). The problem is that neither Raz nor Zagzebski offers tools for determining when a mistake undermines a putative expert's authority.

A related concern Lackey raises strikes even at the case of a doctor who prescribes 4,000 pills an hour: "[I]t is unclear how the testimony of an authority can even strike one as clearly false or outrageous, given that all of one's other relevant evidence has been normatively screened off" (2018a: 235, italics removed). To be sure, one can *experience* a certain amount of outrage at a claim; Zagzebski's account doesn't make claims on our psychological states. Nevertheless, if you have normative reasons to set aside all other evidence, then you have normative reasons to dismiss your outrage as misplaced or misguided. But if this is right, how strongly should we trust the initial evidence we used to adopt the expert in the first place? As Raz explains, "The whole point and purpose of authorities . . . is to preempt individual judgments on the merits, and this will not be achieved if in order to establish whether the authoritative determination is binding individuals have to rely on their own judgment of the merits" ([1986] 1990: 126). Yet, this is precisely the predicament we are in. In other words, even on Raz and Zagzebski's account, authority is neither preemptive nor content-independent.

6.3.3 Expert Domains Overlap with Expertise in Domains of Value

A third problem for the doxastic control account is raised by Lackey's example of the misogynistic minister: Expert domains are rarely value-free affairs. To the degree that expertise overlaps with our values, novices often have a stronger epistemic standing than is often acknowledged in discussions of expertise.

Consider the case of neonatal medicine. Neonatology is a highly specialized domain of medicine for addressing health issues very early in life, often with premature infants. A number of neonatal diseases—such as trisomy 18 (or Edwards syndrome) and hypoplastic left heart syndrome (HLHS)—are known as severely life-limiting. In other words, infants who have them rarely grow to adulthood. Nevertheless, some treatments are available that can increase the amount of life these infants can live. The treatments have a low success rate, and children in these conditions are sometimes in a lot of discomfort. For years, doctors advised families to choose comfort care only, that is, resist the complicated surgeries that would extend the infants' lives a few years. The idea was that the risk of success was so low and the small benefit of a few months of life was not worth the excruciating discomfort to the infant. Neonatologists and bioethicists across the world still agree that comfort measures are ethically appropriate in these cases. But are they the only ethically appropriate option?

Setting aside the uncertainties of the medicine in these cases, the value of the risks and benefits to the infant and their family are best assessed by the family. The doctors can certainly engage the parents in a values conversation and discuss considerations that may be relevant to the family's decision. But *whether the risks are worth taking* are squarely within the purview of the parents to decide.[12] Doctors who presume to appeal to their medical expertise to advise otherwise overstep the boundaries of their expertise.

Quill R. Kukla (published as Rebecca Kukla 2007) contends that this overlap of domains between doctors and patients extends to all medical encounters. Doctors often use the rhetoric of "routine" to encourage deference from patients when patients have good reasons for challenging their doctor's recommendations: "There is an important difference between describing a procedure as strongly recommended and describing it as routine—the first description invites a conversation about the reasons for the recommendation, whereas the second discourages such conversation" (2007: 31–2, references removed). Other examples where "routine" is used to "shut down" conversations include conversations about "'good motherhood' (abstaining completely from alcohol during pregnancy, giving birth in a hospital, avoiding all infant formula in the first few months, 'electing' for a scheduled cesarean birth after a previous cesarean, etc.)" (2007: 31, fn 23). Kukla says that many pregnant women and new mothers in these conversations "do not feel entitled to question their rationality in any serious way" (2007: 31, fn 23). Zagzebski's doxastic control account suggests, contra widespread agreement over the importance of shared decision-making in medical decisions, that patients are not entitled to challenge their doctor's expertise.

6.3.4 Expertise Overlaps with Other Domains of Expertise

A fourth problem is that the doxastic control view presupposes that traditional expert domains, even exempting the domain of values, are cleanly dividable affairs. If someone is an expert in a domain in which a novice has no or little-to-no competence, such as interventional radiology or anesthesiology, perhaps acknowledging that someone is an authority in those domains normatively requires the novice to screen off any of their current reasons relevant to the claims of experts in those domains. Importantly, however, many domains are not like this. Geology overlaps with physics and mathematics. Toxicology overlaps with biochemistry and public health. Real estate overlaps with mortgage brokerage, and many others. A real estate expert, while not an expert in mortgage brokerage, often understands enough about mortgages to recognize when a mortgage broker says something intended to mislead home buyers. The real estate agent does not owe the mortgage broker the same degree of deference that most home buyers do. So, when an expert speaks, the degree of deference normatively required of their authority will be proportionate to how well their audience is placed within the domain most relevant to that claim.

Philosopher Scott Brewer (1998) explains that epistemic authority is "a matter of degree" and not "an all-or-nothing relationship":

> [W]hen B treats A as an epistemic authority, B's deference extends only so far as B recognizes A to be speaking within the subject area of A's expertise. Thus, even in paradigmatic cases of epistemic deference, the nonexpert must police the epistemic boundaries between assertions by A that are within what B recognizes to be the zone of A's expertise and assertions by A that are not within that zone. These borderlines will inevitably be fuzzy. For example, where exactly does the epistemic authority of a physicist end when he is testifying to the nonexpert about the advisability of nuclear energy? Not exactly anywhere. Even if such an expert is testifying as an "instrumentally rational" expert, one who is using his expert knowledge to advise the nonexpert about how best to achieve goals the nonexpert has chosen, the nonexpert must be ever vigilant to keep the expert within his proper epistemic domain. The price of rational deference is eternal vigilance. (1586–7)

Vigilance is in constant tension with the "peremptory and content-independent reason for believing what [an authority] says" (1586), to the point that we should be asking what the norms of preemptiveness and content-independence amount to.

6.3.5 Truth-Conduciveness Is Not Always Relevant to Expert Competence

The fifth, and perhaps most serious, objection to the doxastic control view is that it presupposes, for all domains of expertise, that there is a distinctly "true" belief in that domain that an expert can understand and to which they can testify. Not all domains of expertise engage with truths in this way. Palliative care doctors, therapists, consultants, artists, and attorneys can be helpful—and expertly so—in ways that are functions of their epistemic placement in a domain but that are not a matter of truth-tracking. Recall from Chapter 1, palliative care physician Michael Pottash notes that his role is not to bring a truth from his domain of expertise but rather to "ask the question of every test, intervention, or medication: Does this promote quality of life? Some life-prolonging interventions can be continued without impacting quality, if the patient so chooses. This will all depend on the patient's preferences and the clinical context" (Pottash 2019). Some outcomes will be better, some worse; none will fit a predetermined indicator of competence. What counts as "best" or "good enough" emerges through a certain kind of encounter with an expert. While trust is necessary for this practice to go well, deference to expert authority is neither implied nor epistemically required.

As one last example, consider the ways that seeking expertise can be a tool for coming to understand something yourself rather than for forming true beliefs. For example, I may seek an expert's advice on how to join wood for a woodworking project. While I may try to use their advice, I may find that it doesn't quite work for me, whether because my hands are too small or not strong enough, or I don't have the right tools. Nevertheless, on the basis of the expert's advice, or maybe through some casual discussion with the expert, I might figure out a way to accomplish the task myself. This is analogous to discussions in bioethics of how dependence on others, including medical providers, can "empower" a patient's autonomy without undermining it.[13] The point is that the track-record argument does not sufficiently support preemptiveness or content-independence as necessary conditions for authority because neither is necessary for authorities to put us in better positions than we otherwise might be.

Given all these objections, why keep preemptiveness and content-independence as necessary conditions for authority? One additional reason I find is Raz's contention that this sort of strong deference is the only way to make sense of authority's *bindingness* on non-authorities. But why would we think "binding" authority is called for in epistemic matters? In politics, such binding is supposed to ensure social order (though, see Michael Huemer 2012). What order are we trying to preserve in our doxastic systems? What order *could* we preserve by establishing a norm of strong deference to anyone we regard as authoritative? To be sure, in low-stakes environments and when there seems nothing epistemically problematic about doing so, we are typically happy to defer judgment and well justified in doing so. It is efficient, and, in some cases, it is intellectually virtuous. But to argue that expert authority normatively requires such deference ignores the many high-stakes environments where the domains overlap, degrees of expertise and epistemic weight vary, and disagreement and error are common.

Ultimately, what is likely behind Raz and Zagzebski's commitment to the strong conception of authority is the assumption that novices stand in such an impoverished position relative to experts that there is no good epistemic reason to believe they could adequately assess an expert's competence. If you know A is an expert in Y and that you are not, and you cannot assess the merits of any claim about Y, then you have a rather strong reason to trust A regarding Y. There certainly are cases where novices understand so little about a domain that deference is epistemically justifiable. We will take a closer look at the problems associated with these cases in Chapters 7 and 8. But to restrict an account of epistemic authority to this narrow set of cases overlooks the rich variety of epistemic relationships between experts and novices and among experts. If thin epistemic advantages are possible, if experts can confirm and disconfirm one another's work, if a novices in one domain can contribute authoritatively to collaborative projects in other, overlapping domains (such as building skyscrapers and space shuttles), then we need a richer account of authority than the doxastic control account offers.

6.4 Giving Up Control: Authority as Weak Deference

Where, then, does this leave us? So far, we have seen that three prominent accounts of authority—the physical control account, the ontological control account, and the doxastic control account—fail to fully capture the normative implications of expertise. Happily, there is yet one more option.

Imagine I call an HVAC (heating, ventilation, and air-conditioning) service to get information on how to care for my home's heating and cooling system. Imagine also that they tell me that, to avoid damaging my system, I should change my filter every month and only use a certain kind of filter. To be sure, I have the authority (in the administrative sense) to make decisions about my house, regardless of what an HVAC person tells me I should do. But set that aside. Whether it is epistemically responsible for me to follow their advice depends on a number of epistemic considerations, including, for example, whether I have good reasons to believe the "filter-changing mantra" is a racket for which even many HVAC experts lack solid data.

Why might I think that HVAC experts lack solid data? I take HVAC service people to be extremely competent at inspecting, maintaining, and repairing HVAC systems. I believe, however, that their expertise ends there and does not extend to domains of research. I suspect that their information on these matters comes from manufacturers of HVAC systems, who may be biased in favor of selling more filters. I also suspect that their domain, like many service domains, thrives on opacity.

In some domains, restricting the amount of information about a domain protects at least the veneer of expertise. There may be expertise, but without data, it is hard to tell. One example of this is the science of making copper stills for distilling Scotch whisky. On a trip to Islay, a tour guide at one distillery explained how it is local lore that the different shapes of the stills make a significant difference in the taste of different scotches. This means that the coppersmiths who repair the stills work in strict confidence not to share the distinct features of the stills with other distilleries. But he also explained that any attempts to study this claim are rebuffed because learning whether it is true will hurt each distillery's distinct niche in the market. If it turns out that the still shape does not affect flavor, then part of the mystique of distilling and coppersmithing is undermined. If it turns out that still shape does affect flavor, then others could engage in trial and error and reproduce the flavor of proprietary brands elsewhere and much more cheaply. Historian Andrew Jefford confirms the practice of avoiding research, if not the motivation: "Scotch whisky distillers have been reprehensibly incurious about their craft; they have, historically, resisted research and experiment.... In a frustrating minority of cases, the answers are known, but the residual culture of Scotch whisky secrecy has kept them locked away in company filing cabinets or computers" (2004: 7).

This problem is analogous to doctors who do not keep up with the latest research in their domain. I know of one doctor who says that we should (without the public's consent) put baby aspirin, multivitamins, and statins in the water like we do fluoride to prevent many common chronic illnesses. Yet, while the evidence on statins still seems relatively strong, there is much controversy over whether multivitamins and baby aspirin actually have health benefits. We can imagine the horrors that might ensue if novice politicians took this doctor as an authority in Zagzebski's sense.

The HVAC service person does, however, in virtue of my recognition of their expertise and the fact that I have sought their opinion, have the authority to advise me about when it is appropriate to change the filter. (Note that they do not have this authority when I don't seek their opinion—they don't have the epistemic right to go door-to-door, explaining to people that they need to change their filters. This may help explain our frustration with people who show up at our doors unannounced, such as salespeople, evangelists, and political activists.) But if this is right, what sort of authority is it to be competent to advise me on how to care for my HVAC unit?

In contrast to control accounts, Jennifer Lackey (2018a) offers a weaker version of expertise that she calls the "expert-as-advisor" view (238ff). Lackey argues that it is far more plausible to view experts as advisors rather than authorities in Zagzebski's strong sense. Unlike authorities, advisors offer guidance; that is, their TAP counts as evidence for believing something. Lackey says that an expert witness at a trial is a paradigmatic example of an expert-as-advisor:

> No one would tell the jurors that the testimony of a given expert is authoritative or provides preemptive reasons for belief. Indeed, jurors themselves would be superfluous in many ways if experts functioned authoritatively. Instead, competing expert testimony is often presented from both sides—the prosecution and the defense—with jurors needing to evaluate the full body of evidence in reaching a verdict. The experts here are, then, advising the jurors rather than dictating to them what they ought to believe. (Lackey 2018a: 239)

Lackey wants to replace the word "authority" with the word "advisor." I worry that this is misleading. Anyone can advise anyone else, from friends to ministers to the annoying guy from the office down the hall. Epistemically, we can take or leave such advice. But experts stand in a distinct epistemic position to advise. Their advice comes—I am presuming based on my definition of expertise—with extra epistemic weight. Thus, I will call what Lackey describes a type of epistemic authority, but I will categorize it as "weak deference," or what I will call the "normative presumption," account of epistemic authority:

> **Epistemic authority (normative presumption): A subject S has epistemic authority over subject A in a domain D just in case S is sufficiently epistemically placed in D that S's testimony, advice, or performance in D constitutes *prima facie* justification for that testimony, advice, or performance to the degree that A is justified in believing that S has an epistemic advantage over them in D.**

The idea is that, once I have sufficient reason to believe that someone is well placed in a domain, whether thickly or thinly, I stand under a normative presumption that they are prima facie trustworthy in that domain, in other words, I have a prima facie reason to trust their TAP. If R is justified in regarding S as an expert in D, then R regards her as one of the people in D who, as Collins and Evans put it, "know what they are talking about" (2007: 2). This is different from mere trust that p because S stands in a contingently better epistemic place than R (as with normal instances of trustworthy testimony). It is, rather, that R has reasons to believe that S has a thick epistemic advantage over her with respect to domain D.

How strong is this prima facie justification? That will depend on a number of factors about the domain, S's placement in it, how they hold that placement, and what we are trusting S for. For many claims, a person's testimony will be authoritative because they have a thin epistemic advantage over us. They were at a concert we couldn't attend. They are taller than we are, so they can see what's on the top shelf and we cannot. They can tell us whether they are in pain or in love.

Other claims will derive their authority from thick epistemic placement. Claims by mathematicians or engineers, for example, have a stronger claim to epistemic authority than some other types of experts, such as financial advising and weather forecasting. Further, S may be well enough placed in a domain to qualify as an expert but may not be as qualified as many others in that domain (compare resident physicians, who lack experience and medical license, to attending physicians, who have both). Whether we trust S may depend on whether they are simply giving information about their domain or giving us advice for how to apply information from their domain to our lives. Whether their advice is trustworthy will depend on how well they understand our interests and how well we can follow it (see Section 8.3 for more on the normative difference between testimony and advice).

In the case of the HVAC person and my conspiratorial concerns about filter changing, I should recognize that my suspicions are largely *mere* suspicions, unfounded in actual evidence. Further, filters are relatively inexpensive, the HVAC company doesn't directly benefit from my buying filters, and the costs of fixing an HVAC system are sufficiently high that I would be remiss in my epistemic responsibilities if I didn't accept the expert's filter-changing advice. This is still not, however, the picture of deference implied by expert authority according to Zagzebski.

The key here is that what expertise normatively demands from us is more complicated than Zagzebski describes. Not all expertise is alike, and expert judgments are subject to a number of undermining factors, some of which even novices can navigate.

That justification is not so strong as to constitute a prima facie justification for deferring to the expert's TAP—at least not in a strong sense, suspending all reasons relative to the issue under consideration. Having a prima facie *reason to defer* to an expert's judgment depends on a host of additional epistemic conditions not directly related to the expert's epistemic position in a domain. As demonstrated in the examples earlier, expert authority does not constitute a prima facie justification to accept that

- the expert's TAP *represents the current state of the domain* as opposed to an idiosyncratic position,
- the expert is *trustworthy*,
- the expert has an *interest* in helping the novice achieve their epistemic goals, or
- the expert has (absent extensive conversation) sufficient understanding of novices' goals, interests, or values that their TAP is sufficiently likely to be helpful.

At best, then, recognizing that someone is an expert in a domain constitutes a prima facie justification for accepting the expert's TAP in their domain, where *actual* or *full* justification depends on the expert's meeting additional criteria.

The key here is that what expertise normatively demands from novices is more complicated than how Zagzebski characterizes it. Not all expertise is alike, and expert judgments are subject to a number of compromising factors, some of which even novices can recognize. Thus, rather than having a right to be believed, experts are, under certain circumstances, justifiably believed without additional evidence.

With these considerations in place, the argument for the normative presumption account is straightforward:

(1) **Thick epistemic placement in a domain constitutes a prima facie reason to trust TAP based on that placement.**
(2) **Experts are thickly placed in a domain.**
(3) **Whether experts' placement in a domain is sufficient for justifying their TAP in that domain for novices depends on epistemic factors outside of epistemic placement.**
(4) **Therefore, novices are not fully justified in accepting the expert's TAP in a domain based solely on the expert's thick epistemic placement in that domain.**

Thus, the *normative presumption* account completes our taxonomy of authority (Figure 6.4):

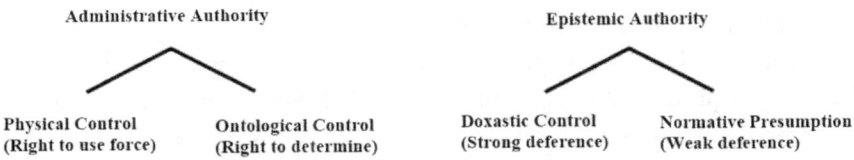

Figure 6.4 Accounts of authority: Normative presumption.

This weaker, presumptive, advisory view of epistemic authority takes seriously the idea that authorities are well placed in a domain and that they have a prima facie thick epistemic advantage over anyone who is not as well placed. But it also accommodates concerns about the fallibility of experts and evidence that they sometimes make audaciously false claims. Further, it takes seriously the fact that experts disagree over claims in their own domains, even domains as highly revered as medicine and physics. And finally, it takes seriously the idea that the relevance of expertise to solving a problem or giving advice is often contingent on a number of contextual and decisional factors, some of which might not be available to the expert.

Most importantly, this account accommodates the many non-truth-functional roles of expert authorities. Lackey gives an example of a clinical ethics consultant in a hospital:

> An ethics consultant serving at a hospital will be effective largely by helping doctors, patients, and their families navigate through difficult medical decisions. Sure, her reliably offering true testimony is important, but equally important are her abilities to clearly explain the terrain, to listen attentively and receptively to the concerns and values of those around her, and to answer questions in a thoughtful and constructive way. (Lackey 2018a: 239)

Similar non-truth-functional competence can be found across expert domains, including medicine, therapy, fitness coaching, writing, and music. Consider the difference between playing a piece of music as it is written and playing with "with feeling." It is hard to explain this "feeling" or "groove" aspect of music. You just have to *feel* it. But an expert music teacher can devise exercises that help students achieve that competence faster than they could on their own. The student still has to "find" the groove on their own, but expert advice can help bootstrap them into finding it.

Note that what distinguishes expert epistemic authority from nonexpert epistemic authority (e.g., in the case of thin epistemic advantage) is not the concept of authority but epistemic placement. Someone can meet the conditions for having epistemic authority regardless of whether they are an expert. But what their authority implies for others will depend on their epistemic placement, how they acquired that placement, and the relative position of others who are considering the authority's TAP.

6.5 Objections to the Weak Deference Account

The normative presumption account does imply that expert authority is, contra Raz and Zagzebski, simply one type of evidence among others. Raz calls this kind of weak deference "profoundly misguided" because it "assumes that people are never bound by authority regarding issues on which they have firm views" ([1986] 1990: 120), and that it "defeats the very point and purpose" (122) of seeking an authority in the first place. But while this may be true in political or institutional contexts, that is, in cases where administrative authority is needed, it is not obviously true in epistemic contexts, for the reasons highlighted earlier. As we also saw earlier, Raz's account allows no exceptions for even systematic mistakes on the part of authorities.

Zagzebski rejects the idea that expert authority functions as independent evidence because she argues that this is not how testimony works: "The testifier does not intend to offer evidence to the hearer, and the hearer does not take it to be evidence. Being invited to trust is not being offered evidence, and accepting it is not taking the testimony as evidence" (2012: 129). To this, I can only reply that I see no evidence that this is true. People regularly ask for deference on the basis of their expertise. They present their credentials and experience and training as evidence that they are well placed in a domain. Their reputation as "leading" or "widely published" or "distinguished" is supposed to count in favor of their ability to judge well all the evidence and formulate a judgment that they offer as authoritative.

Thus, rather than being a defect of the view, rejecting content-independence and accepting that expert authority constitutes a distinct type of evidence to be included among others is a liberating virtue of the normative presumption account. It gives us far more opportunities for forming and enhancing our beliefs and behaviors as we engage with experts in a variety of domains and contexts. As Lackey puts it: "We can evaluate the arguments proffered on behalf of a particular view, we can assess how able the expert in question is at enhancing our understanding of the matter, we can determine how effective the expert is at being an advisor, and so on" (2018a: 239).

6.6 Summing Up: On Good Authority

In Chapter 5, we saw that being well placed in a domain constitutes a type of authority in a domain. In this chapter, we looked at four accounts of what expert authority might entail, dividing them into "control" accounts (physical, ontological, and epistemic) and "normative presumption" accounts. In opposition to control-based accounts of authority, I took insights from Jennifer Lackey's critique of Linda Zagzebski and argued that expert authority entails a weak obligation to respect experts' claims and advice in their domain. This means there are conditions under which novices can challenge, and even reject, expert TAP. However, recognizing just when those conditions are present is tricky. One of the most persistent and challenging problems in the history of expertise studies how to identify genuine experts from people who are merely competent, from charlatans, and from people who have been illegitimately identified as experts. This is the *recognition problem* for expertise, and the final two chapters are devoted to it and its implications for knowing when and how much to trust someone who claims to be an expert.

7

The Easy Recognition Problem for Expertise

Here again arises a very difficult question. For in what way shall we fools be able to find a wise [person].... For by no signs whatever can one recognize any thing, unless [they] shall have known that thing, whereof these are signs. But the fool is ignorant of wisdom.

(Aurelius Augustine, "On the Profit of Believing," §28, trans. C. L. Cornish, 1887)

We seek out experts because they have authority in their domains, whether that authority entails some *control* over our beliefs and behavior or some weaker *normative presumption* over them. Ideally, experts can put us in a better epistemic position (whether gnostic or technical) than we could otherwise be on our own. But in order for them to do this, we have to know who they are; that is, we must be able to distinguish experts from those who are not thickly well placed in a domain.

Presumably, most novices cannot make sense of the arguments or evidence in highly specialized domains, such as quantum electrodynamics or the neurology of movement disorders. Experts in one domain often lack access to the evidence and arguments in other domains. If this is right, then it seems to make sense to conclude that those of us who aren't experts in a putative expert's domain are in no position to assess that person's claims in their domain. We think we can distinguish good guitar players from mediocre ones even if we don't play the guitar, but the reality is that many of the people novices would call *good* are merely *mediocre* by expert standards. Interestingly, we only think we can judge guitarists when we are familiar with the songs or style of music. If the musical piece were non-Western or avant-garde, we would likely not be equipped to judge whether the performance was good or bad (see Collins and Evans 2007: 56). Further, many domains aren't like guitar playing. Many novices wouldn't know where to begin in evaluating a statistician, topologist, aeronautics engineer, actuary, interventional radiologist, climatologist, and so on.

This puts novices in what seems like a classic Catch-22: Novices need experts because experts stand in a better epistemic position than novices; but because novices are less well placed in a domain, they cannot accurately assess whether someone stands in a better place. They would need to be experts in that domain in order to recognize experts in that domain.[1] And if they were to become experts, they would no longer be novices. This is the "recognition problem" for expertise, sometimes called the "novice/expert problem" (Goldman 2001) or the "credentials problem" (Cholbi 2007; Nguyen 2018b).

In this chapter, I start with an exploration of what we mean by a *domain* of expertise (Section 7.1). If experts are authoritative in their domains, and novices and other experts look for experts in specific domains, it is helpful to understand what sort of thing they are looking for. In Section 7.2, I introduce an "easy" version of the recognition problem, which is the problem of accurately identifying experts in a domain. The problem is actually not all that easy to solve because, as domains become increasingly esoteric, both novices and experts face numerous obstacles to picking out experts. Nevertheless, I call it the *easy* recognition problem because I think it can be solved for some types of relatively easily identifiable expertise in some recognizable circumstances. In Sections 7.3–7.6, I explain the conceptual problems we face when trying to identify experts and some of the tools we might use to solve them. In Section 7.7, I close by summarizing the strategy for solving the easy recognition problem and give a nod other versions of the problem that I will explore in Chapter 8.

7.1 What Is a Domain of Expertise? The Boundaries of Expert Authority

Following ancient tradition, I have assumed throughout the book that experts have mastery over a certain area of practice or body of information. Empirical research on expertise has shown us that practice in a domain is highly domain-specific. Katie Ledecky, for example, is an expert competitive swimmer. She likely could not lend much insight or advice about water ballet. Similarly, Jocelyn Bell Burnell is an expert astrophysicist. She likely could not lend much insight into evolutionary biology except in the sort of broad strokes way one might find in an undergraduate textbook. Ledecky and Burnell are examples of how expertise extends to certain boundaries and then stops. These boundaries are aided, to a large extent, by specializations that have emerged in competition, research projects, and academic curricula. Someone studies physics to become a physicist rather than a swimmer.

But as we have also seen, not all types of expertise have clear boundaries. Does an expert video game programmer also have the expertise to program self-driving cars? Could an expert commercial electrician speak authoritatively about a residential electrical problem? I will show that the account of expertise developed throughout this book provides some tools for answering these questions. But before we get there, we need a sense of the difficulties with how domains are related, and, more importantly, how *expert* domains are related.

7.1.1 The Generality Problem for Domains of Expertise

Consider Plato's dialogue *Ion*. Ion is a rhapsode, someone who recites poetry for a living and can explain it to listeners. Ion claims that he is an expert in reciting Homer's poetry but in no other great poet's, and he knows many things about Homer but nothing about other poets. Yet he also claims that he chose to focus on Homer because he knows that Homer far outstrips the other classic poets in beauty and skill. Socrates finds this strange because people who have the mastery (*techne*) to judge which art is best from one artist—whether the artist is a painter, sculptor, musician, or poet—can usually do the same for other artists, as well (533a–c). But if Ion is an expert only on Homer, how can he, with any degree of authority, say that Homer is the best? Ion's competence seems too narrow to be expertise.

Yet, how much would Ion have to know about other poets in order for Ion to be reasonably considered an expert? Today, it doesn't seem odd to call someone an expert in "biology" even if they study only one phenotype of one species in one geographic location. They may know very little about Darwin's finches or Margaret Fountaine's butterflies, but it would be strange to say their expertise is too narrow to call them expert biologists. It also doesn't seem odd to call someone an "expert on Jane Austen" or for them to state in books or articles that Jane Austen was the greatest of the Georgian-society novelists, even if they don't study other Georgian-society novelists. Is Socrates wrong, then, to deny that Ion is an expert in Homer's poetry?

Oliver Scholz (2018) calls this tension between narrow specialization and broad disciplinary categories the "*generality problem for characterizing the domain of expertise*" (32, italics his). He explains: "Often [a domain] is characterized by referring to a whole scientific discipline, e.g., physics, chemistry, biology, psychology, history and so on; but, at least in our days, no one can be a full expert in one of these colossal disciplines" (32). For poetry or rhapsody to be a domain of expertise, we tend to presume unreflectively, one must have expertise in poetry generally or in poets generally. But even Socrates admits that poets rarely know much about poetry generally. They are "not able to make poetry until [they] become[] inspired and go[] out of [their] mind and [their] intellect is no longer in [them]" (534b). And "one can do dithyrambs, another encomia, one can do dance songs, another, epics, and yet another, iambics" (534c). The generality problem emerges: Either one refers to expertise in a broad field, in which case, no one is likely to be an expert, or one refers to expertise in individual activities, which seems merely the ability to do something and not expertise at all. Any combination that includes more than one activity but stops short of a broad field is arbitrary.

Ion agrees with the problem as Socrates formulates it but then asks how Socrates makes sense of that. Socrates responds that this shows that Ion is not an expert (*technein*) rhapsode—someone who acquired the skill through "knowledge [*techne*] or mastery [*episteme*]" (532c, Woodruff translation)—but is rather a representative of the gods through divine inspiration.[2] Just as a magnet pulls iron but also imbues it with power to pull other pieces of iron, so the poets, possessed by the gods, draw people to them, like Ion (533d–e). Thus, according to Plato's Socrates, neither poetry nor rhapsody is a domain of expertise because neither meets the minimum criterion, namely, the ability to learn it without (much) divine intervention.

Thus, for Socrates, an expert domain is a body of knowledge that can be learned (Allen 1994; Bartz 2000), and bodies of knowledge are bounded by the tasks they allow one to do: "[T]he things navigation teaches us—we won't learn them from medicine . . . [T]he things medicine teaches us we won't learn from architecture" (*Ion*, 537c). So, even if Ion cannot compare Homer to other poets without divine inspiration, perhaps he could still study and become an expert on Homer's style and content. Call the idea that a domain of expertise is bounded by the tasks one's training allows one to do the *pragmatic solution* to the generality problem.

Unfortunately, in typical fashion, Socrates calls our attention to a further problem. The pragmatic solution implies that, when a great poet like Homer talks about driving a chariot or fishing, it is not the poet who can tell whether what Homer says is true, but a chariot driver or fisher, since being a poet doesn't allow one to competently drive a chariot or fish. Since Ion can successfully speak about Homer's skill but does not know any of these things, then he did not *learn* about Homer's skill. So, to whatever degree Ion is excellent at extolling the virtues of Homer, it is not a function of expertise. The implication, according to how Socrates draws the distinction between expertise and divine inspiration, is that that even Ion's basic knowledge of Homer must come from divine revelation.

David Coady (2012: 54) makes a similar argument that there are no expert "scientists." Experts in one branch of science can be "quite ignorant of what scientists working in other branches of science do" or "wrongly think that the methods of their branch of science characterize science as a whole." Because no one is an expert in all the relevant subdomains of science, there are no "experts in science." Of course, Socrates thinks that Ion could well be an *excellent* (though not *expert*) rhapsode as long as the gods have seen fit to bestow that excellence on him. Coady, on the other hand, seems to think there is no excellent scientist at all because there is no plausible domain called "science."

A striking implication of the idea that expertise is limited to a single body of knowledge that must be learned, according to Socrates, is that one type of expert cannot make pronouncements about the quality of another type of expertise:

> [T]he same profession must teach the same subjects, and a different profession, if it is different, must teach not the same subjects, but different ones . . . . Then a person who has not mastered a given profession will not be able to be a good judge of the things which belong to that profession, whether they are things said or things done. (538a)

A key premise in this argument is that domains are firmly epistemically sealed off from one another. While we don't typically *act* as if domains are sealed off in this way—as we confidently pronounce on topics like economics, foreign policy, and medical advice, irrespective of our own expertise—this assumption has some intuitive appeal. For example, it helps make sense of concerns about epistemic trespassing, that is, cases where an expert in one domain presumes to speak authoritatively in another domain (see Ballantyne 2019). The primary concern is that experts who trespass mislead nonexperts into thinking they have authority in the trespassed domain, when they may be no more competent than other nonexperts in that domain. Yet, while Ballantyne allows that some cases of trespassing are allowable—through collaborative efforts he calls "easements"—if domains are epistemically sealed off from one another, all cases of epistemic trespassing are problematic.

Hubert Dreyfus (2000) embraces this assumption as a consequence of the embodied nature of expertise. Expert performance is a process that affects the whole body, and experts can rarely explain to novices precisely what they are doing or why when they are performing, yet experts can recognize expertise in one another:

> There is surely a way that two expert surgeons can use language to point out important aspects of a situation to each other during a delicate operation. Such authentic language would presuppose a shared background understanding and only make sense to experts currently involved in a shared situation. (Dreyfus 2000: 308)

As someone acquires increasingly high degrees of expertise, the more embodied their performance is and the less capable they are of explaining themselves to novices.

While these arguments have intuitive force in the abstract, any practical exploration of expertise reveals that Socrates's pragmatic solution to the generality problem falls apart. Melissa Lane (2014) points us to Aristotle to show the implausibility of the idea that domains have hard boundaries, or, as Aristotle puts it, the idea that "just as a doctor should be inspected by doctors, so others should also be inspected by their peers" (*Politics*, Book III, Ch. II, 1282a: 1–3).[3] Aristotle's reply is part of an argument for the claim that democratic processes should include all members of society and not just experts. He begins his case by noting differing "levels of education in most crafts[,] including medicine," or, in other words, that expert competence falls along a continuum. He then points out how practitioners at each level of expertise can, to some degree, "judge . . . even the master crafts[person]" (2014: 103); that is, newly minted experts can recognize the relative merits of masters in their domain.

Recall our distinctions, from Chapter 2: persons of experience, localized, generalized, and specialized expertise. Aristotle draws a similar distinction among three kinds of physicians: "there is the ordinary practitioner, and there is the physician of the higher class, and thirdly the intelligent [person] who has studied the art" (1282a: 3–5). Depending on the domain, an ordinary practitioner could either be a generalized expert or a weak specialized expert. Either way, this is the person who has formal training and can do the normal tasks of an expert but who would not be ranked among the top in their domain. The physician "of the higher class" would be a specialized expert, presumably a strong specialized expert. The intelligent person who has studied the art could either be a person of experience or a localized expert, which might mean a medical student or perhaps a philosopher or sociologist of medicine. Aristotle's aim with these distinctions is to show that physicians along a range of competence in medicine have the competence to judge other physicians, even those who stand in a better epistemic position. If this is right, then it might be that a general practitioner, in virtue of their training, has competence to assess someone who narrowly specializes, such as an anesthesiologist or cardiologist. The general practitioner would, at the very least, have a better idea than a novice of what to look for and how to find it when assessing other specialists.

This example suggests that some domains are "nested" inside of others. For example, endocrinology and hematology are both specialties in the domain of what is called "internal medicine," and therefore, an endocrinologist is better able to assess a hematologist than a patient who has no training in internal medicine. The idea is that, in many cases, an expert in one domain has access to relevant information and evidence regarding another domain in virtue of the relationship between their domains.

These relationships alone are not enough to support Aristotle's conclusion that all citizens should be allowed to participate in democratic processes. At best, they simply expand the kinds of *experts* who should be allowed to participate. But Aristotle goes a step further and says that, in some domains, the user of expertise—even if that user is a novice—is a better judge of expertise than other experts: "A head of household judges a house better than its builder; a captain judges a rudder better than its carpenter; and a guest judges a feast better than its cook" (1282a: 15ff). Lane explains: "As judges, the users are acquainted with the products of the arts and so are able to judge their merits although they lack the *technê* necessary to produce them" (1282a: 19) (2014: 112). Lane thinks that even the "intelligent person" in Aristotle's discussion of doctors includes what we would generally call novices. She says this category "must be more like the involvement of ordinary people, say, in medicating their children at home and so in sharing in medical practice and concerns" (103). Regardless of whether Aristotle had that in mind in the doctor's case, he certainly suggests as much in these later examples. The point is clear: "Aristotle's reply further erodes any sharp boundary between popular and expert knowledge, or what can be more properly considered popular judgment and expert knowledge. They are certainly distinct, but they fall on a continuum, and there will be certain habits of mind shared between them" (Lane 2014: 103).

These examples show that domains are related in more complicated ways than either Socrates or Coady allow. Due to human limitations, a building designer may be able to cultivate only general competence with plumbing, electrical, ventilation, concrete pouring, and so on. But at a certain level of skill, this, competence is reasonably regarded as expertise. That expertise allows building designers to engage with, hire, and critique specialists in plumbing, electrical, and so on. Further, *building designing* constitutes an expert domain in its own right. To the extent that a building designer is successful, they have a high degree of competence in directing specialists in other domains in a way that produces a safe, functional skyscraper. Thus, in addition to nesting domains, there are also *overlapping* domains.

These examples suggest that Socrates and Coady discount the complex ways that information can be organized to accomplish different tasks, and therefore, the way domains are constructed out of information and tasks. They are not epistemically sealed off from one another, and one can be a specialized expert in a domain that encompasses other domains, or at least presupposes a generalized expertise in other domains. Unless we are to believe that food critics and building designers are divinely inspired, Socrates's solution to the generality problem is implausible.

If it is true that domains can be nested and overlap, then it is reasonable to believe that someone in one domain can evaluate the claims of someone in another domain when those claims implicate information in both domains. Thus, even if we accept that an expert domain is a body of information that can be taught, then, so long as we set aside the possibility of divinely inspired competencies, we need not accept the claim that bodies of information have hard boundaries.

Unfortunately, this doesn't solve the generality problem. If anything, recognizing the complex relationships among domains makes the problem harder rather than easier. It doesn't help us determine whether a domain admits of expertise. For example, whiskey-tasting and setting up your new TV both involve bodies of knowledge that can be learned. Yet, can someone be an expert whiskey-taster or TV-setter-upper?

Collins and Evans (2007) reject the idea that simple, learned tasks, such as getting out of bed or flipping a light switch, count as domains of expertise. This is because expertise requires not just the ability to do something but developed skill. "[A]nyone could master [getting out of bed] immediately without practice, so nothing in the way of skill has been gained through the experience" (17). Of course, skill alone will not solve the generality problem, as we still think an oncologist is skilled both in "medicine" and the treatment of cancer.

Psychologists Colin Camerer and Eric Johnson (1991) suggest that some domains are "inherently richer" in some types of indicators than others, that "the presence of feedback and the lack of noise" may be helpful in delineating domains, and that some bodies of knowledge are "more developed" than others (212). But they offer no guidance for how to use these descriptions to distinguish domains or their boundaries.

7.1.2 A Working Solution to the Generality Problem

I think the problem is that extant attempts to solve the generality problem import broad, preconceived notions about which domains count as expert domains, but then they conflate those domains with an overly narrow subset of skills in those domains. For example, we intuitively think "science" is an expert domain but then try define "expert domain" by describing what particular scientific experts, such as biologists and physicists, do. Since a biologist is only one type of scientific expert, we find ourselves at a loss to explain what makes someone an expert in *science*.

In my view, solving the generality problem requires us to understand how various types of expertise are acquired and to recognize how skills and aims overlap or are nested. What we really want to know is whether various skills are structured such that they circumscribe a continuum of competency that allows someone to become an expert and, thereby, constitute an "expert" domain.

Consider the difference between something you can either do or not do, such as turning on a light switch, and something you can do to varying degrees, such as playing tennis. Following Camerer and Johnson (1991: 202), I'll call the maximum competence someone can have in a domain its "performance ceiling." In some cases, such as turning on a light switch, the competence required is low enough that almost anyone can do it, and it doesn't admit of degrees—you either turn on the switch or you don't. The minimal required competence is identical with the performance ceiling. This, then, is not an expert domain. Other tasks require some experience, perhaps even training, to learn, but they still have relatively low-performance ceilings, such as walking, tying your shoes, and manipulating a simple Microsoft Word document on your computer. There is some variation in competence with these tasks, but the performance ceiling is so low that it would be strange to call the ability to do it well "mastery." The target competence is not achieved through cultivation of skill. Tennis is different still, in that it admits of a seemingly endless degree of improvement. To achieve what we might consider expertise, simply getting more and more experience doing it will not help. Achieving mastery requires specialized training.

With this distinction in minds, consider this working definition of an expert domain:

> **Expert domain:** a set of activities for which specialized training (whether formal or informal) improves competence beyond what one can gain by extensive experience alone.

This definition rules out light switch flipping and getting out of bed as expert domains. While the aims of these activities are specifiable, the highest levels of competence in those domains do not require specialized training. The definition rules in astrobiology and chess because those domains do require specialized training. It is worth noting that when I refer to "informal training," this includes self-training and scholarly study, such as teaching yourself computer programming or an ancient language, or studying law so that you can contribute to the philosophy of law.

What about "science" or Homer's poetry? It is reasonable to imagine understanding and skills shared among biologists, physicists, and chemists such that the skills of each may sufficiently establish them as experts in "science," if their expertise extends much further, into subdomains. In fact, expertise in "science" may be circumscribed differently than expertise in "biology" even if there no one with expertise in "science" that isn't also an expert in a narrower subdomain. Every expert in science may necessarily be an expert in more than one domain.

But perhaps I'm shoehorning science into my definition because I am predisposed to believe there are experts in science. To further test the definition, consider whether whiskey-tasting is an expert domain (or "whisky" for my fellow Scotch fans). There are demonstrable differences in competence in whisk(e)y-tasting (some people know the "proper" tasting techniques, and some don't). But these techniques can be picked up with minimal experience: the nose, the body, the finish; sip, don't gulp; try to identify flavors only after your first sip, and so on. There is nothing to suggest expertise in these abilities.

Further, the aim of whisk(e)y-tasting is not clearly specifiable. Is it to taste something specific about the whisk(e)y? In my extensive anecdotal experience (I make no claim to specialized training), I have heard putative whisk(e)y experts from Kentucky to Scotland try to explain what I am "supposed" to taste when I drink whisk(e)y, and the range of options seems limitless: sea salt, cocoa, caramel, brine, cardamom, vanilla, citrus, cherry (in one case "leather," which raises interesting questions), and the list goes on.

Two things are interesting about these experiences. First, the putative expert whisk(e)y-taster almost always says that different people taste different flavors. Some even admit that the process is highly individual because of the way taste evokes memory, as the Master of Malt website explains:

> Smells are often linked to memories: grandfather's desk (leather, wood, age, mustiness), Christmas with the family (Christmas cake, dried fruits, sultanas,

port), a hayloft in summer (dried grass, wood), a barbecue on the beach (salt, smoke, seaweed, cricket). Everyone will have their own memories, thus everyone will find their own descriptive flights of fancy. (How to Taste Whisky, n.d.)

And second, people tend to agree about a flavor more often after they've been primed to notice it. (Someone asks, "Do you taste the vanilla in that?" Everyone nods.) So, is the purpose of tasting to learn *what the whisk(e)y tastes like*, objectively? Or is it to learn *what I taste when I drink a particular whisk(e)y*? If the former, my experience suggests (though, admittedly, not conclusively) that whisk(e)y-tasting does not improve with specialized training, because everyone's taste palettes are slightly different. If the latter, then, since what I taste is affected by a number of variables, including the priming effect, I am not sure there is a specifiable notion of "what I taste when I taste a particular whisk(e)y" because it is likely to change on subsequent tastings. Thus, we have a tentative conclusion that whisk(e)y-tasting is not a domain of expertise but may simply be a means to enjoy whisk(e)y more than we would without the activities associated with it.[4] Thus, our working definition seems to constitute a principled way to distinguish expert domains even if they are nested the way biology is nested inside science.

Can we then extrapolate from what we understand about expert domains to define what a "domain" is, generally? I am doubtful. Does a domain have to be comprised of more than one bit of information related in some way or more than one behavior? Why more than one? (Why not more than two?) What would that relationship be? Logical, causal, explanatory? It seems the best we can do is to let people and groups specify domains according to their interests—vinyl record collecting, 1980s hair bands, feminist science fiction from the 1960s—and then ask whether they admit of expertise by asking whether specialized training would allow one to improve in competence beyond what one can gain by extensive experience alone.

7.1.3 Relationships among Expert Domains

What Socrates misses in *Ion* when he suggests that domains have hard boundaries is that domains are largely grounded in human interests, and human interests are complex in unpredictable ways. Socrates is unaware of the myriad ways of combining information that have led to the variety and narrowness of some of the domains we acknowledge today. The first is that *some domains overlap*. For example, anyone who works in geology must also be highly competent in physics and mathematics. Anyone who works in molecular biology must be competent in chemistry and evolutionary biology. The second is that *some domains are part of other domains*. Topology is a domain within the domain of mathematics.

The third is that *some domains are new(ish)*. To be sure, few domains are wholly new. Recall that, while Aristotle is credited as the "first biologist," this was largely built upon centuries-old husbandry practices. Further, even the designer of a new game has a background in games and can distinguish, for example, competitive from cooperative, fast-paced from slow-paced, strategy from tactical, and so on. But the sorts of technology and social dynamics that emerge to inspire new human interests—like video games and wearable GPS devices—cannot be specified in advance. This makes attempting to offer a general account of "domain" difficult (and somewhat arbitrary).

Relatedly, *some domains are new and emerge from other domains*, such as behavioral economics, which relies on methodologies and information from both psychology and economics, and bioinformatics, which combines medicine and data science. This also allows for the sort of *meta-expertise*—a high degree of competence in more than one domain.

Finally, *some domains supervene on other domains*. For example, and finally returning to our building designer, no one could build a skyscraper if there weren't dozens of experts in other specialized domains, like plumbing, electrical, and structural engineering. When domains overlap or are part of other domains or emerge from other domains, we have a sense that some degree of competence trickles through each of the connected domains. But with increasing specialization and the vast complexity of building, a new kind of expert domain was necessary, namely, the expertise to coordinate other experts. This will prove important later in this chapter, as we try to solve the "recognition problem."

7.1.4 Complications: Fuzzy Domains and Low-performance Ceilings

My account of expert domains is, admittedly, incomplete. One of the most interesting ongoing debates in expertise studies is the effectiveness of psychotherapy, or "talk therapy," with patients experiencing mental health problems. Recall that there is extensive literature showing that people with minimal counseling training have about the same success rate as professionally credentialed psychotherapists. There are a number of explanations for why this might be.

One explanation is that, since specialized training does not improve one's ability to treat mental health issues beyond extensive experience, therapy is not an expert domain. Perhaps mental health issues simply cannot be ameliorated by talk therapy.

But that would be too easy. Therapy is complicated, and it includes multiple aims. So, even if one of the aims of therapy does not admit of achievement through specialized training, others may. For example, the *profession* of psychotherapy (and professionalism is not the same as expertise) creates a space, through legal and professional regulation, for people to talk freely about their problems. It ensures safety, privacy, and an atmosphere of non-judgment. This legally defined protection is clearly a type of administrative authority. But administrative authority is not the only element at work here. Only people who have the training to understand these aspects of therapy are allowed (administratively) to practice as therapists in order to protect potentially vulnerable patients from psychosocial harms. But the ability to listen and respond in such a way that facilitates improvement (whatever that means for a particular patient) rather than harm suggests there is epistemic authority, as well. It is likely that even minimally trained counselors have competencies that may rightly be regarded as "specialized." Therefore, one explanation for the parity in outcomes highlighted in the empirical research on the effectiveness of counseling could indicate that psychotherapy has what Camerer and Johnson call a *low-performance ceiling*.

In 1963, computer scientist J. E. Gustafson found that residents and surgeons predicted post-operation length-of-stay at about the same rate. Radiology researchers Harold Kundel and Paul La Follette, Jr. (1972) found that, while novices and first-year medical students could not detect lesions on radiographs of abnormal lungs, fourth-year students with minimal training in radiography "were as good as full-time radiologists" (Camerer and Johnson 1991: 202).

Camerer and Johnson call domains that require very little training to be as good as the best performers' "low-performance ceiling" domains. Call these limits on performance that are determined by the domain "naturally low-performance ceiling domains."

There are interesting implications of low-performance ceiling domains. For one, we may be able to delegate those tasks to people with less specialization (and whom we don't have to pay as much) so specialists can focus on other areas of their expertise. For example, many of us in the United States are happy to have tax services (like H&R Block) file our annual taxes rather than accountants because trained tax professionals do about as well as accountants for less complicated tax forms, and they cost much less.

Epistemically, this does not imply that they are not expert domains. The plausibility that some domains are low-performance ceiling domains can help inform our judgments about who is an expert, how much to trust them, and how competing claims to expertise can be adjudicated.

Another possibility is more disheartening. There is evidence that some psychiatrists believe that patients with certain mental health problems, like personality disorders, *cannot* get better. This is a phenomenon called "therapeutic pessimism," which is a bias on the part of therapists that their patients will not recover (Chartonas et al. 2017). This bias could lead them to stop using certain treatments too soon. It may also affect their tone or body language. If therapists are pessimistic, this could become a self-fulfilling prophecy. If those failures are then documented in publications, the whole domain could be tainted by that bias (Cereda and Carey 2012).

A similar concern attends some therapeutic surgeries for genetic disorders such as trisomy 18. Trisomy 18, also called Edwards syndrome, is a rare genetic disorder in which there are three copies of chromosome 18 rather than the standard two. This is the same phenomenon that occurs in chromosome 21 to cause Down syndrome (trisomy 21). Unlike Down syndrome, trisomy 18 causes severe birth defects in the head and organs, especially the heart, and this often leads to early death. For years, physicians refused to perform heart surgery to fix the defect because the literature shows that children with trisomy 18 tend to die within fifteen days and only 5–10 percent survive to the age of one (Cereda and Carey 2012). Because of this high mortality rate, surgeons were less inclined to offer heart surgery as a corrective. The thought seemed to be that, since, at most, 10 percent of babies affected would live to one year old anyway, a transition to comfort care rather than surgery was the more beneficent route. Interestingly, though, the morality rates had only been measured for trisomy 18 babies who had not had surgery; few surgeons had attempted surgery, so there was no reliable data. Without knowing the possible benefits of surgery, this—among other considerations—contributed to experts setting an artificial upper limit on mortality. After surgeons began experimenting with the benefits of surgery, we now have evidence that surgery increases the proportion of babies with trisomy 18 who live to one year old from 5–10 percent to 68 percent (Nelson et al. 2016). This suggests that experts' biases can artificially constrain what counts as a "high" level of performance. Call domains like this "artificially low-performance ceiling domains."

What can we take away from this discussion? First, we have a better sense of what Socrates meant by a "body of knowledge," namely, a set of tasks that can be learned and that are aimed at a specifiable goal, and second, we have a working account of an expert domain, namely, a set of activities for which specialized training (whether formal or informal) improves competence beyond what one can gain by extensive experience alone. Third, we have a sense of the complexity of domains—how they emerge, nest, and overlap. This suggests that we should remain rather open as to what an expert domain might look like. Finally, we have seen that what counts as "highly competent" has different success conditions in different domains. Some of those domains have low-performance ceilings (whether natural or artificial) despite forbidding credentialing processes. This suggests that epistemic authority should be assessed in terms of the expert's competence relative to the performance ceiling of their domain and not their credentials or professional accreditation, no matter how seemingly impressive.

7.2 The Easy Recognition Problem

The recognition problem is sometimes used as an umbrella for two distinct problems: the *novice/expert problem* and the *novice/2-expert* problem. The novice/expert problem is the problem I described in the opening: Novices could only identify experts if they became experts, but in that case, they would no longer be novices. In the novice/2-expert problem, novices are faced with the challenge of deciding on which of two (or more) genuine experts to believe when those experts disagree. Since a novice, by definition, does not have the competence to understand the evidence and arguments in an expert domain, it is unclear what resources they might use to choose among competing experts. We will look at the novice/2-expert problem in Section 8.2. But before we know which of *two genuine experts* to believe, we need to be able to accurately identify *genuine experts* in the first place. Notice that, in the novice/2-expert problem, the question is not whether of the two people disagreeing are experts, but rather, which expert to believe. It presupposes that we have solved that question. In the novice/expert problem, on the other hand, novices, who, by definition, do not have competence in a domain, are challenged to figure out who is genuinely an expert in a domain.

I think there are two versions of the novice/expert problem: the *easy recognition problem* (ERP) and the *hard recognition problem* (HRP). ERP has long been the focus of discussion in the philosophical literature on expertise, so

I will focus the remainder of this chapter on it. I discuss HRP and prospects for solving it in Chapter 8.

Perhaps surprisingly, I think the ERP has been solved, or at least can be solved in many cases. Despite its name, it is not easy to solve; rather, it is "easy" in the sense that there is no in-principle reason for thinking it an insuperable obstacle to trusting experts.

The recognition problem is often framed as a dilemma for truth-based accounts of expertise. Truth-based accounts argue that experts have reliable access to true beliefs or knowledge in a domain (see Watson 2021, Chapter 3, for a full discussion of truth-based accounts). Because of this, I'll open the discussion of the novice/expert problem by framing it in terms of accounts that take truth or knowledge to be essential to expertise, ERP-K (the K stands for "knowledge"):

(ERP-K)

(1) **Experts know significantly more in their domain than novices.**
(2) **Novices can know whether some bit of testimony is expert testimony only if novices can know that the testifier has sufficient knowledge in the relevant domain.**
(3) **If novices become experts in that domain, they are no longer novices in that domain.**
(4) **If novices do not become experts, they cannot assess whether the testifier has sufficient knowledge in the relevant domain.**
   Therefore:
(5) **Novices cannot know whether some bit of testimony is expert testimony.**

Some points of clarification are needed. Note that premise 1 is about *genuine experts*, not genuine professionals, people with genuine administrative authority, or people who are posing as experts. This premise is an assumption of the argument. The key is that it does not presuppose that we know who real experts are in any given case; it is simply that, for any given case of a genuine expert, a novice is in no position to recognize that they are, in fact, an expert.

Premise 2 makes the ability to assess a bit of testimony is expert testimony a *necessary but not a sufficient* condition for trust. This avoids the concern about instances where independent reasons about say, a well-known mistake about the facts or reasoning, or a conflict of interest, renders a specific instance of testimony untrustworthy.

Also, premise 2 frames the concern about an expert's epistemic placement *in their domain* rather than *with a particular bit of content or instance of testimony*. This sets the bar according to what we might call the *maximal expectation principle*: The burden of assessing the trustworthiness of an expert should not exceed the abilities of the least qualified person expected to seek the expert's testimony. If we required that novices be able to assess the likelihood that any particular claim of any particular expert is true, then very few novices could justifiably trust experts. If we require that experts be able to convince any individual novice of their expertise, no matter how uninformed the novice may be, the recognition problem would, indeed, be unsolvable. Perhaps an expert in ancient languages cannot explain why she is an expert in Sanskrit to suit the abilities of the average person who knows little about ancient languages, but perhaps she doesn't need to. If the scope of language expert's expertise involves engaging only with her department and other scholars in closely related domains, then expectations about who can justifiably assess her expertise are different from, say, a public scientist like Bill Nye.[5] The maximal expectation principle allows us to require only that experts be able to demonstrate their competence in a domain to some *relevant* subpopulation. This is an epistemically responsible way to formulate ERP-K, and it helps explain why I think this and other versions of ERP can, in principle, be solved.

In cases where that relevant subpopulation includes some kinds of novices, those novices must have some way of assessing experts' competence that does not require a similarly high degree of competence. For example, to recognize the authority of a doctor, novices should have some sense of the relevant differences among medical novices, nurses, and doctors; understand the specializing role of advanced degrees; and so on.[6] But the argument cannot require that they have the discriminatory abilities of an expert, for then they would no longer be a novice.

A final note about premise 2: It states that novices can trust expert testimony *only if* they can tell whether someone is an expert. This is a necessary condition for trusting someone *as an expert*. It doesn't rule out justified trust on other grounds. Trust might also be warranted if the putative expert is your spouse or parent, if trusting this person under these circumstances is useful for non-epistemic reasons, or if the novice has sufficient competence with claim X to assess X on its own merits (e.g., a mathematician testifies to the Pythagorean Theorem).[7] Being able to tell whether someone is an expert, while necessarily, is not sufficient. Even if a novice accurately identifies someone as an expert, there may be good reasons not to trust them. Perhaps they have committed research misconduct or have a clear conflict of interest with respect to what they testified about.

Finally, note that ERP-K is framed only in terms of novices. Standard formulations tend to ignore whether experts can identify one another and whether or to what degree expertise in one domain could help experts identify experts in other domains. I will address this issue in the next chapter. These exclusions, it turns out, have been part of what had made the problem seem so intractable for so long.

And the problem has been around a long time, as the quotation from Augustine at the beginning of this chapter shows. We might even call it a version of the "knowledge paradox" or "Meno's paradox," as Plato frames it in the words of Socrates:

> Do you realize what a debater's argument you are bringing up, that a [person] cannot search either for what [they] know[] or for what [they] do[] not know? [They] cannot search for what [they] do[] know—since [they] know[] it, there is no need to search—nor for what [they] do[] not know, for [they] do[] not know what to look for. (*Meno* 80e, trans. Grube)

Someone who knows absolutely nothing about a domain seems at a loss to justifiably evaluate whether someone else knows something about that domain.

While the ERP is typically aimed at truth-based accounts, it is a problem for all accounts of expertise. Letting "epistemic placement" refer to understanding in a domain, expert-level performance, and whatever combination of those is needed for any particular domain, consider ERP-C:

(ERP-C)

(1) **Experts are significantly better placed in their domain than novices.**
(2) **Novices can justifiably identify that someone is an expert only if they can assess whether the person is sufficiently well placed in the relevant domain.**
(3) If novices become experts in that domain, they are no longer novices in that domain.
(4) If novices do not become experts, they cannot assess whether the person is sufficiently well placed in the relevant domain.
   Therefore:
(5) **Novices cannot justifiably identify that someone is an expert.**

Despite its long pedigree, I call this the ERP because our discussion in this book so far gives us a number of tools for solving it. Specifically, we have reasons to believe that premise 4, under many circumstances, is false.

7.3 Solving the Easy Problem, Take 1: Domain Access and Connection Conditions

An influential attempt to solve the recognition problem is offered by philosopher Elizabeth Anderson (2011). Anderson is optimistic that novices of "ordinary education, using information to which they have ready access" (145) can, with a little effort, successfully identify relevant experts in a domain. By "ordinary education," she means "no more than a high school education, including basic knowledge of how to navigate the Web" and by "ready access," she means "access to the Web, but not to any scholarly sources not posted on the Web" (145). She argues that if a person like this can assess three aspects of expertise, they can know whether to trust that someone is an expert:

(1) Whether a person (the putative expert) is in a position to know (the *expertise* condition);
(2) Whether a person is likely to be truthful and transparent (the *honesty* condition); and
(3) Whether a person is responsive to evidence (as opposed to being dogmatic or arrogant) (the *epistemic responsibility* condition).

A point worth noting (because it will be relevant in Chapter 8) is that Anderson assumes that experts in a specialized domain can separate their *technical knowledge* in their domain from their *judgments about the value of that knowledge*. She acknowledges that "value judgments may play valid roles in constructing and assessing scientific theories" and that "[s]cientists have no special expertise on these value judgments" (146). Nevertheless, she says that "many technical scientific questions . . . require specialized expertise" (146) and "the weight people should accord to others' testimony about a field increases" as they proceed up the hierarchy of specialization to *"leaders"* in a domain (147, italics hers).

A further point worth highlighting is that Anderson's criteria are aimed not only at helping novices identify experts but also to help them justifiably trust experts. Anderson considered the honest and epistemic responsibility conditions strong enough to mitigate the circumstantial concerns surrounding expert testimony, such as conflicts of interest, motivated reasoning, and entrenched value commitments. I will argue in this chapter and the next that such a project faces insuperable obstacles, but here, I will focus on her attempt to help novices identify experts.

The first thing to note about Anderson's solution is that it doesn't presuppose that experts must be able to convince *just anyone* of their expertise. She sets the minimum expectation at novices with an "ordinary education." This is consistent with our aforementioned maximal expectation principle, and it seems a reasonable constraint on the argument given the vast diversity of cognitive abilities in the world. Children, people who have certain cognitive impairments, and people with little background education may not be able to identify experts no matter what tools are available or what the expert does. But this is not a mark against expertise. So, from now own, I will assume that "novice" means "minimally educated novice," where minimally educated just means the ability to be sensitive to evidence appropriate for their need of experts. Children could be sensitive to some types of evidence (a black "X" on an unfamiliar bottle of liquid), but not others (whether the person offering them food is safe because it is from a flight attendant rather than the strange man in the seat next to them). It is their parents' responsibility to be able to draw the latter distinction. John Hardwig is right that "[I]f I do not know and have no way of finding out who the experts are, I will have no way to appeal to the chain of authority" (1985: 333).

But this sort of total ignorance is not the position novices most often find themselves in when they need an expert. If a minimally educated adult needs to find a good cancer specialist, cancer specialists, or at least experts in less esoteric specialties, should be able to explain to them how to do this. This means that a classical assumption of ERP, namely, that everyone is either an expert or knows absolutely nothing about a domain, is false. So, from now own, we will assume that "novice" means "minimally educated novice," where minimally educated just means the ability to be sensitive to evidence appropriate for their need of experts.

How might a novice figure out whether someone meets the expertise, honesty, and epistemic responsibility conditions? Following Goldman (2001), we can start by noting two strategies for assessing an expert: collecting *direct evidence* of expertise and collecting *indirect evidence* of expertise. Collecting direct evidence involves looking at a putative expert's competence in a domain by directly observing or talking with the putative expert. Collecting indirect evidence involves looking at proxy indicators of someone's expertise.

7.3.1 Direct Evidence of Expertise

If the type of expertise in question is performative, such as woodworking, a novice might look at some of the expert's previous work. If the expertise is sports-related, a novice might watch them perform in a scrimmage. If the expert is willing to explain their reasoning and conclusions in nontechnical language, a novice might try to follow those and assess them for apparent defects.

Direct evidence might also take the form of time-limited trust, such as giving the putative expert an opportunity to demonstrate their competence on a contingency basis, such as within the constraints of a contract with an escape clause or a probationary hiring period, so that the novice has a chance to directly observe whether the expert is competent without putting themselves at too much risk. In these cases, the trust is not grounded solely in epistemic considerations but also includes pragmatic considerations of risk. Perhaps these considerations also constitute an incentive for the putative expert to be honest, in which case this enhances one's epistemic reasons for engaging in the time-limited trust. But even if this were right, it would not eliminate the pragmatic element of deciding whether to trust someone as an expert.

Time-limited trust also seems appropriate for low-stakes domains, like most cases of weather forecasting. Imagine you're on vacation at a lake and look forward to kayaking, and the local weather forecaster says it will be a perfect day on the lake tomorrow. Even though you have no idea how good this weather person is, (1) you might as well go ahead and prepare for kayaking since you have no better information to go on, (2) you're already on vacation, so what else are you going to do? And (3), given that you have chosen this time of year carefully, you at least have strong background evidence that there won't be some catastrophic event, like a hurricane, wildfire, or tornado. Worst-case scenario, it rains and you stay inside to play cards. The lost investment of preparing for the lake is not that big of a deal. Again, this kind of trust combines epistemic and pragmatic reasons. On the one hand, the context in which the weather person testifies about the weather (they're on television working as a meteorologist) provides some indirect reasons to enter into the time-limited trust, but the pragmatic reasons are predominant: What choice do you have? What do you have to lose if the putative expert is wrong? If the weather person was right, then you have a small piece of hindsight evidence that the weather person is sufficiently expert at their job.

In higher-stakes cases of weather forecasting, such as piloting a cargo ship around to avoid a storm, this sort of pragmatic or backward-looking evidence is not good enough. You need to know up front whether a storm is likely to drag you off course or threaten your cargo. In many cases like this, there is simply no direct evidence that's relevant; a novice cannot typically look at or speak with a meteorologist and discover sufficient reason to believe they are good at weather forecasting.

7.3.2 Indirect Evidence of Expertise

In such cases, a novice might look for pieces of indirect or proxy evidence of a putative expert's competence. Proxy evidence includes:[8]

- **Contextual cues:** doctors usually wear white coats and work in doctor's offices (not out of unmarked vans); accountants typically work for accounting firms whose reputation may be public (rather than offering services on Craigslist); scientists work for universities or labs (not out of their basements); these work as evidential cues because they are part of institutional processes designed to guarantee competence in a domain
- **Behavioral cues:** smoothness, quickness, and confidence in answering questions, or explaining solutions or answers, as opposed to evasion, double-speak, or overfamiliarity
- **Expert-like qualifications:** education; specialized training certificates; credentials; licenses; rankings; awards; publications (or lack of any of these)
- **A track record of success:** testimony from satisfied clients, professional accolades, important research publications, sports records
- **The consensus of other putative experts in their domain:** getting a second or third opinion, reading popular articles in respectable publications that summarize the state of a domain in nontechnical language, calling or emailing other professionals in their domain; consensus statements by reputable agencies or supposed leaders in the domain
- **Evidence of dishonesty:** media controversies, lawsuits, conflicts of interest, retracted publications, repeating claims that you have good reason to believe are not true
- **The testimony of meta-experts:** people from closely related domains who work with this person; people you are already have good reason to believe are experts, and whose background overlaps enough that they can tell you whether a putative expert is genuine

The idea is that, in cases where direct evidence is not available, these proxies can serve as proxies, that is, as indicators that are correlated with expertise.

What are novices' prospects for actually using this information to successfully identify experts in the real world? In other words, how good is this proxy evidence, and how easy is it for novices to get? Novelist Aldous Huxley makes it sound easy when he discusses trusting scientists:

> For the nonspecialist, a thorough and detailed knowledge of any branch of science is impossible. It is also unnecessary. All that is necessary, so far as the [person] of letters is concerned, is a general knowledge of science, a bird's-eye knowledge of what has been achieved in the various fields of scientific inquiry, together with an understanding of the philosophy of science and an appreciation of the ways in which scientific information and scientific modes of thought are relevant to individual experience and the problems of social relationships, to religion and politics, to ethics and a tenable philosophy of life. (Huxley 1963: 72)

This is a little more robust than what Anderson argues, but not much. Anderson thinks that anyone with a high school education should be able to tell the difference between PhD scientists outside of a domain and PhD scientists inside a domain, between scientists who are research active and those who are leaders in the domain (2011: 146). She also thinks this demographic can judge when someone is cherry-picking data, persistently misrepresenting the views of their opponents, and evading peer review (147). Huxley, by contrast, requires a bit more: a little history of science, a little philosophy of science, and the practical impact of science on daily life. They agree that novices can adequately identify experts, but Anderson sets the bar for the competence needed to do so lower than Huxley.

Whether Huxley or Anderson is right is an empirical matter. But given that most of my college students have trouble distinguishing between philosophy and psychology (much less between an MA degree and a PhD), I am not as optimistic as Anderson. Do nonacademics know that they should be worried about experts' cherry-picking data, persistently misrepresenting the views of their opponents, or evading peer review?[9] People who don't read much, or whose lives do not intersect with the lives of academics or researchers, seem ill-placed to draw such fine-grained distinctions.

But let's set that empirical question aside. Perhaps motivated novices could use indirect evidence, as Anderson suggests. Even still, whether anyone could assess experts depends on *how easy indirect information is to get* and *how well it tracks expertise*. Call the question of how easy proxy evidence is to get the *domain access question*. Call the question of how well proxy evidence tracks expertise the *connection question*.

7.4 The Domain Access Question and the Geography of Expertise

How does anyone access a domain? By "access," I don't mean "become an expert." Rather, I mean *understand a domain well enough to assess claims made by putative experts in that domain*. Recall from Chapter 2 that some domains have content that most anyone can easily understand. We called these *exoteric domains*, and they include competence in activities like music, competitive swimming, and basketball. There are also domains that are so highly specialized that almost no one but those who work in them understand them. We called these *esoteric domains*, and they include specialties like quantum electrodynamics, neurosurgery, and PYTHON computer programming (see Figure 2.1, p. 54).

Interestingly, even though these distinctions lie on a continuum, expert domains turn out to be far more complex than the esoteric/exoteric distinction has it, as Thi Nguyen (2018b) explains.

Evaluating an expert, according to Nguyen involves two processes: *identifying a genuine expert* and *assessing their degree of expertise*. In some cases, they go together. If you tell me you are an expert axe-thrower, then when I see you accurately throw an axe enough times to know it's not luck, I know both that you are a genuine expert and that you have a pretty high degree of expertise. In other cases, knowing one is easier than knowing the other. If you tell me you are an aeronautics engineer, and I find out you are licensed by a professional association of aeronautics engineers, and I know that you are supposed to keep planes from falling out of the sky, and I also know that planes rarely fall out of the sky, then I have some reason to believe you are an expert. That information doesn't let me assess your degree of expertise, but it tells me something about the competence of people in your domain, generally speaking. Nguyen calls domains *obvious* when "they produce, individually or collectively, some result whose successfulness is available to the inexpert observer" (5).

On the other end of the continuum, Nguyen calls domains *subtle* if "there are no such tests available to the inexpert observer" (5). These include domains like number theory and abstract expressionist art.

Importantly, *obvious* and *subtle* do not neatly track our original distinction between *exoteric* and *esoteric*. This is because some subtle domains present novices with opportunities to evaluate experts. They can do this when they are linked to other domains that novices *can* access:

Even in subtle domains, the inexpert are not without resources. Many domains are interlinked, so one can perform what Phillip Kitcher calls "indirect calibration" (Kitcher, 1993, pp. 320-323). That is, some fields are interwoven with other fields; thus, we may be able to link up subtle fields with more obvious ones. For example, nuclear engineers rely on the results of particle physics, and nuclear engineering has some rather dramatic tests, whose failures are available to the inexpert. (5)

This means that some subtle domains are exoteric enough for novices to make sense of them because they understand closely related domains. Nguyen calls these domains *linked*.

Just as obvious and subtle fall along a continuum, domains are linked to various degrees. At some point, there is no link left, and there we find *isolated* domains. These domains are not linked to any domains that novices can access. Not all isolated domains are esoteric, though. Some have obvious indicators of competence despite not being linked to other domains, such as rock climbing.[10] This means that not all isolated domains are subtle. What emerges from this more complex picture of expert domains is Figure 7.1 that I call Nguyen's "Epistemic Geography of Expertise" (for reasons that will become obvious).[11]

If we were to try to map the original exoteric/esoteric continuum onto this figure, it would look like an "S" curve from strongly exoteric over to weakly exoteric, then diagonally up to weakly esoteric, and then right to strongly esoteric.[12]

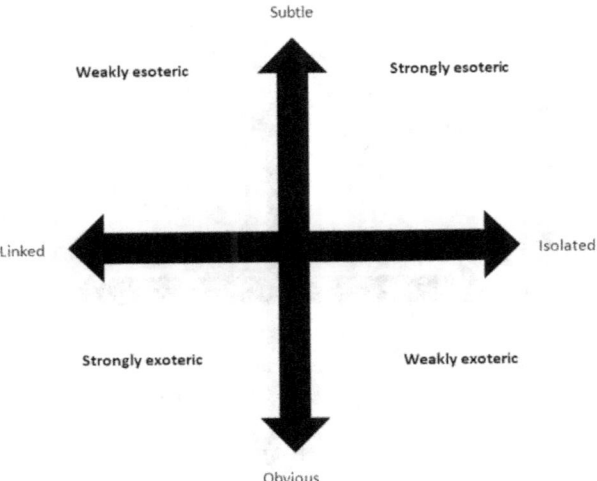

Figure 7.1 Nguyen's epistemic geography of expertise.

The benefit of this conceptual map is that it highlights how some potential problems for identifying experts can be solved. When expertise is obvious and linked, the recognition problem is easily overcome: novices have access both to the domain and to the strong connection between the evidence and competence in that domain. Nguyen says that strongly exoteric domains are on what he called novices' "cognitive mainland," which means that "expertise is unnecessary to decide which experts to trust" (3). As one moves further from the mainland, to weakly exoteric and weakly esoteric domains, the difficulties in recognizing experts increases. One must rely on more abstract, indirect evidence, including the testimony of meta-experts to explain the findings from a specialized domain. This is not a problem as long as the connection between this proxy evidence and competence in a domain is strong. At some point, however, a domain of expertise is too subtle and isolated for novices to access. Nguyen says that domains that are strongly esoteric are on "cognitive islands" (see Figure 7.2).

On cognitive islands, it is difficult even for experts in a domain to evaluate one another's competence. This is because the expertise in those domains is so specialized that, if you work in one of those domains, your judgment about the concepts, methodologies, and evidence in that domain is part of what comprises the state of competence in that domain. So, if another expert in your domain disagrees with you, and the only standard by which to judge their competence is your own judgment, then determining who is right will require a long discussion that may or may not be productive.

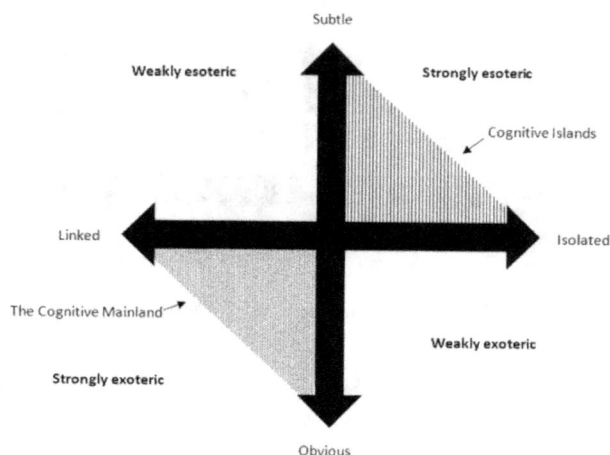

Figure 7.2 Nguyen's epistemic geography of expertise, revised.

Are some domains inherently or necessarily on cognitive islands such that there is no way for people on the mainland to make sense of them without becoming experts themselves? I think it is possible. Consider translating a language like Sanskrit or a domain like quantum electrodynamics. The background information necessary for understanding even basic claims in these domains is so rich and advanced that typically only people in other very closely related domains can access them.

However, as new technology emerges and new pedagogical techniques are developed, what is seemingly impossible comes to pass. The philosopher Martin Heidegger was famously wrong when he said that only the German language has "deep and creative philosophical character to compare with the Greek" ([1982] 2002: 36). Human language is a marvelous thing. There are now cartoons that attempt to explain such complex philosophical concepts as personal identity over time to high school students. With the right metaphors and the right motivation on the part of the novice, it might be that no domain is wholly isolated.

7.5 Solving the Easy Problem, Take 2: Indicators, Time, and Stakes

Now we are in a position to ask *when*, that is, under what conditions, novices are able to use indirect evidence to successfully identify experts. We start by rejecting the assumption that all novices are alike. Expertise need not be accessible to just anybody before it is authoritative for a relevant group of novices. Experts are only obliged to convince novices who stand in need of their competence, and whether a novice needs to be convinced can differ in different contexts. For example, a novice in architectural engineering may be an expert real estate developer. An expert architectural engineer may be able to provide sufficient evidence of expertise to the real estate developer because of the overlap in their domains, even if she could not do so for her doctor or her accountant. Given that the engineer has no need to convince her doctor of her expertise, it is no mark against her expertise that her doctor does not have sufficient access to her domain to evaluate her expertise.

Second, as we have seen, if a domain is on the cognitive mainland, premise 4 of ERP-C ("If novices do not become experts, they cannot assess whether the person is sufficiently competent in the relevant domain") is false for that domain. Novices can assess experts in those domains, either directly, as in watching an axe-thrower, or indirectly, as in looking up an athlete's win/loss record. Further, because domains are related in various complex ways, indirect evidence, such as appealing to meta-experts, renders premise 4 false even as one sets out into the less familiar waters of weakly exoteric and weakly esoteric domains.

The only domains to which novices lack the ability to access are strongly esoteric domains: those on cognitive islands. But since even experts have trouble assessing one another on cognitive islands, this is relatively good news for novices. So far, the ERP is only a problem for accessing subtle and isolated domains.

Of course, the mere *ability* to access a domain is not all there is to domain access. When we actually need experts, other factors affect our access besides our abilities: importantly, time and stakes. So, even if we could access the relevant domain if our need for an expert were not time sensitive and the stakes were low, this is not often how the world works. Consider the case of Dr. Tamika Cross, who tried to help a fellow passenger on a plane who was having health problems but was told by a flight attendant that "We are looking for actual physicians or nurses or some type of medical personnel, we don't have time to talk to you" (Hawkins 2016). The problem wasn't the flight attendant's ability to access Dr. Cross's credentials, but the time-sensitive nature of the problem. Unfortunately, the flight attendant would likely not have been so dismissive if Dr. Cross weren't a black woman. There are good pragmatic reasons to trust someone who says they are a doctor under certain circumstances. The flight attendant's bias led her to ignore those and respond in a discriminatory way. Even still, pragmatic reasons are not epistemic reasons. In some circumstances, the time-sensitive nature of a question or problem makes it difficult or impossible to *responsibly* review indirect evidence.

The stakes involved in a decision can also affect one's domain access. Even if ability and time are not a problem, if a need is serious enough, it may be hard to accurately use proxy evidence. Imagine your child is very sick, and you take them to the emergency room. From the emergency room they are admitted to the hospital for tests. The doctor who evaluates your child tells you your child needs an expensive therapy and that, even though it has certain risks, you should start the therapy soon. The alternative risk is that your child will continue to be sick for many years. Let's say you also look up your child's illness and the treatment on reputable websites, and the authors of that website give a slightly more pessimistic view of the therapy. When you ask the doctor about this, she says that, while that's normally the case, your child has a rare combination of problems that makes this therapy the best shot at treating them.

In this case, neither time nor ability is a factor. Looking up more expert opinions won't help because the doctor has dismissed them as irrelevant *to your child's case* (this happens quite often in children's hospitals). So, you are left on your own to find indirect evidence of whether this doctor is expert enough to make this recommendation. You have time to look up the doctor's education, experience, credentials, accolades, and any controversies or reviews about them. You can ask the nurses about their experience with this doctor (though you know their opinion is likely biased in favor of the person they work with all the time). You can reach out on Facebook to find out if anyone you know has had this doctor. But because of the risk, you are always faced with the question: Is that enough to justify trusting them with my child's health?

Where does this leave us? Our conclusion is less optimistic. It turns out that novices cannot adequately access needed domains when:

- The domain is subtle and isolated.
- The need is time sensitive.
- The need is high stakes.

This is bad news for many important decisions but good news for many of our everyday decisions to trust experts. So long as the domain of expertise is either linked or obvious, and our need is not time sensitive or high stakes, it is possible to access the domains we need. This shows that ERP is not an in-principle insuperable problem, at least from a domain access concern.

7.6 Solving the Easy Problem, Take 3: Wicked and Manipulated Environments

Unfortunately, answering the domain access question is not all that is required for figuring out whether to trust someone as an expert. We must also be reasonably confident that the evidence to which we have access is strongly enough connected to expert competence that it tells us accurately whether someone is an expert. When is proxy evidence strongly connected to expert competence?

In some domains, feedback is immediate and clearly correlated with competence. In other domains, feedback is only loosely or indirectly correlated with competence. Consider the difference between being a good musician and being a good policymaker. Musicians know immediately when they've made a mistake, and they can typically tell whether they have improved when they have been having trouble with part of a piece of music. This is because the musician's environment is what psychologist Robin Hogarth (2001; 2010) calls a "kind learning environment," an environment in which the feedback one gets is immediate and strongly correlated with skill level (2010: 343). Surgery is a kind environment, as is violin performance. So, kind environments allow novices to answer the connection question in the affirmative.

Teaching, on the other hand, takes place in a wicked environment, that is, an environment where "feedback is either missing or distorted" (ibid. 343). Whether a student learns is a function of many different factors—from the interest the child's parent takes in their education, to how well the child is eating, to whether the child is being bullied, has an undiagnosed learning disability, is stressed because of home life or illness, interest in the subject, intelligence, grit, has a fixed or growth mindset, and so on. Determining whether a teacher is successful given this environment is almost impossible. This is not to say that expertise cannot be identified in domains with wicked environments, only that access to this evidence is highly esoteric and, therefore, may be available only to specialists in closely related domains.

In domains with kind environments, daily practice in the field is often enough to enhance competence. Surgeons, for example, tend to get better with experience (Vickers et al. 2007, et al. 2008). But in domains with wicked environments, more specialized training is needed. For example, radiologists and diagnosticians tend to get worse with experience (Elmore, et al. 2009; Choudry et al. 2005; Spengler and Pilipis 2015), and standard continuing education activities do not help much (Davis et al. 1999; Forsetland et al. 2009). To enhance skills in these environments, training must force learners to continually engage with and reflect on practice with others. In medicine, for example, role-play and simulation activities show marginally better results (Forsetland et al. 2012).[13] So, in addition to the domain access question, novices also need to know whether a putative expert's domain is kind or wicked, and then, if the domain is wicked, whether they have had sufficient training to acquire expert-level competence.

We also know that proxy evidence is *not* strongly connected with expert competence when there are confounding factors at stake in the transmission of expertise, that is, where environments are manipulated by cognitive or social factors. Confounding factors affect how novices interpret and use expert testimony, and these include both cognitive and social phenomena such as tribal epistemology, standpoint bias, the Dunning-Kruger effect, filter bubbles, and echo chambers (see Watson 2021).

There are other confounding factors, however, that affect how experts deploy their expertise. These include contexts when the interests of the experts do not align with the relevant interests of the novice, either explicitly or implicitly, and contexts where indirect indicators of expertise are intentionally manipulated. Typically, these contexts are what I call "value-charged" needs for expertise. Value-charged needs are those that both novices and experts have a sensitive personal interest in. What counts as a "sensitive personal interest" will differ from person to person. Many people are indifferent to whether the government bans handguns, while others claim they will stake their lives against it. Many people are indifferent meat-eaters, while others are vociferous vegans or obstinate omnivores. Nevertheless, the moment the need for expertise is value-charged, either for the expert or for the novice, bad things can happen to expertise.

Recall that Anderson says that assessing an expert's honesty can help them decide whom to trust. But note that this works only if the expert's aims align with relevant aims of the novice. One might think that such misalignment would automatically be a case of dishonesty—along the lines of deceitful research showing the safety of tobacco products or the absence of anthropogenic factors in climate change—but this is not always the case. Experts can tell the truth, but in certain ways they think is beneficial to novices. In some cases, an honest judgment can be biased by the nature of the expert's domain. Physician Franz Ingelfinger points out that it "It is understandable . . . that the bulk of biomedical scientists and parascientists will as a group make decisions grossly influenced by their own skills and resources. Under many a circumstance the surgeon will cut when the internist will use antibiotics" (1980: 1508).

In other cases, honest judgments can be biased by what experts *think* are in their audience's interests, and if the novices knew about the other ways of telling the truth, they may not agree. Consider nudge strategies that try to improve patient health decisions by framing health decisions in terms of probabilities rather than frequencies. For example, a doctor might say, "Taking this drug will cut your chances of disease X in half!" rather than, "Taking this drug will cut your chances of disease X from 4% to 2%." Both could be true (2 percent is half of 4 percent), but the doctor thinks the drug is in the patient's interests despite its small effect (it is value-charged for the doctor who feels a duty to make the patient better off). The patient, however, has no idea, and from their perspective, taking more medicines and risking side effects and adverse interactions with their other medications may be more valuable than the 2 percent risk savings.

Some experts do this intentionally, as when a physician understands the nudge literature and applies it to influence patients' decisions, but others do it unintentionally. Perhaps they have no idea that there is a difference in the way patients interpret risks, and they just casually use probabilities instead of frequencies, and, therefore, have no idea what impact it will have on patient's decisions. This sort of value-charged effect can also happen in retail environments. In cases where a retailer is doing well, they can pretty much take or leave your sale. But if a retailer struggles for every penny (as in used car sales), they may frame the truth in a way that intentionally (from selfishness) or unintentionally (from desperation) affects your buying choices in ways that prevent you from getting what you really want.

Alex Guerrero (2017) calls cases where "there is some measure of nonalignment between the expert's interests and the nonexpert's interests" "strategic contexts" (2). As the example shows, this nonalignment can lead to suboptimal decisions even when the expert is honest because "the truth is not always, or not always fully and exclusively, on our side" (5). This challenges Anderson's claim that assessing honesty is a means by which novices can successfully identify experts.

There are also cases where well-intentioned experts can tell the truth with the intent of being honest but leave out information that they are afraid will mislead novices. Stephen John (2018), for example, argues against the idea that experts should be open, transparent, and honest with novices. He points out that public trust in experts is often "fragile," and normal disagreements in science—disagreements that happen even in the most well-supported scientific endeavors—can, if the public knew about them, be viewed by the public as a reason to distrust experts (however misguided this conclusion). Thus, experts have the right, under some circumstances, not to be open or transparent. But, of course, this move may strike novices, if they found out about it, as unacceptably dishonest. This, again, challenges Anderson's idea that assessing honesty is a means by which novices can successfully identify experts.

Value-charged contexts can also lead people who are not experts to manipulate domains to seem like their claims are grounded in their expertise when they aren't. Two examples are epistemic trespassing and manufactured credentials. Epistemic trespassing, as noted earlier, occurs when experts in one domain may pose (sometimes unintentionally) as experts in another (Ballantyne 2019). Consider climate scientists. Climate scientists have a high degree of competence in answering questions about global temperature change, the causes and trends of that change, and potential future trends. But they are often called to support political action to mitigate climate change. Interestingly, climate scientists are not experts in public policy. They have no competence to identify which types of policies actually change people's behavior, which types of policies will lead to the greatest reduction in greenhouse gases, or what unforeseen social, financial, and economic consequences climate policies will have. Therefore, if a climate scientist speaks on claims regarding climate change, they are speaking within the scope of their expertise. But if a climate scientist defends a public policy regarding climate change, they are epistemically trespassing, which can give novices the sense that their testimony is authoritative when it isn't.

Another means of manipulating domains on value-charged issues is manufacturing credentials. Consider the American College of Pediatrics (ACP).[14] It sounds very much like the American Academy of Pediatrics (AAP). Both have political advocacy arms. Both have very professional-looking websites. Both are made up of genuine medical doctors. The difference is that the ACP is a right-wing group of doctors who reject widely accepted therapies (like speech therapy), homosexual families, and abortion. If you didn't look very deep, you wouldn't know that the group only has a couple of hundred members (though that is disturbing enough). But if you were a novice, you might be tempted to think the ACP is a group of experts who constitute another voice of expertise in the medical community, when in reality, they are rejected by the vast majority of pediatricians.

Most people are likely to be skeptical of a group like American Parapsychological Association despite its peer-reviewed journal and affiliation with the American Academy of Science simply on the basis of its content (e.g., ESP and remote viewing). But when the content of a domain is almost indistinguishable from a sham alternative, it is difficult to tell the difference.

7.7 Summing Up: This Is Harder Than It Looks

The ERP contends that novices have no means by which to determine whether someone is an expert. We now have reason to believe that's not true. In the following circumstances, novices can, with a bit of determination, get and use indirect evidence in a domain that tends to be strongly correlated with competence in that domain. These are cases where:

- The domain is not on a cognitive island (either not subtle or not isolated).
- The need for expertise is not highly time sensitive.
- The need for expertise is relatively low stakes.
- The domain's environment is mostly kind.
- The domain's environment is not strongly value-charged.

This suggests that much of our everyday reliance on experts is reasonably justified. When we go to accountants for our annual tax returns, attorneys to write up contracts, engineers to draw up building plans, computer specialists to fix our laptops, logistics managers to get our product from the warehouse to the client, auto mechanics to fix our cars, and so on, we do so under conditions where proxy evidence tracks competence rather well. In these contexts, it is easy for novices to recognize whether their problem or need has been adequately addressed. Technology has improved this epistemic situation through online reviews (though people are always coming up with ways to skew those reviews). And access to the legal system allows dissatisfied or defrauded consumers to seek recourse.

Notice the qualifiers in the list above: "not highly," "relatively low," and so on. Every domain will have some threshold for when a compromising condition will become, in fact, compromising. What that threshold is will depend on the domain, and it won't always be clear or unambiguous. Medicine, for example, is always value-charged to some degree, and it can be extremely high stakes. But, in cases of bacterial infections and broken fingers, the environment is relatively kind. Medicine has proved itself quite good at addressing those problems. So, even when we need an appendectomy, we can be relatively sure we are in good hands.

Does a novice need to have good reasons to believe all of these conditions are met before they can justifiably trust an expert? To some extent, yes. But I don't think they need reasons that involve any great detail. For example, simply having reasons to believe there are checks in place on expertise in relevant cases—such as accrediting bodies, licensing boards, malpractice lawsuits, the Better Business Bureau, firing practices, and organizations that record professional malfeasance—and that these reinforce basic contextual cues, such as *I should only talk with a doctor in what looks like a doctor's office*, and *I should only use an accountant from a respected firm*. These are the sort of reasons we rely on when, for example, we get on an elevator or an airplane. Most of us don't really know how either works. We certainly don't know any details about the expertise or expert coordination that goes into building and maintaining them. Yet, we have a general sense that they are reliable in virtue of their general success and the social structures that make them possible.

Nevertheless, novices must still exhibit epistemic responsibility.

Further, simply identifying someone as an expert is not sufficient for *trusting* someone as an expert. Recall from Section 6.4 that expert authority does not constitute a prima facie justification to accept that

- the expert's TAP *represents the current state of the domain* as opposed to an idiosyncratic position;
- the expert is *trustworthy*;
- the expert has an *interest* in helping the novice achieve their epistemic goals; or
- the expert has (absent extensive conversation) sufficient understanding of novices' goals, interests, or values that their testimony, advice, or performance is likely to be helpful.

It turns out that compromising conditions can compromise a novice's investigation in two ways—they can prevent an accurate assessment of whether someone is an expert and they can constitute reasons not to trust even genuine experts.

We come to understand the track record of a doctor differently than we come to understand the track record of an auto mechanic. So, novices must still *get* and *use* relevant indirect evidence to evaluate experts. They have a responsibility to use it well. Whether they muster the energy to do so, and what social factors may undermine their motivation to do so, is another matter. I speak here only about strategies available to novices for recognizing experts.

Unfortunately, our interest in experts is not always value-neutral, time-neutral, or low-stakes. The experts we need don't always operate in kind environments or on the cognitive mainland. Further, our ability to use our intellectual resources well is often compromised by cognitive or social obstacles, such as filter bubbles and echo chambers. All these factors point to a different version of the recognition problem, to which we now turn.

8

The Hard Recognition Problem, Disagreement, and Trust

> [T]he dealers wholesale or retail who sell the food of the body ... praise indiscriminately all their goods, without knowing what are really beneficial or hurtful. ... In like manner, those who carry the wares of knowledge ... praise them all alike; though I should not wonder, O my friend, if many of them were really ignorant of their effect upon the soul.
> (Socrates in Plato's *Protagoras*, 313c–313e, trans. Jowett, 1892)

In this final chapter, I explore two more versions of the recognition problem: the hard recognition problem (Section 8.1) and the novice/2-expert problem (Section 8.2). While I am pessimistic about the prospects for solving the hard recognition problem (HRP), I do not think it is in-principle unsolvable. I only worry that the social structures needed for solving it—or, at least, mitigating its implications—require a kind of coordination among epistemic agents that is inconsistent with human nature.

In Section 8.3, I explore the normative implications of two different types of expert contribution: testimony and advice. Whether we should trust experts, I argue, depends partly on what their expertise means for us. If an expert is testifying about their domain, and I know little about that domain, then little is at stake for me in trusting them. I contrast, if an expert is asking something of me—to believe or do something—that advice crosses into the domain of my interests, values, and preferences. Since (I will argue) I am an expert on these things, I have epistemic standing relative to whether I accept that advice.

In Section 8.4, I highlight the overall conclusions of this book and identify some remaining questions. If my conclusions in this book are right, experts do stand in a better epistemic position than novices, and even other experts have good reason to seek them out. However, my conclusions also suggest that there are a number of good reasons to be skeptical of experts at times. I hope this book offers some guidance about when to trust experts and how strongly.

8.1 The Hard Recognition Problem

Our solution to the easy recognition problem points toward a harder problem, and one that affects experts no less than novices. If any one of the conditions for solving the easy problem are not met, then others are not well placed to justifiably identify or trust experts:

- The domain is on a cognitive island (both subtle and isolated).
- The need for expertise is time sensitive.
- The need for expertise is high stakes.
- The domain's environment is wicked.
- The domain's environment is value-charged.

Call this set of individually sufficient conditions *compromising conditions* (CCs). The possibility that one of these CCs is present in any given instance of needing an expert suggests the following Hard Recognition Problem (HRP):

(HRP)

(1) **Experts are significantly better placed in their domains than novices.**
(2) **Experts need other experts just as much as novices do.**
(3) **Experts and novices can justifiably believe that some bit of testimony or advice is trustworthy as expert testimony or advice only if experts and novices have sufficient access to a domain and proxy evidence is strongly connected with expert competence.**
(4) **In CCs, either experts and novices lack sufficient access to a domain or proxy evidence is not strongly connected with expert competence.**
    Therefore:
(5) **In CCs, neither experts nor novices can justifiably believe that some bit of testimony or advice is trustworthy as expert testimony or advice.**

Note that HRP combines questions of *identifying* expertise and *trusting* expert testimony. This is because CCs render expertise problematic in both ways. For example, if a domain's environment is value-charged, such as the COVID-19 pandemic, then nonexperts or epistemic trespassers may be incentivized to make themselves seem like genuine experts, which puts novices (and even some experts) at an epistemic disadvantage when deciding whom to trust. Further, in value-charged circumstances, genuine experts may be incentivized to present themselves overly confident or to oversimplify an issue for the sake of convincing novices to accept their testimony. Further still, the COVID-19 pandemic highlighted the ways in which novel situations impact expert authority. Though there were many experts on virology, immunology, and epidemiology, there was no expert consensus about the new SARS-CoV-2 virus. In order to work toward consensus, there was disagreement among experts until the empirical evidence favored one expert judgment over others. This was most apparent to the public in the debate over whether various kinds of masks were effective against transmission of the virus. Thus, CCs make it difficult both to know whether someone is an expert and, even after we have identified genuine experts, to know whether to trust them.

With respect to the argument, premise 1 is the same as ERP-C from Section 7.2. Premise 2 stems from all the instances in this book we have seen where experts justifiably rely on other experts. For example, weak specialized experts in a domain rely on strong specialized experts in that domain to improve their competence; strong specialized experts engage with other strong specialized experts to improve further (as in competition and high-level research); strong specialized experts rely on other specialized experts in their domain to confirm or disconfirm their conclusions; and strong specialized experts in one domain rely on strong specialized experts in other domains in order to complete complex projects (expert coordination). Based on premise 2, premise 3 expands the recognition concern to include experts, since CCs render the trustworthiness of many instances of putative expertise difficult for anyone to assess.

Premise 3 also introduces an ambiguity that emerges from CCs, namely, the ambiguity between whether someone is a genuine expert and whether they are giving testimony or advice on the basis of that expertise. Consider that an epistemic trespasser is a genuine expert in a domain, just not the domain at issue. So, being able to successfully identify someone as a genuine expert *in some domain* is not sufficient for trusting the expert in the domain at issue. For example, consider the case of Andrew Wakefield, who led many people to question the safety of the MMR vaccine (Rao and Andrade 2011). While Wakefield is an expert, both as a physician and as a gastroenterologist, he is not an immunologist, which means that, as the first author on the famously now-retracted article attempting to smear the MMR vaccine, he was an epistemic trespasser.

But even if he had been an expert in the relevant domain, his ability to speak as an expert was compromised by his financial conflict of interest and fraudulent research. ERP frames the problem of whether to trust a person "as an expert"; that is, if we aren't careful, we can be misled into thinking that if we have good reason to believe a person is an expert, we have good reason to trust them. HRP, however, frames the problem as whether "an instance of testimony or advice is trustworthy *as expert testimony or advice.*" In other words, irrespective of whether someone is an expert in a domain, does their putatively expert testimony or advice meet epistemic conditions for trusting that testimony or advice as epistemically authoritative in the domain at issue?

Finally, premise 3 highlights how the recognition problem hangs on the domain access question and the connection question (discussed in Section 7.3). And premise 4 simply states that CCs preclude sufficient answers to either the domain access or connection questions.

Interestingly, even if we agree that this is a hard problem, it might not be all that significant if CCs are rare or insignificant. Whether they are rare is an empirical question. However, CCs seem to me, anecdotally speaking, to be the domains in which we have the highest vested interest in expert testimony or advice—domains related to our health, political and social well-being, climate, and money. If this is right, then we are likely not justified in trusting experts regarding many of the issues that are most important to us.

Of course, confounding factors don't just affect experts or pseudo-experts. Whether, for example, the Dunning-Kruger effect leads a novice to unwarranted arrogance about, say, bathroom tile work or cooking, may matter very little (except to the family members subjected to it). Whether one is trapped in an echo chamber about whether *The Lord of the Rings* trilogy is the greatest fantasy fiction of all time is not very concerning (to most of us). But if they compromise novices' judgments regarding public health behavior, medical decisions, financial planning, and so on, then even the best strategies for addressing CCs will be of little avail when they need experts the most. Confounding factors turn the easy problem into a hard problem, and the hard problem is, seemingly, intractable.

Is there a way to mitigate the hard problem? I am not optimistic. However, I think some recent work on the relationships among domains offers a chance at a way forward.[1] Johnny Brennan (2020), for example, draws an analogy between the social role of experts and an ancient Indian parable, where six blind men attempt to describe an elephant, each from a different angle. After describing quite different experiences, the men proceed to contradict one another over the "true" nature of the elephant. In the parable, the men find themselves in a lamentable stale mate, though we who hear it recognize the simple solution. Rather than arguing about what an elephant is like within the limits of one's own perception, each observer should admit that their perspective is limited and that the others may have information they lack. In that case, they could collaborate on a description of the elephant. If experts are like elephants, novices might not be in the dire position painted by the HRP. Brennan explains: "The ecological as well as the motivational obstacles facing novices can be overcome if they can build the right coalition" (2020: 57).

A *coalition of trust* is a group of novices in a target domain who combine their diversity of competencies (which may include expertise in other, closely related domains) to assess and confirm or disconfirm the authority of an expert in the target domain. How might a coalition of trust accomplish this task? Brennan argues that its feasibility depends, first, on giving up a common assumption in expertise studies, namely, that experts and novices occupy opposite ends of the epistemic spectrum in the domain at issue. Rather than starting from the assumption that all experts are highly competent and all novices are uniformly incompetent, novices should begin from the assumption that "both novices and experts vary widely in their competencies" (Brennan 2020: 55). Second, it depends on "a richer picture of the overlap in domains" including "how competence in those areas of overlap" (Brennan 2020: 56).

Consider that there is little reason to be concerned about a novice who chooses to trust someone as a medical expert when that person is (a) in a hospital, (b) wearing a white coat, (c) has an "MD" badge, and (d) claims to be a doctor. (To be sure, there are cases where trust would not be warranted, but those are rare enough that it would not be a mark against her epistemic responsibility.) Contrast this case with a novice who encounters someone who exhibits (b)–(d), but rather than meeting them in a hospital, they see a video of them on the internet.

A key difference in these cases is how the evidence related to credibility in each case is *linked* to evidence the novice already has good reason to trust. Recall from the previous chapter that novices' prospects for accurately identifying experts depends partly on their ability to assess how close an expert's domain is to what C. Thi Nguyen (2018) calls their "cognitive mainland," that is, how closely their knowledge and skills are related to things they already understand well enough to assess.

But even if this novice were not savvy to the epistemic dangers of internet "doctors," it wouldn't take a physician to explain why trust is not likely warranted in the second case, especially if the question relates to a high-stakes health matter. In fact, groups of novices come together to vet putative expert claims in numerous ways: consumer reviews, patient support groups, and (my favorite example) the CRAAP test (currency, relevance, authority, accuracy, and purpose), developed by a group of librarians in California to help students in all domains evaluate the reliability of academic sources. These strategies work to the degree that novices' competence either overlaps with or is nested with the target domain, or some combination.

If this is right, then coalitions of trust can help novices because they link domains of expertise in ways that support justified trust in experts. This is a noteworthy development given that so much of the expertise literature advises novices to work on their own to track down and assess credentials and track records. In reality, experts rarely conduct extensive background checks on other experts. A nephrologist does not try to find out what place the oncologist graduated in their class, their publication record, whether they have demonstrated trustworthiness, or even whether they have a track record of success. That's not to say that these features do not figure into domain linkages, but simply that those features are not the most accessible or even the most relevant to adequately identifying experts. The nephrologist instead relies on contextual and institutional cues, which involve groups of people who affirm the oncologist's status as an expert, as well as the overlap in their respective domains, to decide whether to trust the oncologist's recommendation on a patient.

To be sure, this coalition strategy can break down. Some imposters do a practically foolproof job of deceiving others. This suggests an additional aspect of successful coalitions of trust that is less evident but no less important. All the examples of linked domains mentioned in this chapter and the previous one operate under accountability conditions—market forces, accreditation requirements, peer evaluations, or easy access to litigation. It is more epistemically responsible to trust a plumber if you and the plumber both know that, if the plumber makes a mistake, you can hold them accountable to fix it. If they know you can hold them accountable, they are less likely to make the mistake in the first place. Stephen Turner calls these "bonding" conditions (2014, 188ff). Bonding conditions introduce transparency into the novice-expert transaction that is not present on, say, the internet or in political speech. Without a means of holding putative experts accountable, a coalition of trust may become subject to its own ideological commitments, and then do more harm than good.

8.2 The Novice/2-Expert Problem and the Problem of Expert Disagreement

In cases where novices have identified genuine experts, they face a further problem, namely, which of two experts to believe when those experts disagree. As we saw in Chapter 1, much is made of this disagreement when the credibility of experts is at stake. We often either appeal to experts to support a claim or appeal to experts to contradict other experts. Sometimes we then point to the disagreement as a reason to suspend judgment about expertise altogether. The significance of this problem becomes clear when we start to understand why genuine experts disagree. I only scratch the surface here, but one key reason for disagreement, namely, assigning different values to risks, is relevant for some of our most pressing social problems, like climate change and vaccines.

8.2.1 Idealized Disagreement versus Everyday Disagreement

Before diving in, it is worth noting that there is a rich philosophical literature on disagreement (Feldman and Warfield 2010; Goldman and Whitcomb 2011; Machuca 2013; Matheson 2015). This literature focuses largely on disagreement among "epistemic peers" (Kelly 2005)—whether those peers are experts or not. This literature is primarily aimed at the epistemic implications of what Jon Matheson (2015) calls "idealized disagreement," that is, what you should do when someone who has all the cognitive abilities that you do and all the same information that you do about a topic but nevertheless disagrees with you. You are both fallible, so you are equally likely to be right or wrong. Should you stand firm? Should you suspend judgment? Should you lower the degree to which you believe (conciliate)?

Matheson writes that two people, S1 and S2, are in an idealized disagreement just in case:

(i) **S1 and S2 genuinely disagree about p at t.**
(ii) **S1 and S2 are qualified epistemic peers about p at t.**
(iii) **S1 and S2 each has access to their own evidence, processing of it, or resultant attitudes relevant to p at t, and this access is no better or worse than their access to the other individual's evidence, processing of it, or resultant attitudes relevant to p at t.**
(iv) **At t, S1 and S2 are not aware of the attitudes of any "third-parties" regarding p. (2015: 114)**

By "qualified epistemic peer," Matheson means that two people are not just equally placed in a domain (using Fricker's terminology of epistemic placement), they are both *well placed* in a domain: "[Q]ualified epistemic peers about p are both good sources about p and equally good sources about p" (25). This still doesn't imply expertise, since it could include one-off positioning, such as S1 and S2's having equal eyesight and looking at a painting from the same distance under the same lighting conditions, and so on.

Interestingly, while Matheson thinks that discussions of idealized disagreement are important for philosophers, they are so idealized that "it is doubtful whether it ever actually occurs" (33), for at least three reasons. First, it is doubtful that any two individuals "ever have *exactly* the same evidence pertaining to any one matter" (115, italics his). Second, "it is doubtful that any two individuals are equally good at processing evidence" (116). Third, even if both had the same evidence and were equally good processors of information, the likelihood that the circumstances under which they evaluate p are exactly alike is implausible. Matheson calls disagreement between qualified peers that fails to meet these idealized conditions *everyday disagreement*.

The fact that expert disagreement is almost always *everyday* and not *idealized* has significant implications for expertise studies. Matheson writes:

> [W]hile it is very improbable that any two individuals are in *exactly* as good of an epistemic position on the topic, neither party may be able to tell *which* party is in the better epistemic position. There simply *being* a difference in the quality of epistemic position needn't give either party a *reason* to give more or less weight to the other party's opinion. (116, italics his)

This means that the novice/2-expert problem is also what Goldman ([2001] 2002: 143) calls the "expert/expert" problem, the problem "in which experts seek to appraise the authority or credibility of other experts." If experts cannot be sure whether fellow experts are epistemic peers, then they, too, face the question of whom to trust when experts disagree.

Because the novice/2-expert problem presupposes that we have solved the recognition problem, I focus on an example that affects both novices and experts. To be sure, not all novice/2-expert problems are also expert/expert problems, as in the case of climate change or the safety of the MMR vaccine. In those cases, experts do have tools by which to formulate good reasons for thinking they are better placed in a domain than those who disagree. Because of this, novices have at least some resources, in the form of meta-experts, to help resolve the question of whom to trust. This solution does presuppose, of course, that there are either no CCs or that they can be mitigated. If there were, then novices would be left with another version of the HRP.

But let us consider the more difficult case of when a novice/2-expert problem is also an expert/expert problem. A question we might think should have a clear answer by now is whether women over forty years old should get a mammogram every year. This is not an especially isolated domain, despite its technical subtlety. It is time sensitive but only on a broad, social scale—the sooner we can identify a cure or effective prophylactic measures, the better. The individual decision of whether to have an annual or biannual mammogram is not emergent or urgent; everyone has time to consult the literature before making a decision. It is certainly a value-charged and high-stakes decision, since life and morbidity are on the line, but, happily, the interests of breast cancer doctors and patients with breast cancer are largely, except in idiosyncratic cases, aligned. This is true on a global level.

Despite all this, and perhaps surprisingly, the domain is sharply divided as to whether screening is effective and to what degree in which demographic of women. Breast cancer surgeons in the United States tend to think the answer is yes—annual mammograms starting at age forty catch cancers earlier, and this leads to fewer deaths from breast cancer. Family medicine doctors in the United States tend to think screening every two years is fine—even if mammograms prevent some deaths, they also lead to unnecessary treatments, anxiety, and fear. In France, mammograms are not recommended until age fifty, and then only every other year.

So, experts offer different recommendations. Who has the better perspective? It turns out this is an incredibly difficult question to answer. Take the simple claim that *mammograms prevent deaths*. How many deaths do mammograms prevent? At what age? Is that number worth the problems with false-positive rates?

A French public health report from 2016 found highly conflicting results on the usefulness of mammograms (see Figure 8.1).

On one hand, you might think: *Well, look, any way you slice it, screening saves more lives than not screening*. But this does not take into account what is traded off by getting the screening, that is, the risks associated with screening. Consider that about 11.4 people per 100,000 died in highway car crashes in 2017. We could reduce that number by lowering the speed limit to 20 miles per hour or requiring all cars to be built like army tanks. But the trade-off is not worth it. We prefer the risk to the costs of avoiding the risk.

What are the risks associated with breast cancer screening? Mammograms are notorious for false positives. False positives lead to more aggressive tests, including surgical biopsies, which have high complication rates. Further, not all

Type	Author, year of publication, reference	Results
Meta-analysis	Gøtzsche PC, Nielsen M. Cochrane Database Syst Rev, 2009 Oct 7;(4) Screening for breast cancer with mammography	50 deaths avoided every 100,000 women screened
	Gøtzsche PC, Nielsen M. Cochrane Database Syst Rev. 2011 Jan 19;(1): Screening for breast cancer with mammography	
	Independent UK Panel on Breast Cancer Screening. Lancet 2012; 380: 1778–86 The benefits and harms of breast cancer screening: an independent review	430 deaths avoided every 100,000 women screened
Literature review	Hofvind S et al. J Med Screen. 2012;19 Suppl 1:57-66. False-positive results in mammographic screening for breast cancer in Europe: a literature review and survey of service screening programmes	700 to 900 deaths avoided every 100,000 women screened
Randomized study	Kalager M et al. N Engl J Med. 2010 Sep 23;363(13):1203-10. Effect of screening mammography on breast-cancer mortality in Norway	40 deaths avoided every 100,000 women screened
	Tabár L et al. Radiology. 2011 Sep;260(3):658-63 Swedish two-county trial: impact of mammographic screening on breast cancer mortality during 3 decades	75 deaths avoided every 100,000 women screened

Figure 8.1 *Rapport Du Comité D'Orientation* 1 (2016: 69). Translated from French by Dr. Loïc Boulanger.

breast cancers are fatal. Yet, the stigma and fear surrounding breast cancer are such that simply knowing they have the cancer will lead some women to start chemotherapy, radiation, or in some cases get a mastectomy, all of which have substantial risks.

Trading off these risks and benefits is hard enough. The same French report cites findings published in *JAMA* (*Journal of the American Medical Association*) in 2014 that attempt to help women decide if screening is worth the risk (see Figure 8.2).

But even if one has a clear sense of how they would trade off the risks versus the benefits if the experts agreed about the deaths averted by breast cancer screening, the experts don't agree, as we saw in Figure 8.1.

Attitudes among physicians vary widely. One surgeon I spoke with simply discounted the data, saying roughly that any hardships associated with further testing and treatment are outweighed by the trauma of dying with breast cancer. Another recognized that the question depends heavily on just how bad those hardships are and how patients experience those hardships.

8.2.2 Resolving Everyday Disagreement among Experts: Independence and Epistemic Election

If this is how experts respond to this disagreement, how should novices respond? Notice that appealing to meta-experts will not help. Given the range of attitudes

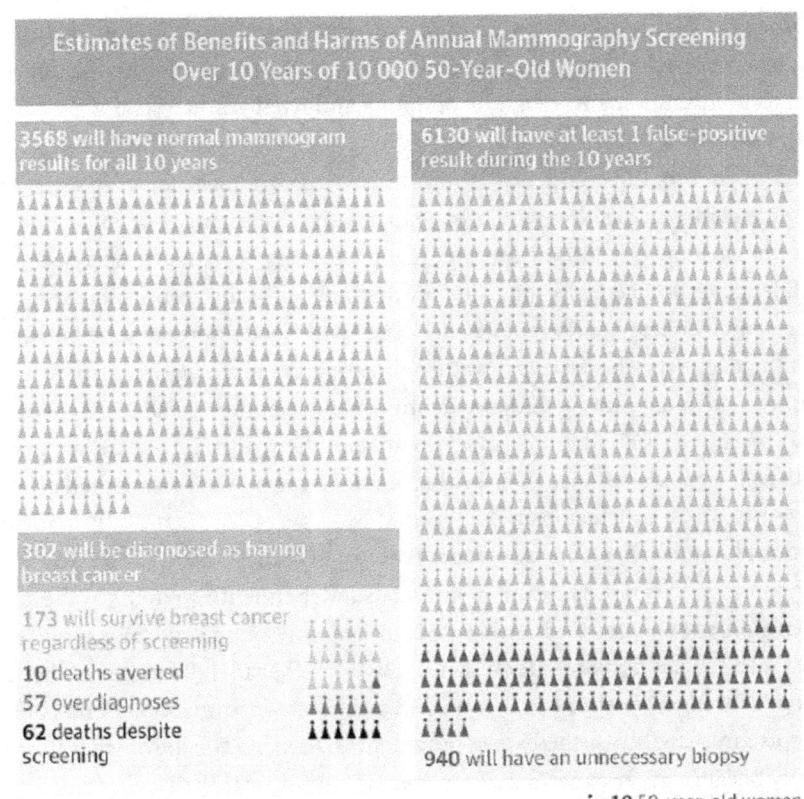

Figure 8.2 *Rapport Du Comité D'Orientation* 2 (2016: 156). Taken from Jin J. (2014).

among experts, any particular meta-expert will simply reflect another sound in the cacophony. Given how many voices have weighed in on cases like this, "the small and subtle differences in epistemic position between any two individuals seems [*sic*] to matter very little in the end" (Matheson 2015: 125).

What might help? One insight from the idealized disagreement literature is the importance of the "independence" of expert judgments. If all experts look at a piece of evidence and come to the conclusion that p, that consensus is better evidence that p than if two experts looked at the evidence and concluded that p, and then all the others testify that p on the basis of those two. The rest are *epistemically dependent* on the first two. Thus, if it turns out that Group A of experts arrive at the conclusion that p largely independently of one another, while Group B of experts arrive at the conclusion that not-p, but they are largely dependent on a few experts' judgments, this is a reason to trust Group A over Group B. Factors like group-think and cultural biases tend to taint dependent judgments. "We are all well aware of the correlations between political opinions and the color of the state you grew up in, philosophical opinions and where you went to grad school, and religious opinions and what country you grew up in" (Matheson 2015: 128).

But epistemic independence is not decisive. As we have seen, investigating the same evidence together with other experts and discussing how you arrived at your conclusion with those experts can appropriately increase or decrease your confidence in your conclusion. This is what epistemically responsible mentors and research colleagues do for one another. David Coady notes that he presumes "that the scientists who believe in anthropogenic climate change have not reached their conclusions entirely independently of one another" (2012: 45). This is partly because it is a rather narrow domain, and their work is well known to one another. It is partly because their evidence is taken from sites distributed around the world. Their conclusions are arrived at by expert coordination. But, for the reasons I have noted, Coady concludes that just because "scientific consensus (or near consensus) is not the result of scientists independently arriving at the same conclusion should not undermine its significance from a novice's perspective. If anything, it should strengthen it" (2012: 45). What this illustrates is that the strength of expert consensus is not primarily a matter of independence but of the epistemic quality of the expert judgments. Do experts believe what they do merely because other experts in their domain say so, or is their belief a function of an assessment of the evidence that includes feedback or input from others who are seemingly as well placed in the domain? Unfortunately, this is not a matter that would be open to novices to evaluate.

Is there an option open to novices? Matheson thinks one possibility is to use an "epistemic election" (Matheson and Carey 2013; Matheson 2015). "The epistemic election is a metaphor for compiling the relevant higher-order evidence and declaring the 'winning' attitude as the result" (Matheson 2015: 126). "Higher-order" evidence is evidence about the quality, nature, and strength of our evidence. So, unlike a democratic election, epistemic elections do not treat all votes equally. Expert votes get more weight than novice votes. Matheson weighs independent expert votes more than dependent expert votes (126–7).

Matheson argues that this strategy helps adjudicate some of the concerning disagreements we face in contemporary US society, such as whether former President Obama was born in Kenya, whether the earth is more than 6,000 years old, whether the MMR vaccine is safe, and whether humans are contributing substantially to increased global temperatures (126–7). But for other controversial beliefs—beliefs about politics, religion, science, and philosophy—the evidence is not so clear. Absent a clear result from the epistemic election, Matheson argues that we are rationally obligated to suspend judgment:

(1) **Regarding many controversial propositions, you should suspend judgment regarding the result of the "epistemic election" regarding those propositions.**
(2) **If (1), then for many controversial propositions you should suspend judgment regarding those propositions.**
(3) **Therefore, for many controversial propositions, you should suspend judgment regarding those propositions. (2015: 129)**

Our breast cancer screening case is a prime example of a disagreement for which the epistemic election yields no clear answer. Experts themselves are at a loss for how to advise women. Many default into a dogmatic position: *Women should be screened every year, irrespective of the consequences.* Others, who are concerned to mitigate the consequences of bad advice (or at least to mitigate their responsibility for those consequences), attempt what is called "shared decision-making" with patients, to elicit from them how much different bad consequences would mean to them, and then to offer their own perspectives on the value of those consequences and to offer advice on the relative and absolute risks of those bad consequences.

Unfortunately, Matheson's conclusion won't help these folks. Suspending judgment is not an option. Women must make a decision about when, if ever, to get screened for breast cancer. The consequences must be risked. Of course, one may have good reasons to do something that are not *epistemic* reasons. One could also have pragmatic reasons. But if listening to experts is not rational under these circumstances, are they stuck doing what's irrational? I think the answer is no, and I think the explanation for why is hidden in an assumption that has filtered its way through the entire book.

8.3 Trusting Experts: Testimony, Advice, and the Specter of Paternalism

Up to now, we have been treating expert testimony and expert advice as if they are, epistemically, of a piece. If an expert is genuinely an expert in a domain, we have assumed there is a prima facie reason to trust them in that domain, regardless of whether they are simply making claims or giving advice. The problem is that testimony and advice come apart in nontrivial ways.

Imagine a horticulturist gives you a list of seven things to do to keep a hydrangea plant alive. This list is, at one and the same time, testimony (a description of what keeps hydrangeas alive) and advice (what you should do to keep this hydrangea alive). In this situation, you can justifiably accept that the horticulturist is an expert and believe their testimony, and still be justified in not taking their advice—for instance, because you couldn't care less about keeping the hydrangea alive, or maybe you care but not enough to spend your time or money doing all seven steps.

8.3.1 Testimony versus Advice

It is clear that giving testimony and giving advice are different acts. One is about beliefs and the other about actions. Yet, someone might believe they are epistemically connected in the case of expertise—you are trusting that a person knows what they are talking about regardless of the content of what they are talking about (i.e., regardless of whether they expect you to believe them or do what they say). Linda Zagzebski (2012), for example, argues that an expert's "conscientious authority" takes our ends into account when giving advice (136–9). Christian Quast (2018a and b) regards it a necessary condition of expertise that experts help agents achieve their ends, which includes offering advice.

But notice that taking advice does not necessarily require belief, as Eric Wiland (2018) points out:

> Advice is advice to do something, not to believe something. So to trust someone's advice is (roughly) to do what is advised. If someone advises you to be patient, or to donate more money to the poor, then you take her advice only if you are patient, or if you donate more money to the poor. Trusting advice requires action. (11)

Interestingly, Wiland argues that giving advice also opens one to moral implications over and above epistemic implications. "If you offer mistaken advice, and your advisee trusts you, you haven't merely *said* something false or bad. You would also be on the hook for what has been done" (12, italics his). Alfred Moore (2017) puts it this way: "The general knows *how* to go to war, but not *whether* to do so. The rhetorician knows *how* to persuade an audience, but not *what* it is good to persuade them of" (19, italics his). This is, perhaps, why some doctors are so careful not to sanction certain behaviors like using marijuana for pain or drinking a little alcohol while pregnant. There is not yet enough data to judge what amount or how often these behaviors are helpful or innocuous. So, instead, doctors sometimes err on the side of extreme caution.

A prominent example of this is that, for many years, pregnant women have been regarded as a "vulnerable population." Only recently have the national research ethics guidelines known as the Common Rule allowed pregnant women to participate in medical research. For decades, it was thought too dangerous to subject fetuses to unknown risks. But today, when diseases like Zika present a special threat to pregnant women, this overcautiousness has proved disastrous because there are few known safe medicines for pregnant women. Researchers have to take responsibility for the fact that their advice not to include pregnant women in research has put pregnant women all over the world at risk.

Trusting advice is distinct from trusting testimony in a further, more important sense, as well. My time, skills, and energy are scarce resources. Every day I have to decide how to behave in light of my short life, basic needs, and varied interests. Thus, if you are expert on the cosmos, and you tell me all sorts of trivia about Pluto, the Big Bang, and the current number of identified exoplanets, I may believe you simply because it is not worth my time to consider the evidence for your expertise and conduct the relevant epistemic election. It requires nothing of my time, skills, or energy, and I will not be affected if you're wrong. But if you tell me I should stop eating meat because it causes unnecessary harm and, as you point out, I don't believe anyone should cause unnecessary harm, suddenly I recognize a reason to reevaluate how I deploy my scarce resources. What should I do?

8.3.2 Taking Advice in Light of Our Interests

On one hand, I don't want to cause unnecessary harm. On the other, I know that many people who are against eating meat have strong emotional and political reasons for advocating. I may also think that "activists" in general tend to overstate some social problems for the sake of causing the sort of changes they want. So, should I invest the time to see if they're right? What am I risking by not doing so? How much am I losing if I do the work and then find out they're wrong, or at least not completely right? Let's say I am concerned enough about harms to do the work.[2]

Here's an interesting possibility. I could do the work, find out they are mostly right, but then decide that the type of harm I would be culpable for in continuing to eat meat is not significant enough to warrant changing my eating habits. I could discover that I could do better by the animal welfarists' own lights by advocating against the harms associated with large-scale farming practices. I could also decide that the harms experienced by, say, fish or shellfish are not comparable to the harms experienced by cattle and chickens, and so become a pescatarian rather than a vegetarian or vegan.

Is such a position rational? I think it could be, depending on the evidence. This is because, in the case of advice, the distribution of authority always extends beyond the expert's domain and into domains where others have important epistemic advantages. So, while animal welfarists may be experts in the domain of morally salient concerns about animals, I am an expert on *what I consider valuable* about the impact of certain behaviors.

To be sure, I could be wrong about what's valuable. For instance, I may weigh the cost of giving up meat-eating too highly relative to the cost of the harm meat-eating imposes on animals. The power of ethical argument is that it allows us to engage with one another about the appropriate values to assign to different costs and benefits in any given case (Rachels and Rachels 2015: ch. 1; see also Matheson, McElreath, and Nobis 2018). This suggests that I may justifiably agree with your expert judgment within the scope of your domain but justifiably disagree with your assessment of its implications for my behavior. This would mean the nature of your argument would need to shift from convincing me *you are right* about claims in your domain to convincing me that *I am not weighing certain values appropriately*. You should offer me a moral argument.

Returning to the case of advice, an expert's advice necessarily implicates something of value to me, namely, my scarce resources as an agent (my limited time, the opportunity costs of taking your advice rather than doing something else, the costs and benefits of that advice for my interests). And, as an adult, no one knows *better* than I do the value of certain behaviors to me. This is true even if I don't know them all that well. I may not be highly competent with my values. I could be wildly mistaken about what is in my interests. But no one else is any *more* competent with them than I am; that is, I am better placed with respect to them even if I am not an expert.

So, let's assume that the typical case of expert testimony distributes authority according to competence in a domain (which, again, could include deep understanding or performative ability) and that the weight of authority heavily favors the experts. As we saw in Chapter 6, expert authority tracks placement in a domain, so people who are highly competent in a domain have more authority than people who are less competent.

It follows that when an expert speaks in a domain in which they are less competent, they have less authority in that domain. Consider the case where domains overlap. An expert in a specialty (such as nephrology, hematology, or vascular surgery) may have some expertise in related domains (such as pharmacy, anesthesiology, or radiology), but because of their specialization, their authority in these other domains is weaker (hence, the attractiveness of what's now called "team-based medicine"). So, what happens when an expert in a specialist domain engages with an expert in a related specialist domain? They should recognize that the expert is better placed in that domain than they are. An expert breast cancer surgeon's competence in radiography is likely higher than a nonmedical professional's; but it is not higher than an expert radiographer's, and vice versa. Nevertheless, their competence overlaps at a certain degree of understanding in one another's domains. We saw a similar sort of overlap in Chapter 5 with Figure 5.1 (see p. 116).

In this case, the overlap is about access to evidence relative to a single belief, namely, whether the patient is in pain. In what remains, I argue that expert advice implicates a much larger portion of information within the advisee's competence.

8.3.3 Overlapping Domains, Conflicts among Interests

How, then, do these relationships relate to our discussion of expert testimony versus expert advice? I argue that *all* instances of expert *advice* constitute cases of overlapping expertise, and that the overlap is with a domain that is strongly in the advisee's purview, namely, the advisee's interests and values. Here is the first half of the argument:

(1) Advice is aimed at changing my behaviors.
(2) My behaviors require scarce time, skills, or resources.
(3) Deciding to use my scarce resources depends on how valuable that use is to me (my interests and preferences).
(4) The strength of authority for me of some advice depends on how well placed in a domain the authority is relative to me.
    Therefore,
(5) The strength of authority for me of some advice depends on how well placed I am relative to the authority regarding my interests and preferences.

Recall from Section 6.1 that many political philosophers contend that political authority is legitimate only if a ruler has: *knowledge* of the people's interests, the *ability* to facilitate citizens' fulfilling those interests, and the *willingness* to facilitate their fulfilling them. Recall, also, that there is good historical evidence that rarely, if ever, are all three conditions met by someone. It turns out that this rarity also pervades the social and interpersonal levels (see Watson 2014).

In some cases, we can know one another's interests, as when we discuss what someone wants for a birthday gift or where we want to go on vacation. But even then, there is no guarantee. If I tell you I want a Sony TV for my birthday, I may have specific models in mind that I don't want. I don't even realize this matters until you show up with one of those models that I didn't want, and suddenly, I don't know how to act. I believe I should be grateful because you tried to get me what I wanted, but there is always some tinge of disappointment.

In some cases, the stakes are much higher. In studies about what medical decisions proxy decision-makers would make for their loved ones when they can't make decisions for themselves, about one-third of proxies choose options the patient wouldn't have (Shalowitz, Garrett-Mayer, and Wendler 2006).

This leads to the second half of the argument:

(6) I am better placed to know my interests and preferences than anyone else (i.e., I am better placed in the domain of my interests and preferences than anyone else).[3]
(7) If I am better placed in a domain than anyone else, then advice based on expertise in another domain is not prima facie authoritative for me. Therefore,
(8) Expert advice is based, necessarily, on expertise in a domain other than my interests and preferences. Therefore,
(9) Expert advice is not prima facie authoritative for me.

Note that the conclusion is not that expert advice is not authoritative for me or that it could not be authoritative for me. It certainly could be. When my and an expert's interests align in the relevant way—for example, when we have talked through what I need from them, when I am confident they are authentically committed to providing what I need—then expert advice is authoritative. This is how contracts and informed consent work. The argument simply concludes that, given that expert advice necessarily implicates me and my values, expert advice is not prima facie authoritative for me. It requires further epistemic (and usually moral) assessment.

Philosopher Evan Selinger (2011) explores this argument through Henrik Ibsen's play, *An Enemy of the People* (1882). In the story, Thomas Stockmann is a doctor at a spa in a small European tourist town. Stockmann discovers that a poison is contaminating the water of the spa and takes this information to the public, confident that they will rally together to clean and protect the water. Surprisingly (for Stockmann, anyway—the title gives it away for the rest of us), the townspeople reject the idea that they should try to fix the problem. Addressing the pollution would likely disrupt their lives and livelihoods, and they perceive that disruption as too great a risk to take to address a problem they are not currently experiencing. They value their current way of life more than the disruption of addressing the poison problem. Stockmann may be an expert on technical matters, but the people are experts on the lives they want to live. Stockmann is shocked at what today we would call their "science denial." He thought he would be the people's hero, but, instead, he's become their enemy.

Initially, this strikes us as a silly example that suggests quite the opposite of my conclusion. Of *course* the people should take Stockmann's advice. By focusing on the value of their current way of life, they are simply ignoring the *fact* that that way of life will be wiped out one way or another, either now, by prophylactic measures, or later, by the poison. At least the former offers them some hope of getting that life back, whereas the latter will dissuade tourists from ever coming back even if they eventually fix the problem. We recognize that Stockmann is not merely an expert about the water supply; he is also better placed with respect to the citizens' interests and values.

But it turns out that the example strikes us as silly only because we are sitting outside that world, with a sort of God's-eye perspective. In the play, the narrative makes it clear who has the "better" sense of the matter: The town *should* trust Stockmann and take the necessary precautions before people start getting sick, which would be an even greater threat to their lives and livelihoods than fixing the problem. We can see this clearly, though, only because we are audience members. As Selinger puts it: "The person in the audience is not standing anywhere, not situated with respect to this aspect; this third position, in short, is not a hermeneutically sensitive one" (2011: 35).

In the real world, however, there is no audience. We are *all* in the play. There is no neutral position from which to evaluate these matters. We have a stake in the choice of whom to trust:

> In any real controversy, . . . no one occupies the audience position; everyone is as it were "on stage" in a situated position, standing someplace with particular involvements which give rise to a particular understanding of the situation and, with it, an inclination to accept some people rather than others as authoritative. (Selinger 2011: 35)

To see how this plays out in real life, consider an example from an international debate over the safety of sewage sludge for use as fertilizer (Rakel 2004).

Sewage sludge is largely organic material that is left over after wastewater has been treated. It is mostly clean enough to be dumped into rivers or oceans. But in its solid state, contaminants "accumulate" (9). To test the safety of sewage sludge, scientists take soil samples from soil treated with the sludge and measure its toxicity. Interestingly, during one international project, scientists from the United States came to very different conclusions about appropriate levels of toxicity than scientists from the EU. This was the case despite the fact that "the research results generated by members of each community . . . were known and available to all" and the "members of the two communities even attended the same conferences" (20). So, they were all similarly trained experts with access to the same evidence. How did the two groups arrive at different conclusions?

What made the difference was how each group *weighed the risks* of toxicity. While the US scientists presumed the soil was safe unless they had strong evidence that it was not, the EU scientists required that the soil was proved safe "beyond a reasonable doubt" (16) before declaring it safe. According to the US group, the evidence was in, yet for the EU group, the tests were far from over. The former were open to certain risks while the latter were closed to them, and this disposition, according to Horst Rakel, is largely driven by cultural values: "Two main factors appear to be responsible for this marked divergence of standards: the value basis shaped by cultural affiliation of the involved scientists and/or the regulatory process" (21). The EU and the United States have a long history of assessing and managing risk differently, and this has shaped how they interpret and weigh the same evidence.

As with the soil scientists, the disagreement between Stockmann and the townspeople is not over Stockmann's expertise or even his claim that the water is polluted (his expert testimony) but how Stockmann weighs that fact against other interests and then concludes how they should act (his expert advice). Selinger explains that "The background and lifeworld involvements of citizens mean that economic and political motives loom much larger than they do for Stockmann . . . and suggest different people to whose advice they should defer in seeking to advance their welfare" (34).

What happens when the misalignment between experts and their audience turns on a domain in which their audience has a non-negligible level of competence, especially when that domain is their values and preferences? Ideally, it would be the same sort of conversation that two experts in the same domain have over how to weigh the evidence. The conversation revolves, inevitably, around value considerations. When the value interests are high stakes, as when deciding whether to take a doctor's advice to get surgery, whether to take a financial advisor's advice about how to save for retirement, whether to take your lawyer's advice to plead guilty, or whether to take a climate scientist's advice to eat less meat, the decision includes more than the relevant expertise of the advisor (though that is significant). It also includes how much you value the possible outcomes.

This is, admittedly, not a conclusive argument against epistemic paternalism. There are likely cases where others are justified in overriding my interests in certain information or epistemic behavior. What this argument shows is that the burden on experts for knowing when they have met the conditions for justification is high, and such evidence is not easy to get.

8.4 Onward and Upward: Conclusions and Remaining Questions[4]

Can the discussions in this book help us navigate the minefield of putative experts we encounter on a daily basis? I think only generally. Recognizing that expertise comes in degrees can help us know what questions to ask when two experts in a domain offer competing perspectives on a question or claim. Understanding how expertise is acquired, incrementally and through specialized training, can instill confidence when we discover that someone is an expert in some fields. Also, understanding that the sort of training needed for expertise in some domains is rather low (low-performance ceiling domains) can help alleviate some of our anxiety about approaching or questioning experts. But even still, we have to work hard to overcome the many obstacles to accurately identifying where someone falls on this continuum. Finally, I think understanding expert authority, from expert testimony or advice, can help us determine whether we have sufficient ability to assess that testimony or advice and, if we do, whether to accept it. Learning where we stand epistemically relative to experts, whether in a nested domain or overlapping domain, whether we are well or poorly placed in a domain, whether we have localized or generalized expertise, and so on, makes an important difference to the assessments we can make about experts.

Ultimately, I think there are five implications of this book for expertise studies:

- Expertise is competence in a domain that falls along a continuum (it is not a distinct kind of competence).

- Experts have authority that is a function of their epistemic placement in a domain and how they achieved that placement.
- Expert authority can be challenged in intellectually responsible ways, even, in some cases, by novices.
- Some experts (weaker experts) have an epistemic obligation to defer to some other (stronger) experts in their domain (i.e., expertise is not all-or-nothing).
- What counts as competence sufficient for expertise is domain-specific; expertise is not inherently knowledge-based, performance-based, and so on.
- Experts and novices stand in more complicated relationships than the domain of expertise studies has traditionally acknowledged (nesting relationships; overlapping relationships).

If all this is right, then expertise studies needs to become more nuanced. Rather than presuming a yawning gulf between novices and experts, scholars must wrestle with the degrees of competence of those engaged in any particular debate. Also, rather than assuming expertise establishes an infallible or indefeasible authority of experts over novices, they must wrestle with the voluminous access to one-off information that novices have (and sometimes understand) and the overlap between experts' competence and their audience's interests and values. Expertise scholars must also accommodate those cases where experts are justified in deferring to other experts in the same domain.

I also hope this book offers a useful framework for addressing the numerous remaining issues in both expertise studies and society generally. Further issues in expertise studies include the relationship between expertise and autonomy (Dellsén 2018), the concept of "understanding" as it informs various accounts of expertise (Elgin 2012, 2017), the relationship between expertise and democracy (Fischer 2009; Brown 2014), and whether expertise makes sense in domains like philosophy (Buckwalter 2014), ethics (McGrath 2008; Watson and Guidry-Grimes 2018), politics (Moore 2017; Fischer 2009; Watson 2017), and religion (Flower 2015).

Issues in society are more pressing, and they are not as straightforward as lamenting the "anti-expert" attitude of *hoi polloi* (see Watson 2021, Chapter 1). The increased promotion of STEM (science, technology, engineering, and math) curriculum in education has added a new dimension to the expectation to trust some types of people as experts. In my teaching, for example, I find it very difficult to persuade science and medical students to take seriously the idea that some scientific claims should be doubted, or that patients might have information that is indispensable to the success of a doctor's treatment plan, or that, once they've graduated, the advice of their peers in other scientific or medical specialties can be challenged in ways that actually lead to better decisions. Paul Feyerabend seemed to have an insight into this phenomenon in 1974, when he expressed concern about the state of science education:

> [C]onsider the role science now plays in education. Scientific "facts" are taught at a very early age and in the very same manner in which religious "facts" were taught only a century ago. There is no attempt to waken the critical abilities of the pupil so that [they] may be able to see things in perspective. ([1974] 2006: 360)

As Feyerabend shrewdly notes, students seem to have few critical tools by which to challenge one another or the information presented to them. So, they rather blithely accept them.

Yet this phenomenon contrasts starkly with evidence that the general public doesn't trust scientists or doctors very much. As a society, it seems we have trained one subpopulation to trust too much and another to trust too little, and we have not given either of them tools for calibrating their beliefs to evidence.

When we take the problems facing understanding, acquiring, and using expertise seriously, it is easy to become pessimistic about the prospects for expertise in helping to solve broad socioeconomic problems. In everyday circumstances, with domains on the cognitive mainland, in relatively kind environments, when the stakes are low and not substantially value-charged, we seem reasonably within our epistemic rights to trust people we perceive to be experts. Unfortunately, our most pressing and significant decisions—even decisions as seemingly straightforward as whether to get a mammogram— are beset by CCs. Further still, all of us must work to overcome potentially confounding factors like tribal epistemology and the Dunning-Kruger effect. Knowing about these problems is the first step, but because many of them are implicit or structural, knowing they exist is not enough.

Individually, when we find ourselves in wicked environments, talking with people whose interests may not align with ours in the relevant ways, or there is a lot on the line, our best option is often some form of pragmatic or ethical reasoning. Epistemic responsibility suggests that we should take experts seriously but also that we should balance expert testimony or advice against its likely impact on our own interests. This is not easy. Not all novices are equipped to do it. But given that we have a perspective on the meaning of a decision that experts do not have, epistemic responsibility should also prevent us from ignoring that perspective in the process. On the sociopolitical scale, things are even worse. Well-meaning experts sometimes endorse heinous policies, and political ideologues sometimes keep well-meaning experts out of places where they could do the most good. Addressing those problems will require expert coordination on a grand scale.

If this book reveals anything useful for our epistemic lives, I hope it is that experts are incredibly important for forming epistemically responsible beliefs and making epistemically responsible decisions, but they are just one factor in epistemic responsibility. Experts are complex, fallible, and culturally embedded epistemic agents just like the rest of us. Their high-stakes, administrative, and often public roles make them susceptible to biasing incentives that novices and other experts cannot fully understand. This means that how we cultivate our epistemic lives and virtues is largely up to us. We are not alone in the struggle, and we should not aspire to be, but not all help will get us where we want to go.

Notes

Preface

1 In Watson (2020: 176), I formulated this as: "A subject S is an expert in domain D if and only if **(a)** S has a high degree of competence in D at a time that **(b)** is acquired through rigorous training along one of two cognitive systems, and **(c)** that is confirmed to be high enough by the current state of skills and information in D at that time." The phrase "at a time" in (a) now seems redundant to that phrase in (c), so I removed it here.
2 Oliver Scholz draws this distinction (2009: 188; 2018: 30).

Chapter 1

1 "Dare to know!"
2 See Collins (2014: 11–16) for a discussion of the details.
3 McMyler (2011: 145) calls these "explanatory" reasons and "justificatory" reasons, respectively.
4 This is another example of base rate neglect. Base rate neglect can also be exacerbated by confirmation bias. If we think there is a correlation between two events, we may only count the times they are correlated and ignore or minimize the significance of the times they are not.
5 See Veatch (2000).
6 See Ritchie (2016) for a fascinating argument that challenges this percentage. The author goes to exceptional detail to argue that "97 percent" is largely a marketing tool, and the consensus could be as low as 80 percent. The question this raises for me is what purpose an argument like this is supposed to serve. Is it a corrective, offered simply in the name of accuracy? If so, why is it published in *Forbes*? As the author points out, any consensus above 80 percent is strong, and really, it doesn't matter if the consensus is 90 percent or 100 percent. So, what should general readers do with this info? The author doesn't say.
7 See Goldman (2002: 150–6) and David Coady (2012: 38–46) for discussions of the following the numbers strategy.
8 In *The New Organon* (1620 [2000]), Francis Bacon gave a similar warning against trusting on the basis of consensus: "A true consensus is one which (after

examination of the matter) consists in liberty of judgment converging on the same point. But the great majority of those who have accepted the philosophy of Aristotle have enslaved themselves to it from prejudice and the authority of others; so that it is rather discipleship and party unity than a consensus" (63).

9. We might have categorized this example of expert skepticism as "conflict-of-interest" skepticism (see Section 1.2.7). But notice that the attorney's conflict of interest motivates them to spark disagreement, and it is the disagreement that is doing the work. So, while there is a conflict of interest at play, that conflict is not the primary locus of skepticism in this case.

10. Physicians who claimed to treat patients using Hippocrates's teachings and principles.

11. Thanks to Markus Seidel for pointing this out.

12. It is not innocent for any source of fallible justification, whether induction, memory, or perception. My point here is simply that, while we often take it in stride in these more fundamental cases, we should be especially concerned by it in the complicated context of expert testimony.

13. See Tetlock and Gardner (2015); Bishop and Trout (2005). See also Mizrahi (2013).

14. Hardwig (1985) does admit that there can be exceptions to the rule that laypeople should defer to experts, as when there are "ad hominem" cases to be made: the expert is not disinterested, is not acting in good faith, is covering for peers, is caving to social pressures, or there is widespread disagreement among experts. Nevertheless, Hardwig's point is that if (a) a person takes someone to be an expert and (b) has no reason to doubt their expertise, then (c) they should defer to that expert on topics within the scope of their expertise.

Chapter 2

1. Kory Stamper, who wrote for *Merriam-Webster Dictionary* for many years, writes of one type of complexity translators face: "English grammar is not Latin grammar. The languages are cousins, but not close ones, because they come from different branches of the Indo-European language tree . . . . Blending grammatical systems from two languages on different branches of the Indo-European language tree is a bit like mixing orange juice and milk: you can do it, but it's going to be nasty" (2017: 47).

2. The root of *temptat* is *tento*, meaning "to feel the pulse" or "to get the sense of," and is also used to mean "to try" or "to test."

3. I say this with all due caveats and conditionals because I realize it is dangerous to say "the earliest known X" about anything.

4. Philosopher Steve Fuller says the noun use of "expert" did not emerge until the start of France's Third Republic, around 1870, when "expert witnesses" were called to detect forgeries in courts of law (2006: 342). This date seems unlikely given the prominent use of specialized witnesses in France two centuries earlier. Further, according to the *Oxford English Dictionary*, the noun form of *expert* is found in R. Johnson's 1630 *Kingdom and Commonwealth*, though I could not locate a copy to verify this.

5. Golan (2008: 889) explains: "The parts of the harbor furthest from the sea became increasingly clogged, and by mid-century the quay became inaccessible to shipping and the greater part of the cargo had to be carried to and from the town by lighters. Wells merchants and the ship owners blamed the deterioration of their harbor on some of the local landlords, who embanked and reclaimed from the North Sea significant tracts of land on both sides of the harbor's main channel. These embankments, Wells inhabitants believed, greatly weakened the body of backwater available for scouring their harbor, thereby causing it to choke up."

6. Even if these terms are *consistent with* "specialized expertise," as we understand it today, the history of these words does not constrain their use to that sense, and thus offers little normative guidance for how to understand it today.

7. Achim Landwehr (2004) follows a similar strategy, searching for conceptual equivalents of "specialized knowledge" in the history before the emergence of the word *expert*. Rather than exploring authority, skill, or artistry, he points to the influential role of "commissioners" in the period between the fifteenth and nineteenth centuries as a close analogue to specialized expertise. I find Landwehr's argument unconvincing, but not because I think it is prima facie implausible. In grouping together certain practices (various crafts, professions, and studies), I am doing something similar. However, I think Landwehr's discussion is too narrow to be helpful. He argues that a commissioner is distinct from a "common official" in that, unlike common officials, commissioners are highly educated and stand outside the normal political hierarchy, reporting directly to the "sovereign." The office of commissioner is "an institution that has to be filled with persons who possess the resources of knowledge, experience, and authority to accomplish relevant tasks" (217). While it sounds like commissioner is an example of an expert, much like blacksmiths and shipwrights, it is not obvious to me that the concept of "commissioner" is broad enough to capture this in a way that illuminates the concept of expertise as we are trying to understand it. One reason is that it is inextricably tied to politics, and, thereby, an overly narrow sense of authority. Another is that it threatens to conflate expertise with professional office, which is highly problematic (see Watson 2021, Chapter 1). So, while the office of commissioner might prove

an interesting case study of a type of expertise, I set it aside as vehicle through which to study the concept itself.
8. Following Emily Wilson (2018: 5–13), I refer to "Homer" in the sense of the "Homeric writers," whether the author was one person or several, or the culmination of many oral voices.
9. See Detienne and Vernant (1991, Chapter 2).
10. In *Protagoras*, Socrates asks a friend what sophists are supposed to be able to do (310dff). There is an interesting play on the various meanings of *sophia* in these passages. "Sophists" are supposed to make one "wise" or "clever" (*sophon*). But Socrates presses his friend to explain what sort of *sophistes* (σοφώτατον) ("expertise," Lombardo and Bell trans.; or "mastery," Lamb trans.) Protagoras has.
11. See Detienne and Vernant (1991, Chapter 2).
12. See Parry (2014).
13. One might point to the heroic 2009 landing of US Airways Flight 1549 into the Hudson River by commercial airline pilot Sully Sullenberger as an instance of "cunning intelligence." While I would agree that Sully demonstrated highly specialized expertise, courage, and a number of other virtues, I am not convinced that he demonstrated cunning in the sense used here, of shrewd plotting or deception.
14. See Watson and Guidry-Grimes (2018) for a variety of perspectives on this question.
15. See Scott and Liddell, *A Greek-English Lexicon*, and Robert Scott and H. G. Liddell, *An Intermediate Greek-English Lexicon*, any editions.
16. Philosopher Gilbert Ryle famously drew this distinction in his 1949 book, *The Concept of Mind*. Hubert and Stuart Dreyfus introduced into the expertise literature in their 1986 book, *Mind over Machine: The Power of Human Intuition and Expertise in the Era of the Computer*. For a contemporary discussion, see Fantl (2008).
17. The alpha (α) at the beginning of a word in Greek (called the alpha privative) is used to negate what comes after it. Knowing this, famous biologist Thomas Huxley, in a speech at a meeting of the Metaphysical Society in 1869, coined the word "agnosticism" by combining the alpha privative with the Greek word *gnosis* (γνῶσις), which comes from *ginosko* (γινώσκω), another word for "knowledge."
18. See Stevenson (2017) for a critique of Bill O'Reilly's "*Killing [So-and-So]*" history books.
19. While there was likely a single person called Hippocrates, the writings attributed to him were written by others. They are simply "early Greek medical treatises which were brought together by the Alexandrian scholars of the third century" (Adams 1952: ix).
20. For this section, I am indebted to Parry (2014).

Chapter 3

1. See Jaeger (1994) for a history of medieval education.
2. "Carolingian" is taken from "Carolus," which was Charlemagne's given name. Charlemagne is a French variant of the Latin "Carolus Magnus," which is translated in English as "Charles the Great."
3. In contrast with the "illiberal arts." See note 4 below.
4. Aristotle explains the "illiberal arts" as "any occupation, art, or science which makes the body, or soul, or mind of the freeman less fit for the practice or exercise of virtue is vulgar; wherefore we call those arts vulgar which tend to deform the body, and likewise all paid employments, for they absorb and degrade the mind" (*Politics* 8.2.1337b.5).
5. From Hugh of St. Victor, *De Institutione Novitiorum*, cited in Jaeger (1994: 248–9).
6. I left these references to "men" (instead of changing them to "people") because, for these scholars, the object of instruction was most certainly only men.
7. See Lindberg (2002a) and (2002b) for a superb introduction to the complex relationship between religion and science in the Middle Ages.
8. "The Catholic church did not impose thought control on astronomers, and even Galileo was free to believe what he wanted about the position and mobility of the earth, so long as he did not *teach* the Copernican hypothesis as a *truth* on which Holy Scripture had no bearing" (Shackelford 2009: 65, italics his).
9. Cf. Shackelford (2009).
10. G. E. R. Lloyd (1987) argues that the Greek thinkers also prized this sort of individualism, which he calls "egotism," setting themselves up in contrast to "dogmatists."
11. The full title is: *Discourse on the Method of Rightly Conducting One's Reason and of Seeking Truth in the Sciences*, translated by John Cottingham, Robert Smotthoff, and Dugald Murdoch (1988).
12. Thanks to Markus Seidel for encouraging me to add this paragraph.
13. Apart, perhaps, from dead languages and logic.
14. To be sure, Xenophanes made a case for this view many centuries before. Clement of Alexandria (in *Stromateis*) records Xenophanes as writing:

    > But if cattle and horses and lions had hands
    > or could paint with their hands and create works such as [people] do,
    > horses like horses and cattle like cattle
    > also would depict the gods' shapes and make their bodies
    > of such a sort as the form they themselves have. (Fr. 15)
    >
    > Ethiopians say that their gods are snub-nosed [σιμούς] and black
    > Thracians that they are pale and red-haired. (Fr. 16)
    > (Translated by Diels-Kranz, Die Fragmente der Vorsokratiker, 1954)

15 This term was introduced into the discussion over the role of science by Jean-François Lyotard (1979). See also Grenz (1996: 44–56).
16 See Chakravartty (2017) for details.
17 Thanks to Nathan Nobis for this point.
18 In a 2011 survey of 100 people with Down syndrome, 99 percent reported being happy with their lives, 97 percent reported being happy with who they are, and 96 percent said they like how they look (Skotko, Levine, and Goldstein 2011).
19 Thanks to Elizabeth Victor for the examples in this paragraph.
20 Though SSK proponent David Bloor (2011) claims to explain this example in terms of relativism.
21 See Kornblith (2002, Section 5.4) for an argument along these lines.
22 Taken from the University of Arkansas for Medical Sciences' (UAMS) "Oath of Hippocrates." What is called the "Hippocratic Oath" varies widely from one medical school to another, and all are very different from the original, and for good reason, as the original is morally problematic in a number of ways. See Veatch and Guidry-Grimes (2020, Chapter 2).
23 It is worth noting that the phrase "do no harm" does not appear in the original Hippocratic Oath.
24 See Veatch and Guidry-Grimes (2020, chapter 2) for a rich discussion of problems with the Hippocratic Oath.
25 See Spier (2002b) and Armstrong (1997).
26 See, for example, the efforts of Retraction Watch, which keeps vast amounts of data on retracted research: https://retractionwatch.com/.
27 Dictionaries are fascinating things. Kory Stamper, former lexicographer [one who writes dictionaries] for *Merriam-Webster*, explains that "To be a lexicographer, you must be able to sit with a word and all its many, complex uses and whittle those down into a two-line definition that is both broad enough to encompass the vast majority of the word's written use and narrow enough that it actually communicates something specific about this word. . . . You must set aside your own linguistic and lexical prejudices about what makes a word worthy, beautiful, or right, and to tell the truth about language" (2017: 19–20).
28 There are also genetic studies of expertise, but the central questions in that domain overlap little with the central philosophical questions I address in this book, so I am setting them aside for the sake of brevity.

Chapter 4

1 See Ericsson (2003) and Shorto (2008, Chapter 5).
2 Thanks to D. Micah Hester for insights into James's theory of learning. See Hester (2001) for how these concepts can inform and help develop good moral reasoning.

3 Of course, for James, there is no meta-self that stands outside this stream to observe it. Consciousness just is the stream, so these descriptions are somewhat metaphorical in their attempts to pick out which parts of attention and effort we are trying to explain.
4 See James ([1890] 1950), especially Chapter 4, "Habit."
5 No relation.
6 As the influential expertise researchers Allen Newell and Herbert Simon explain: "Our theory posits internal mechanisms of great extent and complexity, and endeavors to make contact between them and the visible evidences of problem solving. That is all there is to it" (1972: 9–10).
7 The Analytical Engine was a proposed design for the first "general purpose" computer, developed by Charles Babbage in 1837 as the successor to his difference engine, which was a real mechanical calculator that Babbage had created in 1822. For a fun piece of steampunk fiction tracing alternate origins of the difference engine, see William Gibson and Bruce Sterling, *The Difference Engine* (1990).
8 Turing was actually ahead of the curve. He proposed his test in 1950. For a marvelous discussion of the Turing test, see Alex Garland's (2014) film *Ex Machina*.
9 Though, it is getting better. See Sinkovec (2016). Thanks to Markus Seidel for this reference.
10 Searle's (1980) article is "Minds, Brains and Programs." He revised the experiment and responds to criticisms in his (1984) and (1989). He reflects on the significance of his thought experiment in his (2002).
11 See Hauser (n.d.) for an excellent introduction to the impact of this thought experiment.
12 It is worth noting that even this prediction proved wrong, as there have now been a number of grandmasters aged 14 or younger.

Chapter 5

1 The term "evidence" is used in a number of ways in the epistemology literature. Some might view the fact that x (whether a belief or a mental state) is a reason to believe that p is sufficient to regard x as evidence that p irrespective of whether anyone has x or believes p (called *reasons externalism*). Others argue that for x to be evidence that p, someone has to have x but not necessarily be able to reflectively think about or *access* x or whether x supports p (called *mentalism*). Still others argue that, for x to be evidence that p, someone has to have x and they must be able to access (remember, recognize) x and that x supports p (called *accessibilism*). (See Watson 2016.) In this book, I am using "evidence" loosely to indicate a reason to believe that p regardless of how it is construed. However, be aware that my own

view is a version of accessibilism, and this may influence the way I reason about evidence. Some of my conclusions may not hold if someone accepts, say, reasons externalism.
2. Philosopher Bernard Williams calls this a "purely positional advantage" (2002: 42).
3. See Hardwig (1985) and Gelfert (2014: 12).
4. Note it not always the case that "finding out for myself" releases me from epistemic dependence on you. The more esoteric a domain is, the more likely conferring with others enhances my understanding of and confidence with evidence in that domain. See Section 7.4 for more on esoteric and exoteric domain access.
5. Thanks to Markus Seidel for this point.
6. This is often the case as domains become increasingly esoteric or are on what C. Thi Nguyen (2018b) calls "cognitive islands" (see Section 7.4).
7. This view is prominently attributed to Scottish philosopher Thomas Reid, and ably defended by Tyler Burge (1993) and Richard Foley (1994).
8. See Van Cleve (2006: 59ff).
9. See Sosa (2006) and Van Cleve (2006) for defenses of this view.
10. Or, if it is the case for others, it is for very different reasons. For example, if my mom tells me about something she saw on the show *CBS Sunday Morning*, even if it sounds outlandish, I will typically trust that what she is telling me is right. This is not because she is an expert but because I take her to be a trustworthy person. (Not to mention that in those cases where something has sounded so outlandish that I expressed skepticism, it turns out she was right.)
11. Doctors have a tendency to dismiss such testimony. See Reiheld (2017).
12. This kind of competence is known as "patient expertise" (see Badcott 2005 and Heldal and Tjora 2009).

Chapter 6

1. Hubert Dreyfus (2000) argues that, in fact, experts should not be trusted to testify about their domain because expert knowledge is essentially tacit and non-propositional. If that is right, then expert testimony is more likely to be misleading than enlightening—either a rationalization of the expert's reasons or a poor heuristic for understanding their practice. Unfortunately, Dreyfus's account makes it seem as if the inability to explain one's judgment to novices is essential to expertise, which is empirically suspect. Evan Selinger (2011), Harry Collins and Robert Evans (2007), and I (Watson 2021) raise concerns about this conception of expertise: Even if it is true for some types of expert performance, it not plausible that it is *essential* to expertise.

2. In Section 2.3.4, we saw that Xenophon also expresses this view in *Memorabilia* 1.2.32.
3. Philosopher Joseph Raz calls this the "normal justification thesis": *"[T]he normal and primary way to establish that a person should be acknowledge to have authority over another person involves showing that the alleged subject is likely better to comply with reasons which apply to him (other than the alleged authoritative directives) if he accepts the directives of the alleged authority as authoritatively binding and tries to follow them, rather than by trying to follow the reasons which apply to him directly"* ([1986] 1990: 129, italics his).
4. Logician Joseph Bochenski (1965) calls this "deontic" authority, by which he means the authority to issue commands. However, deontic is typically translated "duty," and duty implies some sort of objective obligation on others. Those who have administrative authority may or may not have it legitimately, so I am resistant to using a term that might implicitly imply the legitimacy of the ability to command. I will stick with "administrative."
5. Hannah Arendt (1954) says that the root of *auctoritas* is not *auctor* but *augere*, which means to "augment" (18). In her account, authority augments the political tradition that has been handed down to them. Despite Arendt's meticulous use of Greek and Latin in her article, I could not find textual support for this root. R. S. Peters (1958: 210) invokes the link between *auctoritas* and authorship to help elucidate the concept of authority.
6. Gilman writes, "[I]s it wise to place experts in charge of experts? The point may be debated, but it is irrelevant. The positive system [of authority] dos not propose to do so, but to give them a share in controlling others. The question—Who shall decide when doctors disagree?—finds its answer when another equal authority is present to add considerations beyond the scope of either" (1914: 776–7).
7. A different way of understanding Arendt is offered by Friedman ([1973]1990: 58–9). Rather than claiming that societies agree on an authority structure and then defer to those who stand in certain roles as authorities, Arendt might be claiming that communities already share sets of beliefs, and that authority derives from this shared-ness. In other words, certain people in those communities have a right to command by pointing to the implications of shared beliefs. If this is right it would constitute a version of "doxastic control" account, discussed in Section 6.1.3.
8. Much ink has been spilled over whether we can believe voluntarily, or at will, or at the request or command of others. I think Zagzebski allays this debate succinctly, and I set it aside on the assumption that we do have some means by which we control what we believe. "Our beliefs are not like pains or passing thoughts. There are no norms for pains or passing thoughts, but there are norms for beliefs. We teach students those norms and remind ourselves to follow them. If there were no norms, there would be no point in inquiring about the rational way to respond to the beliefs of others or to evidence contrary to our beliefs" (2012: 101).

9 Legal scholars John Finnis (1980) H. L. A. Hart (1982) defend versions of this account, as well. Finnis writes: "A person treats something (for example, an opinion, a pronouncement, a map, an order, a rule . . .) as authoritative if and only if he treats it as giving him sufficient reason for believing or acting in according with it *notwithstanding* that he himself cannot otherwise see good reason for so believing or acting, or cannot evaluate the reasons he can see, or sees some countervailing reason(s), or would himself otherwise (i.e. in the absence of what it is that he is treating as authoritative) have preferred not so to believe or act" (176, italics his).
10 For the sake of accuracy, I should note that Zagzebski's account is strictly about authoritative *testimony*. I am presuming that her account—like my account of expertise generally—applies *mutatis mutandis* to expert advice and performance (TAP). If it does not, my critiques should be taken as aimed at Zagzebski's treatment of expert testimony and further elaboration will be needed to tease out its potential implications for advice and performance.
11 Philosopher G. E. M. Anscombe (1975) draws a version of this distinction between believing "a person" and believing "the thing he says."
12 There is a caveat here. Medical providers have a duty not to put patients at risk of active harm (called the duty of non-maleficence, Beauchamp and Childress 2009: 149-96). This entails a moral obligation to not pursue interventions that cause pain with no hope of benefit or that hasten death without hope of alleviating suffering. Whether doctors have a legal right to override parental authority in these circumstances is a matter of state law and hospital policy. But the ethical boundaries are relatively clear—there is a limit to parents' moral authority to subject their children to discomfort and pain.
13 See Veatch and Guidry-Grimes (2020: 94).

Chapter 7

1 And sometimes even that isn't enough. See LaBarge 1997.
2 While expertise is something that can be *learned*, according to Plato's Socrates, it doesn't necessarily require a *teacher*. Bartz (2000: 12) writes: "In *Laches* 185e-186a, Plato noted that becoming an expert in a craft without having a teacher was possible; one who made this claim, however, would be expected to show 'several well-made pieces of work as examples of their skill'" (Lane trans.).
3 All quotations are from the Jowett translation (1943).
4 All the better as far as I'm concerned.
5 See Croce (2019: 33) on the difference between "expert-oriented" and "novice-oriented" abilities of experts.
6 This is one reason research on health literacy has grown so much, both in the United States and in Europe, over the past two decades. If patients cannot get,

understand, and use health information, then they cannot make informed decisions for themselves. But since we cannot improve people's health literacy, we must devise interventions that help providers meet them at their level of understanding. Explaining medical terms and options using plain language and engaging teach-back and shared decision-making empower patients both to recognize which medical providers are offering them choices in their interests and to make those choices (see Watson 2019).

7   With respect to this last example, someone might contend that the novice isn't trusting the expert in this case but simply relying on her own sense of the truth of the Pythagorean theorem. But this would be an overly narrow view of the role of experts. Recall that experts can serve as confirmation/disconfirmation for other experts in their domains, such that if an expert disagrees with an expert, they have a reason to reconsider their judgment. Thus, a novice may justifiably trust an expert as confirming her own judgment (and thereby strengthening her justification) regarding the Pythagorean theorem, even if she didn't need that judgment to have a sufficiently justified belief.

8   This list owes a debt to Goldman ([2001] 2002); Anderson (2011); Coady (2012); Guerrero (2017); and Nguyen (2018b). Walton (1997: 223) also offers a concise list of questions for assessing expertise:

> Expertise Question: How credible is E as an expert source?
> Field Question: Is E an expert in the field F that assertion(?) A is in?
> Opinion Question: What did E assert that implies A?
> Trustworthiness Question: Is E personally reliable as a source?
> Consistency Question: Is A consistent with what other experts assert?
> Backup Evidence Question: Is E's assertion based on evidence?

9   Thanks to Rebecca Mullen for this question.
10 Nguyen, in conversation.
11 Thanks to Thi Nguyen for feedback on this graphic representation of his view.
12 It may not be true for every domain that is "obvious and isolated," like rock climbing, that it is more weakly exoteric than those on the cognitive mainland. I have situated it here because I assume that isolated domains require at least a stronger set of background information to understand what is going in those domains than those who are linked with other domains we are familiar with. Whether this is true should not affect my general points about this geography. But it is important to note it in the event that an example I have yet to come across renders it relevant.
13 Ericsson and Pool (2016: 135) point out that their review of the literatures shows that "no type of continuing medical education is effective at improving complex behaviors, that is, behaviors that involve a number of steps or require considering a

number of different factors." This suggests we still have work to do when it comes to enhancing performance in wicked environments.

14 Thanks to Dr. Angela Scott for this example.

Chapter 8

1 The remainder of this section is adapted from Watson (2021).
2 I might not be. I may decide that I'm really not educated enough to weigh the evidence well, and since this is a controversial issue, I shouldn't be surprised to find strong arguments on both sides. This alone suggests I should avoid the work and stick with omnivorous behavior. For an argument that such a position can be an epistemically responsible position, see Fantl (2018).
3 For a thorough defense of this claim, see Veatch (2000).
4 This phrase is taken from C. S. Lewis (1954), *The Horse and His Boy*: "Onward and upward! To Narnia and the North!"

References and Further Reading

2U (2019), "To Future-Proof Your Career, Start by Embracing Cross-Disciplinary Thinking," *Quartz*, May 2. Available online: https://qz.com/1589490/to-future-proof-your-career-start-by-embracing-cross-disciplinary-thinking/.

AAP Task Force on Sudden Infant Death Syndrome (2016), "SIDS and Other Sleep-Related Infant Deaths: Updated Recommendations for a Safe Infant Sleeping Environment," *Pediatrics*, 138 (5). Available online: https://pediatrics.aappublications.org/content/pediatrics/138/5/e20162938.full.pdf.

AARP (2018), "Online Pharmacy Scams," AARP Fraud Resource Center, December 3. Available online: https://www.aarp.org/money/scams-fraud/info-2019/online-pharmacy.html.

Abagnale, Frank and Stan Redding (1980), *Catch Me If You Can: The True Story of a Real Fake*, New York: Grosset & Dunlap.

Adams, Francis (1952), "Biographical Note: Hippocrates, fl. 400 B.C.," in Robert Maynard Hutchins (ed.), *Great Books of the Western World: Hippocrates, Galen*, ix, Chicago: William Benton, Encyclopedia Britannica.

Agnew, N. M., K. M. Ford and P. J. Hayes ([1994] 1997), "Expertise in Context: Personally Constructed, Socially Selected, and Reality-Relevant?," in Paul J. Feltovich, Kenneth M. Ford and Robert R. Hoffman (eds.), *Expertise in Context*, 219–44, Cambridge, MA: AAAI/MIT Press.

Ahlstrom-Vij, Kristoffer (2013), *Epistemic Paternalism: A Defence*, Basingstoke: Palgrave Macmillan.

Aikin, Scott (2009), "Don't Fear the Regress: Cognitive Values and Epistemic Infinitism," *Think*, 8 (23): 55–61.

Allen, James (1994), "Failure and Expertise in the Ancient Conception of Art," in T. Horowitz and A. Janis (eds.), *Scientific Failure*, 83–110, Lanham, MD: Rowman & Littlefield.

The American Association for the Advancement of Science (AAAS) (n.d.), "Affiliates," AAAS. Available online: https://www.aaas.org/group/60/list-aaas-affiliates#p.

American Academy of Pediatrics (n.d.), American Academy of Pediatrics. Available online: https://www.aap.org/en-us/Pages/Default.aspx.

American College of Pediatricians (n.d.), American College of Pediatricians. Available online: https://www.acpeds.org/.

Anderson, Elizabeth (2011), "Democracy, Public Policy, and Lay Assessments of Scientific Testimony," *Episteme*, 8 (2): 144–64.

Anderson, J. G. and K. Abrahamson (2017), "Your Health Care May Kill You: Medical Errors," *Studies in Health, Technology, and Informatics*, 234: 13–17.

Anscombe, G. E. M. (1975), "What Is It to Believe Someone?," in C. F. Delaney (ed.), *Rationality and Religious Belief*, 141–51, Notre Dame, IN: University of Notre Dame Press.

Arendt, Hannah ([1954] 1961), "What is Authority?," in *Between Past and Future: Six Exercises in Political Thought*, 91–141, New York: Viking.

Ariely, Dan (2010), *Predictably Irrational: The Hidden Forces That Shape Our Decisions*, New York: Harper.

Aristotle (1955), *On Sophistical Refutations*, trans. E. S. Forster, The Loeb Classics Library, Cambridge, MA: William Heinemann Ltd.

Aristotle (2001), "Politics," trans. Benjamin Jowett, in Richard McKeon (ed.), *The Basic Works of Aristotle*, 1113–316, New York: Modern Library.

Arkes, H. R., R. L. Wortmann, P. D. Saville and A. R. Harkness (1981), "Hindsight Bias Among Physicians Weighing the Likelihood of Diagnoses," *Journal of Applied Psychology*, 66: 252–5.

Armstrong, J. Scott (1997), "Peer Review for Journals: Evidence on Quality Control, Fairness, and Innovation," *Science and Engineering Ethics*, 3 (1): 63–84.

Associated Press (2019), "Japan's Supreme Court Uphold Transgender Sterilization Requirement," *NBC News*, January 25. Available online: https://www.nbcnews.com/feature/nbc-out/japan-s-supreme-court-upholds-transgender-sterilization-requirement-n962721.

Audi, Robert (2006), "Testimony, Credulity, Veracity," in Jennifer Lackey and Ernest Sosa (eds.), *The Epistemology of Testimony*, 25–49, New York: Oxford University Press.

Austin, J. L. (1946), "Other Minds, Part II," *Proceedings of the Aristotelian Society*, 148: 148–87.

Bacon, Francis ([1620] 1876), "The Great Instauration," in L. Bacon and J. Devy (eds.), *The Physical and Metaphysical Works*, 15, Bell & Daldy Publishers: London.

Bacon, Francis ([1612] 1980), "Of Studies," in *The Essays of Sir Francis Bacon*, Norwalk, CT: The Easton Press.

Bacon, Francis ([1620] 2000), *New Organon*, Cambridge: Cambridge University Press.

Badcott, D. (2005), "The Expert Patient: Valid Recognition or False Hope?," *Medicine, Health Care, and Philosophy*, 8 (2): 173–8.

Baker, Peter and Julie Hirschfeld Davis (2015), "Obama Chooses Nike Headquarters to Make His Pitch on Trade," *New York Times*, May 7. Available online: http://www.nytimes.com/2015/05/08/business/obama-chooses-nike-headquarters-to-make-his-pitch-on-trade.html.

Ballantyne, Nathan (2019), "Epistemic Trespassing," *Mind*, 128 (510): 367–95.

Barnes, B. and D. Bloor (1982), "Relativism, Rationalism and the Sociology of Knowledge," in M. Hollis and S. Lukes (eds.), *Rationality and Relativism*, 21–47, Oxford: Basil Blackwell.

Bartlett, James C., Amy L. Boggan and Daniel C. Krawczyk (2013), "Expertise and Processing Distorted Structure in Chess," *Frontiers in Human Neuroscience*, 7:

825. Available online: https://www.frontiersin.org/articles/10.3389/fnhum.2013.00825/full.

Bartz, Robert (2000), "Remembering the Hippocratics: Knowledge, Practice, and Ethos of Ancient Greek Physician-Healers," in Mark G. Kuczewski and Ronald Polansky (eds.), *Bioethics: Ancient Themes in Contemporary Issues*, 3–29, Cambridge, MA: The MIT Press.

Baumeister, R. F. (1984), "Choking Under Pressure: Self-Consciousness and Paradoxical Effects of Incentives on Skillful Performance," *Journal of Personality and Social Psychology*, 46 (3): 610–20.

Bealer, George (1992), "The Incoherence of Empiricism," *Aristotelian Society Supplementary Volume*, 66 (1): 99–138.

Beaman, Lori, Reghabendra Chattopadhyay, Esther Duflo, Rohini Pande and Petia Topalova (2009), "Powerful Women: Does Exposure Reduce Bias?," *The Quarterly Journal of Economics*, 124 (4): 1497–540.

Beauchamp, Tom and James Childress (2009), *Principles of Biomedical Ethics*, 6th ed., Oxford: Oxford University Press.

Beckwith, Christopher I. (2012), *Warriors of the Cloisters: The Central Asian Origins of Science in the Medieval World*, Princeton, NJ: Princeton University Press.

Beebe, James R., Maria Baghramian, Luke Drury and Finnur Dellsén (2019), "Divergent Perspectives on Expert Disagreement: Preliminary Evidence from Climate Science, Climate Policy, Astrophysics, and Public Opinion," *Environmental Communication*, 13 (1): 35–50, doi: 10.1080/17524032.2018.1504099.

Beilock, Sian (2010), *Choke: What the Secrets of the Brain Reveal About Getting It Right When You Have To*, New York: Free Press.

Berkman, Nancy, Stacey L. Sheridan, Katrina E. Donahue, David J. Halpern and Karen Crotty (2011), "Low Health Literacy and Health Outcomes: An Updated Systematic Review," *Annals of Internal Medicine*, 155 (2): 97–115.

Berlin, Isaiah (1953), *The Hedgehog and the Fox: An Essay on Tolstoy's View of History*, London: Weidenfeld and Nicolson.

Berman, J. C. and N. C. Norton (1985), "Does Professional Training Make a Therapist More Effective?," *Psychological Bulletin*, 98: 401–7.

Bertamini, M., A. Spooner and H. Hecht (2004), "The Representation of Naïve Knowledge about Physics," in Grant Malcolm (ed.), *Multidisciplinary Approaches to Visual Representations and Interpretations*, 27–36, Amsterdam: Elsevier.

Biederman, Irving and Margaret M. Shiffrar (1987), "Sexing Day-Old Chicks: A Case Study and Expert Systems Analysis of a Difficult Perceptual-Learning Task," *Journal of Experimental Psychology: Learning, Memory, and Cognition*, 13 (4): 640–5.

Bilalić, Merim (2017), *The Neuroscience of Expertise*, Cambridge: Cambridge University Press.

Bishop, Michael A. and J. D. Trout (2005), *Epistemology and the Psychology of Human Judgment*, Oxford: Oxford University Press.

Biss, Eula (2014), *On Immunity: An Inoculation*, Minneapolis, MN: Graywolf Press.

Bloor, David (2011), *The Enigma of the Aerofoil: Rival Theories in Aerodynamics, 1909–1930*, Chicago: University of Chicago Press.

Bochenski, Joseph (1965), "The Logic of Religion," *Journal of Symbolic Logic*, 33 (2): 312–13.

BonJour, Laurence (1985), *The Structure of Empirical Knowledge*, Cambridge, MA: Harvard University Press.

Bornstein, B. H., A. C. Emler and G. B. Chapman (1999), "Rationality in Medical Treatment Decisions: Is There a Sunk-Cost Effect?," *Social Science & Medicine*, 49 (2): 215–22.

Botting, D. (2018), "Two Types of Argument from Position to Know," *Informal Logic*, 38 (4): 502–30.

Bowell, T. (n.d.), "Feminist Standpoint Theory," *Internet Encyclopedia of Philosophy*. Available online: https://www.iep.utm.edu/fem-stan/#H2.

Brainard, Jeffrey and Jia You (2018), "What a Massive Database of Retracted Papers Reveals about Science Publishing's 'Death Penalty,'" *Science Magazine*, October 25. Available online: https://www.sciencemag.org/news/2018/10/what-massive-database-retracted-papers-reveals-about-science-publishing-s-death-penalty.

Breitenstein, Mirko (2014), "The Success of Discipline: The Reception of Hug of St. Victor's *De institutione novitorum* within the 13th and 14th Century," in M. Breitenstein, J. Burkhardt, St. Burkhardt and J. Rohrkasten (eds.), *Rules and Observance*, 183–222, Berlin: Abhandlungen.

Brennan, Johnny (2020), "Can Novices Trust Themselves to Choose Trustworthy Experts? Reasons for Reserved Optimism," *Social Epistemology*. DOI: 10.1080/02691728.2019.1703056.

Brewer, Scott (1998), "Scientific Expert Testimony and Intellectual Due Process," *The Yale Law Journal*, 107 (6): 1535–1681.

Brewer, Scott (2006), "Scientific Expert Testimony and Intellectual Due Process," in Evan Selinger and Robert P. Crease (eds.), *The Philosophy of Expertise*, 111–58, New York: Columbia University Press.

Brown, Mark B. (2014), "Expertise and Democracy," in Stephen Elstub and Peter McLaverty (eds.), *Deliberative Democracy: Issues and Cases*, 50–68, Edinburgh: Edinburgh University Press.

Buchanan, Bruce G., Randall Davis, Reid G. Smith and Edward A. Feigenbaum (2018), "Expert Systems: A Perspective from Computer Science," in K. Anders Ericsson, Robert R. Hoffman, Aaron Kozbelt and A. Mark Williams (eds.), *The Cambridge Handbook of Expertise and Expert Performance*, 2nd ed. 84–104, Cambridge: Cambridge University Press.

Buckwalter (2014), "Intuition Fail: Philosophical Activity and the Limits of Expertise," *Philosophy and Phenomenological Research*, 92 (2): 378–410.

Burge, Tyler (1993), "Content Preservation," *Philosophical Review*, 102 (4): 457–88.

Burgess, Glenn (1992), "The Divine Right of Kings Reconsidered," *The English Historical Review*, 425: 837–61.

Burns-Piper, Annie (2016), "Advocates, Experts and Mothers Call for Action on the Mistreatment of Women During Childbirth," *CBC News*, November 19. Available online: https://www.cbc.ca/news/investigates/childbirth-mistreatment-reaction-1.3857635.

Burnyeat, Myles (1987), "Wittgenstein and Augustine De Magistro," *Proceedings of the Aristotelian Society Supplement*, 61: 1–24.

Camerer, Colin F. and Eric J. Johnson (1991), "The Process-Performance Paradox in Expert Judgment: How Can Experts Know So Much and Predict So Badly?," in K. Anders Ericsson and Jacqui Smith (eds.), *Toward a General Theory of Expertise*, 195–217, Cambridge: Cambridge University Press.

Campbell, D. T. (1977), *Descriptive Epistemology: Psychological, Sociological, and Evolutionary*, Cambridge, MA: Harvard University Press.

Castelvecchi, Davide (2016), "Fermat's Last Theorem earns Andrew Wiles the Abel Prize," *Nature: International Weekly Journal of Science*, March 15. Available online: https://www.nature.com/news/fermat-s-last-theorem-earns-andrew-wiles-the-abel-prize-1.19552.

Cereda, Anna and John C. Carey (2012), "The Trisomy 18 Syndrome," *Orphanet Journal of Rare Diseases*, 7: 81.

Chakravartty, Anjan (2017), "Scientific Realism," in Edward N. Zalta (ed.), *The Stanford Encyclopedia of Philosophy* (Summer 2017 Edition). Available online: https://plato.stanford.edu/archives/sum2017/entries/scientific-realism/.

Chartonas, Dimitrios, Michalis Kyratsous, Sarah Dracass, Tennyson Lee and Kamaldeep Bhui (2017), "Personality Disorder: Still The Patients Psychiatrists Dislike?," *BJ Psych Bulletin*, 41: 12–17.

Chase, William G. and Herbert A. Simon (1973), "Perception in Chess," *Cognitive Psychology*, 4: 55–81.

Chaucer, Geoffrey (2001), *Troilus and Cressida*, trans. A. S. Kline, Poetry in Translation. https://www.poetryintranslation.com/PITBR/English/Chaucerhome.php.

Chisholm, Roderick (1982), "A Version of Foundationalism," in Roderick Chisholm (ed.), *The Foundations of Knowing*, 61–75, Minneapolis, MN: University of Minnesota Press.

Chisholm, Roderick (1973), *The Problem of the Criterion*, Milwaukee, WI: Marquette University Press.

Chlebowski, R. T., K. C. Johnson, C. Kooperberg, M. Pettinger, J. Wactawski-Wende, T. Rohan, J. Rossouw, D. Lane, M. J. O'Sullivan, S. Yasmeen, R. A. Hiatt, J. M. Shikany, M. Vitolins, J. Khandekar, F. A. Hubbell and Women's Health Initiative Investigators (2008), "Calcium Plus Vitamin D Supplementation and the Risk of Breast Cancer," *Journal of the National Cancer Institute*, 100 (22): 1581–91.

Cholbi, Michael (2007), "Moral Expertise and the Credentials Problem," *Ethical Theory and Moral Practice*, 10 (4): 323–34.

Choudry, N. K., R. H. Fletcher and S. B. Soumerai (2005), "Systematic Review: The Relationship Between Clinical Experience and Quality of Healthcare," *Annals of Internal Medicine*, 142 (4): 260–73.

Christensen, David (2007), "Epistemology of Disagreement: The Good News," *Philosophical Review*, 116: 187–218.

Chudnoff, Elijah (forthcoming), "Two Kinds of Cognitive Expertise," *Nous*.
Cicero, M. T. (1988), *De Oratore*, trans. E. W. Sutton, Loeb Classical Library, Cambridge, MA: Harvard University Press.
Cicero (1860), *De Oratore*, trans. J. S. Watson, New York: Harper and Brothers Publishers.
Clifford, W. K. (1877), "The Ethics of Belief," *Contemporary Review*, XXXIX January Edition.
Clifford, W. K. ([1872] 1886), "On the Aims and Instruments of Scientific Thought," a lecture delivered to members of the British Association at Brighton, August 19, 1872, in Leslie Stephen and Frederick Pollock (eds.), *Lectures and Essays*, 2nd ed., 85–109, London: Macmillan and Co.
Coady, David (2012), *What to Believe Now: Applying Epistemology to Contemporary Issues*, Malden, MA: Wiley-Blackwell.
Cohen, I. Bernard (1985), *The Birth of a New Physics*, revised and updated ed., New York: W. W. Norton.
Cohen, Marvin S. (1993), "The Naturalistic Basis of Decision Biases," in Gary A. Klein, Judith Orasnu, Roberta Calderwood and Caroline E. Zsambok (eds.), *Decision Making In Action: Models and Methods*, 51–99, Norwood, NJ: Ablex Publishing Corporation.
Coleman, Clifford, Stanley Hudson and Lucinda Maine (2013), "Health Literacy Practices and Educational Competencies for Health Professionals: A Consensus Study," *Journal of Health Communication*, 18 (Supplement 1): 82–102.
Coleman, Clifford, Stanley Hudson and Ben Pederson (2017), "Prioritized Health Literacy and Clear Communication Practices for Health Care Professionals," *Health Literacy Research and Practice*, 1 (3): e91–e99.
Collins, Harry (2014), *Are We All Scientific Experts Now?* Cambridge: Polity Press.
Collins, Harry and Robert Evans (2006), "The Third Wave of Science Studies: Studies of Expertise and Experience," in Evan Selinger and Robert P. Crease (eds.), *The Philosophy of Expertise*, 39–110, New York: Columbia University Press.
Collins, Harry and Robert Evans (2007), *Rethinking Expertise*, Chicago: University of Chicago Press.
Collins, Harry and Trevor Pinch (2005), *Dr. Golem: How to Think about Medicine*, Chicago: University of Chicago Press.
Conly, Sarah (2012), *Against Autonomy*, Cambridge: Cambridge University Press.
Cook, John, Dana Nuccitelli, Sarah A Green, Mark Richardson, Bärbel Winkler, Rob Painting, Robert Way, Peter Jacobs and Andrew Skuce (2013), "Quantifying the Consensus on Anthropogenic Global Warming in the Scientific Literature," *Environmental Research Letters*, 8 (2): 1–7. IOP Publishing Ltd, doi: 10.1088/1748-9326/8/2/024024.
Cotgrave, Randle (1611), *A Dictionarie of the French and English Tongues*, London: Adam Inslip. Available online: http://www.pbm.com/~lindahl/cotgrave/.

Coughlin, L. D. and V. L. Patel (1987), "Processing of Critical Information by Physicians and Medical Students," *Journal of Medical Education*, 62: 818–28.

Crasnow, Sharon, Alison Wylie, Wenda K. Bauchspies and Elizabeth Potter (2015), "Feminist Perspectives on Science," in Edward N. Zalta (ed.), *The Stanford Encyclopedia of Philosophy*, Summer 2015 edition. Available online: http://plato.stanford.edu/archives/sum2015/entries/feminist-science/.

Croce, Michael (2019), "Objective Expertise and Functionalist Constraints," *Social Epistemology Review and Collective*, 8 (5): 25–35.

Cross, Patricia K. (1977), "Not *Can*, But *Will* College Teaching Be Improved?," *New Directions for Higher Education*, 17: 1–15.

Csikszentmihalyi, Mihaly (1975), *Beyond Boredom and Anxiety*, San Fransisco: Jossey-Bass Publishers.

Csikszentmihalyi, Mihaly (1988), "The Flow Experience and Its Significance for Human Psychology," in M. Csikszentmihalyi and I. S. Csikszentmihalyi (eds.), *Optimal Experience: Psychological Studies of Flow in Consciousness*, 15–35, New York: Cambridge University Press.

Csikszentmihalyi, Mihaly (1990), *Flow: The Psychology of Optimal Experience*, New York: Harper Collins.

Dall'Alba, Gloria (2018), "Reframing Expertise and Its Development: A Lifeworld Perspective," in K. Anders Ericsson, Robert R. Hoffman, Aaron Kozbelt and A. Mark Williams (eds.), *The Cambridge Handbook of Expertise and Expert Performance*, 2nd ed. 33–9, Cambridge: Cambridge University Press.

Dane, Erik, Kevin W. Rockmann and Michael G. Pratt (2012), "When Should I Trust my Gut? Linking Domain Expertise to Intuitive Decision-Making Effectiveness," *Organizational Behavior and Human Decision Processes*, 119: 187–94.

Davis, Dave, Mary Ann Thomson O'Brien, Nick Freemantle, Frederic M. Wolf, Paul Mazmanian and Anne Taylor-Vaisey (1999), "Impact of Formal Continuing Medical Education: Do Conferences, Workshops, Rounds and Other Traditional Continuing Education Activities Change Physician Behavior or Health Care Outcomes?," *Journal of the American Medical Association*, 282 (9): 867–74.

Davis, Edward B. (2009), "That Isaac Newton's Mechanistic Cosmology Eliminated the Need for God," in Ron Numbers (ed.), *Galileo Goes to Jail and Other Myths about Science and Religion*, 115–22, Cambridge, MA: Harvard University Press.

Dawes, Robyn (1994), *House of Cards: Psychology and Psychotherapy Built on Myth*, New York: Free Press.

Dawkins, Richard (1976), *The Selfish Gene*, Oxford: Oxford University Press.

DeCesare, Tony (2012), "The Lippmann-Dewey Debate Revisited: The Problem of Knowledge and the Role of Experts in Modern Democratic Theory," *Philosophical Studies in Education*, 43: 106–16.

De Groot, Adriaan ([1946] 1965), *Thought and Choice in Chess*, The Hague, Netherlands: Amsterdam Academic Archive.

Dellsén, Finnur (2018), "The Epistemic Value of Expert Autonomy," *Philosophy and Phenomenological Research*, 2: 344–61.

Derrida, Jacques (1977), "Signature, Event, Context," in Samuel Weber and Jeffrey Mehlman (trans.), *Glyph*, 1: 172–97.

Descartes, René ([1637] 1988), "Discourse on the Method," in John Cottingham, Robert Stoothoff and Dugald Murdoch (trans.), *Descartes: Selected Philosophical Writings*, 20–56, Cambridge: Cambridge University Press.

Detienne, Marcel and Jean-Pierre Vernant ([1978] 1991), *Cunning Intelligence in Greek Culture and Society*, Chicago: University of Chicago Press.

de Tocqueville, Alexis (2010), *Democracy in America: Historical-Critical Edition of De la démocratie en Amérique*, ed. Eduardo Nolla, translated from the French by James T. Schleifer. A Bilingual French-English editions, Vol. 3, Indianapolis: Liberty Fund.

Dewey, John ([1910] 2009), *How We Think*, U.S.: BN Publishing.

Dewey, John (1922), "Habits as Social Functions," in *Human Nature and Conduct: An Introduction to Social Psychology*, 14–23, New York: Modern Library.

Dewey, John (1927), *The Public and Its Problems*. New York: Holt Publishers.

Dormandy, Katherine (2018), "Epistemic Authority: Preemption or Proper Basing?," *Erkenntnis*, 83, 773–91.

Drake, Jennifer E. and Ellen Winner (2018), "Why Deliberate Practice is Not Enough: Evidence of Talent in Drawing," in David Z. Hambrick, Guillermo Campitelli and Brooke N. Macnamara (eds.), *The Science of Expertise: Behavioral, Neural, and Genetic Approaches to Complex Skill*, 101–28, London: Routledge.

Dreyfus, Hubert (1979), *What Computers Can't Do: The Limits of Artificial Intelligence*, revised, New York: Harper Colophon Books.

Dreyfus, Hubert (1999a), "How Neuroscience Supports Merleau-Ponty's Account of Learning," Paper presented at the Network for Non-Scholastic Learning Conference, Sonderborg, Denmark.

Dreyfus, Hubert (1999b), "The Primacy of Phenomenology over Logical Analysis," *Philosophical Topics*, 27 (2): 3–24.

Dreyfus, Hubert (2000), "Could Anything be More Intelligible than Everyday Intelligibility? Reinterpreting Division I of *Being and Time* in the Light of Division II," in J. Faulconer and M. Wrathall (eds.), *Appropriating Heidegger*, 155–70, Cambridge: Cambridge University Press.

Dreyfus, Hubert L. (2001), *On the Internet*, New York: Routledge.

Dreyfus, Hubert (2006), "How Far is Distance Learning from Education?," in Evan Selinger and Robert P. Crease (eds.), *The Philosophy of Expertise*, 196–212, New York: Columbia University Press.

Dreyfus, Hubert L. and Stuart E. Dreyfus (1986), *Mind Over Machine: The Power of Human Intuition and Expertise in the Era of the Computer*, New York: Free Press.

Dreyfus, Hubert L. and Stuart E. Dreyfus (2005), "Peripheral Vision: Expertise in Real World Contexts," *Organization Studies*, 26: 779–92.

Dreyfus, H., C. Spinosa and F. Flores (1997), *Disclosing Worlds: Entrepreneurship, Democratic Action, and the Cultivation of Solidarity*, Cambridge, MA: The MIT Press.

Driver, Julia (2006), "Autonomy and the Asymmetry Problem for Moral Expertise," *Philosophical Studies*, 128 (3): 619–44.

Duckworth, Angela (2016), *Grit: The Power and Passion of Perseverance*, New York: Scribner.

Dunning, David (2011), "The Dunning-Kruger Effect: On Being Ignorant of One's Own Ignorance," in J. M. Olson and M. P. Zanna (eds.), *Advances in Experimental Social Psychology*, 44, San Diego, CA: Academic Press.

Dunning, David (2016), "The Psychological Quirk that Explains Why You Love Donald Trump," *Politico*, May 25. Available online: https://www.politico.com/magazine/story/2016/05/donald-trump-supporters-dunning-kruger-effect-213904.

Dworkin, Gerald (1988), *The Theory and Practice of Autonomy*, Cambridge: Cambridge University Press.

Edwards, D. and J. Edwards (1977), "Marriage: Direct and Continuous Measurement," *Bulletin of the Psychonomic Society*, 10: 187–8.

Elga, Adam (2011), "Reflection and Disagreement," in Alvin Goldman (ed.), *Social Epistemology: Essential Readings*, 158–82, Oxford: Oxford University Press.

Elgin, Catherine Z. (2012), "Begging to Differ," *The Philosopher's Magazine*, 59: 77–82.

Elgin, Catherine Z. (2016), "Understanding," in *Routledge Encyclopedia of Philosophy*. New York: Routledge.

Elgin, Catherine Z. (2017), *True Enough*, Cambridge, MA: The MIT Press.

Elgin, Catherine Z. (2018), "Epistemically Useful Falsehoods," in Brandon Fitelson, Rodrigo Borges and Cherie Braden (eds.), *Themes from Klein: Knowledge, Skepticism, and Justification*, 25–38, Cham, Switzerland: Springer Nature.

Elliot, Terri (1994), "Making Strange What Had Appeared Familiar," *The Monist*, 77 (4): 424–33.

Elmore, Joann G. et al. (2009), "Variability in Interpretive Performance at Screening Mammography and Radiologists' Characteristics Associated with Accuracy," *Radiology*, 253 (3): 641–51. doi:10.1148/radiol.2533082308.

Elwyn, Glyn, Dominick Frosch, Richard Thomson, Natalie Joseph-Williams, Amy Lloyd, Paul Kinnersley, Emma Cording, Dave Tomson, Carole Dodd, Stephen Rollnick, Adrian Edwards and Michael Barry (2012), "Shared Decision Making: A Model for Clinical Practice," *Journal of General Internal Medicine*, 27 (10): 1361–7, doi: 10.1007/s11606-012-2077-6.

Engeström, Yrjö (2018), *Expertise in Transition: Expansive Learning in Medical Work*, Cambridge: Cambridge University Press.

Epstein, David (2014a), *The Sports Gene: Inside the Science of Extraordinary Athletic Performance*, New York: Portfolio/Penguin.

Epstein, David (2014b), "Are Athletes Really Getting Faster, Better, Stronger?," *TED Talk*. Available online: https://www.ted.com/talks/david_epstein_are_athletes_really_getting_faster_better_stronger?language=en.

Epstein, David (2019), *Range: Why Generalists Triumph in a Specialized World*, New York: Riverhead Books.

Erasmus ([1511] 1876), *In Praise of Folly, Illustrated with Many Curious Cuts, Designed, Drawn, and Etched by Hans Holbein, with Portrait, Life of Erasmus, and his Epistle to Sir Thomas More*, London: Reeves and Turner.

Ericsson, K. Anders (1985), "Memory Skill," *Canadian Journal of Psychology*, 39 (2): 188–231.

Ericsson, K. Anders (1990), "Peak Performance and Age: An Examination of Peak Performance I Sports," in P. B. Baltes and M. M. Baltes (eds.), *Successful Aging: Perspectives from the Behavioral Sciences*, 164–95, New York: Cambridge University Press.

Ericsson, K. Anders (2003), "Valid and Non-Reactive Verbalization of Thoughts During Performance of Tasks: Toward a Solution to the Central Problems of Introspection as a Source of Scientific Data," *Journal of Consciousness Studies*, 10: 1–18.

Ericsson, K. Anders (2008), "Deliberate Practice and Acquisition of Expert Performance: A General Overview," *Academic Emergency Medicine*, 15 (11): 988–94.

Ericsson, K. Anders (2011), "The Surgeon's Expertise," in H. Fry and R. Kneebone (eds.), *Surgical Education: Theorising an Emerging Domain*, 107–21, Dordrecht: Springer.

Ericsson, K. Anders (2018), "An Introduction to the Second Edition of *The Cambridge Handbook of Expertise and Expert Performance*: Its Development, Organization, and Content," in K. Anders Ericsson, Robert R. Hoffman, Aaron Kozbelt and A. Mark Williams (eds.), *The Cambridge Handbook of Expertise and Expert Performance*, 2nd ed., 3–20, Cambridge: Cambridge University Press.

Ericsson, K. Anders and W. G. Chase (1982), "Exceptional Memory," *American Scientist*, 70: 607–15.

Ericsson, K. Anders and Neil Charness (1994), "Expert Performance: Its Structure and Acquisition," *American Psychologist*, 49 (8): 725–47.

Ericsson, K. Anders and Neil Charness (1997), "Cognitive and Developmental Factors in Expert Performance," in Paul J. Feltovich, Kenneth M. Ford and Robert R. Hoffman (eds.), *Expertise in Context*, 3–41, Cambridge, MA: AAAI/MIT Press.

Ericsson, K. Anders and A. C. Lehmann (1996), "Expert and Exceptional Performance: Evidence of Maximal Adaptation to Task Constraints," *Annual Review of Psychology*, 47: 273–305.

Ericsson, K. Anders and Robert Pool (2016), *Peak: Secrets from the New Science of Expertise*, Boston: Mariner.

Ericsson, K. Anders and Jacqui Smith, eds. (1991), *Toward a General Theory of Expertise*, Cambridge: Cambridge University Press.

Ericsson, K. Anders, W. G. Chase and S. Faloon (1980), "Acquisition of a Memory Skill," *Science*, 208: 1181–2.

Ericsson, K. Anders, Robert R. Hoffman, Aaron Kozbelt and Mark Williams, eds. (2018), *Expertise and Expert Performance*, 2nd ed., , UK: Cambridge University Press.

Ericsson, K. Anders, R. Th. Krampe and C. Tesch-Römer (1993), "The Role of Deliberate Practice in the Acquisition of Expert Performance," *Psychological Review*, 100 (3): 363–406.

Euripides (1995), *Andromache*, trans. David Kovacs, Loeb Classical Library, Cambridge, MA: Harvard University Press.

Fantl, Jeremy (2008), "Knowing-How and Knowing-That," *Philosophy Compass*, 3 (3): 451–70.

Fantl, Jeremy (2012), "Knowledge How," in Edward N. Zalta (ed.), *The Stanford Encyclopedia of Philosophy*, Fall 2017 Edition. Available online: https://plato.stanford.edu/archives/fall2017/entries/knowledge-how/.

Fantl, Jeremy (2018), *The Limitations of the Open Mind*. New York: Oxford University Press.

Faulkner, Paul (2000), "The Social Character of Testimonial Knowledge," *Journal of Philosophy*, 97: 581–601.

Feldman, Richard and Ted A. Warfield (2010), *Disagreement*, , UK: Oxford University Press.

Feltovich, Paul J., Michael J. Prietula and K. Anders Ericsson (2018), "Studies of Expertise from Psychological Perspecitves: Historical Foundations and Recurrent Themes," in K. Anders Ericsson, Robert R. Hoffman, Aaron Kozbelt and A. Mark Williams (eds.), *The Cambridge Handbook of Expertise and Expert Performance*, 2nd ed. 59–83, Cambridge: Cambridge University Press.

Feyerabend, Paul ([1974] 2006), "How to Defend Society Against Science," in Evan Selinger and Robert P. Crease (eds.), *The Philosophy of Expertise*, 358–69, New York: Columbia University Press.

Finnis, John (1980), "Authority," in Joseph Raz (ed.), *Authority*, 174–202, New York: New York University Press.

Fischer, Frank (2009), *Democracy and Expertise: Reorienting Policy Inquiry*, Oxford: Oxford University Press.

Flax, Jane, 1983, "Political Philosophy and the Patriarchal Unconscious," in Sandra Harding and Merrill Hintikka (eds.), *Discovering Reality*, 245–81, Dordrecht, Holland: Kluwer.

Flower, Mike (2015), "Religious Expertise," in Esther Eidinow and Julia Kindt (eds.), *The Oxford Handbook of Ancient Greek Religion*, 293–307, Oxford: Oxford University Press. DOI: 10.1093/oxfordhb/9780199642038.013.21.

Foley, Richard (1994), "Egoism in Epistemology," in Frederick F. Schmitt (ed.), *Socializing Epistemology: The Social Dimensions of Knowledge*, 53–73, London: Rowman & Littlefield.

Foley, Richard (2001), *Intellectual Trust in Oneself and Others*, Cambridge: Cambridge University Press.

Forsetlund, Louise, Arild Bjørndal, Arash Rashidian, Gro Jamtvedt and Andrew D. Oxman (2009), "Continuing Education Meetings Workshops: Effects on Professional Practice and Health Care Outcomes," *Cochrane Database of Systematic Reviews*, 2, CD003030.

Foucault, Michel ([1979] 2000), "What is an Author?," repr. in Forrest E. Baird and Walter Arnold Kaufmann (eds.), *Twentieth-Century Philosophy*, 2nd ed., Upper Saddle River, NJ: Prentice Hall.

Fowler, Harold N., ed. (1921), *Plato in Twelve Volumes*, Vol. 12, Cambridge, MA: Harvard University Press; London: William Heinemann Ltd.

Fricker, Elizabeth (2006), "Testimony and Epistemic Autonomy," in Jennifer Lackey and Ernest Sosa (eds.), *The Epistemology of Testimony*, 225–50, Oxford: Oxford University Press.

Freedman, David H. (2010), *Wrong: Why Experts Keep Failing Us—And How to Know When Not to Trust Them*, New York: Little, Brown & Company.

Freiman, Ori and Boaz Miller (forthcoming), "Can Artificial Entities Assert?," in Sanford C. Goldberg (ed.), *The Oxford Handbook of Assertion*, Oxford: Oxford University Press.

Friedman, R. B. ([1973] 1990), "On the Concept of Authority in Political Philosophy," In Joseph Raz (ed.) *Authority*, 56–91, Washington Square, NY: Authority.

Fuller, Steve (2006), "The Constitutively Social Character of Expertise," in Evan Selinger and Robert P. Crease (eds.), *The Philosophy of Expertise*, 342–57, New York: Columbia University Press.

Funk, Cary and Brian Kennedy (2019), "Public Confidence in Scientists has Remained Stable for Decades," Pew Research Center, March 22. Available online: https://www.pewresearch.org/fact-tank/2019/03/22/public-confidence-in-scientists-has-remained-stable-for-decades/?fbclid=IwAR2RsXV-9y1aUHEm5hebd5kWz7Pf85oEEAlCInpyeZi28ES5m-HiwR2kEj0.

Funk, Cary, Brian Kennedy and Meg Hefferon (2018), "Public Perspectives on Food Risks," *Pew Research Center*, November 19. Available online: https://www.pewresearch.org/science/2018/11/19/public-perspectives-on-food-risks/.

Gagné, Francoys (1999), "Nature or Nurture? A Re-examination of Sloboda and Howe's (1991) Interview Study on Talent Development in Music," *Psychology of Music*, 27 (1): 38–51.

Garland, Cedric F., Frank C. Garland, Edward D. Gorham, Martin Lipkin, Harold Newmark, Sharif B. Mohr and Michael F. Holick (2006), "The Role of Vitamin D in Cancer Prevention," *American Journal of Public Health*, 96 (2): 252–61.

Gelfert, Axel (2011), "Expertise, Argumentation, and the End of Inquiry," *Argumentation*, 25 (3): 297–312.

Gelfert, Axel (2014), *A Critical Introduction to Testimony*, London: Bloomsbury Academic.

Gibson, William and Bruce Sterling (1990), *The Difference Engine*, London: Victor Gollancz, Ltd.

Gigerenzer, Gerd (2007), "Fast and Frugal Heuristics: The Tools of Bounded Rationality," in Derek J. Koehler and Nigel Harvey (eds.), *Blackwell Handbook of Judgment & Decision Making*, 62–88, Malden, MA: Blackwell Publishing.

Gigerenzer, Gerd (2008), "Why Heuristics Work," *Perspectives on Psychological Science*, 3 (1): 20–9.
Gilman, Benjamin Ives (1914), "The Day of the Expert," *Science*, 39 (1013): 771–9.
Gilovich, Thomas (1991), *How We Know What Isn't So*, New York: Free Press.
Gilovich, Thomas, Dale Griffin and Daniel Kahneman, eds. (2002), *Heuristics and Biases: The Psychology of Intuitive Judgment*, Cambridge: Cambridge University Press.
Gobet, F. and Charness, N. (2006), "Expertise in Chess," in K. A. Ericsson, N. Charness, P. J. Feltovich and R. R. Hoffman (eds.), *The Cambridge Handbook of Expertise and Expert Performance*, 523–38, New York: Cambridge University Press.
Golan, Tai (2008), "Revisiting the History of Scientific Expert Testimony," *Brooklyn Law Review*, 73 (3), Symposium: A Cross-Disciplinary Look At Scientific Truth: What's the Law to Do?: 879–942.
Goldman, Alvin (1991), "Epistemic Paternalism: Communication Control in Law and Society," *The Journal of Philosophy*, 88 (3): 113–31.
Goldman, Alvin (2001), "Experts: Which Ones Should You Trust?," *Philosophy and Phenomenological Research*, 63 (1): 85–109.
Goldman, Alvin I. ([2001] 2002), "Experts: Which Ones Should You Trust?," in Alvin I. Goldman (ed.), *Pathways to Knowledge: Private and Public*, 139–63, Oxford: Oxford University Press.
Goldman, Alvin (2009), "Replies to Discussants," in Shurz, Gerhard and Markus Werning (eds.), *Reliable Knowledge and Social Epistemology: Essays on the Philosophy of Alvin Goldman and Replies by Goldman*, 245–90, Amsterdam: Grazer Philosophische Studien.
Goldman, Alvin (2018), "Expertise," *Topoi*, 37 (1): 3–10.
Goldman, Alvin I. and Dennis Whitcomb (2011), *Social Epistemology: Essential Readings*, Oxford: Oxford University Press.
Goldstein, Robin, Johan Almenberg, Anna Dreber, John W. Emerson, Alexis Herschkowitsch and Jacob Katz (2008), "Do More Expensive Wines Taste Better? Evidence From A Large Sample Of Blind Tastings," Working Papers 37328, American Association of Wine Economists.
Good, Anthony (2008), "Cultural Evidence in Courts of Law," *The Journal of the Royal Anthropological Institute*, 14: S47–S60.
Goodman, Nelson (1984), *Of Mind and Other Matters*, Cambridge, MA: Harvard University Press.
Gould, John (1955), *The Development of Plato's Ethics*, Cambridge: Cambridge University Press.
Graves, Robert ([1955] 1960), *The Greek Myths*, rev. ed., London: Penguin.
Grenz, Stanley J. (1996), *A Primer on Postmodernism*, Grand Rapids, MI: Wm. B. Eerdman's.
Grob, Gerald N. (2011), "The Attack of Psychiatric Legitimacy in the 1960s: Rhetoric and Reality," *Journal of the History of the Behavioral Sciences*, 47: 398–416.

Groopman, Jerome (2010), *How Doctors Think*, Boston, MA: Houghton, Mifflin, Harcourt.

Groopman, Jerome and Pamela Hartzband (2011), *Your Medical Mind: How to Decide What Is Right for You*, New York: Penguin.

Gross, Samuel R. (1991), "Expert Evidence," *Wisconsin Law Review*, 1991: 1113–232.

Guerrero, Alex (2017), "Living with Ignorance in a World of Experts," in Rik Peels (ed.), *Perspectives on Ignorance from Moral and Social Philosophy*, 156–85, New York: Routledge.

Guidry-Grimes, Laura K. (2017), "Mental Diversity and Meaningful Psychiatry Disabilities," Ph.D. Dissertation, Georgetown University. Available online: http://hdl.handle.net/10822/1043860.

Guthrie, C., Rachlinski, J. and Wistrich, A. (2001), "Inside the Judicial Mind," *Cornell Law Review*, 86: 777–830.

Guthrie, C., Rachlinski, J. and Wistrich, A. (2007), "Blinking on the Bench: How Judges Decide Cases," *Cornell Law Review*, 93: 1–43.

Guthrie, C., Rachlinski, J. and Wistrich, A. (2011), "Probable Cause, Probability, and Hindsight," *Journal of Empirical Legal Studies*, 8: 72–98.

Hallett, Christine (2005), "The Attempt to Understand Puerperal Fever in the Eighteenth and Early Nineteenth Centuries: The Influence of Inflammation Theory," *Medical History* 49 (1): 1–28.

Hardwig, John (1994), "Toward an Ethics of Expertise," in Daniel E. Wueste (ed.), *Professional Ethics and Social Responsibility*, 83–102, Lanham, MD: Rowman & Littlefield.

Hambrick, David Z. Guillermo Campitelli and Brooke N. Macnamara, eds. (2018), *The Science of Expertise: Behavioral, Neural, and Genetics Approaches to Complex Skill*, London: Routledge.

Hampshire, Adam, Roger R. Highfield, Beth L. Parkin and Adrian M. Owen (2012), "Fractionating Human Intelligence," *Neuron*, 76 (6): 1225–37, doi: 10.1016/j.neuron.2012.06.022.

Hand, Learned (1901), "Historical and Practical Considerations regarding Expert Testimony," *Harvard Law Review*, 15 (1): 40–58.

Hardwig, John (1985), "Epistemic Dependence," *Journal of Philosophy*, 82 (7): 335–49.

Hart, H. L. A. (1982), *Essays on Bentham: Jurisprudence and Political Philosophy*, Oxford: Oxford University Press.

Hartsock, Nancy (1987), "The Feminist Standpoint: Developing the Ground for a Specifically Feminist Historical Materialism," in Sandra Harding (ed.), *Feminism and Methodology: Social Science Issues*, 157–80, Bloomington: Indiana University Press.

Haskell, Thomas (1998), *Objectivity is Not Neutrality: Explanatory Schemes in History*, Baltimore, MD: Johns Hopkins Press.

Hauser, Larry (n.d.), "Chinese Room Argument," *Internet Encyclopedia of Philosophy*. Available online: https://www.iep.utm.edu/chineser/.

Hawkins, Derek (2016), "Flight Attendant to Black Female Doctor: 'We're Looking for Actual Physicians,'" *Washington Post*, October 14. Available online: https://www.washingtonpost.com/news/morning-mix/wp/2016/10/14/blatant-discrimination-black-female-doctor-says-flight-crew-questioned-her-credentials-during-medical-emergency/?noredirect=on.

"Healthcare Ethics Consultant-Certified Program," American Society for Bioethics and Humanities, accessed July 11, 2019. Available online: http://asbh.org/certification/hcec-certification.

HEC-C Certification Commission (2019), *Healthcare Ethics Consultant-Certified (HEC-C) Examination Candidate Handbook*, Chicago, IL: American Society for Bioethics and Humanities.

Hecht, Jennifer Michael (2003), *Doubt: A History*, New York: Harper Collins.

Heidegger, Martin ([1982] 2002), *The Essence of Human Freedom: An Introduction to Philosophy*, trans. Ted Sadler, London: Continuum.

Heldal, Frode and Aksel Tjora (2009), "Making Sense of Patient Expertise," *Social Theory and Health*, 7: 1–19.

Hempel, Carl (1966), *Philosophy of Natural Science*, Englewood Cliffs, NJ: Prentice Hall.

Hester, D. Micah (2001), *Community as Healing: Pragmatist Ethics in Medical Encounters*, Lanham: Rowman and Littlefield.

Hinton, Martin David (2015), "Mizrahi and Seidel: Experts in Confusion," *Informal Logic*, 35 (4): 539–54.

Hochschild, Arlie Russell (2016), *Strangers in their Own Land: Anger and Mourning on the American Right*, New York: The New Press.

Hodgson, Robert T. (2008), "An Examination of Judge Reliability at a Major U.S. Wine Competition," *Journal of Wine Economics*, 3 (2) 105–13.

Hodgson, R. (2009), "How Expert are 'Expert' Wine Judges?" *Journal of Wine Economics*, 4 (2): 233–41. doi:10.1017/S1931436100000821.

Hoffman, Diane E. and Anita J. Tarzian (2001), "The Girl Who Cried Pain: A Bias Against Women in the Treatment of Pain," *Journal of Law, Medicine and Ethics*, 29: 13–27.

Hoffman, Kelly M., Sophie Trawalter, Jordan R. Axt and M. Norman Oliver (2016), "Racial Bias in Pain Assessment and Treatment Recommendations, and False Beliefs about Biological Differences Between Blacks and Whites," *PNAS*, 113 (16): 4296–301.

Hogarth, Robin M. (2001), *Educating Intuition*, Chicago: University of Chicago Press.

Hogarth, Robin (2010), "Intuition: A Challenge for Psychological Research on Decision Making," *Psychological Inquiry*, 21: 338–53.

Hogarth, Robin M., Tomás Lejarraga and Emre Soyer (2015), "The Two Settings of Kind and Wicked Learning Environments," *Current Directions in Psychological Science*, 24 (5): 379–85.

Homer (2018), *The Odyssey*, trans. Emily Wilson, New York: W. W. Norton and Company.

Homer (1900), *The Odyssey*, trans. Samuel Butler, London.
How to Taste Whisky (n.d.). *Master of Malt*. Available online: https://www.masterof malt.com/c/guides/how-to-taste-whisky/.
Howard, John W. and Robin M. Dawes (1976), "Linear Prediction of Marital Happiness," *Personality and Social Psychology Bulletin*, 2 (4): 478–80.
Huemer, Michael (2012), *The Problem of Political Authority*, New York: Palgrave Macmillan.
"Human Health Risk Assessment," US EPA, accessed July 15, 2019. Available online: https://www.epa.gov/risk/human-health-risk-assessment.
Hussain, A., S. Ali, M. Ahmed and S. Hussain (2018), "The Anti-Vaccination Movement: A Regression in Modern Medicine," *Cureus*, 10 (7): e2919, doi: 10.7759/cureus.2919.
Huxley, Aldous (1963), *Literature and Science*, New Haven, CT: Leete's Island Books, Inc.
Ingelfinger, Franz J. (1980), "Arrogance," *New England Journal of Medicine*, 303 (26): 1507–11.
International Association of Memory. Available online: http://iam-stats.org/.
Irwin, Alan (1995), *Citizen Science: A Study of People, Expertise and Sustainable Development*, New York: Routledge.
Jackson, M. (1994), "Suspicious Infant Deaths: The Statute of 1624 and Medical Evidence at Coroners' Inquests," in M. Clark and C. Crawford (eds.), *Legal Medicine in History*, 64–86, Cambridge: Cambridge University Press.
Jaeger, C. Stephen (1994), *The Envy of Angels: Cathedral Schools and Social Ideals in Medieval Europe, 950–1200*, Philadelphia: University of Pennsylvania Press.
James, William ([1890] 1950), *Principles of Psychology*, New York: Dover.
Jamieson, Kathleen Hall and Joseph N. Cappella (2010), *Echo Chamber: Rush Limbaugh and the Conservative Media Establishment*, Oxford: Oxford University Press.
Jasanoff, Sheila (2003), "Breaking the Waves in Science Studies: Comment on H. M. Collins and Robert Evans, 'The Third Wave of Science Studies,'" *Social Studies of Science*, 33 (3): 389–400.
Jefferson, Thomas (1776), "A Bill for Establishing Religious Freedom," Available online: https://founders.archives.gov/documents/Jefferson/01-02-02-0132-0004-0082.
Jefford, Andrew (2004), *Peat Smoke and Spirit: A Portrait of Islay and Its Whiskies*, London: Headline.
Jenks, Rod (2008), *Plato on Moral Expertise*, Lanham, MD: Lexington Books.
Jin, J. (2014), "Breast Cancer Screening: Benefits and Harms," *JAMA*, 312 (23): 2585.
Jobs, Steve (2011), "Technology and Liberal Arts," *YouTube*, October 6. Available online: https://www.youtube.com/watch?v=KlI1MR-qNt8.
John, Esther M., G. G. Schwarz, D. M. Dreon and J. Koo (1999), "Vitamin D and Breast Cancer Risk: The NHANES I Epidemiologic Follow-up Study, 1971–1975 to 1992," *Cancer Epidemiology, Biomarkers & Prevention*, 8 (5): 399.

John, Stephen (2018), "Epistemic Trust and the Ethics of Science Communication: Against Transparency, Openness, Sincerity and Honesty," *Social Epistemology*, 32 (2): 75–87.
Johnson, Dave (2015), "Obama to Visit Nike to Promote TPP. Wait, Nike? Really?," *Huffington Post*, May 7. Available online: http://www.huffingtonpost.com/dave-johnson/obama-to-visit-nike-to-pr_b_7233118.html.
Jones, James ([1981] 1993), *Bad Blood: The Tuskegee Syphilis Experiment*, rev. ed., New York: The Free Press.
Journal of Parapsychology (n.d.), Parapsychological Association. Available online: https://www.parapsych.org/section/17/journal_of_parapsychology.aspx.
Kahneman, Daniel (2011), *Thinking Fast and Slow*, New York: Farrar, Straus, & Giroux.
Kahneman, Daniel and Dan Lovallo (1993), "Timid Choices and Bold Forecasts: A Cognitive Perspective on Risk Taking," *Management Science*, 39 (1): 17–31.
Kahneman, D., P. Slovic and A. Tversky (1982), *Judgment Under Uncertainty: Heuristics and Biases*, Cambridge: Cambridge University Press.
Kahneman, Daniel and Amon Tversky, eds. (2000), *Choices, Values and Frames*, Cambridge: Cambridge University Press.
Kaiser, Mary Kister, John Jonides and Joanne Alexander (1986), "Intuitive Reasoning about Abstract and Familiar Physics Problems," *Memory and Cognition*, 14 (4): 308–12.
Kant, Immanuel (1784), "What Is Enlightenment?," trans. Mary C. Smith. Available online: http://www.columbia.edu/acis/ets/CCREAD/etscc/kant.html.
Kant, Immanuel ([1785] 2006), *Anthropology from a Pragmatic Point of View*, trans. Robert B. Louden, Cambridge: Cambridge University Press.
Kellogg, Ronald T. (2018), "Professional Writing Expertise," in K. Anders Ericsson, Robert R. Hoffman, Aaron Kozbelt and Mark Williams (eds.), *Expertise and Expert Performance*, 2nd ed., 413–30, Cambridge: Cambridge University Press.
Kelly, Thomas (2005), "The Epistemic Significance of Disagreement," in T. Gendler and J. Hawthorne (eds.), *Oxford Studies in Epistemology*, Vol. 1, 167–96, Oxford: Oxford University Press.
Keren, G. (1987), "Facing Uncertainty in the Game of Bridge: A Calibration Study," *Organizational Behavior and Human Decision Processes*, 39: 98–114.
Kerényi, Karl (1951), *The Gods of the Greeks*, London: Thames and Hudson.
Khan, Carrie-Ann Biondi (2005), "Aristotle's Moral Expert: The Phronimos," in Lisa Rasmussen (ed.), *Ethics Expertise: History, Contemporary Perspectives, and Applications*, 39–53, Dordrecht: Springer.
Kitcher, Philip (1993), *The Advancement of Science*, New York: Oxford University Press.
Klein, Gary (1998), *Sources of Power: How People Make Decisions*, Cambridge, MA: The MIT Press.
Klein, Gary (2003), *The Power of Intuition: How to Use Your Gut Feelings to Make Better Decisions at Work*, New York: Currency.
Klein, Gary (2013), *Seeing What Others Don't: The Remarkable Ways We Gain Insight*, New York: Public Affairs.

Klein, Gary (2015), "A Naturalistic Decision Making Perspective on Studying Intuitive Decision Making," *Journal of Applied Research in Memory and Cognition*, 4: 164–8.

Klein, Gary A. (2016), "The Naturalistic Decision Making Approach: What We Have Learned by Studying Cognition in the Wild," *Psychology Today*. Available online: https://www.psychologytoday.com/nz/blog/seeing-what-others-dont/201602/the-naturalistic-decision-making-approach?amp.

Klein, G., R. Calderwood and A. Clinton-Cirocco (2010), "Rapid Decision Making on the Fireground: The Original Study Plus a Postscript," *Journal of Cognitive Engineering and Decision Making*, 4: 186–209.

Klein, Gary A., Judith Orasnu, Roberta Calderwood and Caroline E. Zsambok, eds. (1993), *Decision Making In Action: Models and Methods*, 51–99, Norwood, NJ: Ablex Publishing Corporation.

Klein, G., S. Wolf, L. Militello and C. Zsambok (1995), "Characteristics of Skilled Option Generation in Chess," *Organizational Behavior and Human Decision Processes*, 62 (1): 63–69.

Klein, Peter (2005), "Infinitism is the Solution to the Regress Problem," in Matthius Steup and Ernest Sosa (eds.), *Contemporary Debates in Epistemology*, 131–9, Malden, MA: Blackwell.

Klinkenborg, Verlyn (2012), *Several Short Sentences about Writing*, New York: Vintage Books.

Koehler, D. J., L. Brenner and D. Griffin (2002), "The Calibration of Expert Judgment: Heuristics and Biases Beyond the Laboratory," in T. Gilovich, D. Griffin and D. Kahneman (eds.), *Heuristics and Biases: The Psychology of Intuitive Judgment*, 686–715, Cambridge: Cambridge University Press.

Kornbith, Hilary (2002), *Knowledge and Its Place in Nature*, Oxford: Oxford University Press.

Kornblith, Hilary (2010), "Belief in the Face of Controversy," in Richard Feldman and Ted A. Warfield (eds.), *Disagreement*, 40–1, Oxford: Oxford University Press.

Kuhn, Thomas (1962), *The Structure of Scientific Revolutions*, Chicago: University of Chicago Press.

Kukla, Rebecca (2007), "How Patients Know," *The Hastings Center Report*, 37: 27–35.

Kundel, H. L. and P. S. LaFollette (1972), "Visual Search Patterns and Experience with Radiological Images," *Radiology*, 103: 523–58.

Kutrovátz, G. (2011), "Expert Authority and ad verecundiam Arguments," in F. H. van Eemeren, B. J. Garssen, D. Godden and G. Mitchell (eds.), *Proceedings of the Seventh Conference of the International Society of the Study of Argumentation*, 1050–61, Amsterdam: Rozenberg.

LaBarge, Scott (1997), "Socrates and the Recognition of Experts," *Apeiron*, 30 (4): 51–62.

Lackey, Jennifer (2006), "Introduction," in Jennifer Lackey and Ernest Sosa (eds.), *The Epistemology of Testimony*, 1–21, Oxford: Oxford University Press.

Lackey, Jennifer (2018a), "Experts and Peer Disagreement," in Matthew A. Benton, John Hawthorne and Dani Rabinowitz (eds.), *Knowledge, Belief, and God: New Insights in Religious Epistemology*, 228–45. Oxford: Oxford University Press.

Lackey, Jennifer (2018b), "True Story: Echo Chambers Are Not the Problem," *Morning Consult Blog*, Available online: https://morningconsult.com/opinions/true-story-echo-chambers-not-problem/.

Lagay, Faith (2002), "The Legacy of Humoral Medicine," *AMA Journal of Ethics Virtual Mentor*, 4 (7), doi: 10.1001/virtualmentor.2002.4.7.mhst1-0207.

Landman, J. T. and R. M. Dawes (1982), "Psychotherapy Outcome: Smith and Glass' Conclusions Stand Up to Scrutiny," *American Psychologist*, 37: 504–16.

Landwehr, Achim (2004), "The Expert in a Historical Context: The Case of Venetian Politics," in Elke Kurz-Milcke and Gerd Gigerenzer (eds.), *Experts in Science and Society*, 215–28, New York: Kluwer Academic / Plenum Publishers.

Lane, Melissa (2014), "When the Experts are Uncertain: Scientific Knowledge and the Ethics of Democratic Judgment," *Episteme*, 11 (1): 97–118, doi: 10.1017/epi.2013.48.

Lappe, Joan M., D. Travers-Gustafson, K. M. Davies, R. R. Recker and R. P. Heaney (2007), "Vitamin D and Calcium Supplementation Reduces Cancer Risk: Results of a Randomized Trial," *American Journal of Clinical Nutrition*, 85 (6): 1586–91.

Lee, Carole J., Cassidy R. Sugimoto, Guo Zhang and Blaise Cronin (2013), "Bias in Peer Review," *Journal of the American Society For Information Science and Technology*, 64 (1): 2–17.

Leventhal, L., Teasley, B. and Rohlman, D. (1994), "Analyses of Factors Related to Positive Test Bias in Software Testing," *International Journal of Human-Computer Studies*, 41: 717–49.

Leibniz, Gottfried , W. ([1671] 1992), "On the Establishment of a Society in Germany For the Promotion of the Arts and Sciences," trans. John Chambless, *FIDELIO*, The Schiller Institute, Washington, DC, 1 (2).

Lewis, C. S. (1954), *The Horse and His Boy*, London: Geoffrey Bles.

Lewis, C. S. (1960), *The Four Loves*, New York: Harcourt Brace.

Leyva, Arturo (2018), "Embodied Rilkean Sport-Specific Knowledge," *Journal of the Philosophy of Sport*, 45 (2): 1–16.

Licon, Jimmy Alfonso (2012), "Skeptical Thoughts on Philosophical Expertise," *Logos and Episteme*, 3 (4): 449–58.

Lindberg, David C. (2002a), "Early Christian Attitudes Toward Nature," in Gary B. Ferngren (ed.), *Science and Religion: A Historical Introduction*, 47–56, Baltimore, MD: Johns Hopkins University Press.

Lindberg, David C. (2002b), "Medieval Science and Religion," in Gary B. Ferngren (ed.), *Science and Religion: A Historical Introduction*, 57–72, Baltimore, MD: Johns Hopkins University Press.

Linshi, Jack (2015), "10 CEOs Who Prove Your Liberal Arts Degree Isn't Worthless," *Time Magazine*, July 23. Available online: https://time.com/3964415/ceo-degree-liberal-arts/.

Lippmann, Walter (1927), *The Phantom Public*, New Brunswick: Transaction Publishers.
Lippmann, Walter (1922), *Public Opinion*, New York: Harcourt.
Lloyd, G. E. R. (1987), *Revolutions of Wisdom: Studies in the Claims and Practice of Ancient Greek Science*, Berkeley, CA: University of California Press.
Locke, John (1975), *An Essay Concerning Human Understanding*, ed. Peter H. Nidditch, Oxford: Oxford University Press.
London, Alex John (2000), "Thrasymachus and Managed Care: How Not to Think about The Craft of Medicine," in Mark G. Kuczewski and Roland Polansky (eds.), *Bioethics: Ancient Themes in Contemporary Issues*, 131–54, Cambridge, MA: The MIT Press.
Lopez, German (2019), "For the First Time, the Feds Criminally Charged a Pharma Distributor for the Opioid Epidemic," *Vox*, April 23. Available online: https://www.vox.com/policy-and-politics/2019/4/23/18512781/rochester-drug-cooperative-opioid-epidemic-drug-trafficking.
Luscombe, Belinda (2011), "10 Questions for Daniel Kahneman," *Time Magazine*, November 28. Available online: http://content.time.com/time/magazine/article/0917 1209971200.html.
Lyotard, Jean-François ([1979] 1984), *The Postmodern Condition: A Report on Knowledge*, trans. Geoff Bennington and Brian Massumi, Manchester: Manchester University Press. Trans. of La Condition postmoderne: rapport sur le savoir (Paris: Minuit, 1979).
Machuca, Diego E., ed. (2013), *Disagreement and Skepticism*, London: Routledge.
Majdik, Zoltan P. and William M. Keith (2011), "The Problem of Pluralistic Expertise: A Wittgensteinian Approach to the Rhetorical Basis of Expertise," *Social Epistemology*, 25 (3): 275–90.
Makary, Martin A. and Michael Daniel (2016), "Medical Error: The Third Leading Cause of Death in the US," *BMJ*, 353, doi: 10.1136/bmj.i2139.
Marr, Bernard (2017), "Machine Learning, Artificial Intelligence—And the Future of Accounting," *Forbes Magazine*. Available online: https://www.forbes.com/sites/bernardmarr/2017/07/07/machine-learning-artificial-intelligence-and-the-future-of-accounting/#2fc34b1c2dd1.
Martin, Ben L. (1973), "Experts in Policy Processes: A Contemporary Perspective," *Polity*, 6 (2): 149–73.
Martini, Carlo (2015), "The Paradox of Proof and Scientific Expertise," *Journal of Philosophical Studies*, 28: 1–16.
Martinson, Brian C., Melissa S. Anderson and Raymond de Vries (2005), "Scientists Behaving Badly," *Nature*, 435: 737–8.
Maruthappu, Mahiben, Antoine Duclos, Stuart R. Lipsitz, Dennis Orgill, Matthew J. Carty (2015), "Surgical Learning Curves and Operative Efficiency: A Cross-Specialty Observational Study," *BMJ Open*, 5 (3), doi: 10.1136/bmjopen-2014-006679
Mascaro, Jennifer S. Patrick D. Hackett and James K. Rilling (2013), "Testicular Volume is Inversely Correlated with Nurturing-Related Brain Activity in Human Fathers," *PNAS*, 110 (39): 15746–51.

Matheson, Jonathan (2015), *The Epistemic Significance of Disagreement*, New York: Palgrave Macmillan.

Matheson, Jonathan and Brandon Carey (2013), "How Skeptical is the Equal Weight View?," in Diego E. Machuca (ed.), *Disagreement and Skepticism*, 131–49, New York: Routledge.

Matheson, Jonathan, S. McElreath and N. Nobis (2018), "Moral Experts, Deference & Disagreement," in Jamie Carlin Watson and Laura Guidry-Grimes (eds.), *Moral Expertise*, 87–105, Cham, Switzerland: Springer.

Mazza, Ed (2016), "Florida 18-Year-Old Arrested for Allegedly Operating Fake Medical Practice," *Huffington Post*, February 2. Available online: https://www.huffpost.com/entry/malachi-love-robinson-teen-fake-doctor_n_56c40019e4b0c3c5505328df?guccounter=1.

McCain, Kevin (2014), "The Problem of the Criterion," *Internet Encyclopedia of Philosophy*. Available online: https://www.iep.utm.edu/criterio/.

McCloskey, M., A. Caramazza and B. Green (1980), "Curvilinear Motion in the Absence of External Forces: Naïve Beliefs about the Motion of Objects," *Science*, 210: 1139–41.

McGrath, Alister (2007), *Christianity's Dangerous Idea*, New York: Harper Collins.

McGrath, Sarah (2008), "Moral Disagreement and Moral Expertise," in Russ Shafer-Landau (ed.), *Oxford Studies in Metaethics: Volume 4*, 87–108, Oxford: Oxford University Press.

McLean vs. Arkansas Documentation Project (2005), "Statement of Purpose," *AntiEvolution.org*. Available online: http://www.antievolution.org/projects/mclean/new:site/index.htm.

McMyler, Benjamin (2011), *Testimony, Trust, & Authority*, Oxford: Oxford University Press.

McNeil, B. J., S. G. Pauker, H. C. Sox, Jr. and A. Tversky (1982), "On the Elicitation of Preferences for Alternative Therapies," *New England Journal of Medicine*, 306: 1259–62.

Merleau-Ponty, Maurice (1945), *Phenomenology of Perception*, Paris: Éditions Gallimard.

Mie, Axel, Christina Rudén, Philippe Grandjean (2018), "Safety of Safety Evaluation of Pesticides: Developmental Neurotoxicity of Chlorpyrifos and Chlorpyrifos-Methyl," *Environmental Health*, 17 (77): 1–5.

Mieg, Harald and Julia Evetts (2018), "Professionalism, Science, and Expert Roles: A Social Perspective," in K. Anders Ericsson, Robert R. Hoffman, Aaron Kozbelt and A. Mark Williams (eds.), *The Cambridge Handbook of Expertise and Expert Performance*, 2nd ed., 127–48, Cambridge: Cambridge University Press.

Millgram, Elijah (2015), *The Great Endarkenment*, Oxford: Oxford University Press.

Milroy, Chrisopher M. (2017), "A Brief History of the Expert Witness," *Academic Forensic Pathology*, 7 (4): 516–26.

Mitchell, Georgina (2017), "Man Charged After "Impersonating Doctor" at NSW Hospitals for 11 Years," *Sydney Morning Herald*, March 7. Available online: https://

www.smh.com.au/national/nsw/man-charged-after-impersonating-a-doctor-at-nsw-hospitals-for-11-years-20170307-guswh5.html.

Mizrahi, Moti (2013), "Why Arguments from Expert Opinion are Weak Arguments," *Informal Logic*, 33 (1): 57–79.

Mizrahi, Moti (2016), "Why Arguments from Expert Opinion are still Weak: A Reply to Seidel," *Informal Logic*, 36 (2): 238–52.

Mizrahi, Moti (2018), "Arguments from Expert Opinion and Persistent Bias," *Argumentation*, 32 (2): 175–95.

Mlodinow, Leonard (2008), *The Drunkard's Walk: How Randomness Rules Our Lives*, New York: Pantheon Books.

Montero, Barbara (2016), *Thought in Action: Expertise and the Conscious Mind*, Oxford, UK: Oxford University Press.

Montague, Jules (2017), "Trust Me, I'm a Fake Doctor: How Medical Imposters Thrive in the Real World," *The Guardian*, August 14. Available online: https://www.theguardian.com/global/2017/aug/14/trust-me-im-a-fake-doctor-how-medical-imposters-thrive-in-the-real-world.

Moore, Alfred (2017), *Critical Elitism: Deliberation, Democracy, and the Problem of Expertise*, Cambridge: Cambridge University Press.

Morrot, G., F. Brochet and D. Dubourdieu (2001), "The Color of Odors," *Brain and Language*, 79 (2): 309–20. doi: 10.1006/brln.2001.2493. PMID: 11712849.

Mosing, Miriam A., Isabelle Peretz and Frederick Ullén (2018), "Genetic Influences on Music Expertise," in David Z. Hambrick, Guillermo Campitelli and Brooke N. Macnamara (eds.), *The Science of Expertise: Behavioral, Neural, and Genetic Approaches to Complex Skill*, 272–82, London: Routledge.

Murray, Charles and Richard Hernstein (1994), *The Bell Curve: Intelligence and Class Structure in American Life*, New York: Free Press.

Murray-Close, Marta and Misty L. Heggeness (2018), "Manning Up and Womaning Down: How Husbands and Wives Report their Earnings When She Earns More," United States Census Bureau Working Paper Number: SEHSD-WP2018-20, Available online: https://www.census.gov/content/dam/Census/library/working-papers/2018/demo/SEHSD-WP2018-20.pdf.

Nelson, K. E., L. C. Rosella, S. Mahant and A. Guttman (2016), "Survival and Surgical Interventions for Children with Trisomy 13 and 18," *JAMA*, 316 (4): 420–28.

Newell, Allen and Herbert Simon (1972), *Human Problem Solving*, Upper Saddle River, NJ: Prentice Hall.

Newton, Isaac (1952), *Mathematical Principles of Natural Philosophy*, trans. Andrew Motte, rev. Florian Cajori, Chicago: Encyclopedia Britannica Inc.

Nguyen, C. Thi (2018a), "Echo Chambers and Epistemic Bubbles," *Episteme*, 1–21, doi: 10.1017/epi.2018.32.

Nguyen, C. Thi (2018b), "Cognitive Islands and Runaway Echo Chambers: Problems for Epistemic Dependence on Experts," *Synthese*, 1–19, doi: 10.1007/s11229-018-1692-0.

Nichols, Tom (2017), *The Death of Expertise: The Campaign against Established Knowledge and Why It Matters*, New York: Oxford University Press

Nietzsche, Friedrich ([1878] 1986), *Human, All Too Human: A Book for Free Spirits*, trans. R. J. Hollingdale, Cambridge, UK: Cambridge University Press.

Nietzsche, Friedrich ([1886] 2009), *Beyond Good and Evil*, trans. Helen Zimmern, Urbana, IL: Project Gutenberg.

Nippel, Wilfried (2007), "The Roman Notion of *Auctoritas*," in *The Concept of Authority*, 13–34, Rome, Italy: Fondazione Adriano Olivetti.

Norman, Geoffrey R., Lawrence E. M. Grierson, Jonathan Sherbino, Stanley J. Hamstra, Henk G. Schmidt and Silvia Mamede (2018), "Expertise in Medicine and Surgery," in K. Anders Ericsson, Robert R. Hoffman, Aaron Kozbelt and Mark Williams (eds.), *Expertise and Expert Performance*, 2nd ed., 331–55, Cambridge, UK: Cambridge University Press.

Norton, Kevin and Tim Olds (2001), "Morphological Evolution of Athletes Over the 20th Century," *Sports Medicine*, 31 (11): 763–83.

Noveck, Beth Simone (2015), *Smart Citizens, Smarter State: The Technologies of Expertise and the Future of Governing*, Cambridge, MA: Harvard University Press.

Numbers, Ron (2006), *The Creationists: From Scientific Creationism to Intelligent Design*, Cambridge, MA: Harvard University Press.

Oreskes, Naomi and Erik M. Conway (2010), *Merchants of Doubt: How a Handful of Scientists Obscured the Truth on Issues from Tobacco Smoke to Global Warming*, New York: Bloomsbury.

Origgi, Gloria (2015), "What Is an Expert That a Person May Trust Her? Towards a Political Epistemology of Expertise," *Journal of Philosophical Studies*, 28: 159–68.

Ovid (2001), *Metamorphoses*, trans. A. S. Kline, Poetry in Translation.

Pariser, Eli (2011), *The Filter Bubble: What the Internet is Hiding from You*, New York: Penguin Press.

Parry, Richard (2014), "Episteme and Techne," in Edward N. Zalta (ed.), *The Stanford Encyclopedia of Philosophy*, Fall 2014 Edition. Available online: https://plato.stanford.edu/archives/fall2014/entries/episteme-techne/.

Patel, V. [L.] and K. A. Ericsson (1990), "Expert-Novice Differences in Clinical Text Understanding," Technical Report CME90-CS13. Montreal: Centre for Medical Education, McGill, University.

Patel, V. L. and G. J. Groen (1991), "The Nature of Medical Expertise: A Critical Look," in K. Anders Ericsson and Jacqui Smith (eds.), *Toward a General Theory of Expertise*, 93–125, Cambridge, UK: Cambridge University Press.

Patel, V. L. and G. J. Groen (1986), "Knowledge-Based Solution Strategies in Medical Reasoning," *Cognitive Science*, 10: 91–116.

Perceptions of Science in America (2018), Cambridge, MA: American Academy of Arts and Sciences. Available online: https://www.amacad.org/sites/default/files/publication/downloads/PFoS-Perceptions-Science-America.pdf.

Peters, R. S. (1967), "Authority," in Anthony Quinton (ed.), *Political Philosophy*, 83–96, Oxford: Oxford University Press.

Peters, R. S., P. G. Winch and A. E. Duncan-Jones (1958), "Authority," *Proceedings of the Aristotelian Society*, 32: 207–60.

Philips, Jennifer K., Gary Klein and Winston R. Sieck (2007), "Expertise in Judgment and Decision Making: A Case for Training Intuitive Decision Skills," in Derek J. Koehler and Nigel Harvey (eds.), *Blackwell Handbook of Judgment and Decision Making*, 297–315, Malden, MA: Blackwell Publishing.

Pico della Mirandola, Giovanni (1956), *Oration on the Dignity of Man*, trans. A. R. Caponigri, Chicago: H. Regnery Co.

Plato (1903), *Statesman*, trans. John Burnet, Oxford: Oxford University Press.

Plato (1967), *Protagoras*, trans. W. R. M. Lamb. Plato in Twelve Volumes, Vol. 3, Cambridge, MA: Harvard University Press; London: William Heinemann Ltd.

Plato (1968), *The Republic of Plato*, trans Allan Bloom, 2nd edn. New York: Basic Books.

Plato (1992), *Republic*, trans. G. M. A. Grube, revised by C. D. C. Reeve, New York: Hackett.

Plato (1997a), "Ion," trans. Paul Woodruff, in John M. Cooper (ed.), *Plato: Complete Works*, 937–49, Indianapolis, IN: Hackett Publishing Company.

Plato (1997b), "Laches," trans. Rosamond Kent Sprague, in John M. Cooper (ed.), *Plato: Complete Works*, 664–86, Indianapolis, IN: Hackett Publishing Company.

Plato (1997c), "Protagoras," trans. Stanley Lombardo and Karen Bell, in John M. Cooper (ed.), *Plato: Complete Works*, 746–90, Indianapolis, IN: Hackett Publishing Company.

Plato (1997d), "Statesman," trans. C. J. Rowe. in John M. Cooper (ed.), *Plato: Complete Works*, 294–358, Indianapolis, IN: Hackett Publishing Company.

Plutarch (1874), *Plutarch's Morals*, translated from the Greek by several hands, rev. William W. Goodwin, Boston: Little, Brown, and Co; Cambridge: Press of John Wilson and Son.

Polanyi, Michael ([1958] 1962), *Personal Knowledge: Towards a Post-Critical Philosophy*, New York: Harper Torchbooks.

Porter, Roy (2003), *Cambridge History of Science, Vol. 4: Eighteenth-Century Science*, Cambridge: Cambridge University Press.

Porter, Theodore M. (1995), *Trust in Numbers: The Pursuit of Objectivity in Science and Public Life*, Princeton, NJ: Princeton University Press.

Postman, Neil (1985), *Amusing Ourselves to Death: Public Discourse in the Age of Show Business*, New York: Penguin.

Pottash, Michael (2019), "Comfort Care, Whatever Does that Mean?," *Pallimed: A Hospice and Palliative Care Blog*. Available online: https://www.pallimed.org/2019/05/comfort-care-whatever-does-that-mean_4.html.

Prasad, Vinayak K. and Adam S. Cifu (2015), *Ending Medical Reversal: Improving Outcomes, Saving Lives*, Baltimore, MD: Johns Hopkins University Press.

Pratchett, Terry (2013), *Raising Steam*, London: Doubleday.

Putnam, Hilary (1975), *Mind, Language, and Reality: Philosophical Papers Volume Two*, Cambridge: Cambridge University Press.
Quast, Christian (2018a), "Expertise: A Practical Explication," *Topoi*, 37 (1): 11–27.
Quast, Christian (2018b), "Towards a Balanced Account of Expertise," *Social Epistemology*, 32 (6): 397–418.
Rachels, James and Stuart Rachels (2015), *The Elements of Moral Philosophy*, 8th ed., New York: McGraw-Hill Education.
Rakel, Horst (2004), "Scientists as Expert Advisors: Science Cultures Versus National Cultures?," in Elke Kurz-Milcke and Gerd Gigerenzer (eds.), *Experts in Science and Society*, 3–25, New York: Klewer Academic.
Rao, T. S. Sathyanarayana and Chittaranjan Andrade (2011), "The MMR Vaccine and Autism: Sensation, Refutation, Retraction, and Fraud," *Indian Journal of Psychiatry*, 53 (2): 95–6.
Rapport Du Comité D'Orientation (2016), "Ensemble: Améliorons Le Dépistage du Cancer du Sein," Available online: http://www.concertation-depistage.fr/wp-content/uploads/2016/10/depistage-cancer-sein-rapport-concertation-sept-2016.pdf.
Ray, C. Claiborne (2019), "A Barnyard Mystery: Are the Chicks Male or Female?," *New York Times*, June 24. Available online: https://www.nytimes.com/2019/06/24/science/chicken-sexing.html.
Raz, Joseph ([1975] 1999), *Practical Reasons and Norms*, Oxford: Oxford University Press.
Raz, Joseph ([1985] 1990), "Authority and Justification," in Joseph Raz (ed.), *Authority*, 116–41, New York: New York University Press.
Raz, Joseph (1988), *The Morality of Freedom*, Oxford: Oxford University Press.
Reade, Charles ([1868] 1896), *Foul Play*, London: Chatto & Windus, Piccadilly.
Reeves, Josh (2018), "Should Christians Trust Scientific Experts?," *BioLogos Blog*, Available online: https://biologos.org/articles/should-christians-trust-scientific-experts.
Reichenbach, Hans (1958), *The Philosophy of Space & Time*, New York: Dover.
Reiheld, Alison (2017), "What You Don't Know CAN Hurt You: Epistemic Injustice and Conceptually Impoverished Health Promotion," *IJFAB Blog*, November 3rd. Available online: https://www.ijfab.org/blog/2017/11/what-you-dont-know-can-hurt-you-epistemic-injustice-and-conceptually-impoverished-health-promotion/.
Rieder, Gernot and Judith Simon (2016), "Datatrust: Or, the Political Quest for Numerical Evidence and the Epistemologies of Big Data," *Big Data and Society*, 3 (1): 1–6.
Rieder, Travis (2019), *In Pain: A Bioethicist's Personal Struggle with Opioids*, New York: Harper Collins.
Rilke, Rainer Maria ([1910] 1985), *The Notebooks of Malte Laurids Brigge*, trans. S. Mitchell, New York: Vintage.
Ritchie, Earl J. (2016), "Fact Checking the Claim of 97% Consensus on Anthropogenic Climate Change," *Forbes Magazine*, December 14. Available online: https://www.forbes.com/sites/uhenergy/2016/12/14/fact-checking-the-97-consensus-on-anthropogenic-climate-change/#7ad367271157.

Roberts, David (2017), "Donald Trump and the Rise of Tribal Epistemology," *Vox*, May 19. Available online: https://www.vox.com/policy-and-politics/2017/3/22/14762030/donald-trump-tribal-epistemology.

Robertson, Josefina (2014), "Waiting Time at the Emergency Department from a Gender Equality Perspective," MA diss., Institute of Medicine at the Sahlgrenska Academy, University of Gothenburg.

Rogers, J. C., D. E. Swee and J. A. Ullian (1991), "Teaching Medical Decision Making and Students' Clinical Problem Solving Skills," *Medical Teacher*, 13 (2): 157–64.

Rorty, Richard (1979), *Philosophy and the Mirror of Nature*, Princeton, NJ: Princeton University Press.

Rorty, Richard (1990), "Introduction," in John P. Murphy (ed.), *Pragmatism: From Peirce to Davidson*, Boulder, CO: Westview Press.

Rowlands, Mark (2015), "Rilkean Memory," *Southern Journal of Philosophy*, 53 (S1): 141–54.

Russell, Bertrand (1912), "Problems of Philosophy, Home University Library," Available online: http://www.ditext.com/russell/russell.html.

Russell, Bertrand (1968), *The Art of Philosophizing and Other Essays*, New York: Philosophical Library.

Ruthsatz, Joanne, Kimberley Stephens and Mark Matthews 'The Link Between Child Prodigies and Autism," in David Z. Hambrick, Guillermo Campitelli and Brooke N. Macnamara (eds.), *The Science of Expertise: Behavioral, Neural, and Genetic Approaches to Complex Skill*, 87–100, London: Routledge.

Ryle, Gilbert (1945), "Knowing How and Knowing That: The Presidential Address," *Proceedings of the Aristotelian Society*, 46: 1–16.

Ryle, Gilbert ([1949] 2009), *The Concept of Mind: The 60th Anniversary Edition*, New York: Routledge.

Sacks, Oliver (1985), *The Man Who Mistook His Wife for a Hat*, New York: Touchstone.

Sahni, V. A., P. C. Silveira, N. I. Sainani and R. Khorasani (2016), "Impact of a Structured Report Template on the Quality of MRI Reports for Rectal Cancer Staging," *American Journal of Roentgenology*, 205 (3): 584–88, doi: 10.2214/AJR.14.14053.

Samuel, Arthur L. (1959), "Some Studies in Machine Learning Using the Game of Checkers," *IBM Journal*, 3 (3): 210–29.

Saposnik, Gustavo, Donald Redelmeier, Christian C. Ruff and Philippe N. Tobler (2016), "Cognitive Biases Associated with Medical Decisions: A Systematic Review," *BMC Medical Informatics and Decision Making*, 16 (138). Available online: https://bmcmedinformdecismak.biomedcentral.com/articles/10.1186/s12911-016-0377-1.

Schick, Theodore and Lewis Vaughn (2010), *How to Think about Weird Things: Critical Thinking for a New Age*, 6th ed., New York: McGraw-Hill.

Schmitt, Frederick F. (2006), "Testimonial Justification and Transindividual Reasons," in Jennifer Lackey and Ernest Sosa (eds.), *The Epistemology of Testimony*, 193–224, Oxford: Oxford University Press.

Scholz, Oliver (2009), "Experts: What They Are and How We Recognize Them—A Discussion of Alvin Goldman's Views," in Shurz, Gerhard and Markus Werning (eds.), *Reliable Knowledge and Social Epistemology: Essays on the Philosophy of Alvin Goldman and Replies by Goldman*, 187–208, Amsterdam: Grazer Philosophische Studien.

Scholz, Oliver (2018), "Symptoms of Expertise: Knowledge, Understanding, and Other Cognitive Goods," *Topoi*, 37 (1): 11–27.

Schwitzgebel, Eric and Fiery Cushman (2012), "Expertise in Moral Reasoning? Order Effects on Moral Judgment in Professional Philosophers and Non-Philosophers," *Mind and Language*, 27 (2): 135–53.

Scott, Robert and H. G. Lidell (1996), *A Greek-English Lexicon*, Oxford: Oxford University Press.

Scott, Robert and H. G. Lidell (1945), *An Intermediate Greek-English Lexicon*, Oxford: Oxford University Press.

Searle, John (1980), "Minds, Brains, and Programs," *Behavioral and Brain Sciences*, 3: 417–24.

Searle, John (1984), *Minds, Brains, and Science*, Cambridge: Harvard University Press.

Searle, John (1989), "Reply to Jacquette," *Philosophy and Phenomenological Research*, 49: 701–08.

Searle, John (2002), *Consciousness and Language*, Cambridge: Cambridge University Press.

Seidel, Markus (2014), *Epistemic Relativism: A Constructive Critique*. New York: Palgrave Macmillan.

Selinger, Evan (2011), *Expertise: Philosophical Reflections*, U.S.: Automatic Press.

Selinger, Evan and Robert P. Crease (2006), "Dreyfus on Expertise: The Limits of Phenomenological Analysis," in Evan Selinger and Robert Crease (eds.), *The Philosophy of Expertise*, 213–45, New York: Columbia University Press.

Selinger, Evan and John Mix (2006), "On Interactional Expertise: Pragmatic and Ontological Considerations," in Evan Selinger and Robert Crease (eds.), *The Philosophy of Expertise*, 302–21, New York: University of Columbia Press.

Sevin, C., G. Moore, J. Shepherd, T. Jacobs and C. Hupke (2009), "Transforming Care Teams to Provide the Best Possible Patient-Centered, Collaborative Care," *Journal of Ambulatory Care Management*, 32 (1) : 24–31.

Shackelford, Jole (2009), "That Giordano Bruno Was the First Martyr of Modern Science," in Ronald L. Numbers (ed.), *Galileo Goes to Jail: And Other Myths about Science and Religion*, 59–67, Cambridge, MA: Harvard University Press.

Shaffer, Michael J. (2013), "Doxastic Voluntarism, Epistemic Deontology, and Belief-Contravening Commitments," *American Philosophical Quarterly*, 50 (1): 73–81.

Shakespeare, William, *All's Well That Ends Well*. Available online: http://shakespeare.mit.edu/allswell/index.html.

Shakespeare, William, *Antony and Cleopatra*. Available online: http://shakespeare.mit.edu/cleopatra/index.html.

Shakespeare, William, *King Henry VI, Part I*. Available online: http://shakespeare.mit.edu/1henryvi/index.html.
Shakespeare, William, *King Henry VIII*. Available online: http://shakespeare.mit.edu/henryviii/index.html.
Shakespeare, William, *King Lear*. Available online: http://shakespeare.mit.edu/lear/index.html.
Shakespeare, William, *Othello*. Available online: http://shakespeare.mit.edu/othello/index.html.
Shalowitz, David I., Elizabeth Garrett-Myer and David Wendler (2006), "The Accuracy of Surrogate Decision Makers: A Systematic Review," *Arch Intern Med*, 166 (5): 493–97.
Shanteau, J. (1989), "Psychological Characteristics and Strategies of Expert Decision Makers," in B. Rohrmann, L. R. Beach, C. Vlek and S. R. Watson (eds.), *Advances in Decision Research*, 203–15, Amsterdam: North Holland.
Shapin, Steven (1994), *A Social History of Truth: Civility and Science in Seventeenth-Century England*, Chicago: University of Chicago Press.
Shema, Hadas (2014), "The Birth of Modern Peer Review," *Scientific American*, April. Available online: https://blogs.scientificamerican.com/information-culture/the-birth-of-modern-peer-review/.
Shinde, G. R., A. B. Kalamkar, P. N. Mahalle, N. Dey, J. Chaki and A. E. Hassanien (2020), "Forecasting Models for Coronavirus Disease (COVID-19): A Survey of the State-of-the-Art," *SN Computer Science*, 1 (4): 197, doi: 10.1007/s42979-020-00209-9.
Shorto, Russell (2008), *Descartes' Bones: A Skeletal History of the Conflict Between Faith and Reason*, New York: Vintage.
Simon, Herbert (1957a), *Administrative Behavior: A Study of Decision-Making Processes in Administrative Organization*, 2nd ed., New York: Macmillan.
Simon, Herbert (1957b), *Models of Man*, New York: John Wiley.
Simon Herbert, A. and William G. Chase (1973), "Skill in Chess," *American Scientist*, 61 (4): 394–403.
Simonton, Dean Keith (1999), "Talent and Its Development: An Emergenic and Epigenetic Model," *Psychological Review*, 106 (3): 435–57.
Sinkivec, Maja (2016), "How Good is Google Translate Really? Evaluation of Google Translate for the Language Direction Slovenian-German," Master's Thesis at Karl-Franzens-University Graz, Austria.
Skotko, Brian G., Susan P. Levine and Richard Goldstein (2011), "Self-Perceptions From People with Down Syndrome," *American Journal of Medical Genetics Part A*, 155: 2360–9.
Slowik, Edward (2017), "Descartes' Physics," in Edward N. Zalta (ed.), *The Stanford Encyclopedia of Philosophy*, Fall 2017 edition. Available online: https://plato.stanford.edu/entries/descartes-physics/#ForcCartPhys.
Smith, Barry and Roberto Casati (1994), "Naïve Physics: An Essay in Ontology," *Philosophical Psychology*, 7 (2): 225–44.
Smith, J. F. and Thomas Kida (1991), "Heuristics and Biases: Expertise and Task Realism in Auditing," *Psychological Bulletin*, 109 (3): 472–89.

Smith, Tom W. and Jaesok Son (2013), "Trends in Public Attitudes about Confidence in Institutions," *NORC at the University of Chicago*. Available online: http://www.norc.org/PDFs/GSS%20Reports/Trends%20in%20Confidence%20Institutions_Final.pdf.

Solomon, Miriam (2009), "Standpoint and Creativity," *Hypatia*, 24 (4): 226–37.

Sosa, Ernest (2006), "Knowledge: Instrumental and Testimonial," in Jennifer Lackey and Ernest Sosa (eds.), *The Epistemology of Testimony*, 116–23, Oxford: Oxford University Press.

Specter, Michael (2007), "The Denialists: The Dangerous Attacks on the Consensus About H.I.V. and AIDS," *The New Yorker*, March 12. Available online: https://www.newyorker.com/magazine/2007/03/12/the-denialists.

Spence, Charles and Qian Janice Wang (2019), "Wine Expertise: Perceptual Learning in the Chemical Senses," *Current Opinion in Food Science*, 27: 49–56, doi: 10.1016/j.cofs.2019.05.003.

Spier, Raymond (2002a), "The History of the Peer Review Process," *Trends in Biotechnology*, 20 (8): 357–8.

Spier, Raymond (2002b), "Peer Review and Innovation," *Science and Engineering Ethics*, 8 (1): 99–108.

Stamper, Kory (2017), *Word by Word: The Secret Life of Dictionaries*, New York: Penguin Random House.

Starks, J. L. and J. Deakin (1984), "Perception in Sport: A Cognitive Approach to Skilled Performance," in W. F. Straub and J. M. Williams (eds.), *Cognitive Sport Psychology*, 115–28, Lansing, NY: Sport Science Associates Intl.

Steen, R. G., A. Casadevall and F. C. Fang (2013), "Why Has the Number of Scientific Retractions Increased?," *PLOS ONE*, 8 (7): e68397.

Stevenson, Matthew (2017), "Killing Bill O'Reilly: The Disgraced Broadcaster's Distortions of History," *Harper's Magazine*, July.

Stich, Stephen (1990), *The Fragmentation of Reason*. Cambridge, MA: MIT Press.

Stichter, Matt (2015), "Philosophical and Psychological Accounts of Expertise," *Journal of Philosophical Studies*, 28: 105–28.

Sunday, Mackenzie and Isabel Gauthier (2018), "The Neural Underpinnings of Perceptual Expertise," in David Z. Hambrick, Guillermo Campitelli and Brooke N. Macnamara (eds.), *The Science of Expertise: Behavioral, Neural, and Genetic Approaches to Complex Skill*, 200–17, London: Routledge.

Sunstein, Cass (2017), *#Republic*, Princeton, NJ: Princeton University Press.

The Talk Origins Archive (1996), "McLean vs. Arkansas Board of Education," *Talk Origins Archive*, Available online: http://www.talkorigins.org/faqs/mclean-v-arkansas.html.

Tan, Yi Ting, Gary E. MacPherson and Sarah J. Wilson (2018), "The Molecular Genetic Basis of Music Ability and Music-Related Phenotypes," in David Z. Hambrick, Guillermo Campitelli and Brooke N. Macnamara (eds.), *The Science of Expertise: Behavioral, Neural, and Genetic Approaches to Complex Skill*, 283–304, London: Routledge.

Tanesini, Alessandra (2020), "Standpoint Then and Now," in Miranda Fricker, Peter J. Graham, David Henderson and Nikolaj J. L. L. Pedersen (eds.), *The Routledge Handbook of Social Epistemology*, 335–43, New York: Routledge.

Tempere, S., G. de Revel and G. Sicard (2019), "Impact of Learning and Training on Wine Expertise: A Review," *Current Opinion in Food Science*, 27: 98–103, doi: 10.1016/j.cofs.2019.07.001.

Tetlock, Philip E. (2005), *Expert Political Judgment: How Good Is It? How Can We Know?* Princeton, NJ: Princeton University Press.

Tetlock, Philip E. and Dan Gardner (2015), *Superforecasting: The Art and Science of Prediction*, New York: Crown Publishers.

Thaler, Richard H. and Cass R. Sunstein (2003a), "Libertarian Paternalism," *American Economic Review (Papers and Proceedings)* 93 (2, Fall): 175–9.

Thaler, Richard H. and Cass R. Sunstein (2003b), "Libertarian Paternalism is Not an Oxymoron," *The University of Chicago Law Review*, 70 (4): 1159–1202.

Thaler, Richard and Cass Sunstein (2009), *Nudge: Improving Decisions about Health, Wealth, and Happiness*, New York: Penguin.

Thornton, B. (1977), "Linear Prediction of Marital Happiness: A Replication," *Personality and Social Psychology Bulletin*, 3: 674–6.

de Tocqueville, Alexis ([1835] 1963), *Democracy in America*, vol. 2, New York: Knopf.

Turner, Stephen P. (2014), *The Politics of Expertise*, London: Routledge.

Tversky, Amos and Daniel Kahneman (1974), "Judgment Under Uncertainty: Heuristics and Biases," *Science*, 185: 1124–1.

Tversky, Amos and Daniel Kahneman (1981), "The Framing of Decisions and the Psychology of Choice," *Science*, 211: 453–8.

Tversky, Amos and Daniel Kahneman (1986), "Rational Choice and the Framing of Decisions," *The Journal of Business*, 59 (4) Part 2: The Behavioral Foundations of Economic Theory: S251–S278.

United States, Congress, Subcommittee on Health and Long-Term Care (1985), Fraudulent Medical Degrees: Hearing Before the Subcommittee of Health and Long-Term Care of the Select Committee on Aging, House of Representatives, Ninety-eighth Congress, Second Session, December 7, 1984, Washington: US GPO. Available online: https://babel.hathitrust.org/cgi/pt?id=mdp.39015031766556&view=1up&seq=7.

US Census (2014), United States Census Bureau. Available online: https://www.census.gov/programs-surveys/acs/news/data-releases/2014.html.

Van Cleve, James (2006), "Reid on the Credit of Human Testimony," in Jennifer Lackey and Ernest Sosa (eds.), *The Epistemology of Testimony*, 50–74, Oxford: Oxford University Press.

Van Inwagen, Peter (1996), "It is Wrong, Always, Everywhere, and for Anyone, to Believe Anything, Upon Insufficient Evidence," in J. Jordan and D. Howard-Snyder (eds.), *Faith, Freedom, and Rationality*, 137–54, Hanham, MD: Rowman and Littlefield.

Van Noorden, Richard (2011), "Science publishing: The trouble with retractions," *Nature*, 478: 26–8.

Veatch, Robert M. (2000), "Doctor Does Not Know Best: Why in the New Century Physicians Must Stop Trying to Benefit Patients," *Journal of Medicine and Philosophy: A Forum for Bioethics and Philosophy of Medicine*, 25 (6): 701–1.

Veatch, Robert M. and Laura Guidry-Grimes (2020), *The Basics of Bioethics*, 4th ed., New York: Routledge.

Vickers, Andrew J., Fernando J. Bianco, Angel M. Serio, James A. Eastham, Deborah Schrag, Eric A. Klein, Alwyn M. Reuther, Michal W. Kattan, J. Edson Pontes and Peter T. Scardino (2007), "The Surgical Learning Curve for Prostate Cancer Control after Radical Prostatectomy," *Journal of the National Cancer Institute*, 99 (15): 1171–7.

Vickers, Andrew J., Fernando J. Bianco, Mithat Gonen, Angel M. Cronin, James A. Eastham, Deborah Schrag, Eric A. Klein, Alwyn M. Reuther, Michael W. Kattan, J. Edson Pontes and Peter T. Scardino (2008), "Effects of Pathologic Stage on the Learning Curve for Radical Prostatectomy: Evidence that Recurrence in Organ-confined Cancer is Largely Related to Inadequate Surgical Technique," *European Urology*, 53 (5): 960–6.

Vlastos, Gregory (1957), "Socratic Knowledge and Platonic 'Pessimism,'" *The Philosophical Review*, 66 (2): 226–38.

Voyer, Benjamin G. (2015), "Nudging Behaviors in Healthcare: Insights from Behavioural Economics," *British Journal of Healthcare Management*, 21 (3): 130–5.

Wada, Kyoko, Louis C. Charland and Geoff Bellingham (2019), "Can Women in Labor Give Informed Consent to Epidural Analgesia?," *Bioethics*, 33 (4): 475–86.

Wagemans, Jean H. M. (2011), "The Assessment of Argumentation from Expert Opinion," *Argumentation*, 25: 329–39.

Wai, Jonathan and Harrison Kell (2017), "What Innovations Have We Already Lost? The Importance of Identifying and Developing Spatial Talent," in M. S. Khine (ed.), *Visual-Spatial Ability in STEM Education*, 109–24, Cham, Switzerland: Springer.

Walton, Douglas (1992), *The Place of Emotion in Argument*, University Park, PA: Pennsylvania State University Press.

Walton, Douglas (1997), *Appeal to Expert Opinion*, University Park: Penn State Press.

Walton, Douglas (2013), *Methods of Argumentation*, New York: Cambridge University Press.

Walton, Douglas (2014), "On a Razor's Edge: Evaluating Arguments from Expert Opinion," *Argument and Computation*, 5 (2–3): 139–59.

Wang, Q. J. and C. Spence (2019), "Drinking through Rosé-Coloured Glasses: Influence of Wine Colour on the Perception of Aroma and Flavour in Wine Experts and Novices," *Food Research International*, 126: 108678. doi: 10.1016/j.foodres.2019.108678. Epub 2019 Sep 15. PMID: 31732050.

Ware, Mark and Michael Mabe (2015), *The STM Report: An Overview of Scientific and Scholarly Journal Publishing*, 4th ed., The Hague: International Association of Scientific, Technical and Medical Publishers.

Watson, James (1913), "Psychology as the Behaviorist Views It," *Psychological Review*, 20: 158–77.
Watson, Jamie Carlin (2014), "Prolegomena to an Epistemic Case for Classical Liberalism," *Libertarian Papers*, 6 (1): 21–55.
Watson, Jamie Carlin (2016), "Filter Bubbles and the Public Use of Reason: Applying Epistemology to the Newsfeed," in Frank Scalambrino (ed.), *Social Epistemology and Technology: Toward Public Self-Awareness Regarding Technological Mediation*, 47–58, London: Rowman & Littlefield.
Watson, Jamie Carlin (2017), *Winning Votes by Abusing Reason: Responsible Belief and Political Rhetoric*, Lanham, MD: Lexington Books.
Watson, Jamie Carlin (2018), "The Shoulders of Giants: A Case for Non-Veritism about Expert Authority," *Topoi*, 37 (1): 39–53.
Watson, Jamie Carlin (2019), "What Experts Could Not Be," *Social Epistemology*, 33: 74–87.
Watson, Jamie Carlin (2021), *Expertise: A Philosophical Introduction*, London: Bloomsbury.
Watson, Jamie Carlin (n.d.), "Epistemic Justification," *Internet Encyclopedia of Philosophy*. Available online: https://www.iep.utm.edu/epi-just/.
Watson, Jamie Carlin and Laura Guidry-Grimes, eds. (2018), *Moral Expertise*, New York: Springer.
Watson, John B. (1913), "Psychology as the Behaviorist Views It," *Psychological Review*, 20: 158–77.
Watson, Katherine D. (2006), "Medical and Chemical Expertise in English Trials for Criminal Poisoning, 1750–1914," *Medical History*, 50 (3): 373–90.
Wegwarth, Odette and Gerd Gigerenzer (2011), "Statistical Illiteracy in Doctors," in Gerd Gigerenzer and J. A. Muir Gray (eds.), *Better Doctors, Better Patients, Better Decisions: Envisioning Health Care 2020*, 137–52, Cambridge, MA: The MIT Press.
Weinberg, J., S. Nichols and S. Stich (2001), "Normativity and Epistemic Intuitions," *Philosophical Topics*, 29: 429–60.
Wheeler, Gregory (2018), "Bounded Rationality," in Edward N. Zalta (ed.), *The Stanford Encyclopedia of Philosophy*, Fall 2019 Edition. forthcoming. Available online: https://plato.stanford.edu/archives/fall2019/entries/bounded-rationality/.
Wiland, Eric (2018), "Moral Advice and Joint Agency," in Mark C. Timmons (ed.), *Oxford Studies in Normative Ethics*, 102–3, Vol. 8, Oxford: Oxford University Press.
Williams, Bernard (1972), *Morality: An Introduction to Ethics*, New York: Harper Torchbooks.
Williams, Bernard (2002), *Truth and Truthfulness*, Princeton, NJ: Princeton University Press.
Wilson, Emily (2018), "Introduction," in Emily Wilson (trans.), *The Odyssey*, 1–80, New York: W. W. Norton and Company.
Winter, Tom and Elisha Fieldstadt (2019), "First Major Drug Distribution Company, Former Executives, Charged in Opioid Crisis," *NBC News*, April 23. Available online:

https://www.nbcnews.com/news/us-news/former-ceo-major-drug-distribution-company-first-face-criminal-charges-n997571.

Wittgenstein, Ludwig ([1958] 2000), "Philosophical Investigations," in Forrest E. Baird and Walter Kauffman (eds.), *Twentieth Century Philosophy*, 2nd ed., 168–85, Upper Saddle River, NJ: Prentice Hall.

Wolff, Robert Paul (1970), *In Defense of Anarchy*, New York: Harper and Row.

Wolff, Robert Paul ([1970] 1990), "The Conflict between Authority and Autonomy," in Joseph Raz (ed.), *Authority*, 20–31, Washington Square, NY: New York University Press.

Woodward, Thomas (2004), *Doubts about Darwin*, Grand Rapids, MI: Baker Books.

Wouk, Herman (1951), *The Cain Mutiny*. New York: Doubleday.

Wylie, Alison and Lynn Hankinson Nelson (2009), "Coming to Terms with the Value(s) of Science: Insights from Feminist Science Scholarship," in Harold Kincaid, John Dupré and Alison Wylie (eds.), *Value-Free Science? Ideals and Illusions*, 58–86, Oxford: Oxford University Press.

Yarrow, K., P. Brown and J. W. Krakauer (2009), "Inside the Brain of an Elite Athlete: The Neural Processes that Support High Achievement in Sports," *Nature Reviews Neuroscience*, 10: 585–96.

Yates, J. Frank, Laith Alattar, David W. Eby, Lisa J. Molnar, David LeBlanc, Mark Gilbert, Michelle Rasulis and Renáe St. Louis (2011), "An Analysis of Seatbelt Use Decision Making Among Part-Time Users," The University of Michigan Transportation Research Institute, April 2011. Available online: https://deepblue.lib.umich.edu/bitstream/handle/2027.42/85177/102755.pdf?sequence=1&isAllowed=y.

Zagzebski, Linda (2012), *Epistemic Authority: A Theory of Trust, Authority, and Autonomy in Belief*, New York: Oxford University Press.

Zenger, T. R. (1992), "Why Do Employers Only Reward Extreme Performance? Examining the Relationships Among Performance, Pay, and Turnover," *Administrative Science Quarterly*, 37 (2): 198–219.

Zucco, G. M., A. Carassai, M. R. Baroni and R. J. Stevenson (2011), "Labeling, Identification, and Recognition of Wine-Relevant Odorants in Expert Sommeliers, Intermediates, and Untrained Wine Drinkers," *Perception*, 40 (5): 598–607. doi: 10.1068/p6972. PMID: 21882722.

Index

(Transliterated words and titles appear in italics.)

abilities   ix, 4, 14, 40, 62, 66, 74, 90–2, 96, 98, 138, 153, 166, 173, 176, 184, 187, 199, 215, 226 (Ch. 7, n.5)
Activity Theory   32
Addams, Jane   93
administrative authority, *see* authority, administrative
advice, expert   xv, 10, 15, 23, 26, 37, 50–1, 123, 126, 143, 147, 150–1, 153, 193–6, 205–10, 212, 226 (Ch. 6, n.10)
  overlapping expertise (argument)   209–10
Allen James   50, 52, 160
anti-expert   214
anti-vaxxers   1, 5
appert   35, 41
Aristotle   12, 42–3, 51, 52, 56–7, 60–1, 66, 69–70, 78, 162–3, 168, 218 (Ch. 1, n.8), 221 (Ch. 3, n.4)
ars/arte/artium   31, 61–2, 67
art/arts   1 (epigraph), 23, 31, 42, 43, 50–7 (translated from *techne*), 59–62, 66–70, 74, 93, 159, 162–3, 221 (Ch. 3, n.3, n.4)
artificial intelligence (AI)   89, 95–8
auctor   129–30, 225 (Ch. 6, n.5)
auctoritas   44, 225 (Ch. 6, n.5)
auctoritatem   44–5
authoritative   44–6, 71, 88, 110, 121, 123, 132, 134, 136–7, 141, 143–4, 147, 150, 151, 154, 158, 183, 189, 196, 210–11, 225 (Ch. 6, n.3), 226 (Ch. 6, n.9 and n.10)
authority (general)   xi–xiii, xiv, xvi, xvii, 1–29, 31, 42–6
  administrative   xiv, 128–30, 154, 169, 172, 225 (Ch. 6, n.4)

control accounts   xiv, 42, 44, 46, 125–9, 155 (*see also* authority (general), doxastic control accounts; authority (general), ontological control; authority (general), physical control)
doxastic control   133–48, 225 (Ch. 6, n.7)
epistemic   xiv
expert (*see* authority, epistemic)
normative presumption account   xiv, 126, 148–54, 150 (definition)
ontological control accounts   131–3, 148
physical control accounts   129–31, 148
preemption view (*see* authority, doxastic control accounts)
scientific   79 (*see also* authority, epistemic)
thin epistemic authority   120–1
total evidence view (*see* authority, normative presumption)
weak deference account   148, 150, 154 (*see also* authority, normative presumption)
automaticity   93
autonomy   70, 147, 214

Bacon, Francis   3, 36, 45, 62, 74, 217 (Ch. 1, n.8)
Ballantyne, Nathan   12, 161, 188
behaviorism   xiii, 89, 94–5
Boyle, Robert   3, 74–5
Brewer, Scott   115–16, 146

Cavendish, Margaret   ix (epigraph)
Chaucer, Geoffrey   35
chess   31–3, 49, 56, 99–103, 166

Cicero   33–4, 44–5, 54, 61, 66, 67, 70
climate science/climate/climate
    change   6, 9, 12–13, 16, 19–22, 41,
    187–9, 196, 199, 204, 213
Coady, David   xii, 18, 24, 86, 113–14,
    161, 163, 164, 204, 217 (Ch. 1, n.7),
    227 (Ch. 7, n.8)
cognitive bias, *see* heuristics and biases
cognitive island   182–4, 189, 194, 224
    (Ch. 5, n.6)
cognitive systems account of
    expertise   xii, 217 (preface, n.1)
Collins, Harry   xii, 26, 77, 79, 121–2, 143,
    151, 157, 164, 217 (Ch. 1, n.2), 224
    (Ch. 6, n.1)
competence (definition)   xii
confounding of expertise   23, 186–9,
    196, 215
control accounts of authority, *see*
    authority, control accounts
Creation Science   17, 78
Csikszentmihalyi, Mihaly   103
cunning intelligence   31, 42, 46–9, 50, 62,
    220 (Ch. 2, n.8), *see also* metis

Descartes, René   3, 12, 18, 70–2
Dewey, John   93–4
disagreement   xv, 148, 195, 199–205, 212,
    218 (Ch. 1, n.9 and n.14)
    everyday   xv, 199–205
    idealized   199–205
disagreement skepticism, *see* skepticism,
    disagreement
doctor, *see* physician
domain (field of study; subject matter;
    specialization) (definition)
    expert domain (domain of
        expertise)   12, 15, 16, 26, 29, 108,
        115, 147, 158–71, 165 (definition)
    specialized (or specialist)
        domain   144, 175, 182, 209
domain at a time   xii
Dreyfus, Hubert   97, 103, 161–2, 220
    (Ch. 2, n.16), 224 (Ch 6, n.1)
Dreyfus, Stuart   97, 103, 220 (Ch. 2, n.16)
Dunning-Kruger effect   x, 186, 196, 215

echo chambers   x, 186, 191, 196
Elgin, Catherine   214

embodied knowledge   103, 161–2
engineers (engineering)   38, 86, 157, 168,
    180, 181, 183, 214
Enlightenment Mandate   73
episteme   49, 50, 60–2, 67, 106, 160
epistemein   57
epistemic advantage   xiv, 26, 105–9, 107
    (definition), 110, 113–20, 141–3,
    150–1, 153
    thick epistemic advantage   109, 120,
        151, 153
    thin epistemic advantage   114, 115,
        117, 119–20, 141–3, 148, 151, 153
epistemic authority, *see* authority,
    epistemic
epistemic placement   xiv, 4, 56,
    105–9, 107 (definition), 113, 114,
    116–20, 123, 125, 130, 133, 141,
    142, 147, 151–4, 173, 174, 200,
    208, 214
    thick epistemic placement   117, 123,
        151, 152
    thin epistemic placement   117
epistemic trespassing (Ballantyne)   12,
    161, 188–9
Erasmus, Desiderius   45, 70
Ericsson, K. Anders   xi, xii, 91, 98, 99,
    222 (Ch. 4, n.1), 227 (Ch. 7, n.13)
esoteric   54, 55, 62, 84, 85, 123, 158, 176,
    180–6, 224 (Ch. 5, n.4 and n.6)
espert   35, 41
Evans, Robert   xiii, 26, 37, 77, 79, 84,
    98–102, 121–2, 140, 151, 153–8,
    160–1, 163, 164, 180, 206 (n.6), 224
    (Ch. 6, n.1)
exoteric   54, 55, 62, 180–4, 224
    (Ch. 5, n.4), 227 (Ch. 7, n.12)
experience (relevant for expertise)   x,
    xiii, xvi, 4, 14–16, 31, 33–41, 48,
    52–3, 57, 58, 62, 69, 93, 100–3,
    114–18, 121, 143, 151, 154, 162,
    164, 165, 167, 168, 171, 185, 186,
    219 (Ch. 2, n.7)
experience, person of   53, 58, 118, 162
expert (definition)   xii, 217 (Preface, n.1)
expert coordination   190, 195, 204, 216
expertise (types)
    contributory   xii, 122
    default   x, 153, 156

embodied   103, 161
generalized   31, 57, 58 (definition), 121, 162, 164, 213
interactional   xii, 121–2
localized   xvi, 31, 40 (definition), 41, 58, 117, 118, 121, 143, 162, 213
meta-expertise   57, 122, 168 (definition), 178, 182, 184, 200, 202–3
performative   99, 177, 208
specialized   31, 41 (definition), 42, 46, 47, 58, 61, 62, 65, 117, 121–2, 126, 128, 133, 162, 164, 175, 195, 219 (Ch. 2, n.6 and n.7), 220 (Ch. 2, n.13)
expert skepticism   xi, xiii, 3–29, 81, 84, 87, 218 (Ch. 1, n.9), *see also* skepticism, expert
expertus   31–5, 41, 61

filter bubbles   x, 186, 191
flow (optimal experience)   103–4
Folkes v. Chadd   38–41
follow the numbers strategy (Goldman)   20
Fricker, Elizabeth   105–6, 113–15

Gall, Franz Joseph   90–1
Galton, Francis   91
generality problem for expert domains   159–68
genius   xiii, 31, 68, 91–2
geography of expertise   180–3
Gigerenzer, Gerd   101, 142
Gilman, Benjamin Ives   40, 130–1, 225 (Ch. 6, n.6)
Goldman, Alvin   xii, 158, 176, 199, 200, 217 (Ch. 1, n.7), 227 (Ch. 7, n.8)
Gorgias   1 (epigraph), 50

Hardwig, John   26–7, 109, 176, 218 (Ch. 1, n.14), 224 (Ch. 5, n.3)
heuristics and biases   7, 99, 101, 109, 142, 184
anchoring bias   131
confirmation bias   217 (Ch. 1, n.4)
Dunning-Kruger effect   186
framing bias   70
hindsight bias   99

standpoint bias   x, 186
therapeutic pessimism   170
Hippocrates (character in *Protagoras*)   57–8
Hippocrates (Hippocratic writers)   23, 55, 85, 218 (Ch. 1, n.10), 220 (Ch. 2, n.19), 222 (Ch. 3, n.22, n.23, and n.24)
hobbyist   ix, 4, 31, 40, 58, 117

Ibsen, Henrik   210–11
illiberal arts   62, 67, 221 (Ch. 3, n.3 and n.4)
immersion (linguistic or cultural) (Collins)   xii, 67, 114
indicators of expertise (also evidence of expertise and symptoms of expertise)   ix–xi, 54–5, 164, 176, 178, 181, 183–5
direct   ix, 176–8
indirect   ix, 176, 178–9 (types of indirect evidence), 182–5, 187, 189, 191
indirect calibration (Kitcher)   181
insight   47, 71, 158
intelligence   xiii, 42, 68, 74, 81, 89, 91, 92, 94, 186
intuition   103
Ion   53, 159–61, 167

just do it principle (Montero)   103
justification, epistemic   82, 104, 105, 107, 110, 112–13, 138–42, 150–2, 190–1, 213, 218 (Ch. 1, n.12), 225 (Ch. 6, n.3), 227 (Ch. 7, n.7)

Kant, Immanuel (Kantians and neo-Kantians)   3, 73, 83, 139
kind learning environment (Hogarth)   186, 189–91, 215
Klein, Gary   99, 102, 103

Laches   59, 226 (Ch. 7, n.2)
Lackey, Jennifer   113, 126, 143–4, 150, 153, 154
Lane, Melissa   56–7, 162–3
layperson, *see* novice
Leibniz, Gottfried Wilhelm   74
liberal arts   66–7, *see also* illiberal arts
Locke, John   72–3

master (as expert)   49, 53, 57, 65–70, 92, 126, 162, 164
master (as political authority)   42, 43, 45
mastery   43, 47, 88, 92, 127, 129–30, 158–60, 165, 220 (Ch. 2, n.10)
mathematician   2, 12, 19, 20, 27, 48, 77, 90, 96, 101, 151, 173
mathematics (or math)   20, 27, 49, 61, 67, 70–1, 73, 75, 77, 83, 95, 96, 106, 146, 167, 168, 214
mechanic   191
medicine/medical expertise   x, 5, 9–11, 13–15, 24, 27–8, 49, 78, 114–17, 122, 128, 142, 144–5, 163–4, 186, 190, 201, 209
   ancient medicine   43, 52–3, 55–7, 60, 61, 160–3
Memorabilia   50–1, 54, 68, 225 (Ch. 6, n.2)
Meno   59, 174
metis   31, 46–50, 59
Mizrahi, Moti   218 (Ch. 1, n.13)
Montero, Barbara   98, 103

Natural Decision Making (NDM) (Orasanu and Klein)   102
natural expertise   98, 99, 101–3
natural greatness   89, 90
nature *vs.* nurture debate   42, 68, 70, 91–5
neurological approaches to expertise   32, 89, 94, 103–4
Nguyen, C. Thi   158, 180–3, 197, 224 (Ch. 5, n.6), 227 (Ch. 7, n.8, n.10, and n.11)
Nichols, Tom   26
non-expert, *see* novice
nonminded   103
normative presumption account of authority (definition)   150, *see also* authority, normative presumption
novice (or non-expert, layperson) (definition)   xvi
novice/expert problem   158, 171, 172, *see also* recognition problem
novice/2-expert problem   xiv, xv, 171, 193, 199–205

Odyssey   46, 49
operational definition   32

Oppian   47
optimal experience, *see* flow
optimists, expert   98–103

pessimists, expert   98–100
phronesis   50, 59
physician (or doctor)   xi, 2, 4, 9, 11, 13–15, 28, 43, 53, 56–7, 62, 73, 84–5, 112, 114–18, 132, 139, 142–4, 147, 149, 162, 173, 183–5, 187, 190, 191, 195, 197–8, 210–11
physicist   146, 159
physics   xii, xvi, 55, 70, 71, 73, 78, 86, 116, 146, 153, 159, 167, 181
Plato   Epigraph, 1 (epigraph), 23, 43–4, 48–53, 56, 57, 62, 65–6, 69, 107, 126, 127, 129–31, 159, 160, 174, 193 (epigraph), 226 (Ch. 7, n.2)
pragmatic solution to the generality problem   160, 162
preemption view of authority (and total preemption, screening off)   133–48, *see also* authority, doxastic control
presumption of epistemic advantage (PEA)   26–9, 108–9
principle of normative deference (PND)   26–9, 108–9
principle of prima facie trust (PPT)   109
profession   65, 76, 84–7, 109, 110, 126, 161, 169, 219 (Ch. 2, n.7)
professional (adjective)   xiv, 9, 25, 54, 56, 85–7, 98, 132, 134, 135, 169, 171, 178, 180, 190
professional(s)(noun)   32, 48, 58, 84–7, 115, 172, 178, 209
professionalism   85–7, 169
Protagoras   Epigraph, 23, 50, 51–2, 54, 57–8, 59–60, 193 (epigraph), 220 (Ch. 2, n.10)

Quetelet, Adolph   90–1

Raz, Joseph   134–8, 141–2, 144, 147, 148, 154, 225 (Ch. 6, n.3)
Recognition-Primed Decision Making (Klein)   103

recognition problem for expertise, easy (ERP)   157–8, 171–91
  easy recognition problem-competence (ERP-C)   174 (argument)
  easy recognition problem-knowledge (ERP-K)   172 (argument)
recognition problem for expertise, general   xiv, 4, 141, 155, 168, 200
recognition problem for expertise, hard (HRP)   xiv, 193–8, 194 (argument)
relativism, epistemic   78–80, 83, 222 (Ch. 3, n.20)
reliability   5, 12, 23, 41, 52, 65, 112, 135, 137, 139, 172 (reliable access to truth), 190, 198
Republic   50, 53, 59, 107, 126–7, 130
Russell, Bertrand   77

Scholz, Oliver   159, 217 (Preface, n.2)
Selinger, Evan   210–12, 224 (Ch. 6, n.1)
Shakespeare   35–6, 62
skepticism, expert (types of expert skepticism)   xi, xiii, 2, 3–4 (Enlightenment), 4–7 (contemporary), 26–9, 81–7, 89, 218 (Ch. 1, n.9)
  anecdotal   7–11
  conflict of interest   7, 23–5
  disagreement   7, 16–24
  scope   7, 11–16
  skill   x, xii, xiii, 3, 31, 34–7, 41, 42, 46–9, 50–3, 59, 60, 68, 80, 85, 88, 91, 93, 106, 114, 119, 125, 128, 129, 159, 160, 163–5, 186, 219 (Ch. 2, n.7), 226 (Ch. 7, n.2)
Sociology of Scientific Knowledge (SSK)   32, 79
Socrates   1 (epigraph), 23, 43, 50–3, 57, 59–60, 108, 126–7, 129, 159–61, 163–4, 167, 170, 174, 193 (epigraph), 220 (Ch. 2, n.10), 226 (Ch. 7, n.2)
sophia   xiv, 48–9, 50, 59, 220 (Ch. 2, n.10)
sophos   49
specialized (or specialist) domain   144, 175, 182, 209
specialized training or skills   x, 34, 48, 49, 69, 120, 129, 165–9, 171, 178, 186, 213

Stamper, Kory   218 (Ch. 2, n.1), 22 (Ch. 3, n.27)
standard response to skepticism about expertise   26–9
standpoint bias, *see* heuristics and biases
Statesman   43
strong deference   137, 147 (distinct from Elizabeth Fricker's 2006 usage)
strong specialized expert or expertise   122, 162
subject matter   xiv, 27, 115, *see also* domain
symptoms of expertise, *see* indicators of expertise
System 1 Cognitive Processing (Kahneman)   91, 100
System 2 Cognitive Processing (Kahneman)   101

tacit knowledge   224 (Ch. 6, n.1)
TAP (testimony, advice, performance)   126, 133, 135–7, 139, 141, 142, 150–2, 154, 155, 191, 226 (Ch. 6, n.10)
technai   60
techne   51–62, 66–7, 105, 159, 160, 163
tektonoi   50
testimony   xiv, xv, 4, 10, 12, 15, 19, 38–9, 45, 72, 75, 105, 106, 108, 109–13, 126, 153, 154, 172–3, 175, 178, 189, 224 (Ch. 5, n.11), 226 (Ch. 6, n.10)
  expert testimony   3, 15, 21–3, 37, 108 (how expert testimony is distinct), 109, 113–20, 123, 126, 140, 143–4, 150–1, 172–3, 176, 178, 182, 186, 191, 193–6, 205–13, 215, 218 (Ch. 1, n.12), 224 (Ch. 6, n.1), 226 (Ch. 6, n.10)
Tetlock, Philip   xi, 15, 135, 218 (Ch. 1, n.13)
therapeutic pessimism   170, *see also* heuristics and biases
thick expertise   115–17
thin expertise   114–17, 121
tribal epistemology   x, 186, 215
trust (in experts)   xiv, 4, 15, 26, 74, 76, 86, 109, 123, 139, 172, 173, 175, 185, 188, 193–4, 196, 198, 205–13
  public trust   5–6, 43, 85, 188

truth-based accounts of expertise   172, 174
Turing test   96–7, 223 (Ch. 4, n.8)
Turner, Stephen   9–10, 51, 76, 77, 198

violin   103, 186

Wakefield, Andrew   5, 25, 195
whisk(e)y-tasting   149, 164, 166–7
wicked learning environment
 (Hogarth)   55, 185–9, 194, 215,
 228 (Ch. 7, n.13)

Williams, James   92–3, 95, 97, 223 (Ch. 4,
 n.3 and n.4)
Wilson, Emily   46–7, 220 (Ch. 2, n.8)
wine-tasting   15–16

Xenophon   49, 50, 54, 89 (epigraph), 225
 (Ch. 6, n.2)

Zagzebski, Linda   125–6, 128, 133–48,
 151, 152, 154, 155, 206, 225
 (Ch. 6, n.8)

www.ingramcontent.com/pod-product-compliance
Lightning Source LLC
Chambersburg PA
CBHW052217300426
44115CB00011B/1729